200 Years of National Philologies

Christoph Strosetzki
Editor

200 Years of National Philologies

From Romanticism to Globalization

Editor
Christoph Strosetzki
Romanisches Seminar
Universität Münster
Münster, Germany

ISBN 978-3-476-05924-6   ISBN 978-3-476-05925-3 (eBook)
https://doi.org/10.1007/978-3-476-05925-3

© The Editor(s) (if applicable) and The Author(s), under exclusive licence to Springer-Verlag GmbH, DE, part of Springer Nature 2023
This book is a translation of the original German edition „200 Jahre Nationalphilologien" by Strosetzki, Christoph, published by Springer-Verlag GmbH, DE in 2022. The translation was done with the help of artificial intelligence (machine translation by the service DeepL.com). A subsequent human revision was done by the authors primarily in terms of content, so that the book will read stylistically differently from a conventional translation. Springer Nature works continuously to further the development of tools for the production of books and on the related technologies to support the authors.
This work is subject to copyright. All rights are solely and exclusively licensed by the Publisher, whether the whole or part of the material is concerned, specifically the rights of translation, reprinting, reuse of illustrations, recitation, broadcasting, reproduction on microfilms or in any other physical way, and transmission or information storage and retrieval, electronic adaptation, computer software, or by similar or dissimilar methodology now known or hereafter developed.
The use of general descriptive names, registered names, trademarks, service marks, etc. in this publication does not imply, even in the absence of a specific statement, that such names are exempt from the relevant protective laws and regulations and therefore free for general use.
The publisher, the authors, and the editors are safe to assume that the advice and information in this book are believed to be true and accurate at the date of publication. Neither the publisher nor the authors or the editors give a warranty, expressed or implied, with respect to the material contained herein or for any errors or omissions that may have been made. The publisher remains neutral with regard to jurisdictional claims in published maps and institutional affiliations.

This Palgrave Macmillan imprint is published by the registered company Springer-Verlag GmbH, DE, part of Springer Nature.
The registered company address is: Heidelberger Platz 3, 14197 Berlin, Germany

Preface

At the time of its emergence at the beginning of the nineteenth century, national-language-oriented philology set itself the task of searching for its own in the foreign or the foreign in the foreign. For a long time, the philological subjects at universities and secondary schools had the task of transmitting the works of Balzac, Cervantes, Dostoyevsky, Goethe and Shakespeare. Herder's concept of the "people's spirit", which manifested itself in language, literature, art, customs and law, gave rise to the idea of the "Romania", i.e. the totality of languages and cultures descended from Roman Latin. The doctrine of the "people's spirit" was supported in the second half of the nineteenth century by the psychology of peoples, which Moritz Lazarus, Heymann Steinthal and Wilhelm Wundt had turned into an independent scientific discipline. Latin as a common source language appeared at the same time as the basis for a homogeneous mentality in the Romania.

The doctrine of the people's spirit found a continuation in the ideologically charged cultural studies after the First World War, which had a nationalistic orientation and, for example, contrasted a profound German spirit with a brilliant but superficial French *esprit*. After Germany's defeat in the First World War, there was a current of regional studies that focused on contemporary France and set itself the task of exploring the "essence" of France's hereditary enemy in order to be better able to defeat it in a later confrontation. Although Karl Voretzsch opposed such "cultural studies" at the twentieth Neuphilologentag in Düsseldorf in 1926, National Socialism was able to pick up where it left off. Not long after the National Socialist takeover in 1933, almost a quarter of the professors of romance philology had been dismissed for racist and political reasons. Among them were Helmuth Hatzfeld, Victor Klemperer and Leo Spitzer. The latter initially went to Istanbul in 1933 as a professor of "European philology". When he moved to the USA three years later, Erich Auerbach took over his position in Istanbul, where he wrote his work *Mimesis*. A direction oriented towards stylistic research emanated from the professors who emigrated to the USA. Ernst Robert Curtius, who in his work *Europäische Literatur und lateinisches Mittelalter (European Literature and the Latin Middle Ages,* 1948) focused on topoi as constants of European literature, or Erich Auerbach, who in *Mimesis* (1946) made the representation of reality an aesthetic distinguishing feature, suggested the abolition of the study of Romance studies as a single discipline.

What changes occur with increasing globalization? Are national literatures, with their values and narratives, becoming more and more absorbed into what we tend to call world literature? The term is not meant in the sense of Goethe, who relied on literature that has the value of a "world cultural heritage" and was created out of a cosmopolitan spirit, but rather in relation to a postcolonial and postmodern understanding of literature, in which the opposition of center and periphery is abolished.

Globalization also raises the question of whether there are universal values. Hans Küng summarized them in his project "Global Ethic". Globalization, supported by digital communication technologies, brings international interdependencies also in cultural areas. As in the times of colonialism, on the one hand the "Christian occidental culture" or what is today called the "western lifestyle" is spread, on the other hand a hyperculturality arises in which cultural ideas detach themselves from their original space, interconnect and mix. What happens to the traditions of local cultures in the process? Are they modified, repressed or forgotten? Is the previous diversity lost in the process of homogenization? Or does this very process provoke a counter-reaction under the keyword of localization, which opposes the merging of cultures by strengthening traditional and local elements?

Is there a national or European Leitkultur and if so, is it desirable? For Bassam Tibi, the values of a desirable guiding culture are: democracy, secularism, enlightenment, human rights and civil society, which roughly corresponds in meaning to what is understood as a "free democratic basic order". If integration means a certain assimilation to the German Leitkultur and its values, then this contrasts with multiculturalism, in which everything applies at the same time and thus nothing really applies any more. Former Bundestag President Lammert commented on this: "If a Europe of diversity is to preserve national identities and yet develop a collective identity, it needs a political guiding idea, a common foundation of values and convictions. Such a European guiding idea necessarily refers to common cultural roots, to common history, to common religious traditions".[1] Supplementing and clarifying this, Lammert proposes a European Leitkultur. Such a culture, based on the "cultural modernity" (Habermas) according to Bessam Tibi, should give reason priority over religion, separate religion and politics and demand democracy, pluralism and tolerance. Also from the party of the Greens come demands for a Leitkultur. In the *Stern of* 20.01.2016 the following sentence of the politician Özdemir can be read: "The Basic Law is our Leitkultur." However, these are purely political-legal positions that say little about motivations, lifestyles and guiding values. In any case, the question of the possibility of a Leitkultur arises in view of the widespread multiculturalism and transculturalism of contemporary societies. To what extent are today's cultures characterized by a diversity of possible identities and thus have a transnational character?

---

[1] Die Welt, 13 December 2005.

Modern philologies such as German studies, Romance studies, English studies, and Slavic studies emerged at German universities in the nineteenth century from the Romanticists' efforts to define a respective national Volksgeist. Similar attempts were made in jurisprudence, where the Germanists preferred the German legal tradition to the Roman tradition, which the Romanists represented. Like classical philology, which always took cultural and philosophical contexts into account, the modern philologies were concerned from the outset with the *realia*, i.e. the practical realities of a culture. The first professorships in German philology were filled in Münster in 1801, in Göttingen in 1805, and in Berlin in 1810; the first German Studies seminar was established in Rostock in 1858. In early German studies, as in Romance studies, the focus was on securing sources and editing texts, following the example of classical philology. In the middle of the nineteenth century, "German Studies" was the study of, in particular, medieval manifestations of Germanic culture in history, law, literature and language. It corresponded to the political desire to create a sense of national identity, a national consciousness for a Germany that had for centuries disintegrated into small states. In 1846, the historians broke away from the Germanists' Assembly in Frankfurt and, like the lawyers later, founded their own association. By the end of the nineteenth century, the Dutch and Scandinavian scholars had also left German studies.

Romance studies also developed in the nineteenth century. Romance Studies, like German Studies, was supported by the educated middle classes, which placed more value on cultural and ethical elements of knowledge than on functional areas of knowledge that serve as professional qualifications. Wilhelm von Humboldt, who founded the Berlin University, propagated an educational idea according to which science is something that is never completely found, but always to be sought out, so that the focus should be on problem-oriented research, in which the state would only be an obstacle if it interfered. The state should not demand anything from the universities, but be convinced that they work optimally from a higher point of view in his sense, if it does not interfere. As a result of Humboldt's revolution, the university has been transformed from an expedient function of the state into a space of purpose-free research without the previous school character, its dignity is that of the claim to validity of the free spirit of modern science, whereby the Faculty of Philosophy in particular has a paradigmatic character. According to Immanuel Kant, it is primarily concerned with finding the truth and with erudition, while in the other faculties useful purposes are in the foreground: "to be blessed after death, to be assured in life among other fellow men of one's own by public laws, finally to be assured of the physical enjoyment of life in itself (i.e. of health and long life)."[2]

With the Pisa study, which looks at the learning success of language teaching at all levels, i.e. in the secondary school, in the Berlitz School or at the university, at three-year intervals, there was a drastic change in the positioning of the philologies in Europe from the year 2000 onwards. Now, the content of the respective culture or literature was of less interest, but instead above all the communicative competences,

---

[2] Kant, Immanuel: Streit der Fakultäten, Klaus Reich (ed.). Hamburg 1959, p. 23.

i.e. coping with communicative situations, writing texts appropriate to the addressee and grammatically correct, and understanding different types of texts. The latter could be measured and tested by language tests. Those who wanted to do well in a future Pisa study had to correctly fill in cloze texts and be prepared for everyday communication, e.g. when explaining the way to a foreign acquaintance. Literary and cultural knowledge, which cannot be tested quantitatively, was neglected. The canon of important authors to be read has been largely abolished in favour of everyday problems that can also be dealt with using newspaper cuttings.

For the philologies at the universities, the change in priorities that Pisa brought about for secondary schools was not without consequences. In the Bachelor's and Master's programmes for teaching at secondary schools in North Rhine-Westphalia, at the beginning of the study programme, students are accompanied by pedagogues and spend time observing at the schools they have just left, later they spend an entire semester accompanied by pedagogues at the school, and there are numerous subject didactic and practical language courses, so that cultural and literary content is pushed to the margins. Whereas even before Pisa a canon of texts to be read at grammar schools was prescribed to schools by decree, the content, especially in foreign language philologies, is now arbitrary and secondary. A rethink is therefore needed. Is it worthwhile, in view of globalisation, to develop elements of a national or European guiding culture? How can these promote intercultural competence? How would these elements relate to universal values? What position can philology take in times when it is no longer supported by an educated bourgeoisie, as it was in the nineteenth century, and state requirements, unlike in the Humboldtian model, become the consequences of a pisa study. Should the study of Balzac, Cervantes, Dostoyevsky, Goethe and Shakespeare be dispensed with in grammar schools in future?

These are the main questions from which an interdisciplinary conference on "200 Years of National Philologies: From Romanticism to Globalization" was held in June 2019. The contributions collected in the present volume were partly presented during the conference, partly they were acquired later. The first part of the articles undertakes a redefinition with a view to the history of the subjects; a second part demonstrates how the framework of the national is blown open by colonies and the concept of world literature; finally, the third part shows newer perspectives, for example through the most recent history of the subject, the demonstration of transversal relationships, but also through paradigm shifts such as that of 1968 and reorientations or newer key concepts such as competence and Leitkultur.

Starting with Romance philology in the second half of the nineteenth century, Ursula Bähler shows how a return to the founding texts in France and Germany offers important reflections for today's debates, with a thematic constant being the confrontations of the self with the foreign. Here, national and universalist conceptions such as that of a *littérature européenne*, a *civilisation occidentale* or a world literature are opposed to each other. The worldliness and value of philology has always made it a decidedly uncomfortable science. It already appeared uncomfortable to Nietzsche, who saw it as confronting an age of haste with the slowness of the goldsmith's art. – Alexander Kalkhoff shows how, in the late eighteenth and nineteenth centuries, knowledge of Spanish and Portuguese literature in Germany moved from an extra-academic aristocratic and bourgeois audience to academic university circles and developed from literary and historical literacy to historical grammar and positivist literary history. – Manfred Tietz explains the same development from the perspective of the universities, into whose canon of subjects the modern philologies integrated themselves in the nineteenth century. Factors such as the secularization of knowledge and worldview as well as an educational ideal conceived by Wilhelm von Humboldt, in which literature is understood as educational, play a role. – Tom Kindt, Hans-Harald Müller and Myriam Richter show how the representative subject encyclopaedias of the modern philologies, which representatively depicted the entire subject that had emerged at the beginning of the nineteenth century in a systematic context, were replaced around 1900 by Grundrisse (outlines) that were limited to individual important and particularly sought-after subfields. Publishers and editors thus took account of a development that finally continued with the transformation of the Grundrisse into book series.

National conceptions are the results of political constellations. France, too, had to come to terms with the loss of its colonies in the eighteenth century, as Spain did at the end of the nineteenth century, but did so differently from the Spanish 1898 generation. While the latter retreated to a national *intrahistoria*, colonial fantasies of a restituted geo- and cultural-political hegemony of France were developed in France, as Hendrik Schlieper demonstrates with the example of Prévost's *Manon Lescaut,* Lesage's *Les mariages de Canada* and the opera of Jean-Philippe Rameau and Louis Fuzelier *Les Indes galantes.* – Gesine Müller asks where contemporary French-language literature from the Caribbean stands in the field of tension between national literature and world literature. Whereas the concept of Francophonie still had clear ideas of France as the centre and the former colonies as the periphery, a "littérature-monde en français" is now being proclaimed that propagates an archipelisation in which an island can only be thought of in conjunction with others, i.e. as an archipelago, and the regions are more important than national borders. After all, in recent years the Gallimard publishing house has increasingly represented authors from the Francophone Caribbean.

When a Chinese student of German studies wants to compare the work of the Swiss idyll poet Salomon Gessner (1730–1788) with that of the Chinese poet Tao Yuanming from the fourth century of the Christian era, it is astonishing to find parallels, despite temporal and spatial distance, in the praise of the simple and unspoiled country life as a counterpart to the restless urban life. For Albrecht Koschorke, the idyll is one of those cultural isomorphies to which greater weight is to be attached as transcultural universals. – It is the intercultural competence postulated by educational curricula that Frank Reiser sees promoted by the study of Héctor Abad Faciolince's *El olvido que seremos,* where cultural-space-specific Colombian social and political conflicts are individualized and fictionalized. If the utility of literature consists in knowledge of the world or knowledge of possibilities with the potential to irritate, then orientation knowledge is provided here. – Roland Weidle subsumes a broad spectrum of cultural, hermeneutic, epistemological and ethical competences under the keyword of understanding the world, which he exemplifies using the example of the academic examination of Shakespeare. The latter's characters not infrequently fail because they misjudge the behavior of characters. "Deciphering world" is thus a competence, as is the ability to take the perspectives of others. Skeptically questioning sources of information, rationally debunking mysteries, enduring breaks with the familiar as well as contradictions and uncertainties, and the ability to empathize with others are further competencies that are trained in the course of literary studies. – Thomas Klinkert shows that fictionality as a symbolically generalized medium of communication is a form of self-description of societies by using the example of the novel *Le donne di Messina*, in which the Italian author Elio Vittorini mediates through a collective and polyphonic narrative process to a village abandoned and destroyed after the Second World War. The claim to reality of the action in the village, the various travel stories, the eyewitness accounts and a village diary is complemented by the failing claim to realisation of the utopia of a dispossessed village community. The conflict between artistic autonomy and political-moral commitment is resolved in accordance with Niklas Luhmann's communication theory, when, unlike in historiography or philosophy, the opposition of truth and falsehood has no validity in fiction, since the latter makes the unobservable visible.

In the nineteenth century, literacy was the goal of educated bourgeois reading practice. Jochen Strobel asks whether the acquisition of competence and the possession of education are actually mutually exclusive. In the course of the 1968 movement, however, the dominance of theory and social relevance increased, as evidenced by a basic curriculum from 1973 that aims to make clear to students the social conditionality of literature as work and the ruling interest of the capitalist state in stabilizing the status quo, thus making literary studies a part of social science – a tendency that is also evident in the introductory literature. While the canon of works to be read is not shattered, it does appear as something pre-theoretical. – A literary canon is as normative as the guiding culture it can serve. For Christian Bermes, the respective national philology is the object of Leitkultur, namely what one might point to when asking about Leitkultur. After looking at Gehlen's understanding of commentary literature as a component of art, Husserl's "lifeworld," and Heidegger's "basic phenomenon of everydayness," he concludes that the Leitkultur is "neither simply the commentary nor the lifeworld, understood as the resistance of the doxa against which the commentary rubs itself." – According to Gesa Singer, from the perspective of South African "German studies abroad", the expansion of the traditional literary canon to include migration literature seems to make sense as a cultural studies approach to the exploration of Afro-German identities. If *German Studies* in southern Africa was initially conducted by native speakers of German from the German minorities and, with the revaluation of African heritage after the end of apartheid, black academics are increasingly being recruited, the category of belonging, not only as a category of analysis when dealing with German-language literature, is becoming more and more central. – Klaus-Dietrich Ertler approaches the recent history of Romance studies from the biographical side. In five volumes already published, he has given 126 emeritus or retired colleagues a chance to speak with autobiographical accounts of their careers and formative experiences. In his article he provides an insight into the broad spectrum of what Romance scholars of different generations consider important and worth communicating in addition to their academic findings. The period of the generation of 68, but also the respective religious orientation, prove to be particularly formative.

After the self-mythification of the founders of German philology, the talk of the end of German studies seems to Lothar Bluhm to be no more than a topos of modern academic reflection that repeatedly points to the need for redefinition. If it was originally a national science borne by patriotic euphoria with the task of contributing to the formation of national identity, it now has to respond to the challenges of a plural, heterogeneous and hybrid society with a migration share of 22.5% in 2018, one proposal being the separation of language education and cultural education fields. – A new structuring of philological subjects is also proposed by Christoph Strosetzki. If Romanticism and the philosophy of German Idealism brought a new impetus to physics and philology, and if physics and philology had both emerged from the propaedeutic tradition of the *artes liberales* at the beginning of the nineteenth century, the different development they have taken in the following two hundred years is astonishing. While physics now has numerous professorships in a wide variety of specialties, the philologies are still referred to sweepingly by uninitiated lawyers as "language teaching" because they continue to be defined institutionally by national languages rather than by specialties, even though, like the physicists, they have their respective specialties.

Thanks are due here to Reinhard and Gertraud Horstmann, who provided financial support for the conference, which was held in cooperation with the *Center for Literature,* Burg Hülshoff.

Münster, Germany   Christoph Strosetzki

Contents

Open Philology: Dealing with Foreign Worlds...... 1
Ursula Bähler

Cervantes, Camões and the Elementary/Basic Elements of the Spanish Language: The Functions of Knowledge About the Iberoromania in Nineteenth-Century Germany...... 21
Alexander M. Teixeira Kalkhoff

On Why the Modern Philologies Were Included in the University Canon of Subjects in the Nineteenth Century...... 35
Manfred Tietz

On the Transformation of Philological Knowledge Orders and Information Stores at the Turn of the Nineteenth and Twentieth Centuries: Developments and Causes...... 57
Hans-Harald Müller, Tom Kindt, and Myriam Isabell Richter

The 'Empire' Writes Back: Literary Recolonizations in Eighteenth Century France (Prévost, Lesage, Fuzelier/Rameau)...... 71
Hendrik Schlieper

National Literature – World Literature – Literatures of the World: The Example of French-Language Contemporary Literatures from the Caribbean...... 89
Gesine Müller

Transversal Similarities: Philology Beyond Tradition, Influence and Interconnectedness...... 101
Albrecht Koschorke

Social Traumas and the Literary Canon: Reflections on the Function of Literary Education for Intercultural Competence Using the Example of *El olvido que seremos* by Héctor Abad Faciolince...... 109
Frank Reiser

"What do you read, my lord?": Purposes and Potential of English Literary Studies... 123
Roland Weidle

Systems Theory Reflections on the Relationship Between Literature and Society: With a Case Study on Elio Vittorini 137
Thomas Klinkert

Theory Instead of 'Belesenheit'? Undergraduate Studies of German Literature After 1968 155
Jochen Strobel

Leitkultur: The Need for Commentary in Modern Society and the Lifeworld 177
Christian Bermes

Approaches to Interculturality and Decolonization in German Studies in Southern Africa... 185
Gesa Singer

Romanistics as a Passion: Narratives from the Recent History of the Discipline 195
Klaus-Dieter Ertler

On the Beginning and End of the Science of the German Language and Literature in Germany 215
Lothar Bluhm

Philology and Physics in Romanticism and Today.................... 227
Christoph Strosetzki

Open Philology: Dealing with Foreign Worlds

Ursula Bähler

Abstract One moment condemned as hotbeds of racism, colonialism and nationalism, and the next praised as places of origin of cross-cultural conviviality, the modern philologies have long been the subject of heated discussions. Indeed, their conceptual realizations span, in terms of content and ideology, two diametrically opposed positions: a hegemonic-destructive one and a democratic-constructive one. In the history of the discipline, the first position has been brought into focus far more often than the second, so that the modern philologies have come under a kind of ideological general suspicion. Coming to terms with their darker sides is indispensable for the self-reflection of the philological disciplines. However, it is equally indispensable for their self-understanding and further development to reflect on the positive potential they have provided from the beginning and which a "future philology" (Sheldon Pollock) can make fruitful. Under these auspices, the following remarks focus on the founding texts of Romance philology in the second half of the nineteenth century. The aim is to show how a return to the beginnings of this discipline can provide relevant considerations for today's debates on the much-cited "crisis" of modern philologies.

Philology [is] the science that seeks to understand human beings insofar as they express themselves in words (language) and in word formations. (Leo Spitzer) (Spitzer 1945/46, p. 576) (Translation Lauren Mulholland (hereafter: transl. L. M). My thanks to Lauren Mulholland for her invaluable help with the translation of the text into English)

Teaching students how to become better readers of texts, let alone better readers of life, seems to be the last thing we're supposed to be doing and the last thing the dusty philologer would be thought to be able or inclined to teach. (Sheldon Pollock) (Pollock 2009, p. 959)

U. Bähler (✉)
Romanisches Seminar, Universität Zürich, Zürich, Schweiz
e-mail: ubaehler@rom.uzh.ch

© The Author(s), under exclusive license to Springer-Verlag GmbH, DE, part of Springer Nature 2023
C. Strosetzki (ed.), *200 Years of National Philologies*,
https://doi.org/10.1007/978-3-476-05925-3_1

"[P]hilology is irreducibly complex, and repels as strongly as it attracts".[1] With this sentence, Geoffrey Galt Harpham succinctly summarizes the reception history of the modern philologies, i.e. those disciplines that deal with the languages and literatures of the Middle Ages and modern times. One moment condemned as hotbeds of racism, colonialism and nationalism, and the next praised as places of origin of cross-cultural conviviality, the modern philologies have long been the subject of heated discussions.[2] Indeed, in terms of content and ideology, their conceptual realizations span two diametrically opposed positions: one that we can call hegemonic-destructive and one that we can call democratic-constructive. In the history of the discipline, the first position has been brought into focus far more often than the second, so that the modern philologies have come under a kind of ideological general suspicion, not least among their own representatives.[3] Coming to terms with their problematic, dark sides is indispensable for the purification process and self-reflection of the philological disciplines.[4] However, it is equally indispensable for their self-understanding and further development to reflect above all on the positive potential they have provided from the beginning and which a "future philology" (Pollock 2009) can make fruitful. Disciplinary history always means a simultaneous differentiation of shortcomings and possibilities, of aberrations and opportunities. This is the "work on the heterogeneity of philological discourses"[5] that Markus Messling rightly calls for.

With this in mind, the following remarks focus on the founding texts of Romance philology in the second half of the nineteenth century, the time of its disciplinary institutionalization. The aim is to show how a return to the beginnings of this discipline can provide relevant considerations for today's debates on the much-cited "crisis"[6] of the modern philologies. The thematic thread is provided by the confrontations of the self with the foreign, which permeate philological discourse on all its meta- and autoreflexive, methodological and substantive levels and model socially relevant forms of the coexistence of people and communities.[7] I confine myself to

---

[1] Harpham 2009, p. 55.

[2] See also Rabault-Feuerhahn 2014 and Feuerhahn and Rabault-Feuerhahn 2014.

[3] See also Pollock 2009, p. 38.

[4] Representative examples in chronological order are: Said 1978, Bloch and Nicholson 1996, Hausmann 2000, Olender 2009, Messling 2016.

[5] Messling 2013, p. 78. Incidentally, the heterogeneity of content and ideology characterizes the discourses of Romance philology in Germany precisely in their institutional beginnings, as Wolf 2012 points out.

[6] On this crisis, see for instance Messling 2013, pp. 70–71, with the relevant data, and Gumbrecht 2015.

[7] When Axel Horstmann remarked more than thirty years ago in an ironically self-deprecating tone that the title of his inaugural lecture at the University of Hamburg, "Das Eigene und das Fremde" ("The Own and the Foreign"), would not win any prizes for originality in the philosophical-hermeneutical context (1986/7, p. 7), then this is also and especially true for the study of philological discourse, since the article published by Leo Spitzer at the end of the Second World War with the title of the same name is still echoing in many ears (1945/46). But originality is one thing, relevance another. The conceptual pair of the self and the foreign still provides one of the most meaningful approaches to understanding philology.

Germany and France, the two countries where Romance philology established itself as a modern humanities discipline most early and intensively. Within philology, the accent is on literary studies.[8]

1 Foreign Worlds I: Romance Philology

The nineteenth century is generally regarded as the golden age of a philology that was exempt from all public accountability and widely accepted by society. Thus one reads, for example, in Heinz Schlaffer:

> So reflexionslos konnte das Leben der Philologen auf dem historischen Höhepunkt ihres wissenschaftlichen und gesellschaftlichen Ansehens dahingehen, weil ihnen die kulturelle Bedeutung von Literatur als wesentlicher Bestandteil klassischer Bildung, humanistischer Tradition, bürgerlichen Bewusstseins und nationaler Identität von vornherein gesichert zu sein schien. Da Philologie als wissenschaftliche Disziplin an den Universitäten eingerichtet, also von Staat und Gesellschaft approbiert war, konnte sie sich jeder Begründung ihrer Existenz enthoben glauben. Solche Selbstverständlichkeit musste im 20. Jahrhundert erst erschüttert werden, damit die Philologen wieder auf die Frage stießen, wozu es denn gut sei, dass es sie gebe.[9]

While the above may be applicable to Classical Philology, it does not reflect the situation of Romance Philology. On the contrary, its founding texts display a great density of auto- and meta-reflexive elements, i.e. those reflections that have as their object their own actions and their meaning.[10] Romance philology was never a self-evident discipline, neither as a foreign nor as a national philology.[11] The ultimately economically motivated reasons for the pressure to legitimize under which it, like the modern philologies in general, stands today, are certainly new in this particular form, but not the pressure to justify in and of itself. Such a pressure has been inscribed in Romance philology from the very beginning. The circumstances that led to this fact and the argumentation that arose in response to it are the subject of the following chapters.

One could go so far as to claim that Romance Philology has been a discipline in "crisis" from the very beginning, if one understands by a crisis not, as is usually the case today, a cyclical and largely externally determined phenomenon at the end of

---

[8] On the conceptual history of philology, see Bähler 1995.
[9] "The lives of philologists at the historical peak of their scientific and social prestige could pass by without reflection because the cultural significance of literature as an essential component of classical education, humanist tradition, civic consciousness and national identity seemed to them to be assured from the outset. Since philology was established as a scientific discipline at the universities, i.e. approved by state and society, it could believe itself absolved of any justification for its existence. Such self-evidence had to be shaken in the twentieth century in order for philologists to be confronted again with the question of why it was good that they existed", Schlaffer 1990, p. 226, transl. L. M.
[10] On this point, Bähler 2004, pp. 311–372.
[11] See also Wolf 2012, p. 182, p. 209 *et passim*.

which one's own disappearance threatens, but a principle inherent and self-determined in the discipline that contributes to its vitality. A crisis then does not primarily call for the compensation of a deficiency, but for the visualization and development of a potential, in the sense of the Greek etymon *krinein*, "*to distinguish*", "to sort", that is, in relation to our object, of a constant (out-)differentiation of the aims and purposes, contents and methods of philology.

Thus, the dialogue between philology and society, the negotiation of *esoteric* knowledge with an *exoteric* audience, to express it with the pair of terms introduced into the philosophy of science by Ludwik Fleck, can be considered a first form of confrontation of the own with the foreign.[12] The founders of Romance philology can be an inspiration to us here insofar as they presented their subject with verve and, in doing so, certainly displayed a certain desire for legitimacy that would be a useful strategy even today, given the often larmoyant-accusatory or else self-ironically autodestructive tone of current debates about the place of philologies in universities and in public discourse. Indeed, we could make a habit of informing about the content and aims of our research and writing without seeing it as an imposition *per se*. This is not so much a matter of justifying a utilitarian-economic activity that cannot be directly exploited, but rather of sharing knowledge that is socially and individually meaningful. Unlike an externally imposed, onerous burden, explaining one's own activity can be understood as a quite normal process of accountability – and not justification – to others and oneself, ultimately coming from within science. Such an approach seems to me more urgent than ever today, not only because of public pressure, but also in view of a certain self-indulgence, at best virtuosic, that too often makes of our subjects an expendable playground of the arbitrary. We should again increasingly take a stand instead of hiding behind a chimerical value neutrality.[13] Philology, like every science, is *worldly* and *value-laden*. It deals with linguistically constituted references to the world and, for its part, refers to the world in a specific way and with a specific intention. To openly present this worldliness and its ideological premises could (again) become a matter of course, which would benefit the exchange with the public, the dissemination of esoteric knowledge and thus the overall social relevance of our disciplines.

But what exactly did the founding philologists account for in their texts? This will be answered in the following sections.

2 Foreign Worlds II: Literatures of the Middle Ages

The modern philologies were essentially modelled on classical philology and at the same time developed differently from it. The subject matter of Classical and especially Greek Philology was preferably texts that, in the New Humanist reading,

---

[12] Fleck 1980 [1935].
[13] See also Pollock 2009.

opened access to the "eternal norm"[14] of human being and creation and thus pursued a moral as well as aesthetic purpose of knowledge and education that no one seriously questioned. Thus, for Wilhelm von Humboldt, the greatest benefit of studying Greek consisted

> [...] nicht gerade in dem Anschauen eines solchen Charakters, als der Griechische war, sondern in dem eignen Aufsuchen desselben. Denn durch dieses wird der Aufsuchende selbst auf eine ähnliche Weise gestimmt; Griechischer Geist geht in ihn über; und bringt durch die Art, wie er sich mit seinem eignen vermischt, schöne Gestalten hervor [...].[15]

The subjects of Romance philology, however, were now literatures and languages that until then, if known at all, had been neither aesthetically nor ethically valued, let alone classified as educationally valuable, namely those of the medieval era. Why texts of the period bracketed between antiquity and humanism should now suddenly become important objects of research and teaching had first to be explained. Thus, from the very beginning, Romance philology has been characterized by a heterodox gesture that breaks with the New Humanist ideal of education and whose subversive power has not been sufficiently emphasized in the historiography of the discipline. It is precisely *not a* matter of continuing to work on the "fabric of a normative culture",[16] but of weaving a *new fabric*. The emancipatory act of the modern philologies consists in this break with the normative.

The confrontation with the normative can be observed particularly clearly in France. Here, however, it was less classical philology than the tradition of the so-called *Belles-Lettres* that determined the horizon of expectations against which it was necessary to stand out. The *Belles-Lettres* had paradigmatically substituted French Classicism for Antiquity within Modernism. For the representatives of the classicist position – Désiré Nisard and Ferdinand Brunetière are emblematic here – French literary history in a serious sense only begins with the literature of the seventeenth century. Compared to this, the literature of the Middle Ages was considered clearly inferior, both aesthetically – medieval texts were mostly perceived as repetitive-monotonous compositions without structure and logic, their language as unduly irregular in orthography, grammar and syntax – and ethically: in the *chansons de geste*, for example, one saw primarily stagings of brutal violence, and in the *fabliaux* one finds very crude obscenities.[17]

In the field of literary studies, then, two normative models oriented towards aesthetic and ethical rules were valid in France: the classical antique and the classical *Belles-Lettres*. Against these, Romance philology, although essentially a national philology – medieval France is indeed the country of origin of practically all

---

[14] See Horstmann 1986/87, p. 21.
[15] "[...] not just in looking at such a character as the Greek one was, but in seeking it out oneself. For by this the seeker himself is tuned in a similar way; Greek spirit passes into him; and by the way it mingles with his own produces beautiful figures [...]", Humboldt, "Über das Studium des Alterthums, und des Griechischen insbesondre" (1793), quoted in Horstmann 1986/87, p. 22, transl. L. M.
[16] Messling 2013, p. 70.
[17] See Bähler 2011.

'modern' literary genres within Romania had to fight for its place. The softening of the normative view can be seen very clearly in Gaston Paris, arguably the most important founder of Romance philology in France alongside Paul Meyer. In 1885, in the preface to his collection of texts *La Poésie au moyen âge*, addressed to a wider public, he expressed himself as follows:

> La poésie du moyen âge offre assurément même aux esprits les plus délicats et les plus cultivés, pourvu qu'ils ne se refusent pas de parti pris à les accepter, de véritables jouissances : elle frappe souvent l'imagination et touche le cœur par sa grandeur naïve, par sa simplicité, par l'intensité du sentiment qui la pénètre, ou elle plaît par la grâce svelte et la vive allure de l'expression. Il est sûr, d'autre part, que non seulement elle ne répond pas aux exigences du goût classique et qu'elle heurte toutes les habitudes dont nous trouvons souvent commode de faire des règles, mais encore qu'elle a des défauts généraux, des pauvretés et des faiblesses incontestables : on y relève souvent un singulier mélange de bizarrerie et de banalité, de grossièreté et de convention; enfin il faut bien reconnaître que le plus habituel des défauts qu'elle présente, comme le plus insupportable, est la platitude. C'est malheureusement l'écueil que l'esprit français, à toutes les époques, côtoie volontiers et touche trop souvent, comme d'autres l'obscurité, le vague ou l'emphase.[18]

In the early years of the institutionalization of Romance philology in France, medieval literature was a foreign literature in its own country. It was the great unknown and thus a suitable projection surface for everything that was to be excluded in the name of the traditional ethical-aesthetic canon. One of the merits of Romance philology was to soften these norms and to give a place to the diverse. Even if this did not directly entail a radical reshaping of the classicist canon, it did pave the way for integrating the deviant and leaving behind the position of bias ("parti pris") and comfortable rule-belief ("les habitudes dont nous trouvons souvent commode de faire des règles"). With subtle irony, Gaston Paris suggests that weaknesses of the "esprit français" that one generally prefers not to see come out particularly well in medieval French literature. In the foreign (of medieval literature), the repressed of the own (of classical literature) becomes visible, entirely in the sense of the basic psychological defense mechanism against that which must not be in the own, as described by Arno Gruen in his book *Der Fremde in uns (The Stranger in Us)*.[19]

At the same time, Germany's *own* medieval literature and German philology also had a very difficult time. However, this was not so much due to the tense relationship to a modern normative understanding of language and literature, but rather to

---

[18] "The poetry of the Middle Ages certainly offers real enjoyment to even the most discerning and cultured minds, provided that they do not refuse to accept it out of bias: it often strikes the imagination and touches the heart with its naive grandeur, its simplicity, and the intensity of feeling that runs through it, or it pleases due to its elegant grace and lively pace of expression. It is certain, however, that not only does it not meet the requirements of classical taste and that it clashes with all the habits that we often find it convenient to establish as rules, but also that it has widespread faults, deficiencies, and undeniable weaknesses: there is often a peculiar combination of the bizarre and the banal, of crudeness and convention; finally, it must be acknowledged that the most common of its defects, as well as the most unbearable, is triteness. This is unfortunately the pitfall that the French spirit, in all eras, willingly encounters and too often touches, as others do with obscurity, vagueness, or grandiloquence", G. Paris ⁶1906 [1885], VII–IX, transl. L. M.

[19] Gruen 2002.

the competition with the normative educational claims and offerings of classical philology.[20] The common notion of a universally celebrated heyday of medieval German studies in the nineteenth century, which emerged to a certain extent organically from the Romantic period's veneration of the Middle Ages and the patriotic embedding of medieval literature in the ideology of the wars of liberation, seems in any case in need of revision.[21] The fact that Romance philology, which dealt not only with *medieval* but also with *foreign* medieval literatures, was all the more unable to play its traditional educational card in Germany is all the less surprising. Gustav Gröber takes the subject out of the game himself in his *Grundriss*:

> Unleugbar ist sie [die Romanische Philologie] nicht berufen zu vielseitigem praktischem Wirken und unfähig das zu leisten, was durch die Erfassung des idealen Geistes des Altertums die klassische Philologie für die Menschenbildung und Menschenerziehung geleistet hat; denn jener Geist ist in ihren Urkunden minder wirksam.[22]

We will see later that there were far more fruitful answers to the question of the ethical content of Romance philology in the German-speaking world at the time. The fact is that, from the very beginning, the modern philologies, by virtue of their subject matter, were designed for a departure into diversity, which could either be normatively blocked or consistently tackled.

3 Foreign Worlds III: Nations and Cultures

For the philologists of the nineteenth century, literature was the most essential expression, irreplaceable by any other kind of historical document, of two basic human experiences: that of being human in itself and that of belonging to a social collective, first and foremost the nation. Various strands of argumentation converged in these two basic assumptions: in the *longue durée*, the Aristotelian remarks on the superiority of poetry as an expression of the essential over the discursive forms of the accidental, especially historiography; in the *courte durée*, the notion of an indissoluble connection between peoples, languages and literatures, which had reached its full form in (German) Romanticism.

Like practically all political, social and scientific discourses of the time, modern philologies in the second half of the nineteenth century thought primarily in national categories. In the eyes of its representatives, medieval literary studies advanced to become the true supreme discipline of the humanities, called upon to provide access to the beginnings of national identity through the study of medieval texts. In this

---

[20] On the history of ancient German studies see in detail Hunger 1994, Krohn 1994, Meves 1994 and Wegmann 1994.

[21] Krohn 1994, p. 321.

[22] "It is undeniable that it [Romance philology] is not called to versatile practical work and is incapable of doing what classical philology has done for the formation and education of mankind by capturing the ideal spirit of antiquity; for that spirit is less effective in its documents", Gröber 1904, p. 202, transl. L. M.

context, two radically different conceptions of the nation and of national literature emerged. An exclusive one, fixated on delimitation and preservation, and an inclusive one, oriented towards exchange and transformation. The exclusive conception and its destructive consequences have been extensively analyzed and commented upon by scholars, and today often serve to discredit Modern Philologies *in globo* as incubators of imperialist, colonialist, and racist Europe already ominously conceived in their premises.[23] Far less well known is the simultaneously present integrative version of the nation and national literature. In France, this is exemplified again by Gaston Paris.

The French nation – as well as the whole of Romania, for that matter – is constructed by Gaston Paris as a space of perpetual integrative fusion, we would say today: of *métissage*. Starting from the Old French epic, which is conceived as a synthesis of Germanic and Romance elements, the principle of the blending of ethnic elements acquires in the philologist's discourse the status of a an *ideologem*, according to which any kind of fusion is positively creative and marks a cultural progress.[24] In this view, national identity is at any point in time the historically unique, but always only provisional result of various ethnic mixing processes, coupled with the free decision of each individual citizen to know, participate in and continue writing this national history.[25]

The principle of ethnic fusion *within* the development of the nation and national literature is paralleled by the idea of exchange and cross-fertilization, on the one hand, and the idea of competition, on the other hand, at the level of contact *between* the individual nations and their literatures. This competition does not revolve around the hegemony of each nation's own literature in its particularity, but around the primacy of each nation's own literature, insofar as it knows how to express superordinate values and ideals that can be shared by others and thus transcend the particular. According to Gaston Paris, different nations have won this competition: for example France in the Middle Ages and in the seventeenth century, Italy during the Renaissance and Germany at the end of the eighteenth and in the nineteenth century.

The experience of the common, coupled with the experience of the difference of each particular, provides the foundation of a civilization. In 1870, in the midst of the Franco-Prussian War, this idea, related to Europe, reads like this in Gaston Paris:

> L'opposition des nations les unes aux autres, qui complète la conscience intime de chacune d'elles, a malheureusement trop souvent pour conséquence la jalousie, la haine, l'étroitesse d'esprit. Réduite à ses justes limites, elle ne doit donner aux peuples divers que la jouissance de leur variété dans une unité plus haute: cette unité plus haute se compose de ce que chaque peuple a de meilleur; elle forme ce qu'on appelle la civilisation, et plus particulièrement la civilisation européenne, patrie agrandie où nous ne désespérons pas, même dans les cruels moments que nous traversons, de voir se donner la main toutes les nations qui y participent. Mais l'opposition des nations les unes aux autres est nécessaire pour qu'elles

---

[23] For an example, see Harpham 2009.

[24] Bähler 2004, pp. 475–478.

[25] Gaston Paris is very close to Ernest Renan here, but developed his ideas largely independently of him, see Bähler 2004, pp. 445–448.

apprennent, non seulement à apprécier les autres, mais à se comprendre elles-mêmes. Elles y puisent un attachement plus vif à ce qui fait leur vie propre; elles peuvent, si elles savent en profiter, y perfectionner leurs qualités et y corriger leurs défauts.[26]

The Swiss Adolf Tobler, holder of the first chair of Romance philology in Berlin, formulated the same vision in his speech on the occasion of his assumption of the rectorate at the Royal Friedrich-Wilhelms University on 15 October 1890 in the following words:

[Wir sehen] die beteiligten Völker in steter Wechselwirkung, jedes rasch sich aneignen, was das andere an wertvollem Neuem erzeugt hat, dann aber wieder auf seine Eigenart sich besinnen und zu ihr zurückkehren, doch nicht ohne erkennen zu lassen, wie aus der vorübergehenden Hingabe an das Fremde Wachstum des eigenen Wesens ihm doch geworden ist. So treiben auch Völker Philologie.[27]

Philology, in further development of the basic hermeneutic principle of *understanding,* meets us here as a guiding metaphor for intercultural exchange *par excellence,* understood as the knowledge and growth of one's own through the knowledge and partial assimilation of the Other.

This leads us to the complex relationship between the particular and the universal that the respective philological discourses construct. Based on a comparison between Gaston Paris and Ferdinand Brunetière, I have elsewhere distinguished two types of *universalism*: a *"universalisme universel"* and a *"universalisme particulariste"*.[28] According to the latter, each nation thinks it is in possession of the universal by itself, while the former understands the universal as a process in which sometimes one's own and sometimes a foreign nation realize a model that all others consider divisible and in whose further shaping they participate, each again in its own form.

The following quotations are intended to illustrate the two divergent positions, which, because they often use the same metaphor, can appear identical at first

---

[26] "The opposition of nations to one another, which completes the intimate consciousness of each of them, unfortunately often results in jealousy, hatred, and narrow-mindedness. Reduced to its proper limits, it can only give to diverse peoples the enjoyment of their variety in a higher unity: this higher unity is formed of that which is best in each people; it forms that which we call civilization, and more particularly European civilization, an expanded homeland where we do not lose hope – even in the cruel times that we live through – of seeing all the nations that participate in it joining hands. But the opposition of nations to one another is necessary for them to learn not only to appreciate others but to understand themselves. They draw from it a stronger attachment to that which makes up their own life; they can, if they know how to benefit from it, perfect their qualities and correct their faults", G. Paris, "La *Chanson de Roland* et la nationalité française [1870]," in G. Paris 1906 [1885], pp. 98–99, transl. L. M.

[27] "[We see] the peoples involved in constant interaction, each rapidly appropriating what the other has produced in the way of valuable new things, but then again reflecting on its own character and returning to it, yet not without showing how the temporary surrender to the foreign has resulted in the growth of its own essence. Thus peoples also pursue philology", Tobler 1908 [1890], pp. 194–195, transl. L. M.

[28] Bähler 2011.

glance, although on closer examination they stand for two radically different conceptions of one's own identity and its relation to other identities. First Brunetière:

> [...] notre [i.e. la France] mission littéraire n'a consisté qu'à nous rendre en quelque manière les médiateurs de la circulation des idées, ou encore à leur donner, – quelle qu'en fût la première origine, anglaise, italienne, allemande, espagnole, orientale, arabe ou chinoise au besoin, – le titre, la forme et le coin qu'il fallait pour en faire la valeur universelle d'échange [...].[29]

Brunetière attributes to France alone the role of universalizing what other nations have put into circulation. To stay with the economic metaphor, in this model the French *franc* becomes the universal means of payment.

Gaston Paris is quite different:

> L'histoire littéraire du monde moderne est celle de l'influence des peuples les uns sur les autres et de leur successive hégémonie: c'est tantôt l'un tantôt l'autre, qui se trouve avoir fait le premier l'évolution que tous doivent accomplir à sa suite. Il ne faut donc pas nous indigner et nous révolter si, à certaines époques, notre développement intellectuel dépend étroitement de celui des peuples voisins: c'est en se suivant qu'on se dépasse, et nous pouvons dire avec une fierté rassurante pour l'avenir que nous sommes la seule nation qui, par deux fois, ait été la tête de colonne des autres, qui ait, par deux fois, soumis ses rivales à l'ascendant de son génie.[30]

Leaving aside the problematic metaphors of war typical of the time, this model negotiates a competition for the universally divisible, in which each nation is equally anxious to win. In other words, if a nation is able to express in its literature that which also speaks to (all) others, then this is not inherent in its nature, but results from a historical cultural process.

Freely following Rabelais, Gaston Paris formulates a principle for a fruitful exchange between modern literatures:

> Aimez, et on vous aimera; ouvrez-vous, et on s'ouvrira à vous; en un mot, comme le démontre si magnifiquement Panurge: Empruntez pour qu'on vous emprunte. Qui ne veut être débiteur, dans ce commerce d'idées, de sujets et de formes, ne sera pas créancier.[31]

---

[29] "[...] our [i.e. France's] literary mission consisted only in making ourselves in some way the mediators of the circulation of ideas, or else in giving them – whatever their first origin may have been, English, Italian, German, Spanish, Oriental, Arabic or Chinese if need be – the title, form, and place necessary to make it a universal exchange value [...]", Brunetière, "Le cosmopolitisme et la littérature nationale" [1895], in Brunetière 1899, p. 308, transl. L. M.

[30] "The literary history of the modern world is that of the influence of peoples on one another and of their successive hegemony: it is sometimes one and sometimes the other that is found to have made the first evolution that all must accomplish in its wake. We should therefore not be shocked and outraged if, at certain times, our intellectual development depends closely on that of neighboring peoples: it is in following each other that we surpass ourselves, and we can say with reassuring pride for the future that we are the only nation that has twice been the head of the column of others, who twice submitted her rivals to the ascendancy of her genius", G. Paris, "La poésie du moyen âge" [1866], in G. Paris 1906 [1885], p. 34, transl. L. M.

[31] "Love and you will be loved; open up, and you will be opened up to; in a word, as Panurge so superbly demonstrates: Borrow so that others will borrow from you. Whoever does not want to be a debtor, in this trade of ideas, subjects and forms, will not be a creditor", G. Paris 1906 [1885], XII, transl. L. M.

When Brunetière also repeatedly sings the praises of the *"littérature européenne"* and the *"civilisation occidentale"*, of what "tous les grands peuples, après l'avoir comme élaboré lentement dans leur isolement national, ont reversé au trésor commun de l'esprit humain",[32] then this civilisation is nothing other than a sum of individual self-contained and unchanging national identities. Moreover, despite the author's occasional assertions to the contrary, these are clearly hierarchical in terms of values, with France at the top. For Gaston Paris, on the other hand, this is a dynamic process in which both the various national characters and that which is considered universal – because it is shared as such – are each in the process of becoming and mutually mix with one another in the sense of the emergent.[33]

The ideas of Gaston Paris and Adolf Tobler correspond to Goethe's conception of world literature, as outlined by the poet in a letter of 15 July 1827 to his friend Eckermann, among others:

> Es ist aber sehr artig, dass wir jetzt, bei dem engen Verkehr zwischen Franzosen, Engländern und Deutschen, in den Fall kommen, uns einander zu korrigieren. Das ist der grosse Nutzen, der bei einer Weltliteratur herauskommt und der sich immer mehr zeigen wird.[34]

Joachim Schrimpf's commentary clarifies this position:

> Das heisst jedoch auch, und hier wird bei allem Respekt vor der Geschichte Goethes weltbürgerlich selektives Denken wieder deutlich, dass immer die Literatur mit Vorrang zur Wirkung gelangen und vernommen werden sollte, in der das allen Menschen Zukommende und Zukömmliche und Gemeinsame in der wie auch immer gearteten besonderen Ausprägung am stärksten zum Tragen kommt.[35]

The universalistic orientation of the modern philologies in this sense can be traced back to the present day, both within and outside Europe. Five examples in chronological order may serve to illustrate this here. In Leo Spitzer's article "Das Eigene und das Fremde" ("The Own and the Foreign") which we have already quoted, the idea of universalism comes to us in the form of a "philological attitude that is equally open to all that is beautiful and always ready to celebrate the spirit", which

---

[32] "all the great peoples, after having slowly worked it out in their national isolation, have returned to the shared wealth of the human spirit", Brunetière 1899, p. 275, transl. L. M.

[33] When Leo Spitzer, on the basis of his experiences with French philology at the beginning of the twentieth century, concludes that the "Toleranz des Franzosen [...] allem Französischen gilt" ("tolerance of the Frenchman [...] applies to everything French"), "Fremdes, das sich nicht unter die ägide Frankreichs begibt [...] höflich ignoriert [wird]" ("foreign things that do not come under the aegis of France [...] are politely ignored") and that the European has little place before the national (1945/46, 581), this 'diagnosis' clearly does not apply to the founding fathers of Romance philology (transl. L. M.).

[34] Quoted in Schrimpf 1968, p. 47. "It really is a very good thing that with this close intercourse between Frenchmen, Englishmen and Germans we have a chance of correcting each other's errors. This is the great advantage that world literature affords, one which will in time become more and more obvious", quoted in Strich 1949, p. 249.

[35] "However, this also means – and here even with Goethe's respect for history, his cosmopolitan selective thinking becomes clear again – that the literature that should always be given priority and be heard is the literature in which that which comes to all people and is common to all people is most strongly expressed in whatever special form it takes", Schrimpf 1968, p. 47, transl. L. M.

is supposed to act as an antidote to the corrosive effect of "narrow nationalism".[36] Spitzer's "celebration of the spirit" corresponds in Léopold Sédar Senghor's work to the idea of the *"Civilisation de l'Universel"*, which he developed in various places in his work with reference to Aimé Césaire, Gaston Berger and Teilhard de Chardin, for example in his address at the "Colloque sur la Négritude" in Dakar on 21 April 1971:

> [...] la civilisation du XXIe siècle sera celle de l'universel, à laquelle chaque ethnie, chaque nation, pourra apporter sa contribution. Je dis 'pourra', car il n'est pas inéluctable que chacune soit, comme l'écrivait Césaire, 'présente au rendez-vous du donner et du recevoir'. Seules y seront présentes, contribueront à bâtir la *Civilisation de l'Universel*, les ethnies et les nations qui croient avoir un message que nulle autre ne possède et qui veulent, consciemment, proférer ce message.[37]

Edward W. Said, for his part, refers directly to Goethe in his "Introduction" to Auerbach's *Mimesis*:

> During the 1820s [his] earlier thoughts carried him [Goethe] toward a conviction that national literatures had been superseded by what he called *Weltliteratur*, or world literature, a universalist conception of all the literatures of the world seen together as forming a majestic symphonic whole. / For many modern scholars – including myself – Goethe's grandly utopian vision is considered to be the foundation of what was to become the field of comparative literature, whose underlying and perhaps unrealizable rationale was this vast synthesis of the world's literary production transcending borders and languages but not in any way effacing their individuality and historical concreteness.[38]

Finally, Boubacar Boris Diop, with whom we end this short tour, follows Senghor in his text "Carona, village planétaire". With a view to the difficulties that arise despite the theoretical globalization of the world in the concrete acquaintance with the Other, the foreign, he writes:

> Une des solutions, la plus évidente au fond, c'est l'échange culturel, c'est-à-dire la possibilité de nouer le dialogue autour de visions singulières du monde qui en expriment, au bout du compte, la rassurante homogénéité. Entre les années 1960 et 1980, Senghor soutenait avec une rare obstination que l'an 2000 serait, pour toutes les nations de la terre, celui du „donner et du recevoir".[39] C'était à une époque où les intellectuels, surtout ceux des pays en développement, n'imaginaient la mondialisation que sous la forme de la dictature universelle du prolétariat. Le Grand Soir n'a pas eu lieu. Le „Banquet de l'universel"non plus. Une belle leçon d'humilité: il ne s'agit plus aujourd'hui que de savoir qui, de Senghor ou de ses détracteurs, s'est le moins lourdement trompé. Même si rien n'indique que la haine soit sur le point de nous accorder un peu de répit, le poète avait peut-être eu plus de bon

---

[36] Spitzer 1945/46, p. 592.

[37] "The civilization of the twenty-first century will be that of the universal, to which each ethnicity, each nation can bring its contribution. I say 'can' because it is not inevitable that each one will be, as Césaire wrote, 'present at the moment of giving and receiving'. Only the ethnicities and nations who believe that they have a message that no other has and who consciously want to deliver that message will be present and will contribute to the building of the *Civilisation de l'Universel*", Senghor 1977, p. 289, transl. L. M.

[38] Said 2013, pp. XV–XVI.

[39] Senghor himself, we have seen, attributes this expression to his friend Aimé Césaire (see quote above).

sens. Il est difficile de concevoir de nos jours une autre voie de sortie de l'intolérance que la culture. Elle s'est imposée en quelque sorte par défaut, comme l'unique réponse au langage des armes. La culture est surtout d'essence démocratique dans la mesure où le fait qu'une nation soit riche ou pauvre peut ne pas y être un facteur décisif. Elle est peut-être le dernier lieu de l'activité humaine où il soit permis d'envisager des relations fondées sur l'équité et le respect mutuel.[40]

All the considerations cited are ultimately based on the same structural logic in dealing with the self and the foreign, the core element of which is the idea of the mutual assimilation of the foreign, through which the self is always transformed without dissolving itself.[41] This structural logic is a fundamental principle of hermeneutics, so that the philological disciplines are specifically called upon here to demonstrate this foundational mechanism, teach it, and repeatedly practice it themselves. The principle at issue here is of course valid not only at the national, but also at all infra- and supranational levels of human coexistence.

In an article in *Le Monde* on May 25, 2019, Julia Kristeva diagnosed the nation with a deep depression and urged it to reclaim its cultural self-awareness on the psychoanalytic couch:

Face à un patient déprimé, le psychanalyste commence par rétablir la confiance en soi, à partir de laquelle il est possible d'établir une relation entre les deux protagonistes de la cure, afin que la parole redevienne féconde et qu'une véritable analyse critique du mal-être puisse avoir lieu. De même, la nation déprimée requiert une image optimale d'elle-même, avant d'être capable d'efforts pour entreprendre, par exemple une intégration européenne, ou une expansion industrielle et commerciale, ou un meilleur accueil des immigrés. „Les nations, comme les hommes, meurent d'imperceptibles impolitesses", écrivait Giraudoux. Un universalisme mal compris et la culpabilité coloniale ont entraîné de nombreux acteurs politiques et idéologiques à commettre, sous couvert de cosmopolitisme, bien pis que d'„imperceptibles impolitesses" à l'égard de la nation. Ils contribuent à aggraver la dépression nationale, avant de la jeter dans l'exaltation maniaque, nationaliste et xénophobe. Les nations européennes attendent l'Europe, et l'Europe a besoin de cultures nationales fières d'elles-mêmes et valorisées, pour réaliser dans le monde cette diversité culturelle dont nous

---

[40] "One of the solutions, in fact the most obvious one, is cultural exchange, that is to say the possibility of establishing a dialogue around different visions of the world that ultimately express a reassuring homogeneity. Between 1960 and 1980, Senghor maintained with unusual obstinacy that the year 2000 would be the time of 'giving and receiving' for all the nations of the world. This was at a time when intellectuals, especially those from developing countries, only imagined globalization in the form of the universal dictatorship of the proletariat. The *Grand Soir* did not happen. Nor did the *Banquet de l'universel*. A good lesson in humility: today it is only a question of knowing who – Senghor or his detractors – was the least mistaken. Although there is no indication that hatred is about to give us any respite, perhaps the poet might have had more sense. Nowadays it is difficult to see any way out of intolerance than through culture. It has become the only response to the language of arms, as it were, by default. Culture is above all democratic in the sense that whether a nation is rich or poor need not be a decisive factor. It is perhaps the last place in human activity where it is possible to envisage relationships based on fairness and mutual respect", Diop 2009, p. 186, transl. L. M.

[41] See also Horstmann 1986/87.

avons donné le mandat à l'Unesco. Une diversité culturelle nationale est le seul antidote au mal de la banalité, cette nouvelle version de la banalité du mal.[42]

The idea expressed here by Kristeva is, as we have seen, already at least 150 years old and stands proudly at the beginning of Romance philology in the founding texts. National, infra- and supranational philologies understood in this way already have value because they oppose the *"banalité"* of the *"globish"* that levels everything and uphold diversity. If we rightly criticize the Modern Philologies of the nineteenth century in some respects, we should not throw the baby out with the bathwater. As historical disciplines, the modern philologies were and are always a place of insight into the diversity and complexity of peoples and nations; in this respect, they were and are always useful correctors of any temptation to essentialize, normativize and uniformize. The fact that there have also been opposing tendencies among philologists, which in the course of history have again and again become disastrously prevalent, should not prevent us from seeing in the founding discourses of the modern philologies also the intellectual potential to which it is necessary to link up. Not to do so is not only scientifically uneconomic in terms of advancing knowledge, but also unhistorical and profoundly unphilological What is ultimately at stake, then, is nothing less than the coherence of our self-image.

4 Foreign Worlds IV: Human Beings

The second basic experience that modern philological discourse locates in literature in the founding years of the nineteenth century is, as I mentioned, that of being human in itself, again both in its universality and in its specific individuality. We find here exactly the same structural elements that we have worked out in the field of collective entities. In this context, we again cite a passage from the pen of Adolf Tobler:

> [Der Philologe verlangt] Auskunft über Regungen fremden Gefühls, über Weltanschauungen, über Lust und Wehe, Streben und Ruhen, Wagen und Zagen, die da und dort, früh oder spät

---

[42] "When dealing with a depressed patient, the psychoanalyst begins by restoring self-confidence, from which it is possible to establish a relationship between the two protagonists involved in the treatment, so that the discussion becomes fruitful again and a true critical analysis of the malaise can take place. In the same way, the depressed nation requires an optimal self-image before it is able to undertake, for example, European integration, industrial and commercial expansion or a better reception of immigrants. 'Nations, like human beings, die from imperceptible impoliteness,' wrote Giraudoux. A misunderstood universalism and colonial guilt have led many political and ideological figures to commit much more than 'imperceptible impoliteness' towards the nation, under the guise of cosmopolitanism. They contribute to the deepening of the national depression, before throwing it into manic, nationalistic and xenophobic exaltation. The European nations are waiting for Europe, and Europe needs national cultures that are proud of themselves and valued, in order to achieve the cultural diversity in the world that we have entrusted to UNESCO. A national cultural diversity is the only antidote to the evil of banality, this new version of the banality of evil", Kristeva 2019, transl. L. M.

im Worte sich kundgegeben haben; ihm ist zu tun um die ungeheure Fülle fremden geistigen Lebens, das in irgendwie fassbarer Redegestalt der Betrachtung sich darbietet und den Betrachter bereichert entlässt nicht um einen flüchtigen Genuss, sondern um das Selbsterleben von Gedanken, Empfindungen, Neigungen, Hoffnungen und ängsten, Freuden und Schmerzen, die aus fremdem Geiste in den eigenen übergegangen sind. Er sucht eine Erziehung zu vollerer, reicherer Menschlichkeit im vertrauten Umgang mit fremdem Geiste, mit den erlesensten Vertretern der glanzvollsten Epochen menschlicher Geschichte, aber auch mit dem Kindessinn solcher Zeiten, da erste Versuche künstlerischer Behandlung der Rede nur tastend gewagt werden [...].[43]

What finds expression here, and is equally valid for dealing with foreign nations, literatures and people, is once again the fundamental impulse of wanting to understand the Other, the confrontation with the unknown, and the partial assimilation of the foreign through philological work on the text. It is the endeavor to first see the foreign as the Other and to understand it as such, in a long, critical and precise work, the aim of which is no less than the "education to fuller, richer humanity in familiar contact with foreign spirit". *Nihil humanum a me alienum puto.* To take the measure of the human, not only in the realizations of any classical-normative canon, but in its entire aesthetic and ethical breadth, this too is therefore a merit of the modern philologies. Neither the metaphor of childhood, which is problematic for us today and whose use is inscribed in the evolutionary theories of the time, nor the idea attached to it of a hierarchy of ethical and aesthetic values that still exists despite all axiological softening, can diminish the basic philological gesture at issue here: the endeavor to trace the human condition in all its breadth and depth through the study of literature. One can dismiss this endeavor as naïve and pathetic; but one can also take it seriously as a hopeful, promising, and meaningful impulse. For this hermeneutic principle is based on the epistemological assumption of something common to and divisible among all human beings, which ultimately makes mutual understanding possible. The philosopher and classical philologist Friedrich Ast expressed this in his *Grundlinien der Grammatik, Hermeneutik und Kritik* in 1808:

Alles Verstehen und Auffassen nicht nur einer fremden Welt, sondern überhaupt eines Anderen ist schlechthin unmöglich ohne die ursprüngliche Einheit und Gleichheit alles Geistigen und ohne die ursprüngliche Einheit aller Dinge im Geiste. Denn wie kann das Eine auf das andere einwirken, dieses die Einwirkung des anderen in sich aufnehmen, wenn

---

[43] "[The philologist demands] information about the stirrings of foreign feeling, about world views, about desire and woe, striving and resting, daring and trembling, which have made themselves known in words here and there, early or late; he is concerned with the immense abundance of foreign spiritual life, which presents itself to the observer in a somehow comprehensible form of speech and enriches him, not with a fleeting enjoyment, but with the self-experience of thoughts, feelings, inclinations, hopes and fears, joys and pains, which have passed from a foreign spirit into his own. He seeks an education to fuller, richer humanity in familiar contact with foreign minds, with the most distinguished representatives of the most glorious epochs of human history, but also with the childlike sense of those times when first attempts at artistic treatment of speech are only tentatively dared [...]", Tobler 1908 [1890], p. 187, transl. L. M.

nicht beide sich verwandt sind, das eine also dem anderen sich zu näheren, sich ihm ähnlich zu bilden oder umgekehrt dasselbe sich ähnlich zu bilden vermag.[44]

Tobler also explains that such an attitude does not necessarily lead to radical relativism and self-sacrifice – such a fear seems typical of 'end-time epochs' such as the last third of the nineteenth century and also our time. As a distant answer to the danger of the dissolution of the self in an all-relativizing whirlpool of historicizing philology, criticized by Friedrich Nietzsche in 1874 in the second of the *Unzeitgemäße Betrachtungen*, "Vom Nutzen und Nachteil der Historie für das Leben" ("On the Advantage and Disadvantage of History for Life"), in which, according to Tobler, "beyond the understanding of everything that has been somewhere and sometime [...] one fails to be something and someone oneself", he writes further:

> [...] dies kann freilich geschehen, obschon ein liebevolles Eingehen auf fremde Art, ein verständnisvolles Nachleben einst gewesenen Geisteslebens solche Frucht keineswegs zu tragen braucht. Philologie läßt uns volle Freiheit eigenen Wachstums; unsere besondere Art auszugeben haben wir nicht nötig, um im Wiederhall für uns ertönender Musik Saiten in uns erklingen zu lassen, die zuvor stumm waren. Was an dauerndem Erfolg, an nicht wieder schwindendem Auswachsen des eigenen Geistes aus der Einwirkung fremder Sinnesart sich ergeben mag, das dürfen wir mit Fug doch als das Erträgnis eigener Anlage ansprechen, als Entwickelung von Keimen, die in uns selbst lagen; und auf der anderen Seite wird das Fernhalten mit nachsichtigem Verständnis durchdrungener fremder Denkweise von unserm eigenen Wesen uns dadurch nicht erschwert, daß wir uns vielleicht sagen müssen: auch in uns lag, was zu solchem Wuchs hätte gedeihen können; wohl uns, daß es neben Besserem aufzukommen nicht vermocht hat, daß die heute entwickelte Art unseres Wesens es in sich nicht duldet. Freiheit der Bewegung besteht also sehr wohl neben philologischem Streben; ja dieses führt geradezu zu Befreiung – aus dem Banne engherziger Pfahlbürgerei, vorurteilsvoller Selbstgerechtigkeit, kümmerlicher Verknöcherung.[45]

Philology, then, is here in the service of "individual liberation", the emancipation of the individual from the narrowness of everything preconceived.

---

[44] "All understanding and comprehension, not only of a foreign world but of another world at all, is completely impossible without the original unity and equality of all spiritual things and without the original unity of all things in the spirit. For how can the one influence the other, how can the latter absorb the influence of the other, if the two are not related to each other, if the one is not able to approach the other, to form itself similar to it, or, conversely, if the one is not able to form itself similar to it", quoted in Horstmann 1986/87, p. 27, transl. L. M.

[45] "[...] This can happen, of course, although a gentle approach to foreign ways, an understanding afterlife of former intellectual life, need by no means bear such fruit. Philology leaves us full freedom for our own growth; we do not need to abandon our particular way of doing things when we let strings sound in us in the reverberation of music that was silent before. Whatever may be the influence of foreign attitudes on the lasting success and definitive growth of our spirit, we may justifiably speak of it as the yield of our own disposition, the development of seeds that lay within ourselves; and, on the other hand, the keeping away from our own being of foreign ways of thinking that have been penetrated with a lenient understanding is not made more difficult for us by the fact that we may have to say to ourselves: there was also in us that which could have flourished into such growth; we are glad that it has not been able to arise alongside something better, that the nature of our being as it is today does not tolerate it in itself. Freedom of movement, therefore, does exist alongside philological striving; more than this, the latter leads to liberation – from the spell of narrow-minded parochialism, prejudiced self-righteousness, stunted ossification", Tobler 1908 [1890], pp. 187–188, transl. L. M.

5 Foreign Worlds V: Heterodoxies

The modern philologies, as our remarks on Romance philology have shown, have always been vectors of modernity, understood as a permanent progression into the new, and that also means into the divergent, into the diverse. The discovery of medieval literature and folklore in the nineteenth century is as much due to this heterodox will of philologists as post-colonialism and the opening up to popular cultures a hundred years later. Contrary to prevailing opinion, the modern philologies were not bourgeois-elitist in their beginnings, but democratic at their core, not only in terms of their objects, but also regarding their methods, which were oriented towards clarity, intelligibility and intersubjective control.[46] The democratic, anti-dogmatic potential of historical-critical work was demonstrated in a particularly striking way in the Dreyfus Affair, in which philologists such as Paul Meyer explicitly invoked their methods to expose the 'facts' underlying the legal error as lies for all and in a generally comprehensible way.[47] Philology in the nineteenth century was clearly intended and perceived as a defiant discipline. After his election to the Académie française in 1896, which was successful only on his third attempt, Gaston Paris wrote to his Swedish friend Per Johan Vising on 1 June of the same year, asking him whether it had been his friendliness towards German that had been his undoing in his first two candidacies:

> Je ne crois pas trop que ce soit mon „teutonisme", – qui ne m'empêche pas, vous le savez, d'être très Français, – qui m'a empêché d'entrer plus tôt à l'Académie; c'est surtout le peu de goût qu'avait cette compagnie pour la philologie et la crainte que cette science chicanière ne mît le nez trop avant dans ses petites affaires.[48]

Philology can and perhaps should once again be a decidedly uncomfortable science. When Boris Boubacar Diop says of the writer: "L'écrivain est, par définition, un traître. Cela veut dire aussi: un être de pur amour",[49] then this characterization could also apply to philologists. At any rate, this is how many of those in the circle of Gaston Paris and Paul Meyer understood themselves.

---

[46] This clarity, understood as democratic participation in critical knowledge, is also called for by Said 2013.

[47] Bähler 1999/2001.

[48] "I don't really believe that it was my "teutonism", – which does not prevent me, as you know, from being very French – that prevented me from entering the Academy earlier; it is above all the little enthusiasm that this company had for philology and the fear that this chicanery science would poke its nose too much into their little affairs", quoted in Bähler 2004, p. 145, transl. L. M.

[49] "The writer is, by definition, a traitor. This also means: a being of pure love", Diop 2009, p. 168, transl. L. M.

6 Foreign Worlds VI: Texts

Finally, I would like to add one more to the various configurations of the self and the Other that we have taken from the philological discourse of the nineteenth century: Literature not only allows us access to the always Other in terms of content, it is also, *as literature* itself, in each individual text, in each of its *singular* manifestations, an initially foreign thing to me, knowledge of which I must acquire in dialogue with it. This form of exchange and of wanting to understand in dealing with the most complex and multi-layered expressions of human language, this form of discipline, of practice, of precision, which always prefers *lectio difficilior* to any rash statement, can also be learned in the modern philologies as nowhere else (with the exception of classical philology).[50] Perhaps no one has expressed this more beautifully than Nietzsche, who otherwise did not spare harsh criticism of philology – or perhaps rather of philologists:

> Philologie nämlich ist jene ehrwürdige Kunst, welche von ihrem Verehrer vor Allem Eins heischt, bei Seite gehn, sich Zeit lassen, still werden, langsam werden —, als eine Goldschmiedekunst und -kennerschaft des *Wortes*, die lauter feine vorsichtige Arbeit abzuthun hat und Nichts erreicht, wenn sie es nicht lento erreicht. Gerade damit aber ist sie heute nöthiger als je, gerade dadurch zieht sie und bezaubert sie uns am stärksten, mitten in einem Zeitalter der ‚Arbeit', will sagen: der Hast, der unanständigen und schwitzenden Eilfertigkeit, das mit allem gleich ‚fertig werden'will, auch mit jedem alten und neuen Buche: — sie selbst wird nicht so leicht irgend womit fertig, sie lehrt *gut* lesen, das heisst langsam, tief, rück- und vorsichtig, mit Hintergedanken, mit offen gelassenen Thüren, mit zarten Fingern und Augen lesen…![51]

In this sense, I understand philology as an eminently performative discipline that does what it says by also fulfilling in its work on texts what it demands on the level of content: an in-depth and approachable engagement with the unknown.

---

[50] In this context, it is worth noting that the 'racist strand' of philologies, as Harpham 2009 beautifully demonstrates, is based to a not inconsiderable degree on inaccurate, selective and therefore *unphilological* readings of philological texts!

[51] Nietzsche 1999 [1881], pp. 614–615. "For philology is that venerable art which exacts from its followers one thing above all—to step to one side, to leave themselves spare moments, to grow silent, to become slow—the leisurely art of the goldsmith applied to language: an art which must carry out slow, fine work, and attains nothing if not *lento*. For this very reason philology is now more desirable than ever before; for this very reason it is the highest attraction and incitement in an age of "work": that is to say, of haste, of unseemly and immoderate hurry-scurry, which is intent upon "getting things done" at once, even every book, whether old or new. Philology itself, perhaps, will not "get things done" so hurriedly: it teaches how to read *well*: i.e. slowly, profoundly, attentively, prudently, with inner thoughts, with the mental doors ajar, with delicate fingers and eyes … my patient friends, this book appeals only to perfect readers and philologists: *learn* to read me well", Nietzsche 1911/2012, p. 9.

References

Bähler, Ursula: Notes sur l'acception du terme de philologie romane chez Gaston Paris, in: Vox Romanica, 54, 1995, pp. 23–40.
Bähler, Ursula: Gaston Paris dreyfusard. Le savant dans la cité, préface de Michel Zink. Paris: Éditions du CNRS 1999/2001.
Bähler, Ursula: Gaston Paris et la philologie romane. Geneva: Droz 2004.
Bähler, Ursula: Universalisme universel ou universalisme particulariste?, in: Pascale Casanova (ed.): Des littératures combatives. L'internationale des nationalismes littéraires, avec un inédit de Fredric Jameson. Paris: Raisons d'agir 2011, pp. 147–171.
Bloch, R. Howard and Nichols, Stephen G. (ed.): Medievalism and the Modernist Temper. Baltimore/London: The Johns Hopkins University Press 1996.
Brunetière, Ferdinand: Études critiques sur l'histoire de la littérature française, 6e série. Paris, Hachette 1899.
Diop, Boubacar Boris: L'Afrique au-delà du miroir. Paris: Philippe Rey 2009.
Feuerhahn, Wolf and Rabault-Feuerhahn, Pascale: La philologie peut-elle s'exporter ? À propos de l'itinéraire identitaire et disciplinaire de Leo Spitzer, in: Revue germanique internationale, 19, 2014, pp. 155–177.
Fleck, Ludwik: Entstehung und Entwicklung einer wissenschaftlichen Tatsache. Einführung in die Lehre vom Denkstil und Denkkollektiv, Lothar Schäfer und Thomas Schnelle (ed.), Frankfurt a. M.: Suhrkamp 1980 [1935].
Gröber, Gustav: Aufgabe und Gliederung der Romanischen Philologie, in: Gustav Gröber (ed.): Grundriss der Romanischen Philologie, 2. verbesserte und vermehrte Auflage, Bd. I. Strassburg: Karl J. Trübner 1904, pp. 186–202.
Gruen, Arno: Der Fremde in uns. Stuttgart: Klett 2002.
Gumbrecht, Hans Ulrich: Die ewige Krise der Geisteswissenschaften – und wo ist ein Ende in Sicht?, in: Beiträge zur Hochschulpolitik, 4, 2015.
Harpham, Geoffrey Galt: Roots, Races, and the Return to Philology, in: Representations, 106, 2009, pp. 34–62.
Hausmann, Frank-Rutger: „Vom Strudel der Ereignisse verschlungen". Deutsche Romanistik im „Dritten Reich". Frankfurt a. M.: Vittorio Klostermann 2000.
Horstmann, Axel: Das Fremde und das Eigene – ‚Assimilation' als hermeneutischer Begriff, in: Archiv für Begriffsgeschichte, 30, 1986/87, pp. 7–43.
Hunger, Ulrich: Die altdeutsche Literatur und das Verlangen nach Wissenschaft: Schöpfungsakt und Fortschrittsglaube in der Frühgermanistik, in: Jürgen Fohrmann und Wilhelm Vosskamp (ed.): Wissenschaftgeschichte der Germanistik im 19. Jahrhundert Stuttgart/Weimar: Metzler 1994, pp. 236–263.
Kristeva, Julia: La culture européenne est la voie pour une Europe plus solide, in: Le Monde, 25.05.2019, http://www.kristeva.fr/le-monde-du-25-mai-2019.html [25.09.2020].
Krohn, Rüdiger: ‚...dass Alles Allen verständlich sey...' Die Altgermanistik des 19. Jahrhunderts und ihre Wege in die Öffentlichkeit, in: Jürgen Fohrmann und Wilhelm Vosskamp (ed.): Wissenschaftgeschichte der Germanistik im 19. Jahrhundert. Stuttgart/Weimar: Metzler 1994, pp. 264–333.
Messling, Markus: Nach der Theorie? Der ‚philological turn' und das Erkenntnisinteresse der Fachgeschichte, in: Geschichte der Germanistik, 43/44, 2013, pp. 70–78.
Messling, Markus: Gebeugter Geist. Rassismus und Erkenntnis in der modernen europäischen Philologie. Göttingen: Wallstein 2016.
Meves, Uwe: Zum Institutionalisierungsprozess der Deutschen Philologie: Die Periode der Lehrstuhlerrichtung (von ca. 1810 bis zum Ende der 60er Jahre des 19. Jahrhunderts), in: Jürgen Fohrmann und Wilhelm Vosskamp (ed.): Wissenschaftgeschichte der Germanistik im 19. Jahrhundert. Stuttgart/Weimar: Metzler 1994, pp. 115–203.

Nietzsche, Friedrich: Morgenröthe, Vorrede 5. In: G. Colli und M. Montinari (ed.): Friedrich Nietzsche, Sämtliche Werke. Kritische Studienausgabe (KSA), 3, 1980, 219–88. Neuausgabe Berlin: De Gruyter 1999 [1881], pp. 614–615.

Nietzsche, Friedrich: The Dawn of day, translated by John McFarland Kennedy. New York: The Macmillan Company 1911 (https://www.gutenberg.org/files/39955/39955-h/39955-h.html#toc5).

Olender, Maurice: Race sans histoire. Paris: Galaade Éditions 2009.

Paris, Gaston: La Poésie au moyen âge, leçons et lectures, 1re série. Paris: Hachette ^{6}1906 [1885].

Pollock, Sheldon: "Future Philology? The Fate of a Soft Science in a Hard World", in: Critical Inquiry, 35/4, 2009, pp. 931–961.

Rabault-Feuerhahn, Pascale: Un humanisme nomade: Edward Said et la philologie allemande, in: Pascale Rabault-Feuerhahn (ed.): Théories intercontinentales. Voyages du comparatisme postcolonial. Paris: Demopolis 2014, pp. 47–68.

Said, Edward W.: Orientalism. New York: Pantheon Books 1978.

Said, Edward W.: Introduction to the Fiftieth-Anniversary Edition, in: Erich Auerbach, Mimesis. The Representation of Reality in the Western Literature, translated from the German by Willard R. Trask [1953], with a new introduction by Edward W. Said [2003], Princeton/Oxford, Princeton University Press, 2013, pp. IX–XXXII.

Senghor, Léopold Sédar: Négritude et civilisation de l'universel ?, in: Liberté 3. Paris: Seuil 1977, pp. 268–289.

Schlaffer, Heinz: Poesie und Wissen. Frankfurt a. M.: Suhrkamp 1990.

Schrimpf, Hans Joachim: Goethes Begriff der Weltliteratur. Essay. Stuttgart: Metzlersche Verlagsbuchhandlung 1968.

Spitzer, Leo: Das Eigene und das Fremde. Über Philologie und Nationalismus, in: Die Wandlung, 1, 1945/46, pp. 576–594.

Strich, Fritz: Goethe and World literature. London: Routledge & K. Paul, 1949.

Tobler, Adolf: Romanische Philologie an deutschen Universitäten (Rede bei der Übernahme des Rektorats gehalten in der Aula der Königlichen Friedrich-Wilhelms-Universität zu Berlin am 15. Oktober 1890), in: Vermischte Beiträge zur Französischen Grammatik, 3. Reihe, zweite, vermehrte Auflage. Mit einem Anhange: Romanische Philologie an deutschen Universitäten. Leipzig; Verlag von S. Hirzel 1908, pp. 181–204.

Wegmann, Nikolaus: Was heisst einen ‚klassischen Text' lesen?, in: Jürgen Fohrmann und Wilhelm Vosskamp (ed.): Wissenschaftsgeschichte der Germanistik im 19. Jahrhundert, Stuttgart/ Weimar: Metzler 1994, pp. 334–450.

Wolf, Johanna: Kontinuität und Wandel der Philologien. Textarchäologische Studien zur Entstehung der Romanischen Philologie im 19. Jahrhundert. Tübingen: Narr Francke Attempto Verlag 2012.

Cervantes, Camões and the Elementary/Basic Elements of the Spanish Language: The Functions of Knowledge About the Iberoromania in Nineteenth-Century Germany

Alexander M. Teixeira Kalkhoff

Abstract In the late eighteenth and nineteenth centuries, an increase in the production of knowledge about Spanish and Portuguese literature and language can be diagnosed in Germany. This knowledge constituted a new knowledge space that also demanded homage from foreign philologists. This article uses an object-historical approach to describe the sociological, institutional and epistemic changes in the functional frame of reference of this knowledge production in the period mentioned. This process of change can be characterized as a shift from a non-university aristocratic-bourgeois audience interested in general education to an academic-educational-bourgeois functional elite, from the library to the university, and from literary and historical textual knowledge to historical grammar and positivist literary history.

1 Functions of Knowledge

There is an extensive research literature on prehistory and early history, on the history of ideas, on ideological and institutional aspects of the preoccupation with Ibero-Romance in eighteenth and nineteenth century Germany.[1] On the whole, research has established an increased interest in Iberoromania – almost synonymous with its literatures – and an increase in a corresponding provision and production of

---

[1] Including Voretzsch 1930; Hoffmeister 1976; Briesemeister 1984; Gauger 1984; Hinterhäuser 1984; Tietz 1988 and 1989; Schrader 1991; Kalkhoff 2010a, b; Strosetzki 2010; Briesemeister 2014.

A. M. Teixeira Kalkhoff (✉)
Romanisches Seminar, Universität Heidelberg, Heidelberg, Deutschland
e-mail: alexander.teixeirakalkhoff@rose.uni-heidelberg.de

© The Author(s), under exclusive license to Springer-Verlag GmbH, DE, part of Springer Nature 2023
C. Strosetzki (ed.), *200 Years of National Philologies*,
https://doi.org/10.1007/978-3-476-05925-3_2

knowledge from the second half of the eighteenth century onwards in Germany. Keywords of this new knowledge dynamic are a general enthusiasm for Spain, an interest in the Spanish and Portuguese authors Cervantes, Lope de Vega, Calderón de la Barca, Quevedo and Camões as well as in popular romance poetry, a romantic transfiguration of Spain as a mysterious, dark counterpart to the rational, rule-governed French classicism as well as the religious-ideological field of tension between Catholicism and Protestantism in the form of the Reformation in Spain. The places of this knowledge dynamic are first libraries, later also universities.

This article is based on the sociological premise that knowledge is always anchored in the social context of societies and creates and structures realities at a given time within the boundaries of what is knowable and worth knowing.[2] From this premise and the above-mentioned findings in the history of science of increasing knowledge production and increased interest in Iberoromania, the research question is derived as to which members of society the knowledge production and thus this new knowledge space about Iberoromania in nineteenth-century Germany functionally relates to.

My hypothesis is that there was a profound change in the sociological profile of the main frame of reference, and thus in the social function, of this knowledge of Iberoromania in the course of the nineteenth century, which can be characterized, roughly speaking, as a shift from an extra-university aristocratic-bourgeois audience interested in general education to the academic-educational-bourgeois functional elites. This transformation shifts the institutional frame of reference, namely from the library to the university, and has profound consequences for the content and presentation of this knowledge. This transformation is firmly embedded in the German educational dynamics of the nineteenth century, in the formation of an academically trained educated bourgeoisie and in the differentiation of the canon of subjects, especially in the Faculty of Philosophy.[3]

2 Order and Places of Knowledge

In 1769 Johann Andreas Dieze (1729–1785), professor of philosophy and first librarian of the Göttingen University Library, published his translation of Luis José Velásquez's (1722–1772) *Orígenes de la poesía castellana* (1754) under the title *Geschichte der Spanischen Dichtkunst*. In his preface, he formulates a sobering assessment of the state of knowledge and dissemination of Spanish literature among Germans:

> In the eager and manifold efforts to spread the knowledge of foreign literature among us, Spanish literature has hitherto been paid very little, or rather no attention at all. Not only does one live in a complete ignorance of it, but one is also so indifferent to it that one does

---

[2] E.g. Berger and Luckmann 1969; Dux 1982.
[3] Bildungsbürgertum im 19. Jahrhundert 1985–1992.

not even take the trouble to examine whether it deserves our respect; indeed, one is so unjust as to utterly despise it without examining it. The difficulty of obtaining scholarly information from the Spaniards, the rarity of their writings among us, the fact that our knowledge of their language is completely lost, but more than all these circumstances, our prejudices have contributed much to the fact that Spanish literature is neglected.[4]

A lack of appreciation of Spanish literature correlated not only with prejudices about it, but also with the scant availability of texts and a lack of knowledge of the language. Friedrich Johann Bertuch (1747–1822) made a similar judgment barely ten years later in 1780 in the introduction "Ein Wort dem Leser" ("A Word to the Reader") to the *Magazin der spanischen und portugiesischen Literatur* (Magazine of Spanish and Portuguese Literature) that he edited.[5] But to whom do Dieze and Bertuch address their appeals to finally take care of the Ibero-Romance literatures? In his preface, Bertuch speaks of "We Germans" and their "thirst for knowledge", of "our busy national spirit", thus including himself in a group of recipients defined as nation and people. Dieze, too, speaks pluralistically and including himself of "among us". But sociologically this group is not further specified and can ultimately only be infered by the socio-economic power to procure the corresponding books by purchase or through the lending system of the libraries. And these were certainly not the common people of the people. But in principle they do not exclude them from their address.

In order to nevertheless be able to make statements about the reference audience of the production of knowledge about Iberoromania, I propose as a heuristic the path via the form of presentation of knowledge in the sense of an object history. Object history is an empirical approach in cultural studies, according to which objects of use are understood as tools for the practices of everyday life common in a historical period.[6] It is always books in which knowledge about Iberoromania is presented, but the books manifest themselves in the form of different types of texts. An anthology, such as August Wilhelm Schlegel's (1767–1845) *Blumensträuße italienischer, spanischer und portugiesischer Poesie* (Bouquets of Italian, Spanish and Portuguese Poetry) (1803), is aimed at a different audience in terms of target group and certainly also in terms of sales strategy than Friedrich Diez's (1794–1876) three-volume *Grammatik der Romanischen Sprachen* (1836–38) or – even more contrasting – Gustav Gröber's (1844–1911) *Grundriss der romanischen Philologie* (Outline of Romance Philology) (1888–1902).[7] Each of the aforementioned books has a use value all its own within fixed social practices.

But we must first ask ourselves what knowledge of Ibero-Romance is made available in Germany from the second half of the eighteenth to the end of the nineteenth century. I propose the following systematization here: (i) Don Quixote translations: Paradigmatic here is, for instance, Ludwig Tieck's (1773–1853) *Leben und*

---

[4] Dieze 1769, "Preface of the Translator."
[5] Bertuch 1780, "A Word to the Reader."
[6] Ruppert 1993, p. 15 f.
[7] A.W. Schlegel 1803; Diez 1836–38; Gröber 1888–1902.

Thaten des scharfsinnigen Edlen Don Quixote von la Mancha by Miguel de Cervantes Saavedra (1799–1801).[8] (ii) Folk poetry: In keeping with the Romantic interest in folk poetry, Johann Gottfried Herder (1744–1803), Jacob Grimm, Friedrich Diez, and Victor Aimé Huber (1800–1869), for example, publish folk songs, *romances*, and heroic songs of the Middle Ages.[9] (iii) Literary History: In addition to the already mentioned, effective Dieze's *Geschichte der Spanischen Dichtkunst*, Friedrich Bouterwek (1766–1828), Eduard Brinckmeier (1811–1897), and Adolph Friedrich von Schack (1815–1894) published extensive literary histories of Spain and Portugal.[10] (iv) Readings resp. Anthology: In order to make literary texts available to a wider audience in German translation, collections of texts are published, for example Friedrich Johann Bertuch publishes/edits between 1780 and 1782 the three-volume *Magazin der spanischen und portugiesischen Literatur* (Magazine of Spanish and Portuguese Literature).[11] (v) Language history: Although the predominant interest is in Spanish and Portuguese literature, works on the linguistic history of the Iberian languages within the Romance language family also appear.[12]

In this way, German philologists sifted through, arranged, translated, disseminated and commented on the hitherto unexploited treasure of Spanish literature. Around the middle of the century, the Spanish literary historian Augustin Durán (1789–1862) paid tribute to these efforts of German scholarship in the preface to the new edition of his *Colección de romanceros y cancioneros*. Diezes and Bertuch's appeals were thus heard by the German scholarly world:

> Por eso las primeras antologías de romances regularmente concebidas y bien pensadas se han hecho en Alemania. Alemanes son los que mejor han publicado la historia de nuestra literatura y teatro; los que sabia y filosóficamente han reimpreso, comentado y juzgado algunas de nuestras crónicas.[13]

Dietrich Briesemeister's work in the history of science impressively demonstrates that the history of Hispanic and Lusitanian studies in the nineteenth century is essentially a history of libraries, i.e. a history of book holdings and the availability of texts.[14] Knowledge is always available knowledge. Here, the University Library of Göttingen deserves special mention, where Johann Andreas Dieze acquired numerous works in Spanish for the university library. Jacob Grimm (1785–1863), for example, drew on the Göttingen University Library's copy of the *Cancionero de*

---

[8] Besides Tieck 1799–1801 also Bertuch 1775–78 and Soltau 1825.
[9] Besides Herder 1779; Grimm 1815; Diez 1821; Huber 1821 also Depping 1817 and 1844; Bellermann 1840, 1864.
[10] Besides Dieze 1769; Bouterwek 1804; Brinckmeier 1844; Schack 1845–46 also Wolf 1859; Gröber 1897.
[11] Besides Bertuch 1780–82 also A.W. Schlegel 1803.
[12] Diefenbach 1831; Diez 1836–38; Delius 1850; Engelmann 1861; Gröber 1888; see also Wilhelm von Humboldt's Betrachtungen zum Baskischen (1821).
[13] Durán 1849, p. VIII.
[14] Briesemeister 1984, 2014.

Amberes (1555) when compiling his *Silva de romances viejos* (1815), which he tells the reader in the preface: "es el exemplar de la bibliotheca publica de Gotinga que me ha sido comunicado toda franqueza y bondad".[15] Without access to Spanish-language book collections, editions, translations and research do not take place.

But the study of Ibero-Romance literatures also found its way into German universities. In the first half of the nineteenth century, a comparative history of literature was institutionalized as a new university subject at some universities, for example in Berlin in 1810, in Munich in 1826, in Marburg in 1836 ("Ordinariat für abendländische Literatur/ Ordinariate for Occidental Literature") and in Rostock in 1837 ("Ordinariat für Ästhetik und neuere Literatur/Ordinariate for Aesthetics and Modern Literature").[16] The main ideology of this comparative history of literature is the Romantic postulate of a universal human spirit uniting all the great classical literatures of the Occident, which was to be traced through comparison. In the canon of this occidental world literature (including Dante, Tasso, Byron, Shakespeare), Cervantes, Calderón and Camões play key roles. This romantic project of a comparative history of literature, however, could not assert itself institutionally, but also ideologically at the universities of the nineteenth century and largely broke off again around the middle of the century. The academic preoccupation with Ibero-Romance literatures would only be continued in the second half of the nineteenth century through the new project of a Romance philology – now, however, in the spirit of particular national literatures.

3 Disciplining Knowledge

Whereas knowledge about Ibero-Romance appeared until the first half of the nineteenth century primarily in the form of Spanish and Portuguese literatures and literary history, the second half of the century saw a fundamental change, both in terms of the knowledge itself and its supporting institutions and reference audience. The various dimensions of this change can be described as a shift from literature and literary history to historical-comparative linguistics and positivist literary studies, from the library to the university, and from an inquisitive, generally educated, non-university middle-class audience to professionalized academic Romance philologists.

The works of Friedrich Diez are firmly inscribed in this process of change. He received his mission to deal with troubadour poetry and the literature of the European Middle Ages in general, mythically exaggerated, from none other than Johann Wolfgang von Goethe (1749–1832).[17] His *Grammatik der romanischen Sprachen* (Grammar of Romance Languages), hailed by the history of Romance studies as the

---

[15] Grimm 1815, "Al lector."
[16] Kalkhoff 2010a, p. 86 f.
[17] E.g. Bähler 2012.

founding document of the discipline, must, however, be seen in continuity with his preoccupation with literary texts of the Romance Middle Ages, such as *Altspanische Romanzen* (Old Spanish Romances) (1821), *Die Poesie der Troubadours* (The Poetry of the Troubadours) (1826), *Leben und Werk der Troubadours* (Life and Works of the Troubadours) (1829), *Zwei altromanische Gedichte* (Two Old Romance Poems) (1852), and *Über die erste portugiesische Kunst- und Hofpoesie* (On the First Portuguese Art and Court Poetry) (1863).[18] Grammar and Etymological Dictionary[19] are first of all tools he needs to be able to read and edit the texts critically. Notwithstanding Diezen's activity as a medieval philologist, however, his grammar unfolds a totalizing force that converges in the concept of a 'Romance philology' both in the disciplinary discourse (historical-comparative linguistics of the Romance language family with a strong positivist bias) and at the level of institutions with the founding of chairs, seminars and seminar libraries usually for improved French teacher training.[20] The readership to which Diez addressed his Grammar 1836 is still quite diffuse:

> The present book is dedicated to a field that is also recommended by geographical expansion and literary education and has primarily the practical purpose of promoting the scientific study of the causes of phenomena, both individual and all languages belonging to it. The importance of historical grammar has recently been emphasized by its equally learned and meaningful application to the German languages, and this science has also been enriched by important observations from other sides. That such languages, which have emerged from the decline of others, also offer highly instructive sides to it, must not first be acknowledged, but I know of no researcher who, from this point of view, would have appreciated the Neo-Roman area as much as W. von Humboldt in his work on the emergence of grammatical forms.[21]

Diez treats Italian, Spanish, Portuguese, Provençal, French, Churwälsch (Rhaeto-Romanic) and Walachian (Romanian) in his grammar. Diez draws his knowledge of the Ibero-Romance languages Spanish and Portuguese, as he himself states, from grammars, literary histories and text editions of the seventeenth to nineteenth centuries. For example, in chronological order, from Duarte Nunez de Lião's *Origem da lingoa portuguesa* (1606), Sebastián de Covarrubias' *Tesoro de la lengua castellana, o española* (1611), Bernardo Aldrete's *Del origen y principio de la lengua castellana, o Romance que oy se vsa en España* (1674), Gregorio Mayáns i Siscár's *Orígenes de la lengua española* (1737), Tomás Antonio Sánchez's *Colección de poesías castellanas anteriores al siglo XV* (1779–1790), João Pedro Ribeiro's *Observações históricas e criticas para servirem de memorias ao systema da diplomática Portugueza* (1798), *Fuero Juzgo en Latín y Castellano, cortejado con los más antiguos y preciosos códices por la Real Academia Española* (1815) and *Las Siete Partidas del sabio rey Don Alonso el IX* (1829). Diez built up a corresponding library collection in Bonn, where he was hired as a lecturer of

---

[18] Diez 1821, 1826, 1829, 1836–44, 1853, 1863.
[19] Diez 1853.
[20] Kalkhoff and Wolf 2014, esp. pp. 139–147.
[21] Diez 1836, p. iii.

southwestern European languages in 1821, promoted to extraordinarius in 1823 and to full professor of middle and modern literatures in 1830, much of which is still in the Bonn Seminary Library.[22]

However, something quite fundamental happens with this knowledge, namely it is transformed from a knowledge about a historical epoch deposited in literary and legal texts into a knowledge about the diachronic development of Romance languages. On the one hand, Diez needed this knowledge to make manuscripts of the Romance Middle Ages critically text-philologically readable, on the other hand, he oriented himself methodologically to the Grimm model of historical-comparative grammar. The result is a new body of knowledge that is addressed to a body of experts and no longer directly to an inquisitive educated public (the "Teutschen" as a whole). Yet somehow Diez still stands between these two worlds, namely a textual philology committed to general education and an autonomous knowledge of the development of Romance languages, as expressed here, for example, in the preface to *Über die erste portugiesische Kunst- und Hofpoesie* (On the First Portuguese Art and Court Poetry) (1863):

> The songs printed in the original language, since the editions are not available to all friends of this literature, can, in connection with the grammatical outline and the glossary, give the opportunity for some acquaintance with the old Portuguese language state, which does not give great results, but the knowledge of which provides a not insignificant contribution to the completeness of the Romance language study.

At this point it is interesting that Diez on the one hand addresses the "friends" of Portuguese literature, i.e. a still very open horizon of recipients, similar to Bertuch's "Teutschen" (Germans), but also refers to the old Portuguese linguistic state, the knowledge of which, however, "does not grant these friends of Portuguese literature any great results", but to the completeness of Romance language history "makes a not insignificant contribution".

Who are these new experts in the "study of Romance languages" for whom Diez writes his grammar? We know from the excerpt from the preface of the grammar quoted above that they are those who deal scientifically with Romance languages. But even at the University of Bonn, the "Mecca of all German philologists", Diez hardly finds listeners who want to follow his scientific explanations. Some of his courses have to be cancelled altogether.[23] One hears something similar from Rostock, where Victor Aimé Huber (1800–1869), appointed professor of aesthetics, art history and rhetoric in 1833, announces courses on Ibero-Romance authors in the sense of a comparative history of literature in the lecture catalogue.[24] In July 1835, Huber wrote to his father-in-law in resignation:

> If I have not written anything to you about my lectures since then, it is for a very good reason that I have not been able to give any. Four hours of English with 3 to 4 students, actually privatissime, only that nothing is paid for it, can hardly be counted. [...] I had

---

[22] Hirdt 1993.
[23] Hirdt 1993, vol. 1, p. 47.
[24] Kalkhoff 2010b, pp. 66 f. and pp. 71–73.

announced History of Europe from the end of the fifteenth century to the Peace of Westphalia and History of the Poetry of the Romance Peoples, – but not a single enthusiast was found for these, just as no historical or literary-historical college [...] has come into being either in this or the previous semester. [...] Not having an audience is the rule, and it is considered to be in order.[25]

Let us stay in Rostock. In 1858, the medieval philologist Karl Bartsch (1832–1888) was appointed professor of German and modern literature at the University of Rostock.[26] In the same year, he refounded the philosophical-aesthetic seminar, which had existed since 1839, as a German philological seminar, which is generally regarded as the first university seminar for German studies.[27] The philosophical-aesthetic seminar had been founded in 1839 with the aim of "providing students from all faculties with an opportunity for scientific study of national literature and that of related peoples or peoples who mediate the education of modern times".[28] Instead of spending leisure hours in "beer and wine houses", the students were to be given the opportunity and encouraged to pursue a general education.

From 1858 onwards, Bartsch will orient the seminar towards a Germanic and Old Romance medieval philology, although it will still be open to students of all faculties. In a letter to Jacob Grimm, however, he initially complains: "the greatest obstacle is only that there are no philologists here" (07/18/1858).[29] In this respect, Bartsch agrees with the lament about the lack of philology students more than 20 years after Huber. However, this would change in the course of his 13-year tenure at the University of Rostock.

It was a stroke of luck that Bartsch's successor Reinhold Bechstein (1833–1894) published a list of members on the occasion of the 25th anniversary of the German-philological seminar.[30] With the introduction of the state teaching examination in Mecklenburg around 1865, a clear change in the composition of the seminar's members became apparent. While in the first years almost exclusively theology and law students (stud. Theol. and stud. Jur.) attended the seminary, now philology students (stud. Phil.) formed the majority. The length of stay in the seminary also increases (Roman numerals in front of the name indicate the semesters spent in the seminary). Since the professions of the former seminarists are also recorded, we see that now only later Gymnasium and Realschule teachers leave the German-philological seminar. Here for comparison the seminar members of the summer semesters 1859 and 1873:

"Summer term 1859. – Members: 2.
II Stud. theol. F. A. F. Philippi from Rostock,
Pastor to Hohen-Kirchen.
Stud. jur. C. H. Hall from Retschow,

---

[25] Elvers 1872–1874, vol. 2, p. 36 f.
[26] Teixeira Kalkhoff 2019.
[27] Kalkhoff 2010a, pp. 78–81.
[28] Expert opinion of the responsible Schwerin Ministry of Justice quoted after Kalkhoff 2010, p. 79.
[29] Breuer, Jaehrling and Schröter 2002, p. 36.
[30] Bechstein 1883, pp. 13–16.

Dr. jur., Mayor and City Judge of Sülze.
[…]
Summer semester 1873. – Members: 3.
V. Stud. phil., Christian Starck from Rostock,
Dr. phil., teacher at the grammar school in Doberan.
Stud. theol. u. phil. Alfred Rische a. Schwenckendorf,
ord. Teacher at the secondary school in Ludwigslust.
Stud. phil. Ernst Fritzsche from Rostock,
Dr. phil., teacher at the grammar school in Wismar."[31]

Although texts from the Ibero-Romance Middle Ages did not play a role in Bartsch's seminar and lectures, the well-documented example of the University of Rostock should make it clear that with the introduction of the philological or new-language state examination in the 1850s and 1860s, a new-language student and teaching body emerged at German universities. These new philologists, who were active at universities, secondary schools and grammar schools, made sure of themselves for the first time in 1863 in Meissen by founding the Germanic and Romance section of the *Verein deutscher Philologen und Schulmänner (Association of German Philologists and Schoolmen) and* finally in 1886 in Hanover by founding the *Deutscher Neuphilologen-Verband (German Association of New Philologists)*. From about 1875 onwards, chairs and seminars in Romance philology were systematically founded at all German universities.[32] Although these foundations were aimed at improving French teacher training, all Romance idioms found a home at German universities under the broad umbrella of Romance Philology. On a discursive level, Diez's *Grammatik der romanischen Sprachen* (Grammar of Romance Languages) plays *a* decisive role in the constitution of the broad Romance object area.

This is the historical place where the Spanish and Portuguese language and literature, after the strand of romantically inspired Comparative Literary History had come to its end around the middle of the century, found its place in the canon of the teaching content of the Faculty of Philosophy, under changed premises of knowledge ideology, up to the present day. In addition to language masters and later lecturers who already taught French, Italian, Spanish and Portuguese in the early modern and modern university, professors now regularly appear who read about Spanish and Portuguese linguistic and literary topics or treat them in their seminar exercises. For example, Hermann Suchier (1848–1914), full professor of Romance languages at the University of Halle, offers Spanish grammar, Calderón's *La vida es sueño,* and an introduction to Portuguese in the summer semester of 1877. Academic careers are now also emerging that are exclusively committed to Hispanic topics, such as Gottfried Baist (1853–1920) in Erlangen, later full professor of Romance philology in Freiburg (1891–1918).[33]

---

[31] Bechstein 1883, p. 13 f.
[32] Kalkhoff 2010b.
[33] Zauner 1924.

The Hispanist Baist also wrote the chapters on Spanish language and literature in Gustav Gröber's monumental *Grundriss der romanischen Philologie* (Outline of Romance Philology) in 1888 and 1897, respectively.[34] The chapter on the Spanish language comprises only 25 pages, 14 of which are devoted to historical Phonetics. This emphasis is entirely in keeping with the Young Grammarian zeitgeist, which places the positive facts about the sounds of a language at the centre of linguistic interest. In the chapter on Spanish literature, also written by Baist, data and titles between late antiquity and the *siglos de oro* are crowded together on 83 pages in the spirit of a positivist history of literature.

The chapter on the Portuguese language was written by the Swiss Romance philologist and dialectologist Jules Cornu (1849–1919).[35] In addition to his work on the dialects of western Switzerland, Cornu was considered an expert on Portuguese phonology, morphology and syntax. Like Baist, Cornu devotes his chapter almost exclusively to historical Phonetics.[36] Carolina Michaëlis de Vasconcellos (1851–1925) and Theophilo Braga (1843–1924) write the extensive and fact-filled chapter on Portuguese literary history from the thirteenth to the nineteenth century.[37]

For whom are these chapters on Spanish and Portuguese in Gröber's *Grundriss*, overflowing with detailed information and difficult to digest, intended? In his preface, Gröber does not address a specific group of recipients *expressis verbi*.[38] But of course for Gröber the recipients are narrowly defined, they are the "Romanists" of whom he speaks elsewhere in the *Grundriss* as a matter of course. Gröber does not need to infer this separately. Bursting with *self-confidence*, the *Grundriss* would meet "an undoubted need – the current sales of over 1000 copies confirm the same – for a comprehensive overview of the whole of Romance philology".[39] The research output of the last 50 years has also made the question of the justification of a Romance philology just as superfluous as it has dispelled doubts about its scientificity.[40]

But these Romanists are no longer the "Germans" as a whole; they are "always only narrower circles" who, through their scientific findings, "enlighten" the Romance peoples as well as the Germans "about themselves" in the spirit of a *national philology*.[41] These Romanists are specialist scholars, i.e. numerically few, academically trained experts in the field of Romance philology, the object area of which has been hemmed in by Gröber's *Grundriss*. And this broad Romance philological object

---

[34] Baist 1888, pp. 689–714 and Baist 1897, pp. 383–466.
[35] Fryba-Reber 2009, pp. 38–40; Crivelli 2008.
[36] Cornu 1888, pp. 715–803.
[37] Michaëlis de Vasconcellos and Braga 1897, pp. 129–382.
[38] Gröber 1888, vol. 1, pp. V–VII.
[39] Gröber 1888, vol. 1, p. V.
[40] Gröber 1888, vol. 1, p. 141.
[41] Gröber 1888, vol. 1, p. 154.

domain mediatizes the professional production of knowledge about Spanish and Portuguese language and literature. Of course, Spanish and Portuguese authors continue to be read and discussed by an interested public, it is just that the discourse arising from this is a marginalized private affair that at best belongs in the feuilleton.

References

Bähler, Ursula: Vocations de philologue (Friedrich Diez et Gaston Paris). Fleur de l'enfer ou fruit du paradis?, in: Patricia Oster-Stierle und Karlheinz Stierle: Legenden der Berufung. Heidelberg: Winter 2012, S. 217–230.

Baist, Gottfried: Die spanische Sprache, in: Gröber, Gustav: Grundriss der romanischen Philologie, Bd. 1. Straßburg: Trübener 1888, Bd. 1, S. 689–714.

Baist, Gottfried: Die spanische Literatur, in: Gustav Gröber: Grundriss der romanischen Philologie, Bd. 2.2. Straßburg: Trübener 1897, S. 383–466.

Bechstein, Reinhold: Denkschrift zur Feier des fünfundzwanzigjährigen Bestehens des deutschphilologischen Seminars auf der Universität zu Rostock am 11. Juni 1883. Rostock: Universitäts-Buchdruckerei 1883.

Bellermann, Christian Friedrich: Portugiesische Volkslieder und Romanzen. Leipzig 1864.

Bellermann, Christian Friedrich: Die alten Liederbücher der Portugiesen oder Beiträge zur Geschichte der portugiesischen Poesie vom dreizehnten bis zum Anfang des sechzehnten Jahrhunderts nebst Proben aus Handschriften und alten Drucken. Berlin: Dümmler 1840.

Berger, Peter L. und Luckmann, Thomas: Die gesellschaftliche Konstruktion der Wirklichkeit. Eine Theorie der Wissenssoziologie. Frankfurt a. M.: S. Fischer 1969.

Bertuch, Friedrich Johann: Magazin der spanischen und portugiesischen Literatur, 3 Bde. Weimar: Hoffmann 1780–1782.

Bertuch, Friedrich Johann: Leben und Thaten des weisen Junkers Don Quijote von Mancha. Neue Ausgabe aus der Urschrift des Cervantes, nebst der Fortsetzung des Avellaneda, 6 Bde. Leipzig: Fritsch 1775–78.

Bildungsbürgertum im 19. Jahrhundert, 4 Bde.: Bd. 1 (1985, hrsg. von Werner Conze und Jürgen Kocka): Bildungssystem und Professionalisierung in internationalen Vergleichen (Industrielle Welten; 38); Bd. 2 (1990, hrsg. von Reinhart Koselleck): Bildungsgüter und Bildungswissen (Industrielle Welten; 41); Bd. 3 (1992, hrsg. von M. Rainer Lepsius): Lebensführung und ständische Vergesellschaftung (Industrielle Welten; 47); Bd. 4 (1989, hrsg. von Jürgen Kocka): Politischer Einfluß und gesellschaftliche Formation (Industrielle Welten; 48). Stuttgart: Klett-Cotta 1985–1992.

Bouterwek, Friedrich: Geschichte der (spanischen und portugiesischen) Poesie und Beredsamkeit. Göttingen: Röwer 1804.

Breuer, Günter, Jaehrling, Jürgen und Schröter, Ulrich (Hg.): Briefwechsel der Brüder Jacob und Wilhelm Grimm mit Karl Bartsch, Franz Pfeffer und Gabriel Riedel (Briefwechsel der Brüder Jacob und Wilhelm Grimm, Kritische Ausgabe in Einzelbänden 2). Stuttgart: Hirzel 2002.

Briesemeister, Dietrich: Entre irracionalismo y ciencia. Los estudios hispánicos en Alemania durante el siglo XIX, in: Arbor 119, 1984, S. 105–122 und 467–468.

Briesemeister, Dietrich: Wege und Motive der Beschäftigung mit dem Portugiesischen in Deutschland: Ein geschichtlicher Überblick. 2014. (http://lusitanistenverband.de/wp-content/uploads/sites/9/Briesemeister-Betrachtungen_zur_Lusitanistik.pdf) (25.11.2019).

Brinckmeier, Eduard: Abriss einer documentirten Geschichte der Spanischen Nationalliteratur nebst einer vollständigen Quellenkunde, von den frühesten Zeiten bis zum Anfange des siebzehnten Jahrhunderts. Leipzig: Wienbrack 1844.

Cornu, Jules: Die portugiesische Sprache, in: Gustav Gröber: Grundriss der romanischen Philologie, Bd. 1. Straßburg: Trübner 1888, S. 715–803.

Crivelli, Paola: Jules Cornu, in: Historisches Lexikon der Schweiz (HLS), Version vom 25.11.2008. Online: https://hls-dhs-dss.ch/fr/articles/044806/2004-03-02/, konsultiert am 9.12.2019.
Depping, Georg Bernhard: Sammlung der besten alten Spanischen Historischen, Ritter- und Maurischen Romanzen. Altenburg: Brockhaus 1817.
Delius, Nicolaus: Die romanische Sprachfamilie. Bonn: Lechner 1850.
Depping, Georg Bernhard: Romancero Castellano, ó colección de antiguos romances populares de los Españoles. Leipzig: Brockhaus 1844.
Diefenbach, Lorenz: Über die jetzigen romanischen Schriftsprachen, die spanische, portugiesische, rhätoromanische, französische, italienische und dakoromanische, mit Vorbemerkungen über Entstehung, Verwandtschaft usw. Leipzig: Ricker 1831.
Diez, Friedrich: Über die erste portugiesische Kunst- und Hofpoesie. Bonn: Weber 1863.
Diez, Friedrich: Etymologisches Wörterbuch der romanischen Sprachen, 2 Bde. Bonn: Marcus 1853.
Diez, Friedrich: Zwei altromanische Gedichte. Bonn: Weber 1852.
Diez, Friedrich: Grammatik der romanischen Sprachen, 3 Bde. Bonn: Weber 1836–44.
Diez, Friedrich: Leben und Werke der Troubadours: Ein Beitrag zur näheren Kenntniß des Mittelalters. Zwickau: Schumann 1829.
Diez, Friedrich: Die Poesie der Troubadours. Zwickau: Schumann 1826.
Diez, Friedrich: Altspanische Romanzen besonders vom Cid und Kaiser Karls Paladinen. Berlin: Reimer 1821.
Dieze, Johann Andreas: Don Luis Joseph Velazquez *Geschichte der Spanischen Dichtkunst*. Göttingen: Bossiegel 1769.
Durán, Agustin: Romancero general, ó Colección de Romances castellanos anteriores al siglo XVIII, 2 Bde. Madrid: Rivadenyera 1849–51.
Dux, Günter: Die Logik der Weltbilder. Sinnstrukturen im Wandel der Geschichte. Frankfurt a. M.: Suhrkamp 1982.
Engelmann, Wilhelm H.: Glossaire des mots espagnols et portugais dérivés de l'arabe. Leyde 1861.
Elvers, Rudolf: Victor Aimé Huber, Sein Werden und Wirken, 2 Bde. Bremen: Müller 1872–1874.
Fryba-Reber, Anne-Marguerite: De Gustav Gröber à Arthur Piaget (1872–1895). L'institutionnalisation de la philologie romane en Suisse, in: Ursula Bähler et Richard Trachsler avec la collaboration de Larissa Birrer (Hg.): Portraits de médiévistes suisses (1850–2000): Une profession au fil du temps. Genève: Droz 2009, S. 33–58.
Gauger, Hans-Martin: Los orígenes de la lingüística hispánica, in: Arbor 119, 1984, S. 59–68 und 467–468.
Grimm, Jacob: Silva de romances viejos. Wien: Mayer 1815.
Gröber, Gustav: Grundriss der romanischen Philologie, 4 Bde. Straßburg: Trübner 1888–1902.
Hinterhäuser, Hans: La hispanística alemana y el siglo XIX, in: Arbor 119, 1984, S. 135–142 und 467–468.
Hirdt, Willi (Hg.): Romanistik. Eine Bonner Erfindung (Academica Bonnensia 8), 2 Bde. Bonn: Bouvier 1993.
Humboldt, Wilhelm von: Prüfung der Untersuchungen über die Urbewohner Hispanien vermittelst der Vaskischen Sprache. Berlin: Dümmler 1821.
Hoffmeister, Gerhart: Spanien und Deutschland: Geschichte und Dokumentation der literarischen Beziehungen (Grundlagen der Romanistik 9). Berlin: Schmidt 1976.
Herder, Johann Gottfried: Volkslieder. Leipzig: Weygand 1779.
Huber, Victor Aimé: Sammlung spanischer Romanzen aus der früheren Zeit. Aarau 1821.
Kalkhoff, Alexander M.: El desarrollo conceptual e institucional de los estudios hispánicos en las universidades alemanas desde el siglo XIX hasta nuestros días, in: Katharina Wieland, Kirsten Süselbeck und Vera Eilers (Hg.): Aspectos del desarrollo de la lingüística española a través de los siglos (Romanistik in Geschichte und Gegenwart, Beiheft 18). Hamburg: Buske 2010a, S. 85–99.
Kalkhoff, Alexander M.: *Romanische Philologie im 19. und frühen 20. Jahrhundert: Institutionengeschichtliche Perspektiven* (Romanica Monacensia 78). Tübingen: Narr 2010b.

Kalkhoff, Alexander M. & Wolf, Johanna: Kontingenz: Zufall und Kalkül. Zur Fachgeschichte der Romanischen Philologie (1820–1890), in: Wulf Oesterreicher und Maria Selig (Hg.): Geschichtlichkeit von Sprache und Text: Philologien – Disziplingenese – Wissenschaftshistoriographie. Paderborn: Fink 2014, S. 131–152.

Michaëlis de Vasconcellos, Carolina und Braga, Theophilo: Geschichte der portugiesischen Literatur, in: Gustav Gröber: Grundriss der romanischen Philologie, Bd. 2.2. Straßburg: Trübner 1897, S. 129–382.

Ruppert, Wolfgang: Zur Kulturgeschichte der Alltagsdinge, in: Ruppert, Wolfgang (Hg.): Fahrrad, Auto, Fernsehschrank. Zur Kulturgeschichte der Alltagsdinge. Frankfurt a. M.: Fischer 1993, S. 14–36.

Schack, Adolph Friedrich von: Geschichte der dramatischen Literatur und Kunst in Spanien, 3 Bde. Berlin 1845–46.

Schlegel, August Wilhelm: Blumensträuße italienischer, spanischer und portugiesischer Poesie. Berlin: Morawe & Scheffelt 1803.

Schrader, Ludwig: El interés por el mundo ibérico y los orígenes del hispanismo científico en los países de lengua alemana (siglo XIX), in: Christoph Strosetzki, Jean-François Botrel und Manfred Tietz (Hg.): Actas del I Encuentro Franco-Alemán de Hispanistas (Mainz 9.-12.3.1989). Frankfurt a. M.: Vervuert 1991, S. 1–18.

Soltau, Dietrich Wilhelm: Der sinnreiche Junker Don Quixote von La Mancha von Miguel de Cervantes Saavedra (Bibliothek classischer Romane und Novellen des Auslandes), 4 Bde. Leipzig: Brockhaus 1825.

Strosetzki, Christoph: August Wilhelm Schlegels Rezeption spanischer Literatur, in: York-Gothart Mix und Jochen Strobel (Hg.): Der Europäer August Wilhelm Schlegel: Romantischer Kulturtransfer – romantische Wissenswelten (Quellen und Forschungen zur Literatur- und Kulturgeschichte 62). Berlin: de Gruyter 2010, S. 143–157.

Teixeira Kalkhoff, Alexander M.: Der Mittelalterphilologe Karl Bartsch in Rostock, in: Rafael Arnold, Albrecht Buschmann, Steffi Morkötter und Stephanie Wodianka (Hg.): Romanistik in Rostock: Beiträge zum 600. Universitätsjubiläum (Rostocker Studien zur Universitätsgeschichte 32). Rostock: Universität Rostock 2019, S. 59–79.

Tieck, Ludwig: Leben und Thaten des scharfsinnigen Edlen Don Quixote von la Mancha von Miguel de Cervantes Saavedra, 4 Bde. Berlin: Unger 1799–1801.

Tietz, Manfred: Geschichte der deutschen Hispanistik vor 1900, in: Fritz Nies und Reinhold R. Grimm, (Hg.): Ein ‚unmögliches' Fach: Bilanz und Perspektiven der Romanistik. Tübingen: Narr 1988, S. 131–144.

Tietz, Manfred (Hg.): Das Spanieninteresse im deutschen Sprachraum: Beiträge zur Geschichte der Hispanistik vor 1900. Frankfurt a. M.: Vervuert 1989.

Voretzsch, Karl: Die spanische Sprache und Literatur in der deutschen Romanistik der Frühzeit, in: Estudios eruditos in memoriam de Adolfo Bonilla y San Martín (1875–1926), vol. 2. Madrid: Imprenta Viuda e Hijos de Jaime Ratés 1930, S. 319–358.

Wolf, Ferdinand: Studien zur Geschichte der spanischen und portugiesischen Nationallitteratur. Berlin 1859.

Zauner, Adolf: Gottfried Baist als Hispanist, in: Archiv für das Studium der neueren Sprachen und Literaturen 147, 1924, S. 102–106.

On Why the Modern Philologies Were Included in the University Canon of Subjects in the Nineteenth Century

Manfred Tietz

Abstract The highly significant inclusion of the (modern) philologies in the subject canon of German universities and the system of secondary schools in terms of the history of science and educational policy is owed to a number of factors that date back to the eighteenth century. In addition to the general secularization of worldview and knowledge, these factors include a new understanding of education, as exemplified by Wilhelm von Humboldt, as well as a largely new evaluation of the phenomena of language and literature as cultural achievements and media of human imprinting. Some examples show that the integration and institutionalization of the philologies into the existing system of traditional 'bread-and-butter' courses of study in theology, law and medicine – just as in the case of the modern natural sciences – took many decades and was not accomplished without resistance on various local grounds, but also not without occasional overestimation of one's own capabilities and ideological misdevelopment. The legitimation of the philologies at the time as a multifactorial experience of alterity has lost none of its topicality and is certainly suitable for inclusion in today's debates about the fundamental scientific and social relevance of the philological subjects.

1 Preliminary Considerations on the Term "Philology"

"Philology" as a procedure or art of an appropriate interpretation of texts is – no matter under which conceptual conception and designation – an integral part especially of every written culture. For the area of the European-Christian culture only

M. Tietz (✉)
Romanisches Seminar, Ruhr-Universität Bochum,
Bochum, Deutschland
e-mail: Manfred.Tietz@rub.de

Augustine's *De doctrina christiana* (written between 397 and 426)[1] is to be referred to here, a text significant for the whole 'Occident', whose aim was to ensure in books 1–3 the adequate reading of the – not only in religious respect par excellence – text, the heterogeneous corpus of the Bible, whereby Augustine's efforts extended to a very wide field – from grammar to the complex cultural and theological issues – since it was a matter of making texts and ideas understandable in a systematic way, which had originated linguistically and spiritually far outside the Bishop of Hippo's own Roman-Latin world. The concluding fourth book of the *Doctrina* presents – based on ancient rhetoric – how these contents can be effectively communicated to readers and listeners in a Christian homiletic. From all this emerges the extraordinary range of what can be grasped under the term philology[2] – ultimately an entire life teaching. The classical philologist Karla Pollman has taken this into account by rendering the title of the *Doctrina as The Christian Formation* rather than *On Christian Doctrine,* as is customary (Augustinus 2013). Johanna Wolf and Alexander Kalkhoff are also to be understood in this sense when they speak – on the basis of their insightful dissertations in Romance studies[3] – of the thesis of "becoming human through experiencing alterity" [sc. through a scholarly engagement with language and literature],[4] which – in the last instance – underlies both classical and modern philologies. In historical reality, however, this high dignity has by no means always been accorded to the philologies.[5] In the medieval educational system, it was distributed among various subfields and had to function, each without its own end in itself, as a servant of the all-encompassing leading science of the time, theology, which was oriented towards the canonized sacred texts. Philology only acquired an alternative end in itself in the context of humanism and the Renaissance in the form of the "studia humaniora" in its application to Greek and Roman-Latin, i.e. profane, pagan-ancient texts, which were now assigned the content and propagation of a new, largely different model than the traditional Christian image of man. From these *studia,* "classical philology" developed as a university discipline in its own right and, for a long time, as the dominant school subject in the higher education

---

[1] Cf. the new translation of the work into German and the afterword by Karla Pollmann 2002, p. 260 ff.

[2] Thus, for example, Zedler's *Großes vollständiges Universal-Lexicon aller Wissenschaften und Künste* (vol. 27 (Pe-Ph, col. 1985 [1741]) also referred to this breadth: "With the ancients, philology had a broad scope, and extended also to history, so that it was set against philosophy. [...] Today, this word is used in a broader and narrower sense. According to the former, the historical sciences, especially the knowledge of antiquities, also belong to it, so that philology and litterae humaniores are indifferent words; according to the latter, however, it is understood to mean the study of the [sc. newer] languages, their nature, composition, and differentiated use, and actually includes the art of language, the art of speech, poetry, and criticism. [...]."

[3] Wolf 2012 and Kalkhoff 2010 as well as 2007. Older insightful case studies here include Koch 2019 [1955] and Seidel-Vollmann 1977.

[4] Kalkhoff and Wolf 2014, p. 147.

[5] According to Lepper, the use of the term "philology" ranges from "high value term" to "swear word" (Lepper 2012a, p. 9).

system, which, however, was ultimately curtailed again by Catholic and Protestant orthodoxy in its alternative ideological potential, as Manfred Fuhrmann has shown.[6]

The so-called "modern philologies" only gradually acquired a status corresponding to the earlier "studia humaniora" from the end of the eighteenth century onwards. However, before these "modern philologies", with which we are familiar today, were given a systematic and institutional place in the university knowledge system and in the faculties of the universities of the time, profound intellectual reorientations were required, which will be discussed in more detail below in order to explain the highly complex "why" mentioned in the title of this article, even at the risk of eventually having to state with Johanna Wolf (and Bertolt Brecht) – albeit in question form: "The curtain closed and all questions open?[7] Even if the history of the (modern) philologies may by no means be understood as a teleologically conceived and triumphalistically accomplished 'heroic history', as already emphasized in the older accounts by Thomas Finkenstaedt on the history of English studies,[8] by Hans Helmut Christmann on the history of Romance studies[9] as well as by Jost Hermand on the history of German studies,[10] it must nevertheless be noted that the number of publicly perceptible philologists increased to such a great extent in the course of the nineteenth century that the number of philologists in the field of German studies increased to such an extent that it became more and more important. In his essay "Wir Philologen" (We Philologists), written around 1874/75, the professional (classical) philologist Nietzsche – who in the meantime had fallen out with his established guild everywhere – polemically demanded a radical "restriction of the philological profession"[11] in view of their – from his contemporary point of view – excessive number. He did this with the unflattering statement for the university philologies that ninety-nine out of a hundred philologists were out of place in the true intellectual life[12] and that, moreover, these philologists, together with the philological "schoolteachers", were the "most educated and conceited of all scholars",[13] because – incidentally, just like the positivist natural scientists of the time – they did not know how to appreciate the only true and important science, philosophy, because of all their fact-hoarding. Thus, although the "young discipline" of philology became a "leading science of the 19th century" in certain areas,[14] at the same time the various individual philologies, which had in the

---

[6] Fuhrmann 2001.

[7] Ch. 6 of her dissertation is entitled: "The Curtain Closed and All Questions Open? – An Attempt at Typological Categorization and Concluding Observations." Wolf 2012, pp. 379–387.

[8] Finkenstaedt 1983.

[9] Christmann 1985.

[10] Reinbek bei Hamburg 1994; Rowohlt Repertoire 2017. The book is cited here according to the 1994 edition. Hermand warns against an "overly linear pattern of interpretation" (1994, p. 9).

[11] Nietzsche 1963, vol. 3, p. 326. There, Nietzsche repeats and specifies his criticism, which he had already vehemently put forward in more detail in 1872 in his Basel lecture series "On the Future of our Educational Institutions". Nietzsche 1963, vol. 3, pp. 175–263.

[12] Nietzsche 1963b, vol. 3, p. 324.

[13] *Beyond Good and Evil*. Sixth major piece, "We Scholars. 204", Nietzsche 1963, vol. 2, p. 663.

[14] Lepper 2012a, pp. 113–117.

meantime differentiated themselves, also fell into the reputation outside their own world of being the "science of the uninteresting facts".[15] This is a reservation that is certainly made to the philologies even in the present university system (and in the general public),[16] albeit rather 'behind closed doors', because at times of a quantitative view of the university, the philological subjects are at least welcome as 'majority procurers' due to their, surprisingly for many observers, still very high student demand. But also the philologies themselves were and are, at least since the 1980s, repeatedly of the opinion that they must constantly reassure themselves of their

---

[15] This formulation, often cited, as also by Hans Helmut Christmann (1987, p. 4) – though without citation of sources – goes back to the Hungarian man of letters (and classical philologist with a doctorate) Lajos Hatvany (1880–1961) and his book *Die Wissenschaft des nicht Wissenswerten; ein Kollegheft*. Leipzig 1908 (Berlin 1911, Munich 1914, Oxford et al. 1986), whereby the author by no means condemned every form of philology, but in a fictitious student transcript with his ironically polemical "rebel work" (Hatvany 1911, p. 35) only wanted to criticize the philological practice of the classical philologists of that time, who, instead of filling the classical text with new life, as "dawdlers of science, poet nerve-splitters, document sniffers, radices raspers" (p. 5) suffocated this very text and its intellectual statement under a jumble of scholarly knowledge piled up as mere end in itself. The concluding metaphorical characterization of philology also refers, as the context – the author's dream of life as the director of an altsprachliches "Gymnaaaasium" (sic) (p. 114) – shows, only to the classical philologists of the time, who also expressed themselves in polemical replicas as those affected:

> "The philology of today is like a crazy enterprise, which in a hitherto inhospitable, unknown region is paving roads, erecting dams and bridges, running trains amid great tinkling and clattering, even posting timetables, and not allowing anyone to board on the lines, which have long since been completed, until the whole network has been completed... Year after year the work is delayed, ever new obstacles get in the way, ever strange valleys open up, and the workers strive on and on. With the shovel, with the hammer they work restlessly. No one has the time or the inclination, and the area that has already been cleared remains as unknown as before.
> Now it is high time that some bold travellers should storm this strange railway to set out for ancient Greece and Italy. A guide would have to be found, and at his first call – I have no doubt – hundreds would gather around him.
> How I would like to be that caller!." (p. 113)

On the intention of this book at the time – not without the knowledge of Nietzsche – cf. Bognár 2018, pp. 243–257.

[16] When the Ruhr-Universität Bochum was founded in 1964 – the first new university to be founded in Germany since the First World War, especially in the Ruhr region, which until then had been deliberately kept 'university-free' – 'Philology' was programmatically placed in a prominent fifth position in the sequence of the 20 (!) faculties, directly behind the faculties for 1) Protestant and 2) Catholic Theology, for 3) Philosophy and Educational Science, and for 4) History, which were traditionally placed in first position. In the meantime, 'my' Ruhr-Universität has retained this ranking, but – probably signalling a different understanding of science – has tacitly abandoned the numerical representation, which was undoubtedly meant to be judgmental at the time, and thus removed the stigma of the natural sciences being named late in the universal round of the sciences.

scientific-systematic and social legitimacy[17] or even describe their scientific actual state as extraordinarily precarious.[18] Against the backdrop of this constant talk of the crisis of the philologies (or even of the humanities as a whole), we will therefore ask here in what intellectual contexts and with what objectives the philology(ies) were conceived as academic disciplines at the beginning of the nineteenth century and integrated in the further course of the century as thoroughly respected units into the canon of subjects of the considerably professionalizing university system of the time.

2 The Constitution of the New Philologies: Preconditions and Objectives. Philology as 'True Humanity Education'

Let us return, then, to the institutionalized beginnings of the modern philologies, whose development, despite quite possible reservations and historical contingencies, has certainly not been the path to a 'science of the uninteresting facts', but rather a necessity in the history of science and the humanities, and thus ultimately also a 'success story' that has been and will continue to be achieved, albeit sometimes only by crooked means. In the following, essentially from the perspective of a Romance scholar, two aspects in particular will be treated here in the required – and therefore perhaps sometimes misleading – brevity as 'worthy of questioning': on the one hand, the intellectual and cultural-historical background for the conceptual foundation of the new philologies as independent academic fields and, on the other hand, very sketchily, the phases and arguments for the institutional integration of the philologies into the university structures of the time.

Beyond the 'statistical' interests of the European states in their mutual, above all economic, condition, which certainly cannot be completely questioned, and which in trade and change required knowledge of the language and subject matter of the other, there can be no doubt that the upswing of the modern philologies is to be seen in the context of the early modern secularization[19] and the Enlightenment, which stripped the phenomena of this world of their – in the thinking of the Baroque period still omnipresent – theological function of referring to an otherworldly reality and made them into thisworldly objects *sui generis,* worthy of their own consideration and

---

[17] As symptomatic contemporary documents of this self-contemplation and self-doubt, reference should be made to the two volumes that give broad space to the philologies and their more recent actual state *The so-called humanities:* (vol. 1) *Innenansichten (*ed. by Wolfgang Prinz and Peter Weingart) and (vol. 2): *Außenansichten* (ed. by Peter Weingart, Wolfgang Prinz, Maria Kastner, Sabine Maasen, Wolfgang Walter), 1990 and 1991.

[18] One example is Thomas Finkenstaedt's (1990, pp. 248–253) highly critical account of the situation of English studies in the last third of the twentieth century. Friedrich Wolfzettel's comments on the situation of Romance literary studies (1990, pp. 254–258) are somewhat more positive.

[19] Even if the term is repeatedly called into question – cf. for example Maria Böhmer (2006), Pohlis (2008) or Hartmut von Sass (2019) – in the present context there is no doubt about the fundamental facts.

analysis, from which new approaches to questions arose,[20] to which philology attempted to develop the appropriate answers. This also includes the insight into the fundamental historicity of the world, the insight that became firmly established in the course of the eighteenth century. This also includes the insight into the fundamental historicity of the world, the insight – which became firmly established in the course of the eighteenth century – that the world is by no means only five or six thousand years old, as theologically inferred from the creation and other biblical accounts, but has a hitherto unimaginable age of hundreds of thousands or even millions of years, which not only makes possible but virtually forces a completely new way of thinking about development processes and "historicity", as the term is used by Oesterreicher and Selig.[21] Finally, a fundamental dignification of the phenomena of language and literature, which are central to human self-understanding and mutual communication, should be mentioned here. This dignification was initiated in the aforementioned process of early modern secularization and completed in the Enlightenment and Romanticism, and made it possible to place them as scientific objects in a slow but nevertheless profound process as independent objects of consideration alongside those of the traditional leading science of theology. As far as the phenomenon of language is concerned, we should refer by way of example to its new understanding as *ergon* and *energeia* in Wilhelm von Humboldt (1767–1835),[22] which was thus accorded a completely new significance for the thinking and idiosyncrasies of individuals and nations, as already prefigured by Herder. In addition, the enormous increase in knowledge of other non-European languages with their – as in the case of Sanskrit[23] or the gradual readability of Egyptian hieroglyphics[24] – extraordinarily far-reaching history made possible language comparisons that could be scientifically justified to an ever greater extent. This consideration of language and human communication followed completely different methods and aims than the – still not overcome – religiously inspired speculations about form and rank disputes regarding an Adamite original language. As far as the complementary phenomenon of literature and its fundamentally changed understanding is concerned, reference should again be made in an exemplary manner to Friedrich Schlegel (1772–18,299), who was also

---

[20] On the complex of the 'question' as a research approach and, where appropriate, as a paradigm shift, cf. the contributions in Kevin Drews et al. (eds.): 2019.

[21] Oesterreicher and Selig 2014.

[22] Extraordinarily important for Humboldt's innovative view of language was his discovery of languages other than the hitherto common European languages. Thus he 'discovered' the pre-Indo-European Basque language on his two journeys to Spain. The numerous Jesuits who had been forced to leave the Spanish overseas possessions in 1767 by decree of the Spanish King Charles III had already brought a rich material of American and Oceanic languages – acquired for the purpose of evangelising the indigenous populations – back to Europe with them. Humboldt was able to make use of these materials due to his personal contacts with the exiled Jesuit Lorenzo Hervás y Panduro (1735–1809).

[23] The discovery of Sanskrit "by Western scholars [was] to play a decisive role in the development of [sc. science-historically revolutionary] comparative philology of the nineteenth century." Lyons 1995, p. 21. Decisive impulses for further philological studies were given by Friedrich Schlegel in 1808 with his work *Über die Sprache und Weisheit der Indier.*

[24] In 1822, the Frenchman Jean-François Champollion (1790–1832) finally succeeded in developing a comprehensive system for reading Egyptian hieroglyphs.

committed to the new thinking of the time and for whom, as it says in his *Geschichte der alten und neueren Literatur (History of Old and Newer Literature)*, literature in the broadest sense of the word is the "epitome of all the intellectual abilities and achievements of a nation".[25] Like Humboldt's statements on the history of language, however, Schlegel's definition of literature has a long prehistory that goes far back into the seventeenth of even the sixteenth century,[26] in which literature developed into a secular, autonomous place of man's reflection on man, which during this period gradually took its place alongside the hitherto authoritative text of the Bible and its conceptions of norms.[27] In the course of Romanticism, this state of affairs was to lead up to the idea of the replacement of religion by art and literature[28] and of the biblical prophet by the artist and author[29] and to be broken down to the individual national literatures as new and weighty media of world knowledge. However these facts may be assessed, they are evidence of a new, extraordinarily positive valuation of literature in general and of vernacular literature in particular, which thus acquired an eminently important cognitive and educational function.

This new valuation of language and literature also gave (modern) philology, as the science that dealt with their objects, a new, hitherto unknown intellectual dignity, which prepared its gradual acceptance into the canon of subjects worthy of university treatment, even if at the official level it was to remain for a long time in the shadow of theology as the still all-important leading and key science.

Due to the Romanticists' conviction that the good and true of cultures could not be found in the present, but rather in the distant past (for the Christian world, specifically in a mythically transfigured, temporally vaguely circumscribed Middle Ages), the academic-university study of literature received a long-lasting medievalist orientation, This was especially true for the European epic, in the case of Germany also for the folk books and fairy tales, in the case of Spain for the romances, to which even Jacob Grimm (1785–1863) dedicated one of his first publications (*Silva de romances viejos,* 1815). This was also true of the 'France' complex, where Friedrich Diez (1794–1876), in the first phase of his philological work, was concerned with the Provençal minnesingers (*Poesie der Toubadours,* 1826), and in 1830 was to become the holder of the first neo-philological Romance chair at the University of Bonn, the denomination of which, however, was still 'for medieval languages and literatures').[30] He opened the preface of the volume dedicated to

---

[25] Quoted from Brüggemann 1964, p. 259.

[26] According to Jost Hermand (1994, p. 17), the birth of German studies dates back to the sixteenth century, "when the historical-philological zeal of the professors teaching there was first combined with a German national consciousness directed against the patronizing encroachments of the Roman Catholic Church at the universities that had been founded in the meantime." On the early forums of German studies in the eighteenth century, cf. Lepper 2012b.

[27] Aleida Assmann (1998, pp. 95–112) has reduced this juxtaposition and succession to the image of (Christian-theological) Jordan and (secular-literary) Helicon.

[28] Cf. Auerochs (2009) and for the analogous phenomena in France Bénichou (1996).

[29] On the author's positive self-assessment in the context of humanism, especially in Spain, see, among others, Christoph Strosetzki (1987) and Manfred Tietz (2011).

[30] On Friedrich Diez in the context of Bonn Romance studies, see Richard Baum 1993 I, pp. 45–140 and II, pp. 457–913.

August Wilhelm Schlegel with a sentence that is characteristic of the epochal consciousness and the state of modern philology at that time:

> In a time such as ours, which makes epochs through the versatility of scientific endeavours [!], it could not be lacking, after the knowledge of national literature [!] and the languages of the Middle Ages had already developed into a subject of its own [!], that the poetry of the Troubadours, which was considered by many to be the source of later poetry, was introduced into the circle of that study [!], into which it had hitherto been known almost only by reputation.[31]

But before we go into the question of the state of development and institutionalization of the modern philologies in more detail, we should briefly mention two further preconditions for the possibility of establishing the modern philologies as a scientific and then also university subject. These are the "secularization of higher education"[32] in the second half of the eighteenth and in the course of the nineteenth century, as emphatically described by Manfred Fuhrmann from the point of view of a classical philologist, and its fundamental turning away from both the Catholic-Jesuit and the Protestant-Lutheran "Latin school of the early modern period", which until then had been regarded as exemplary.[33] We are talking about the school reforms of philanthropism and new humanism, which, according to Fuhrmann, were characterized by "the will to radically turn away from religion, from that tradition handed down from the Middle Ages, to which the school was considered to belong to the church".[34] "Both directions," according to Fuhrmann, sought and achieved that 'secular' content be taught in state institutions, and if possible by teachers "who were not primarily theologians."[35] He goes on to say:

> The main difference between the two directions, the turning to the bourgeois practice of life on the one side and the Greek faith as a kind of substitute religion on the other, is of less importance compared with [their] similarities; in both camps that spirit prevailed which, as in all spheres of culture, so also in schooling and education, brought about the sharpest caesura which European mankind has experienced since Christianization in late antiquity and the early Middle Ages.[36]

---

[31] Diez 1826, p. V.

[32] Fuhrmann 2001, p. 93. Kalkhoff and Wolf (2014, p. 135) have traced this process of emancipation from theology under the heading of a *philologia philosophica* as the emergence of a universal philology that developed over time towards a comprehensive 'neo-philology', which in turn was to differentiate into the various 'national philologies' over the course of the nineteenth century.

[33] Fuhrmann 2001, pp. 29–73.

[34] Fuhrmann 2001, p. 93.

[35] Fuhrmann 2001, p. 93.

[36] Fuhrmann 2001, p. 93. Regarding this caesura, it says: "[…] in the course of secularization, large parts of the European cultural tradition were able to free themselves from the grip of Christian doctrine: philosophy and literature, the sciences and the fine arts." Fuhrmann 2001, p. 95. In the specific case of Wilhelm von Humboldt (1767–1835), this meant distancing himself both from positive religions (he had been a student of radical Enlightenment thinkers such as Johann Heinrich Campe (1746–1834) in his youth) and from the emotion-based renewal of religion of a Friedrich Schleiermacher (1768–1834) (whom Humboldt knew personally). A general, but rather undogmatic religion in the sense of Kant, which also left room for a 'Greek faith', was, however, by no means alien to him, especially as he grew older.

As far as the 'Greek faith' of New Humanism, of Weimar Classicism and finally (in its school and university implementation) of Wilhelm von Humboldt's reforms – conceived and implemented especially between 1809 and 1810[37] is concerned, it contains the conviction that in Greekism (beyond Christianity, which is seen negatively, and beyond the equally negatively connoted rationalism and utilitarianism of the – predominantly French – Enlightenment) the ideal of human education, the absolute ideal of being human, and that especially the Germans are called to revive[38] this ideal of the totality of a comprehensive humanistic education, that is, "the personality as the highest ideal of the human being called to self-perfection, an ideal that can only be realized through the harmonious development of all talents and powers [sc. just not the knowledge useful for professional life and the state] can be realized".[39] The core of this 'Greek faith' is the – in the present context – eminently important conviction that education is possible through a model language and art, and here in particular through a philologically exact reading of the texts of Greek (and Roman) literature, and this exclusively when it is pursued as an end in itself and not – as in the centuries before as *ancilla theologiae* or as a mere instrument of the legal system or, as in the case of French and other modern languages – oriented towards an immediately practical use. However, the Humboldtian system, based on the three pillars of "ancient languages", "history" and "mathematics", gave little space to these newer foreign languages.[40] Rather, the focus on the 'old languages' shaped the timetable and the educational goal of the high school, which was long regarded as exemplary.[41] At the same time, it gave the university subject of 'classical philology' an eminent dignity and – despite the reservations of a Nietzsche or Hatvany mentioned above – made the 'classical philologist' in the image of himself and of others the bad-natured incarnation of the academic scholar who had little respect for the scholars who had gradually emerged in the course of the nineteenth century. As another anecdote about the 'Pope of Classical Philology' Ulrich von

---

[37] On the new university organization of the cooperation of research and teaching, cf. his expositions on the "inner and outer organization of the higher scientific institutions in Berlin" 1809/1810, pp. 229–241.

[38] Harold James counts this 'Greek faith' among the "building blocks of German national identity" (1991, esp. pp. 30–32).

[39] Fuhrmann 2001, p. 121.

[40] "French as well as other modern languages were [sc. in the planned gymnasium timetable of 1816] peculiarly provided for only as an optional addition." Fuhrmann 2001, p. 148.

[41] However, this was contradicted as early as 1828 – albeit initially without consequence – by the Protestant theologian and educator Heinrich Stephani (1761–1850), who insisted that true humanity education – the author's key term – was by no means possible only through the ancient languages. He saw the tedious learning of Latin and Greek as a waste of time and took the view that the content of the ancient authors could also be received in German translation or via texts by modern authors. The pupils should altogether deal with only two languages, German and – depending on the neighbouring region – English, French or Italian. These novel theses, advocated in his book "Ueber Gymnasien, ihre eigentliche Bestimmung und zweckmäßige Einrichtung", earned Stephani an extraordinarily long, radically dismissive and largely derisive review (signed FRHT.) penned by an 'Altsprachler' in the Jenaische Allgemeine Literaturzeitung (no. 216–219, Nov. 1829, sp. 281–304, 289–296, S). Cf. Ulbricht 1998.

Wilamowitz-Moellendorff (1848–1931) reports, he tried to reduce his English colleague Alois Brandl (1855–1940) to an academic dwarf[42] with the remark "the little bit of English one learns through private lessons".[43] Nevertheless, the modern philologists – who were gradually professionalizing and institutionalizing themselves in schools and universities – increasingly adopted the neo-Humanist idea that language and literature were the appropriate instruments for the education and formation of youth by postulating a modern 'faith in foreign languages' in analogy to Humboldt's faith in Greece. It is – as it is programmatically stated in the much quoted preface to the first volume of the *Archiv für das Studium der neueren Sprachen und Literaturen* ('Herrig's Archiv') from 1846 – the conviction "that the study of the languages and literatures of the newer cultural peoples, if it is pursued in the right way, is true humanity study, that in it flows a rich source of genuine human education,"[44] or, in the formulation of Kalkhoff and Wolf, that the modern human being "through the occupation with the foreign [sc. a constant cultural experience of alterity] can form him into an ennobled individual".[45] This pedagogically weighty statement undoubtedly also includes the proof of a "social relevance of the new science" of Neuphilologie[46] and the attempt to legitimize it both as a university and school subject, even if its full implementation in both cases should still take considerable time.[47]

3 The Role of the Modern Philologies in the Process of National Identity Formation in Post-Napoleonic Europe

Among the modern philologies, however, the mother tongue of the students of the higher educational institutions, German, had in the meantime experienced a very weighty revaluation for the subject German Studies, which is exemplarily reflected in the timetable of Humboldt's six-level high school, in which German is on a par

---

[42] Brandl, for his part, was a pioneer of specialization and professionalization within the new philologies. At his instigation, an Institute for English and American Studies was spun off from the former Romance English Institute at the Humboldt University in Berlin in 1895.

[43] Quoted from Christmann 1985, p. 19.

[44] Herrig 1846, p. 1. With this formulation, Herrig sees himself in the succession of the "sprightly pioneer of modern school education" (1846, p. 1), the pedagogue Karl Wilhelm Eduard Mager (1810–1858). In order to ensure the educational mission of the Neusprachliche Unterricht, Mager – who died at an early age – had written a groundbreaking – but unfinished – history of French literature, which was also intended to open up the philosophical, cultural and social components of France to teachers and pupils and thus could well have competed with Humboldt's concept of the educational function of Greek. In doing so, he assumed that literature is "the most concentrated expression of the overall education of a people." Thus the statement of the reviewer Ernst Susemihl (1938).

[45] Kalkhoff and Wolf 2014, p. 135.

[46] Selig 2008, p. 24.

[47] Selig et al. 2006, pp. 21–40.

with Latin in the Sexta and Quinta (6 lessons per week), only to drop from the Quarta to the Prima to half (4 lessons) compared to Latin (8 lessons) and Greek (5 to 7 lessons). This – at least to some extent perceptible – revaluation of German is – like so many other things at that time – due to the epochal events of the time, the temporary supremacy of the Napoleonic Empire and its defence in the anti-Napoleonic wars of liberation by the other European states. The general consequence was a resolutely demanded and promoted return to national identities that supposedly already existed, but were in fact often first constructed, in which – in a conglomeration of the most diverse intellectual and cultural currents, some of which have already been mentioned here – the national languages and literatures played a very important ideological role. This reorientation implied a turning away from the older concept of a 'universal philology' and transnational 'world literature' as well as from the privileging of the old languages. It ultimately led to the constitution of the individual national philologies both as academic disciplines and as school and university subjects. Fuhrmann used the Brothers Grimm as an example to illustrate this process for German, whose goal – which was certainly also political – was to create a 'world literature',

> to penetrate through the language and literature of the Germans to their 'spirit' and 'essence'. Herder had already initiated these efforts at identification; Jacob Grimm, however, saw the goal of his enormous life's work in proving the spiritual unity of the Germans in language, myth, law and custom. He was so eager to do this because the Germans lacked political unity. Belonging to the belief in the unity of essence was also the assumption that the poets, in particular, were called upon to proclaim this essence. Thus the works of German classicism became the most distinguished object of the new Germanic science; there, if anywhere, had unfolded in unadulterated purity the most precious thing that was common to all Germans: their nature, guaranteed by their language.
> The increasing thrust of national thought led to the humanistic tradition of the high school being weakened and eventually relegated to second place; in short, the subject of German took the top spot in the curriculum hierarchy.[48]

This conditional turning away from Humboldt's 'Greek faith' and turning towards the respective national identities brought with it a gradual strengthening of the new philologies overall, required their use in school teaching, where they served

---

[48] Fuhrmann 2001, p. 182. This process received "its strongest impetus from reading instruction," especially the reading books, which "focused on the Weimar Classical period as an outstanding educational resource." A constant canon quickly emerged: "Klopstock, Herder, Lessing, Goethe, and Schiller formed the core of grammar school reading, with a clear preference for the dramatic genre. Shakespeare and occasionally Calderon also appeared frequently; on the other hand, contemporary literature tended to be neglected. The classical core was then gradually extended into both earlier and later times; the Middle Ages and the Reformation, Romanticism and Realism surrounded Weimar Classicism." Fuhrmann 2001, pp. 182 and 184.

National interests have also played a significant role in the emergence of other national philologies, in France, for example, in the emergence of Hispanic studies there, which, as Antonio Niño Rodríguez (1988) has shown, emerged in the context of the Franco-German War of 1870/71, when defeated France attempted to forge an alliance of the "peuples latins" against the overpowering 'Germanic Germany' and in doing so also very clearly relied on scientific-cultural cooperation between Spain and France. The fundamental conclusiveness of Antonio Niño's explanatory approach remains despite the vehement opposition of Bartholomé Bennassar (1991, pp. 19–25).

precisely not only the mere acquisition of language, but also greater consideration in the university sphere as the increasingly unambiguous place of academic, science-based teacher training with the corresponding official study and examination regulations. This unambiguous function of study contributed decisively to the legitimation of German studies, but also of Romance and English studies, as academic subjects, whereby, at least in the field of foreign language philologies, the subject areas of language and literature were privileged over other possible areas such as history or art. At the same time, however, this also – and perhaps even above all – encouraged the study of the subject matter not directly related to education, i.e. the relevant basic research.[49] However, even in this early phase of the modern philologies, a danger became apparent that was to accompany them in all their national manifestations, regardless of whether they were conducted as research on their own national identity or as research on the identity of other peoples: their ideologization and their – sometimes quite acceptable – use for the most diverse political purposes.[50]

This danger, implicit in the modern philologies of the nineteenth century, has already been pointed out by Jost Hermand for the early phases of German studies. Here it was often "less the literary than the patriotic in the broadest sense" that determined interest in specific subjects, such as the *Nibelungenlied,* on the one hand, and was used as a welcome legitimation for one's own activities on the other.[51] However one may judge this state of affairs, Jost Hermand's observation that without the "patriotic activities" of the early Germanists "it would certainly have taken much longer for the subject of German studies to emerge" is certainly correct. Crucial for our question is the fact that with this basic attitude, modern German studies could by no means be qualified as the "knowledge of what is not worth knowing", but that with its – quite democratic – nationalism it represented an answer to a central question of the first decades of the nineteenth century, i.e. the national demand for identity, and could thus rightly expect to be incorporated into the university system in accordance with its social performance. However, this expectation was to flatten out again considerably after the euphoric phase of the freedom wars and their immediate aftermath, partly because German studies, now constituted as a scientific subject, was initially – before its integration into teacher training – "not a bread-and-butter but an ethos study",[52] which did not open up any career prospects

---

[49] The first major sum of this research work in the field of Romance studies was the monumental "Grundriss der romanischen Philologie" (1888–1902) published by Gustav Gröber (1844–1911) and the "Zeitschrift für Romanische Philologie" founded by Gröber as early as 1877. Another important organ of this research is the journal "Romanische Forschungen", founded by Karl Vollmüller (1848–1922) in 1883 and still existing today.

[50] For the – later – period, that of the 'Third Reich', but also its intellectual precursors, Frank-Rutger Hausmann (2000, 2003 and 2011) has illustrated this with great meticulousness and detail for the humanities as a whole and for Romance and English studies in particular. It should also be remembered, however, that Hispanic Studies owes its first more decisive institutionalization to the fact that after the First World War voices were raised calling for a move away from French as the language of the hereditary enemy in research and teaching. Tietz 2012, pp. 932–933.

[51] Cf. on this from a political science perspective Jansen 1993, pp. 199–278.

[52] Hermand 1994, p. 36.

for students under the sobering conditions of the Restoration period. And yet this decline in academic demand and the move away from the 'national relevance requirement' also had a positive side. In the everyday university life of the subject, it led to a "strict objectivity that saw itself as increasing philologization and thus scientification",[53] which, following the strict criteria of classical philology, for example in the editions of medieval texts by a Karl Lachmann (1793–1851) and those of his students, reached a standard that was soon to become a model for all new philologies in the Europe of the time, although this also had the consequence that the subject of German studies – with the help of the "modern philology" of the Restoration era – was no longer able to meet its own requirements, that the subject of German studies – and with it certainly other new philologies that followed their understanding of science – in the long term became the concern of "a marginal academic elite"[54] and thus led to a self-isolation – also lamented again today – which in the view of the educator Clemens Menze (1928–2003) ultimately meant a turning away, especially among the philologists, from Humboldt's basic ideas contained in his 'Greek faith', which were designed to have a broad impact.[55]

The philologization and strict scientificity that was combined in the branch of literary studies – which as a rule was represented by a teacher in personal union with linguistics under the overarching denomination of 'philology' – with an erudite, self-sufficient research into sources, also became the recipe for success – at least scientifically – of another modern philology, Romance studies, which, on the one hand, continued the medieval orientation of the Romantic origins of the new philologies, but, on the other hand, became the par excellence drill ground of diachronic linguistics, since it had the unique privilege of possessing not only a precise knowledge of the numerous, diversified individual Romance 'daughter languages', but a no less comprehensive knowledge of their source language, Latin. This fact made it possible to survey and – in an increasingly positivist manner with the historical-comparative method – to investigate far more than 2000 years of a linguistic history.[56] The 'father' and 'master' of this subject, Romance studies, was certainly the Bonn professor Friedrich [Christian] Diez (1794–1876), whose understanding of the subject was subsequently to be received far beyond Germany.[57] Nevertheless, without taking into account the contexts outlined here, one should not be too quick to describe the neo-philological subject of Romance studies as an "invention of Bonn" that took place *ex nihilo,* as it were.[58] It, too, is preceded by a complex plethora of different forms of interest in France, Italy or Spain, which can certainly be subsumed under the concept of a 'humanitarian experience of alterity',

---

[53] Hermand 1994, p. 37.
[54] Hermand 1994, p. 39.
[55] Menze 1975, p. 119, quoted in Ellwein 1997, pp. 118–119.
[56] On the unity of the "impossible subject" of Romance Studies founded in this approach, cf. Selig 2008, pp. 19–36.
[57] For France, see Gumbrecht 1984, Frýba-Reber (2013) and Ursula Bähler 2004.
[58] Cf. the material-rich description of Romance studies as a "Bonn invention" in Willi Hirdt et al. 1993.

but which would have to be analysed specifically in each individual case.[59] Certainly not only for the field of Hispanic studies it can be stated that the literary side of modern philology at that time, unlike the linguistic side, showed deficits for a long time, which were compensated for even longer by enthusiastic and quite competent non-university 'non-specialists' such as Johann Andreas Dieze (1729–1785), Friedrich Ludwig Bouterwek (1766–1829),[60] Friedrich Justin Bertuch (1747–1822), von Schack (1815–1894) or Hedwig Dohm (1831–1919).[61]

4 The Institutionalization of Modern Philology in German Universities

Despite some reservations in detail, there can be no doubt that the philologies managed to become an integral part of the academic system in the academic discourse of the decades around the turn of the eighteenth and nineteenth centuries. It seems all the more astonishing, therefore, with what slowness and under what coincidences in the specific case the neo-philological subjects, which were by all means coherently conceived in terms of their subject matter, were able to be integrated into the university as an institution at that time.

Hans Helmut Christmann presented an early sketch of this history – which was also marked by colleagues' envy – in 1985, which then led to a fairly complete picture of the conceptual and institutional history of Romance philology for the field of Romance studies with the works of Alexander Kalkhoff and Johanna Wolf already mentioned, as well as their pioneers, even though there is certainly still a lot to be done in detail, especially in terms of archival work. Here, we can only briefly refer to Christmann's outline of the institutional history of Romance philology, which can be extended to all new philologies in summa summarum, whereby reference should be made to the works of the authors just mentioned for all details.

In his, as Alexander Kalkhoff rightly points out, "successful synopsis of the establishment of modern philology",[62] especially Romance and English studies at the German universities of the nineteenth century, Christmann distinguishes six – in each case according to the local circumstances quite strongly overlapping – phases, in which he presents the relatively early establishment of professorships and chairs on the one hand (pp. 7–28) on the one hand, and the establishment of seminars, institutes and libraries (pp. 29–39), which usually took place later, on the other. Contrary to what one might imagine in view of today's institutional 'success story'

---

[59] For the Spanish area, see the contribution by Ludwig Schrader 1991, pp. 1–18.
[60] On his position as a precursor, see Ludwig Schrader 1989, pp. 60–78.
[61] Tietz 2012, pp. 931–932.
[62] Kalkhoff 2010, p. 263, note 1. In his work, Kalkhoff verified and modified Christmann's theses on the basis of extensive contemporary documents for the universities of Heidelberg, Rostock, Halle, Berlin, and Hamburg.

of the philologies, this is a decidedly "protracted process that takes up the entire (sc. 19th) century"[63] and which, one might add, generally involves quite small numbers of teachers and students – which, however, also applied to other disciplines at the time.

The first phase, which in part goes far back into the beginnings of the university system itself, is that of the "language masters or lectors (until about 1850)", whose teaching, even if it was not limited to the mere acquisition of language, but also – in the case of teachers who were thoroughly versed in the subject – included literary texts and elements of cultural history, did not belong to the actual 'professorial teaching' and was therefore hardly appreciated.[64] Phase 2 is that of the "'genuine' professors who, coming from other subjects such as philosophy, history, ancient literature or occasionally still rhetoric, turned to the newer literature and gave lectures with an aesthetic-rhetorical orientation, which [sc. in the sense of a universal philology] usually encompassed many peoples and countries",[65] an approach that covers the period from the end of the eighteenth century to the entire first third of the nineteenth century. In contrast to the dilettantism still frequently found here in the analysis of language and literature, universities and ministries attempted in a further phase "to establish a solid, recognized science".[66] This very important third phase, which is "quite actually the academic beginnings of modern philology,"[67] is characteristic of the 1st half of the century with its "first efforts to establish specific professorships of modern languages and literatures."[68] This is an extraordinarily important phase in the history of the discipline, in which modern philology – German studies with Georg Friedrich Benecke (since 1805 in Göttingen) or Romance studies with Ludwig Gottfried Blanc (since 1822 in Halle) or Friedrich Diez (since 1823 in Bonn) – is institutionally constituted as a scientific subject.[69] With regard to the 4th phase, Christmann states: "The school demanded the establishment of neo-philological professorships for the training of grammar school

---

[63] Christmann 1985, p. 5.

[64] Cf. the anthology on this – like today's 'lectors' sometimes not too appreciated – group of academic teachers by Mark Häberlein (2015) as well as the case study by Dietrich Briesemeister (2008).

[65] Christmann 1985, p. 8. This includes August Wilhelm Schlegel (1818–1845 in Bonn) and Valentin Schmidt (1819–1831 in Berlin), the latter of whom can be considered "the most deserving forerunner of Romance philology in Germany". Christmann 1985, p. 9. Victor Aimé Huber (Professor of Modern Literatures and History (1833–1836 in Rostock, 1836–1843 in Berlin) is also to be counted here, who expanded the subject area of modern philology (in his case above all English and Hispanic studies) beyond the realm of the linguistic-literary into that of regional studies and cultural studies, thus offering a very early example of the later controversial 'de-philologization' of the subject. Cf. Rodiek (1989).

[66] Christmann 1985, pp. 10–11.

[67] Christmann 1985, p. 11.

[68] Christmann 1985, p. 11.

[69] The relevant terms "Germanists" and "Romanists" are first documented in this period – 1840, and 1846, respectively – by the pedagogue Carl Wilhelm Mager (1810–1858). Christmann 1985, p. 15 and 20.

teachers – habilitations for modern philology (ca. 1850 to ca. 1860)".[70] Of course, it was advantageous that the takeover of teacher training in the new philological subjects, which was now desired and supported by the state, meant not only their official recognition and legitimation in terms of scientific theory, but also their ministerial and university guarantee of existence. A positive aspect was undoubtedly that the faculties were thus forced to adequately equip the individual new philologies and to introduce quality standards, which were ensured by a respective subject-specific habilitation. In the long run, however, this in itself gratifying process also had something of a Danaer's gift or a less than happy marriage. Put somewhat strictly, it implied the 'life lie' of our subjects, namely that as a rule university teachers with no experience of school, for example those concentrating on language history and medieval literature, were to ensure that future teachers with completely different fields of work received sufficient specialist training, a paradox which is being countered in the present day by the massive expansion of subject didactics and specific professorships. In Phase 5 (c. 1860 to c. 1875), attempts were made to accommodate the costly teacher training mandate by establishing so-called 'double professorships' that had to cover several subject areas, usually English and Romance.[71] However, these 'double professorships', which were not based on a coherent scientific-theoretical concept, proved to be unfeasible in research and teaching, given the increasing breadth of the subjects to be covered beyond a *de facto* medievalism towards the inclusion of more modern epochs of literature. It was therefore only in keeping with the logic of the matter that between 1860 and 1875, in a 6th phase, a "separation of Romance and English philology by founding separate professorships for English (ca. 1870 to ca. 1900)"[72] took place, even if Romance philology – despite its concentration on teacher training for French – remained in its entirety, despite all kinds of "contradictions and tensions".[73] It was not until the end of the twentieth century that – as a result of the establishment of subject-specific Master's and teacher training courses (for French, above all, also for Spanish and Italian, which were in great demand) – an already de facto internal differentiation was gradually implemented institutionally as well – moreover, long since separated into linguistics and literary studies – and supplemented in a still ongoing process by separate professorships for subject didactics and cultural studies.

---

[70] Christmann 1985, pp. 19–23.
[71] Christmann 1985, pp. 23–27.
[72] Christmann 1985, pp. 27–28.
[73] Selig 2008, p. 21.

5 (Modern) Pilological Expertise and Professional Self-Confidence

Of course, such a – basically primarily informative – outline of the subject and institutional history of the modern philologies is not yet proof of their 'timeless' relevance and social legitimacy. These are, however, part of the humanities (and social) sciences – so named only later – which deal with objects produced by man and his creative mind, just as the natural sciences deal with objects and phenomena as given in 'nature', 'creation' or the 'material world'. In this respect, neither the humanities have a position of primacy, as they accorded themselves until well into the nineteenth century, nor the natural sciences, whose claim to hegemony and legitimation has become one of the most publicized topoi of the twentieth and twenty-first centuries. In my view, the development of the modern-philologies in the nineteenth century can also be read as the history of legitimation – not always free of errors and (self-) doubts – in which they established themselves alongside other models of world interpretation, especially alongside theology and philosophy. Philology is not the "science of the uninteresting facts", nor is it a failed and merely "melancholic project".[74] Especially in times of a boundless, ultimately even self-destructive utilitarianism, it can be – in the well understood sense of Nuccio Ordine's manifesto – the science "of the usefulness of the [sc. only apparently] useless", that is, of that which is not directly economically usable,[75] whereby, it must be conceded to its critics, it must be careful that the "not worth knowing", which undoubtedly also exists, does not obscure the view of its significant core in the hectic everyday business. The philologies can – especially in times of modern secularization and reflection on the limitations of man and nature – be the place beyond the temptation of closing oneself off in the academic ivory tower and of mere career optimization, where it becomes clear that philosophy and literature are (have become) vital, as the American educator and science organizer Abraham Flexner (1866–1959) emphatically demonstrated as early as 1939.[76] On the university level, Jochen Hörisch therefore sees in literature – and thus also in philology – the valuable storehouse of a 'dissident knowledge' open to the alternative and utopian,[77] which Humboldt once propagated in concrete form with his 'Greek faith' and which the neo-philologies of the second half of the nineteenth century initially applied to the medieval and the classical period. This is what the new philologies of the second half of the nine-

---

[74] Thus the conclusion of Lepper 2012a, p. 153: "Philology is not a melancholic project. Contemporary societies need philological expertise, the sensorium for the historicity of word use, insight into the problems of translation – but also explorative daring, self-conscious dialogue of the philologies with the adjacent information and life sciences."

[75] Ordine 2016.

[76] Flexner's thought-provoking essay "The Usefulness of Useless Knowledge" is reprinted in Ordine (2016, pp. 211–242). The unambiguous German translation of the title – "Die Nützlichkeit unnützen Wissens" – takes away the intended ambiguity from the "useless" of the original.

[77] Hörisch 2007, p. 33.

teenth century transferred first to the medieval and then, to an ever greater extent, to the aesthetic-creative knowledge of the works not only of the respective 'classics' of the individual national literatures, but nowadays (also in the sense of a renewed universal philology) opened up to the contemporary literatures. Since university philology and modern language teaching in schools are closely linked by virtue of teacher training, it is highly welcome that the intellectual and 'humanitarian' potential of reading literary texts has recently been increasingly perceived and propagated again – also within the framework of professionalised and university-based subject didactics.[78]

References

Aichinger Wolfram et al. (ed.): Literaturwissenschaft in schwierigen Zeiten, in HeLix. Dossiers zur romanischen Literaturwissenschaft 11, 2018, pp. 11–107 (https://journals.ub.uni-heidelberg.de/index.php/helix/zweiKultureninderissue/view/4299).
Assmann, Aleida: Jordan und Helikon – der Kampf der zwei Kulturen der abendländischen Tradition, in: Jürgen Ebach und Richard Faber (ed.): Bibel und Literatur. München: Fink ²1998, 2., pp. 95–112.
Auerochs, Bernd: Die Entstehung der Kunstreligion. Göttingen: Vandenhoeck & Ruprecht 2009, 2.
Augustinus: Die christliche Bildung (De doctrina christiana). Übersetzung, Anmerkungen und Nachwort von Karla Pollmann. Stuttgart: Reclam 2013, 2. ed.
Bähler, Ursula: Gaston Paris et la philologie romane, avec une réimpression de la Bibliographie des travaux de Gaston Paris publiée par Joseph Bédier et Mario Roques. Genève: Droz 2004.
Bénichou, Paul: Le sacre de l'écrivain moderne: 1750–1830: essai sur l'avènement d'un pouvoir spirituel laïque dans la France. Paris: Gallimard 1996, 2. ed.
Bennassar, Bartolomé: El hispanismo francés (hasta 1945), in: Jean-François Botrel et al. (ed.): Akten des Hispanistentages Mainz 1989, 9.–12.3.1989. I Encuentro Franco-Alemán de Hispanistas. Frankfurt am Main: Vervuert 1991, pp. 19–25.
Baum, Richard: Friedrich Diez, in: Willi Hirdt et alii: Romanistik. Eine Bonner Erfindung. Teil I: Darstellung. Bonn: Bouvier 1993a, pp. 45-140.
Baum, Richard: Friedrich Diez (Dokumentation), in: Willi Hirdt et alii: Romanistik. Eine Bonner Erfindung. Teil. T. II: Dokumentation. Bonn: Bouvier 1993b, pp. 457-914.
Böhmer Maria: Tagungsbericht: Säkularisierung in der Frühen Neuzeit: begriffliche Überlegungen und empirische Fallstudien, 09.12.2006–10.12.2006, in: H/Soz/Kult. Kommunikation und Fachinformation für die Geschichtswissenschaften, 28.01.2006. (<www.hsozkult.de/conferencereport/id/tagungsberichte-1035>).
Bognár, Zsuzsa: Ludwig Hatvanys Großessay *Die Wissenschaft vom Nichtwissenswerten* vor dem Hintergrund seiner deutschsprachigen Rezeption, in Tamás Hamat und Zsuzsa Soproni (ed.): Verschränkte Kulturen. Polnisch-deutscher und ungarisch-deutscher Literatur- und Kulturtransfer. Berlin: Frank & Timme 2018, pp. 243–257.
Briesemeister, Dietrich: Sprachmeister und Lektoren im Vorlesungsangebot für die neueren Fremdsprachen an der Universität Jena (1750–1830), in: Thomas Bach et al. (ed.): Gelehrte

---

[78] Here, exemplary reference is made to Wolfram Aichinger et al.: Literary Studies in Difficult Times, in HeLix. Dossiers zur romanischen Literaturwissenschaft 11, 2018, pp. 11–107 (https://journals.ub.uni-heidelberg.de/index.php/helix/issue/view/4299), especially Hertrampf 2018) and Junkerjürgen (2018), as well as to the anthology Haarmann and Rok (eds.) (2019), especially Ißler (2019). Cf. also Schwindt 2009.

Wissenschaft. Das Vorlesungsprogramm der Universität Jena um 1800. Stuttgart: Steiner 2008, pp. 265–282.

Brüggemann, Werner: Spanisches Theater und deutsche Romantik. Münster/Westf.: Aschendorff 1964.

Christmann, Hans Helmut: Ernst Robert Curtius und die deutschen Romanisten, in: Akademie der Wissenschaften Mainz. Abhandlungen der Geistes- und sozialwissenschaftlichen Klasse. Wiesbaden, Stuttgart: Steiner 1987, pp. 3–28.

Christmann, Hans Helmut: Romanistik und Anglistik an der deutschen Universität im 19. Jahrhundert. Ihre Herausbildung als Fächer und ihr Verhältnis zu Germanistik und klassischer Philologie. Stuttgart: Steiner 1985.

Diez, Friedrich: Die Poesie der Troubadours. Nach gedruckten und handschriftlichen Werken derselben dargestellt von Friedrich Diez, außerordentl. Professor der königlich preußischen Rheinuniversität [sc. Bonn]. Zwickau: Gebrüder Schumann 1826.

Drews, Kevin et al. (ed.): Die Frage in den Geisteswissenschaften: Herausforderungen, Praktiken und Reflexionen. Berlin: Frank & Timme 2019.

Ellwein, Thomas: Die deutsche Universität. Vom Mittelalter bis in die Gegenwart. Wiesbaden: Fourier 1997.

Finkenstaedt, Thomas: Kleine Geschichte der Anglistik in Deutschland. Eine Einführung. Darmstadt: Wissenschaftliche Buchgesellschaft 1983.

Finkenstaedt, Thomas: Zur Situation der Englischen Philologie, insbesondere ihrer Literaturwissenschaft, in: Wolfgang Prinz und Peter Weingart [...] (ed.): Die sog. Geisteswissenschaften: Innenansichten. Frankfurt a. M.: Suhrkamp 1990, pp. 248–253.

Frýba-Reber, Anne-Marguerite: Philologie et linguistique romanes – Institutionnalisation des disciplines dans les universités suisses (1872–1945). Louvain [..]: Peeters 2013.

Fuhrmann, Manfred: Latein und Europa. Geschichte des gelehrten Unterrichts in Deutschland. Von Karl dem Grossen bis Wilhelm II. Köln: DuMont 2001.

Gumbrecht, Hans Ulrich: Un souffle d'Allemagne ayant passé: Friedrich Diez, Gaston Paris und die Genese der Nationalphilologien, in: LiLi (Zeitschrift für Literaturwissenschaft und Linguistik) 14, 1984, pp. 37–78.

Häberlein, Mark (ed.): Sprachmeister. Sozial- und Kulturgeschichte eines prekären Berufsstandes. Bamberg: University of Bamberg Press 2015.

Haarmann, Andreas und Rok Cora (ed.): Wozu Literatur(-wissenschaft)? Methoden, Fumktionen, Perspektiven. Göttingen: V&R unipress. Bonn University Press 2019.

Hatvany, Lajos: Die Wissenschaft des nicht Wissenswerten; ein Kollegheft. Zweite vermehrte und veränderte Auflage. Berlin Concordia 1911.

Hausmann, Frank-Rutger: „Vom Strudel der Ereignisse verschlungen". Deutsche Romanistik im ‚Dritten Reich'. Frankfurt am Main: Klostermann 2000.

Hausmann, Frank-Rutger: Die Anglistik und Amerikanistik im „Dritten Reich". Frankfurt am Main: Klostermann 2003.

Hausmann, Frank-Rutger: Die Geisteswissenschaften im „Dritten Reich". Frankfurt am Main: Klostermann 2011.

Hermand, Jost: Geschichte der Germanistik. Reinbek bei Hamburg: Rowohlt 1994 (Reinbek: Rowohlt Repertoire 2017).

Herrig, Ludwig: Vorwort, in: Archiv für das Studium der Neueren Sprachen und Literaturen 1, 1846, pp. 1–4.

Hertrampf, Marina Ortrud M.: (K)eine Zukunft für den fremdsprachlichen Literaturunterricht an Schulen?! Perspektiven und Ansätze, in: HeLix 11, 2018, pp. 42–62.

Hirdt, Willi et al.: Romanistik. Eine Bonner Erfindung. Teil I: Darstellung. T. II Dokumentation. Bonn: Bouvier 1993.

Hörisch, Jochen: Warum lügen und was wissen die Dichter? Plädoyer für eine problem- und themenzentrierte Literaturwissenschaft, in Jochen Hörisch: Das Wissen der Literatur. München: Fink 2007, 15–42.

Humboldt, Wilhelm von: Über die innere und äussere Organisation der höheren wissenschaftlichen Anstalten in Berlin (1809/10), in: https://doi.org/10.18452/4653, pp. 229–241.
Ißler, Roland:: Wozu romanische Literaturwissenschaft im Lehramtsstudium? Zur kulturellen und ästhetischen Bildungsverantwortung der Romanistik in der universitären Lehrerbildung, in: Andreas Haarmann und Cora Rok (ed.): Wozu Literatur(-wissenschaft)? Göttingen: V& R unipress. Bonn University Press 2019, pp. 61–82.
James, Harold: Deutsche Identität. 1770–1990. Frankfurt/New York: Camous 1991.
Jansen, Christian: ‚Deutsches Wesen', ‚deutsche Seele', ‚deutscher Geist'. Der Volkscharakter als nationales Identifikationsmuster im Gelehrtenmilieu, in: Reinhard Blomert et al. (ed.): Transformationen des Wir-Gefühls. Studien zum nationalen Habitus. Frankfurt a. M.: Suhrkamp 1993, pp. 199–278.
Junkerjürgen, Ralf: Neun Todsünden romanistischer Literaturwissenschaft. Ein Erfahrungsbericht, in: HeLix 11, 2018, p. 63–81.
Kalkhoff, Alexander M.: Begriff und Umfang der Neuphilologie im 19. Jahrhundert – Ein Plädoyer für ein historisches Bewusstsein, in: Dagmar Schmelzer et al. (ed.): Handeln und Verhandeln. Beiträge zum 22. Forum Junge Romanistik (Regensburg, 7.– 10.6.2006). Bonn: Romanistischer Verlag 2007, pp. 433–451.
Kalkhoff, Alexander M.: Romanische Philologie im 19. und frühen 20. Jahrhundert. Institutionengeschichtliche Perspektiven. Tübingen: Narr 2010.
Kalkhoff, Alexander und Wolf, Johanna: Kontingenz und Kalkül. Zur Fachgeschichte der Romanischen Philologie (1820–1890), in: Wulf Oesterreicher, Maria Selig (ed.): Geschichtlichkeit von Sprache und Text. Philologien – Disziplingenese – Wissenschaftshistoriographie. Paderborn: Fink 2014, pp. 131–152.
Koch, Herbert: Die „Geschichte der Romanistik an der Universität Jena" von Herbert Koch. Eine um Professoren-Porträts und ein Schriftenverzeichnis Kochs ergänzte Edition. Bearbeitet von Christian Faludi und Joachim Hendel. [1955] Stuttgart: Steiner 2019.
Lepper, Marcel: Deutsche Philologie im 18. Jahrhundert. Ein Forschungsbericht mit Bibliographie, in: Das achtzehnte Jahrhundert 36, 2012b, pp. 71–105.
Lepper, Marcel: Philologie zur Einführung. Hamburg: Junius 2012a.
Lyons, John: Einführung in die moderne Linguistik. München: Beck 1995, 8. ed..
Menze, Clemens: Die Bildungsreform Wilhelm von Humboldts. Hannover: Schroedel 1975.
Nietzche, Friedrich: „Wir Gelehrten", in: Werke in drei Bänden. Bd. 2. Darmstadt: Wissenschaftliche Buchgesellschaft 1963a, pp. 662–665.
Nietzche, Friedrich: „Wir Philologen", in: Werke in drei Bänden. Bd. 3. Darmstadt: Wissenschaftliche Buchgesellschaft 1963b, pp. 323–332.
Niño, Antonio: Cultura y diplomacia. Los hispanistas franceses y España de 1875 a 1931. Madrid: Consejo Superior de Investigaciones Científicas 1988.
Oesterreicher, Wulf, Selig, Maria (ed.): Geschichtlichkeit von Sprache und Text. Philologien – Disziplingenese – Wissenschaftshistoriographie. Paderborn: Fink 2014.
Ordine, Nuccio: Von der Nützlichkeit des Unnützen. Ein Manifest. Warum Philosophie und Literatur lebenswichtig sind. Mit einem Essay von Abraham Flexner. München: Graf 2016, 3. ed..
Pohlis, Matthias et al. (ed..): Säkularisierung in der Frühen Neuzeit: begriffliche Überlegungen und empirische Fallstudien. Berlin: Duncker & Humblot 2008.
Prinz, Wolfgang und Weingart, Peter (ed.) […]: Die sog. Geisteswissenschaften: Innenansichten. Frankfurt a. M.: Suhrkamp 1990.
Rodiek, Christoph: Die hispanistischen Forschungsschwerpunkte Viktor Aimé Hubers, in: Manfred Tietz (ed.): Das Spanieninteresse im deutschen Sprachraum. Beiträge zur Geschichte der Hispanistik vor 1900. Frankfurt am Main: Vervuert 1989, pp. 79–92.
Sass, Hartmut von: Von Deutungsmächten wunderbar verborgen. Habermas, Taylor und die Metakritik der Säkularisierungstheorie, in Irene Dingel und Christine Tietz (ed.): Säkularisierung und Religion. Europäische Wechselwirkungen. Göttingen: Vandenhoeck & Ruprecht 2019, pp. 11–38.

Schrader, Ludwig: «El interés por el mundo ibérico y los orígenes del hispanismo científico en los países de lengua alemana (siglo XIX)», in: Jean-François Botrel et al. (ed.): Akten des Hispanistentages Mainz 1989, 9.–12.3.1989. I Encuentro Franco-Alemán de Hispanistas. Frankfurt am Main: Vervuert 1991, pp. 1–18.

Schrader, Ludwig: Bouterweks Urteile. Zur Literaturgeschichtsschreibung zwischen Rationalismus und Romantik, in: Manfred Tietz (ed.): Das Spanieninteresse im deutschen Sprachraum. Beiträge zur Geschichte der Hispanistik vor 1900. Frankfurt am Main: Vervuert 1989, pp. 60–78.

Schwindt, Jürgen Paul (ed.): Was ist eine philologische Frage? Beiträge zur Erkundung einer theoretischen Einstellung. Frankfurt am Main: Suhrkamp 2009.

Seidel-Vollmann, Stefanie: Die romanische Philologie an der Universität München (1826–1913). Berlin: Duncker & Humblot 1977.

Selig, Maria et al. (ed.): ‚... daß das Studium der neueren Sprachen und Literaturen ein ächtes Humanitätsstudium werde.' Les débuts de la philologie romane et la question éthique, in: Ursula Bähler (ed.): Éthique de la philologie. Ethik der Philologie. Berlin: Berliner Wissenschafts-Verlag 2006, pp. 21–40.

Selig, Maria: Zur Einheit der Romanischen Philologie im 19. Jahrhundert, in: Ursula Schaefer (ed.): Der geteilte Gegenstand. Beiträge zu Geschichte, Gegenwart und Zukunft der Philologie(n). Frankfurt a. M.: Lang 2008, pp. 19–36.

Strosetzki, Christoph: Literatur als Beruf: zum Selbstverständnis gelehrter und schriftstellerischer Existenz im spanischen Siglo de Oro. Düsseldorf: Droste 1987.

Susemihl, Ernst: K. W. E. Mager: Versuch einer Geschichte und Characteristik der französischen National-Litteratur. Nebst zahlreichen Schriftproben. Zweiter. Vierter Bd., Berlin, 1837, bei K. Heymann, in: Hallische Jahrbücher für deutsche Wissenschaft und Kunst, nr. 111–112 vom 9.–10. Mai 1838, Sp. 886–888, 889–890.

Tietz, Manfred: El nacimiento del ‹autor› moderno y la conflictividad cultural del Siglo de Oro: cultura teológico-clerical versus cultura literario-artística laica, in: Manfred Tietz und Marcella Trambaioli (ed.): El autor en el Siglo de Oro. Su estatus intelectual y social. Vigo: Academia del Hispanismo 2011, pp. 439–459.

Tietz, Manfred: »Hispanistik in Geschichte und Gegenwart«, in: Handbuch Spanisch. Sprache, Literatur, Kultur, Geschichte in Spanien und Hispanoamerika. Für Studium, Lehre, Praxis. ed. Joachim Born, Robert Folger, Christopher F. Laferl und Bernhard Pöll. Verlag 2012 Berlin: Erich Schmidt, 929–938.

Ulbricht, Günter: Heinrich Stephani (1761–1850) – ein großer Pädagoge der Aufklärung in Bayern. Aachen: Shaker 1998.

Wolf, Johanna: Kontinuität und Wandel der Philologien: textarchäologische Studien zur Entstehung der Romanischen Philologie im 19. Jahrhundert. Tübingen: Narr 2012.

Wolfzettel, Friedrich: Zur Situation der Romanischen Literaturwissenschaft, in: Wolfgang Prinz und Peter Weingart […] (ed.): Die sog. Geisteswissenschaften: Innenansichten. Frankfurt a. M.: Suhrkamp 1990, pp. 254–258.

On the Transformation of Philological Knowledge Orders and Information Stores at the Turn of the Nineteenth and Twentieth Centuries: Developments and Causes

Hans-Harald Müller, Tom Kindt, and Myriam Isabell Richter

Abstract In the transition from the nineteenth to the twentieth century, a fundamental change occurs in the communication system of the knowledge order of the philological sciences, in which the publishing system is also involved. Our contribution shows in an exemplary case study how the text type of the scientific *encyclopaedia* is replaced by that of the *Grundriss in the* major national philologies. Whereas the subject encyclopaedia served to present the unity and systematic structure of the subject, the explosive growth of knowledge in the philologies means that the *Grundriss* must confine itself to a pragmatically ordered empirical performance record of the individual subject areas.

In the history of scholarly publishing, the turn of the nineteenth and twentieth centuries is regarded as the "age of collected works".[1] The need for such works was justified by the jurist Fritz Blüthgen in 1913 with the constantly growing quantity and increasing specialization:

---

[1] On the origin of the quotation, cf. Müller 2000, p. 191, note 7 – Cf. also Müller 2004, p. 137.

H.-H. Müller (✉)
Institut für Germanistik, Universität Hamburg, Hamburg, Deutschland
e-mail: harrym@uni-hamburg.de

T. Kindt
Departement für Germanistik, Universität Friburg, Fribourg, Schweiz
e-mail: tom.kindt@unifr.ch

M. I. Richter
Hamburgische Wissenschaftliche Stiftung, Universität Hamburg, Hamburg, Deutschland
e-mail: myriam.richter@uni-hamburg.de

© The Author(s), under exclusive license to Springer-Verlag GmbH, DE, part of Springer Nature 2023
C. Strosetzki (ed.), *200 Years of National Philologies*,
https://doi.org/10.1007/978-3-476-05925-3_4

> The restless diligence of the last generation in all fields of science and the constantly growing number of scientific workers have brought us an almost endless abundance of scientific successes and progress. [...] If we disregard the great diversity of the individual subjects which the philosophical faculty encompasses, then in the circle of the other faculties one could still assume a few decades ago that it was possible for a serious academic to have a sufficient overview of the individual branches of his faculty. Today this has thoroughly changed. Each individual faculty has developed within its framework a quite considerable number of subsidiary subjects into independent disciplines, a process which continues with undiminished force.[2]

Blüthgen also immediately recommended a remedy:

> These are the hand dictionaries and encyclopaedias. In the hand dictionaries the whole field of science is divided into selected headwords, which, arranged in alphabetical order, allow with great ease a brief survey of any subject. The encyclopaedias are different. They, too, owe their origin to the desire for a uniform summary of the whole field while preserving scientific depth. They endeavour, after a presentation of the fundamental disciplines, also to bring before the reader's eyes the results of the individual special researches, but they present these in connection, albeit in a concise form, and thus offer the reader the possibility of becoming fully informed in a systematic way about the whole field of a single subject and of studying all the important and fundamental questions in connection with it.[3]

Helen Müller explained the explosive growth in demand for collected editions in her study of "Science and the Market around 1900" against the background of a fundamental change in the communication system of science: "The more the pluralism of content *and* organization in the sciences progressed, the greater the desire for standardization became, and the more control over whether and how scientific communication reached its audience shifted to the publishers, who thus became part of this communication process."[4] To determine more precisely this process, which had different causes and effects in the individual disciplines, requires more differentiated investigations than we can undertake here. We therefore limit ourselves to an exemplary case study in which we present the change of the text type of the "encyclopaedia" to the "Grundriss" in connection with the growing influence of scholarly publishing on the knowledge orders of the philologies. We can at best hint at connections to other knowledge orders or stores, which, like the ones mentioned, all stem from the differentiation of the *historia literaria* of the eighteenth century.[5] The transformation processes examined in the present context appear informative not least because they reveal commonalities and interactions between the developments in the national philologies, which are quite different in detail and fundamentally independent of one another.

It is well known that the newer philologies, such as German studies, took their cue from the programmatic, theoretical, and practical aspects of classical philology in their efforts to gain scholarly recognition and academic representation.[6] The type

---

[2] Blüthgen 1913, p. 3 f.
[3] Ibid., p. 5 f.
[4] Müller 2004, p. 138 f.
[5] Cf. Gierl 1992 – on the state of research, cf. also Gruner and Vollhardt 2007.
[6] Cf. fundamentally Stierle 1979.

of text in which classical philology had freed itself from the reproach of being "aggregate"[7] and had attained the "dignity of a well-ordered philosophical-historical science"[8] was that of the "encyclopaedia," which needs to be characterized somewhat more precisely. We shall not be concerned here with the long history of the term,[9] but with the definition of the concept of the Fachenzyklopädie[10] in the narrower sense, which in the course of the differentiation of the sciences formed its own type of text.[11] In the philologies of the nineteenth century, subject encyclopaedias were texts of scholarly self-understanding in which scholarly claims were raised, justified and redeemed by means of an ideal-typical, more or less systematic presentation of all areas of the subject in research and possibly also in teaching. Characteristic for the encyclopaedia is its oral origin: most encyclopaedias go back to lectures.[12] Encyclopaedic lectures were regularly offered in the philological subjects at most universities in the nineteenth century, and this was done in the context of hodegetics,[13] the general guide to scientific study; the number of encyclopaedias in print does not give an adequate idea of the spread of this type as an oral genre.

The neo-philologies wanted to assert their claim to equal rights with classical philology and to representation among the academic subjects[14] not least by means of encyclopaedic presentations. In 1858, the grammar school teacher Carl Sachs wrote in the oldest journal of modern philology, the "Archiv für das Studium der neuen Sprachen und Literaturen" (Archive for the Study of New Languages and Literatures), that the unscientific teaching of languages in the past had "given the classical philologists cause and, unfortunately, good reason" to "look down on modern philology with scornful side glances and half contempt".[15] The remedy against this could only be "strict scholarship" and the orientation towards classical philology; therefore it was necessary to "base an encyclopaedia of modern philology on the already existing one of classical philology".[16] Which elements could be taken over from the encyclopaedia of classical philology and which would have to be modified, Sachs made more detailed suggestions.

The ways and successes with which the Neophilologies strove for academic recognition and representation in the second half of the century have been researched

---

[7] Cf. Kindt and Müller 2004, p. 24 f.
[8] Wolf 1985, p. 5.
[9] Cf. for example Dierse 1977; Yeo 2000; Schneider 2008.
[10] Hackel points out on p. 246 that the term "Historik" has become established for the historical encyclopaedias in the Droysen succession and cites the work of Horst Walter Blanke, which has contributed significantly to the clarification of the term.
[11] The branch of alphabetical reference works and universal encyclopaedias, which have been subsumed under the term "encyclopaedia", remains completely unconsidered; cf. on this Spree 2000.
[12] Cf. Hackel 2013, p. 247.
[13] Cf. for an overview Kern 1996.
[14] Cf. especially the works listed in note 17.
[15] Sachs 1858, p. 1.
[16] Ibid., p. 2.

in broad outline and will not be reviewed here.[17] A new generation of specialized encyclopedic texts began to appear in the period from about 1850 to 1880, when the neo-philologies had achieved their first institutional successes in establishing professorships as a result of educational policy activities and solid empirical research.[18] The most important encyclopaedia of modern languages, which also concluded this genre at the end of the nineteenth century, was Gustav Körting's "Encyklopädie und Methodologie der romanischen Philologie" (Encyclopaedia and Methodology of Romance Philology),[19] which followed August Boeckh not only in its title. Körting explicated the task of an encyclopaedia[20] against the background of the history of the genre, he provided a careful definition of the concept and task of philology in historical change[21] as well as a demarcation of the concepts of method, methodology and hodegetics,[22] which had often hardly been distinguished from each other in the encyclopaedias of the nineteenth century. The "Encyklopädie" itself, which aimed to give systematic but not complete overviews of the subfields of Romance philology,[23] contained three parts: "the first discusses the preliminary concepts and gives an introduction to the study of Romance philology; the second is to deal with the Encyklopädie der romanischen Gesammtphilologie, the third finally deals with the Encyklopädie der romanischen Einzelphilologien."[24]

Körting's encyclopaedia, despite its comprehensive foundation in cultural studies and its call for modern New French linguistic and literary research to be placed on an equal footing with research on the older languages and literatures of the Romania,[25] received little attention. The reason for this is probably far less to be found in errors or shortcomings[26] of Körting's "Encyklopädie" than in the fact that his work was completely eclipsed by Gustav Gröber's "Grundriss der romanischen Philologie"[27] only four years after its publication. In addition to the always emphasized "monumental character"[28] of Gröber's Grundriss, the fact that its editor[29] enjoyed an incomparably higher reputation in Romance philology than Körting

---

[17] Cf. Christmann 1985; Kalkhoff 2007; Wolf 2012.
[18] Cf. Kalkhoff 2007, p. 441.
[19] Körting 1884–1886.
[20] Cf. ibid., pp. VI, 110–113.
[21] Cf. ibid., pp. 110 f., 156.
[22] Cf. ibid., p. 115.
[23] Cf. ibid., p. VI: "An encyclopaedia cannot and should not be a complex of compendia on all the individual disciplines of the science in question, nor can it and should it be a complete bibliography of the disciplines in question". Cf. Boeckh 1877, p. 3: "The concept of a science or scientific discipline is not given by enumerating piece by piece what is contained in it."
[24] Ibid., p. V.
[25] Cf. Wolf 2012, p. 238.
[26] Wolf 2012 treats Körting under the heading "Neuphilologische Enzyklopädien als didaktische Projekte" (p. 238), using an anachronistic notion of didactics.
[27] Gröber 1888 ff.
[28] Wolf 2012 p. 329, cf. also Kalkhoff 2007, p. 238.
[29] Cf. Curtius 1960.

certainly contributed to this. The real reason for the success of Gröber's collected works, however, lay in the conception of the *Grundriss* itself. Körting's work had still belonged to the genre of the neo-philological encyclopaedia, with which a scientific and academic claim to validity was established – with the recognition of this claim and the institutionalisation of the discipline,[30] however, the genre of the specialist encyclopaedia had gradually become obsolete. This was recognized even in the leading philological discipline of the nineteenth century. In 1893, the classical philologist Oscar Froehde stated that his discipline represented "as it is today, not a unified science demanded by the unity of the idea, but a field of study of antiquity which will one day rise to the range of a science as true classical antiquity or as the national history of the Greeks and Romans."[31] In his Grundriss, Gröber replaced a unified idealistic conception of science with an empirical record of achievement in all fields of research in the Romania.[32]

Gröber marked the novelty of his undertaking very clearly in his introduction to the "Grundriss":

> The beginnings of the book, the first volume of which is now complete, date back to 1883, when the publisher decided to publish a work that would meet an undoubted need – the current sales of over 1000 copies confirm this – for a comprehensive overview of the whole of Romance philology, for a summary of the knowledge gained in the various fields, laid down in widely divergent places. The editor dared to undertake the task of helping to carry out such a Romance Studies Encyclopaedia in outline, after he had repeatedly, for a decade, read about Encyclopaedias of Romance Philology, and his connections entitled him to hope for the support of authoritative contributors to the work, to obtain the support of important collaborators for the work, which, in order to fulfil its purpose of instructing reliably and without one-sidedness about Romance philology and to represent it worthily to the outside world, could not be offered to the reader from the hand of a single person, or only false ambition could advise him to offer it.[33]

What was new about Gröber's enterprise was that the initiative for a very extensive scientific collective work did not come from a scientist, but from a publisher who issued a "commission" to a scientist. What was also new was that the publisher based the conception of the work on the "need" of the users. These users, however, were no longer concerned with an ostensible justification of the unity of the discipline and the systematic coherence of its parts, but with a compact and clear documentation of the empirical research results of the discipline and its increasingly differentiated fields of research.[34] The changed "need" of the users corresponded

---

[30] Cf. Gröber 1888 ff., p. 141: "The question of the legitimacy of a Romance philology can therefore no longer be answered. Even a doubt as to whether it may be regarded as a science, in the strict sense of the word, can no longer exist after the achievements of the last 50 years in various of its fields and after that expectation of the representatives of Indo-Germanic linguistics."

[31] Froehde 1893, p. 445.

[32] On the change in the understanding of science in the nineteenth century, which is the background of Gröber's position, cf. Schnädelbach 1983, pp. 89–117.

[33] Gröber 1888 ff, p. V.

[34] Accordingly, Richard Heinzel (1889, p. 773) formulates in his review of Paul's "Grundriß": "After the classical, the English and the Romance philology have preceded, we now also receive a 'Grundriß' for the Germanic languages, i.e. a summary of what is or is considered to be the certain result of research in the philological branches of knowledge that refer to Germanic peoples."

with fundamental transformations in the sciences and in the position and self-image of the scientists: The rapid growth of knowledge in the disciplines had created a strong pressure for material, which made new kinds of documentation efforts necessary, which could no longer be achieved by an individual.[35] These requirements led the editor to justify his qualification for the project not only by his expertise, but also by the fact that he possessed "connections" by means of which he could secure the "support of authoritative collaborators for the work".

Johannes Hirschfeld had already emphasized how 'close' and 'markedly reciprocal the influences' were that 'existed between the publishing book trade and science (in the broadest sense of the word)' at the end of the nineteenth century,[36] in his study on 'Science and the Publishing Book Trade in Imperial Germany', and summed up: "Without exaggeration, one can state that the German publisher has fully recognized and fulfilled his duty in this respect, and with his knowledge and experience has rendered infinite services to German science and culture."[37] Among the 'shining examples of the noblest bookseller's spirit' Hirschfeld also named Karl J. Trübner (1846–1907), one of the outstanding publishing personalities in scholarly publishing. Trübner had founded his publishing house, which concentrated on linguistics and literature, in Strasbourg in 1872 with the plan "to create, as far as possible, large, uniform encyclopaedias for the entire field of linguistics, which would bring together knowledge for the first time and give it a firm, secure foundation".[38] It was not only Trübner who suggested Gröber's "Grundriss", but he also initiated the following philological compilations, some of which were completed by Walter de Gruyter only after Trübner's death:

> *Grundriß der romanischen Philologie* (1888 ff.)
> *Grundriß of Germanic Philology* (1891 ff.)
> *Grundriß der iranischen Philologie* (1895 ff.)
> *Grundriß der indoarischen Philologie und Altertumskunde* (1896 ff.)
> *Grundriß der vergleichenden Grammatik der indogermanischen Sprachen* (1886 ff.)
> *Reallexikon der germanischen Altertumskunde* (1910 ff.)
> *Reallexikon der indogermanischen Altertumskunde* (1901 ff.)[39]

With Trübner's offensive, the term "Grundriss" (outline), which had previously served for compendia of all kinds, became predominantly common for the new type of compendium, in German studies especially for bibliographical overviews of the subject and its parts.[40]

In the scholarly publishing world of his time, Trübner was by no means alone with his "Grundrissen". His colleague Paul Siebeck, for example, the owner of a

---

[35] On "material pressure" as a founder of disorder in classification systems and stimulator of innovative orders, cf. the example of Linné Müller-Wille 2001.

[36] Hirschfeld 1921, pp. 1421–1424, 1434–1439, sp. 1421.

[37] Ibid., sp. 1434.

[38] Lüdtke 1920, sp. 4. cf. also Ziesak 1999.

[39] Data according to Jäger 2001, p. 462.

[40] Cf. for example Hoffmann 1863 and, following on from him, Bahder 1883, who for reasons of space, however, already excluded more recent literary history (p. VI).

medium-sized publishing house, also initiated influential collective works in the Empire with the "Grundriß der theologischen Wissenschaften", the "Grundriß der philosophischen Wissenschaften" as well as the "Grundriß der Sozialökonomie" (Grundriß of Social Economy) conceived by Max Weber.[41] Although it was not only in the humanities that there was obviously an interdisciplinary need for such compendia, which were called "Grundriss", "Handbuch" or "Real-Enzyklopädie", the expectations placed on them in the individual sciences were as heterogeneous as the compendia themselves.

Gustav Körting had already pointed out in a description of Gröber's "Grundriss" that these compendia, written by numerous authors in the philological disciplines, were a different scholarly genre from the specialized encyclopaedias of the nineteenth century:

> The "Grundriss" is not the unified work of *one* man, but rather almost *thirty* scholars have worked on it. Such a collaboration, since it must of course not be a work according to a template, inevitably results in disparity of the individual contributions in terms of scope, structure and intrinsic value, even if, as has happened in the present case, the editor has sketched out the plan of the complete work with the greatest expertise and the most careful consideration.[42]

Körting recognized the importance of Gröber's "Grundriss" and emphasized that all its sections were "in factual relation" at the "necessary level of research";[43] he called, however, for a more uniform orientation of the contributions:

> Something, however, must be done in this direction, otherwise the book will continue to give the impression that it is composed of a series of individual works only externally joined together, but not internally closely connected, that it represents a collection of monographs, but not a unified whole.[44]

The conceptual differences between the genres "Fachenzyklopädie" and "Grundriss" can be demonstrated even more clearly by Hermann Paul's "Grundriss der germanischen Philologie", due to the state of tradition. Karl J. Trübner described the genesis of the "Grundriss" in a letter to Wilhelm Scherer dated 14 July 1886:

> Following the 'Grundriss der romanischen Philologie', of which the first volume has been published, I intend to publish a similar one for Germanic philology. Originally, Prof. Gröber wanted to publish both Grundrisse as a joint work and had already worked out a plan for me, which Prof. Martin also saw and approved. However, Prof. Gröber soon became convinced that the work had to be divided into two independent works – Romanic and Germanic – and handed over the editorship of the Germanic part to Prof. Sievers, from whose hands the editorship passed over to Prof. Paul after some time. Thus I have come into contact with a circle of scholars who have hitherto been far removed from my business activities; I dare to hope, however, that you, esteemed Professor, will accompany the work with your participation, despite the fact that it will not be edited exclusively by your students. It would also be my most ardent wish if, by getting to know the representatives of the

---

[41] Cf. Knappenberger-Jans 2011, pp. 20, 80, 182, 232, 320.
[42] Körting 1896, p. 81.
[43] Ibid.
[44] Körting 1892–1895, pp. 148–149.

different directions of Germanic philology, I could contribute with my modest powers something to the reconciliation of the existing personal differences.[45]

Paul confirmed this genesis in the preface to the "Grundriss"; but he added:

> It was not without grave misgivings that I took over the editorship in his [Sievers'] place. The agreements with the collaborators were for the most part concluded in the spring of 1885. For some sections it was not possible to find a collaborator until later, for several the scholars who had originally agreed had to be replaced by others, some that had originally been planned had to be dropped, others were newly added. The disposition of the whole thus shifted not insignificantly.[46]

Paul then described how there were time delays due to the necessary re-scheduling and concluded:

> I am probably as well aware as anyone of the imperfections of the work. In particular, I am well aware of the great unevenness in the treatment of the various sections, and of the many gaps that remain to be filled. I have every reason to ask for kind indulgence, which perhaps a fair judge will not refuse, who realizes the difficulties with which one has to contend in such an undertaking. Perhaps in later editions it will be possible to remove more and more of the defects of the first attempt.[47]

Paul was aware of the conceptual inconsistency of the "Grundriss", and his correspondence with Friedrich Kluge reveals that he repeatedly expressed doubts about the sense of the entire project.[48] It should also be borne in mind that the "Grundriss", as it is bound up for us today, assumed a uniformity that was not initially present, for it appeared as a "continuation work"[49] in individual deliveries that could also be obtained separately, and Trübner's correspondence with Paul reveals that the positions of individual articles in the complete work were still disputed during publication; the date of delivery often played a decisive role.

The only positive news that Trübner was able to send Paul concerned the sales figures of the 'Grundrisses', which Trübner continued to refer to as the

---

[45] Trübner's hope to be able to "contribute to the reconciliation of the existing personal differences" with the "Grundriss" was deceived. On the occasion of the second edition of Paul's "Grundriss", August Sauer (1896) gave vent to his anger in a letter to Bernhard Seuffert about "how badly the newer Lit. Gesch., its representatives in general, Scherer & s. Schule insbesondre come off in it" and demanded: "The Schererische Schule should get together and publish a Grundriß (or a handbook) of the newer German Lit. Gesch.; because of mine of the German Lit. Gesch. in general (but not: the Germanic) [...]." – Here it becomes clear that Grundrisse could serve not only scientific and commercial, but also politico-scientific purposes.

[46] Paul 1891, p. V.

[47] Ibid., p. VI.

[48] Cf. Kluge to Paul in a postcard (no. 31) dated 19.10.1890 (postmark): "By the way, you must not think so pessimistically about the outline, which does so much good and is received so joyfully everywhere, which, according to K. Trübner, is also shown in the paragraph. The fact that everything is uneven [Kluge gives examples], that and other such things do not change the overall character of the book and I think you may rightly be pleased with your work." Kluge also addresses Paul's displeasure with the project once again in a letter dated 3.1.1891 (no. 34).

[49] On the term, cf. Mensching 2003, p. 9.

"Encyklopädie".[50] On November 7, 1889, Trübner stated that, with more than 900 subscribers, sales were "better than for the Romance Grundriss",[51] and on December 23, 1890, he wrote: "I am very satisfied with sales. Apart from about 1600 regular subscribers",[52] far higher numbers of individual deliveries had been sold. However, Paul took little comfort from the sales figures; he continued to doubt the sense of the project and asked Trübner to relieve him of the obligation to publish a second edition of the 'Grundriss'.[53] Trübner succeeded in talking Paul out of this request; upon completion of the entire first edition, he wrote to him:

> At this solemn moment of the completion of our great enterprise, I am compelled to express my gratitude to you from the bottom of my heart for the trust you placed in me at the time when I presented the project to you to carry it out properly in business terms, and for the fact that you yourself have put all your influence and your high reputation into bringing about a work of the first order. I can safely say that this Grundriß will remain the most important work of my publishing house for a long time to come.[54]

While Paul had expressed the hope in the preface to the first volume of the "Grundriss" that it would be possible "in later editions" to "eliminate more and more of the deficiencies of the first attempt",[55] he had to realize during the work on the second edition that, on the contrary, the deficiencies were multiplying. Even for the second edition, Paul had not succeeded in finding an editor for the history of modern German literature.[56] Some of the editors from the first edition left and new ones had to be recruited. Individual sections of the "Grundriss" appeared with the 2nd edition as "special editions",[57] and about the printing Paul had to report: "The hope that the printing would proceed more evenly and rapidly than with the first edition has unfortunately not been fulfilled. The contrary has been the case."[58] During the printing of the first and third volumes, "stagnations" had occurred, and the third volume had "swelled into a shapeless mass" due to the completely disproportionate size of the "Geschichte der friesischen Sprache".[59] Of the second volume

---

[50] Cf. for example Trübner's letters to Paul no. 3 (10.6.1885) and no. 16 (4.6.1888).
[51] Trübner to Paul no. 49 (7.11.1889).
[52] Trübner to Paul no. 74 (23.12.1890).
[53] These facts can be gathered from Trübner's letter to Paul no. 75 (2.1.1891).
[54] Trübner to Paul no. 122 (14.6.1893).
[55] Paul 1891, p. VI.
[56] On June 30, 1890 (No. 65), Trübner had written to Paul: "Since there will probably be a four-week break, I will take the liberty of making two intemperate suggestions in the interest of our enterprise. The first is that you ask Prof. Brandl to extend his Middle English literary history to the New English, including Shakespeare[…] However, German literary history only goes as far as Middle High German. But here, if I remember correctly, the reason was that you did not find a suitable editor and preferred to take over this important area yourself in a new delivery. […]". Later, Trübner had wanted to win Erich Schmidt for the history of modern literature; however, he had declined after a short period of consideration, cf. Trübner to Paul no. 126 (February 25, 1894) and 127 (March 8, 1894).
[57] Paul 1901, p. VI.
[58] Ibid.
[59] Ibid.

he could only announce the first delivery for "soon" and concluded: "Whether an even progress will be possible depends on the collaborators."[60]

Even before the 2nd edition of the 'Grundriss' was completely finished, Trübner announced to Hermann Paul that, due to his age, he had decided "to accept a partner with the right of legal succession on January 1, 1906. It is Dr. W. de Gruyter, owner of the company Georg Reimer in Berlin."[61] A year later, the publishing house began to think about a completely new division of the "Grundriss"; after Trübner's death, the publishing house sent Paul the minutes of a conversation that had taken place between de Gruyter, Trübner's publishing director Dr. Lüdtke, and Paul, which stated:

> Finally, Dr. Lüdtke and I expressed this suggestion: whether, in view of the increasingly differentiated treatment of individual languages in research and study, it would not be advisable, from the third edition onwards, to divide the outline into volumes according to language branches. In this way, one would place a German, an English and a Nordic volume next to a general Germanic one. In this way, we would give the new edition a new incentive – and, what seems particularly important to us – counter the danger that new individual floor plans of this kind appear from other sources.[62]

The term "individual outline" [Einzelgrundriss], which appears in the minutes of the discussion, is an indication that the participants had not only lost the awareness of the connection between the subject encyclopaedia and the outline, but that the concept of the "Grundriss" itself was also threatening to become obsolete: the trend was inevitably moving away from a general overview of the subject to an overview of only the most important – i.e. the most sought-after – singular subject areas.

Paul's reaction to the minutes of the conversation has not survived. However, when he received a precise list from the publisher on October 14, 1910, which envisaged dividing the "Grundriss" into 27 individual volumes, Paul seems to have announced his intention to give up the overall title "Grundriss der germanischen Philologie" in this case and to resign from the editorship.[63] Thereupon, the publisher wrote to him on October 3, 1910, among other things:

> The Grundriss der germanischen Philologie has achieved such a position in German scholarship and brought so much honor to the publishing house that we would feel it like the fall of a cornerstone of the publishing house if the title were to fall. The memory of the founder of the company, which the publishing house must hold high and in honour, would forbid this.
>
> But it is equally certain that just as the Grundriss is linked to the name of the publisher, it is also linked to that of the editor, and that this connection may be preserved is a feeling that is just as deeply rooted as the attachment to the Grundriss. I would therefore like to sincerely ask you, dear Privy Councillor, not to allow the thought that the moment has given rise to to grow any further, and to replace it with the remembrance of the long-standing connections with the publishing house.
>
> We are well aware that it is not easy to abandon the old form of the 'Grundriss', and it was only after long deliberations and after examining all the economic bases of the enter-

---

[60] Ibid.
[61] Trübner to Paul no. 285 (2.8.1905).
[62] Trübner-Verlag to Paul no. 294 (24.10.1907).
[63] This can be seen in letter no. 328 (3.10.1910) from the publisher to Paul.

prise that the publisher decided at the time to submit the proposal to you. I think I may speak quite frankly. The costs associated with the floor plan are very high.[64]

The publisher claimed that, on the one hand, the number of subscribers for the second edition had fallen and, on the other hand, "the distance between the individual volumes, as far as stocks were concerned, had become ever greater",[65] so that "economic necessity" had made it necessary to provide for the division into individual volumes. In a letter of September 2, 1911, Dr. Lüdtke expressed less sinuously what the publisher was concerned with: "The purpose of the new arrangement in the outline is, after all, to increase the saleability of the individual parts and to make the good ones for new editions independent of each other."[66] Through the measure proposed by the publisher and subsequently actually implemented, the "Grundriss" is transformed from an originally cohesive collective work into a "book series"[67] in which the scientific knowledge of the discipline is represented in a novel way.

Let's draw a cautious conclusion:

1. Encyclopaedias of disciplines are nineteenth century texts written by individual authors in the phase of the disciplines' striving for recognition as sciences or for equal rights with already recognised sciences. Their focus is on the presentation of the systematic interrelationship of the individual subject areas of the discipline.
2. The philological "Grundrisse" examined here as examples are works from the end of the nineteenth and beginning of the twentieth century, which were initiated by publishers, conceived in agreement with scholarly editors, and written by numerous authors. They are transitional works which, on the one hand, still adhere to the presentation of the "concept and task of philology" inherited from the subject encyclopaedia, but on the other hand place the main emphasis on the summarising presentation of the research results[68] in the individual subject areas which were accumulated in the previous phase of intensive empirical research activity.
3. In the course of their realization, these "Grundrisse" are confronted with two quite different problems. On the one hand, the editors have to carry out a number of coordinating and editorial tasks with authors and publishers that require a new kind of extraordinary time commitment and, for the most part, other than exclu-

---

[64] Trübner-Verlag to Hermann Paul no. 328 (3.10.1910).
[65] Ibid.
[66] Trübner-Verlag to Paul, no. 351 (2.9.1911).
[67] On the genus of book series, cf. Bry 1917. Bry already draws attention to the transformation of encyclopedic collective works into book series, cf. p. 14, note 1: "For example, the well-known collection Die Kultur der Gegenwart (Teubner) is both a collective work (encyclopaedia) and a book series, although the former character predominates."
[68] Friedrich Kluge believed that the Grundriss should not only summarize research results, but also present new ones. In order to characterize the importance of the Grundriss, he wrote to Paul: "It is an important impulse for science, but it is only if everyone can bring not only what is known, but also new things of their own. [...] I cannot refrain from bringing something new for the English either; one must overtake Körting and Elze." Kluge to Paul no. 27, postcard dated 24.5.1890 (postmark).

sively scientific qualifications. It is perhaps no coincidence that Trübner-Verlag offered Hermann Paul to take on a large part of these tasks, even though they extend into the realm of (scholarly) editorial responsibility.[69] The second problem, which only became apparent with the new edition of the Grundrisse, is that its recipients are showing less and less interest in purchasing the complete work than in purchasing individual volumes which they wish to obtain separately for reasons of research or teaching. Publishers responded to this interest by gradually transforming the Grundrisse into book series.

References

Bahder, Karl von: Die deutsche Philologie im Grundriss. Paderborn 1883.
Blüthgen, Fritz: Zweck und Notwendigkeit der Rechts-Enzyklopädie, in: Forschung und Wissen. Nachrichten vom Wissenschaftlichen Büchermarkt für Gelehrte und Ungelehrte. Hg. von den verbündeten Verlagen Göschen, Guttentag, Reimer und Trübner. Jg. 1913, S. 3–6.
Boeckh, August: Enzyklopädie und Methodologie der philologischen Wissenschaften. Hg. von Ernst Bratuschek. Leipzig 1877.
Bry, Carl Christian: Buchreihen. Fortschritt oder Gefahr für den Buchhandel? Gotha 1917.
Christmann, Hans Helmut: Romanistik und Anglistik an der deutschen Universität im 19. Jahrhundert. Ihre Herausbildung als Fächer und ihr Verhältnis zu Germanistik und klassischer Philologie, in: Akademie der Wissenschaften und der Literatur Mainz, Abhandlungen der geistes- und sozialwissenschaftlichen Klasse Jg. 1985, Nr. 1, Stuttgart 1985, S. 1–40.
Dierse, Ulrich: Enzyklopädie. Zur Geschichte eines philosophischen und wissenschaftstheoretischen Begriffs. Bonn 1977 (Archiv für Begriffsgeschichte. Supplementheft 2).
Froehde, Oscar: Der Begriff und die Aufgabe der Literaturwissenschaft, in: Jahrbücher für classische Philologie 39, 1893 = Neue Jahrbücher für Philologie und Pädagogik 63, 147, S. 433–445.
Gierl, Martin: Bestandsaufnahme im gelehrten Bereich: Zur Entwicklung der „Historia literaria" im 18. Jahrhundert, in: Denkhorizonte und Handlungsspielräume. Historische Studien für Rudolf Vierhaus zum 70. Geburtstag. Göttingen 1992, S. 53–80.
Gruner, Frank und Friedrich Vollhardt (Hg.): Historia literaria. Neuordnungen des Wissens im 17. und 18. Jahrhundert. Berlin 2007.
Gröber, Gustav (Hg.): Grundriss der romanischen Philologie. Strassburg 1888 ff.
Curtius, Ernst Robert: Gustav Gröber und die romanische Philologie [1952], in: Curtius: Gesammelte Aufsätze zur romanischen Philologie. Bern et al. 1960, S. 429–455.

---

[69] Cf. Trübner-Verlag to Paul, No. 328 (3.10.1910): "In order to spare you, dear Privy Councillor, any inconvenience, I am gladly prepared, if you so wish and authorise me, to explain the situation to the individual gentlemen in writing or orally and to ask them to approve the step that the publishing house must take in the interests of the whole and of science. I believe that no one who knows how much trouble large undertakings cause a publisher will disagree. I would, of course, submit the letters to you for your perusal before sending them. Please allow me, however, to emphasize once again that I am only making this suggestion in order to prevent you from being inconvenienced by the economic considerations of the publisher, without wanting to interfere in any way with the rights of the publisher. Just as all communications, inquiries, and suggestions should only serve the purpose of easing your troubles in publishing the third edition, which are, after all, double in the changed situation, to the best of my knowledge and ability, which unfortunately could not be the case with the second edition."

Hackel, Christiane: Philologische Fachenzyklopädien. Zu Charakter und Funktion eines wenig beachteten Genres, in: Christiane Hacke und Sabine Seifert: August Boeckh: Philologie, Hermeneutik und Wissenschaftspolitik. Berlin 2013, S. 243–274.

Heinzel, Richard: [Rez.:] Hermann Paul: Grundriß der germanischen Philologie. In: Zeitschrift für die österreichischen Gymnasien 40, 1889, S. 773–777.

Hirschfeld, Johannes: Wissenschaft und Verlagsbuchhandel im kaiserlichen Deutschland, in: Börsenblatt für den Deutschen Buchhandel 88, Nr. 227 (28.9.1921), S. 1421–1439.

Hoffmann, Heinrich von Fallersleben: Die deutsche Philologie im Grundriss. Ein Leitfaden für Vorlesungen. Breslau 1863.

Jäger, Georg: Der wissenschaftliche Verlag, in: Geschichte des deutschen Buchhandels im 19. und 20. Jahrhundert. Das Kaiserreich 1870–1918. Teil 1. Im Auftrag der Historischen Kommission herausgegeben von Georg Jäger in Verbindung mit Dieter Langewiesche und Wolfram Siemann. Frankfurt a. M. 2001, S. 423–472.

Kalkhoff, Alexander: Begriff und Umfang der Neuphilologie im 19. Jahrhundert – ein Plädoyer für ein historisches Bewusstsein, in: Handeln und Verhandeln. Beiträge zum 22. Forum Junge Romanistik (Regensburg 08.–10.06.2006). Bonn 2007, S. 433–45.

Kern, Manfred: Hodegetik, in: Historisches Wörterbuch der Rhetorik Bd. 3, 1996, Sp. 1450–1454.

Kindt, Tom und Hans-Harald Müller: Die Einheit der Philologie, in: Walter Erhart (Hg.): Grenzen der Germanistik. Rephilologisierung oder Erweiterung? Stuttgart, Weimar 2004 (Germanistische Symposien XXVI), S. 22–44.

Knappenberger-Jans, Silke: Verlagspolitik und Wissenschaft. Der Verlag J.C.B. Mohr (Paul Siebeck) im frühen 20. Jahrhundert. Wiesbaden 2011 (Mainzer Studien zur Buchwissenschaft; 13).

Körting, Gustav: Encyklopädie und Methodologie der romanischen Philologie. Mit besonderer Berücksichtigung des Französischen und Italienischen. Heilbronn, 3 Bde., 1884–1886.

Körting, Gustav: Handbuch der romanischen Philologie. Gekürzte Neubearbeitung der „Encyklopädie und Methodologie der romanischen Philologie". Leipzig 1896.

Körting, Gustav: [Rez.: Gustav Gröber: Grundriss der romanischen Philologie] In: Kritischer Jahresbericht über die Fortschritte der Romanischen Philologie. Unter Mitwirkung von hundertfünfzehn Fachgenossen herausgegeben von Karl Vollmüller und Richard Otto 1, 1892–1895, S. 147–149.

Kluge, Friedrich: Briefe/Postkarten an Hermann Paul: Nr. 31 (19.10.1890), Nr. 27 (24.5.1890), Nr. 34 (03.01.1891), Nachlass Hermann Paul, Universitätsbibliothek München.

Lüdtke, Gerhard: Karl J. Trübner. Die Geschichte eines Verlages im deutschen Elsaß (1872–1919), in: Das literarische Echo 23, Heft 1 (1.10.1920), Sp. 1–6.

Mensching, Eckart: Zur Entstehung eines Fortsetzungswerks: Die ‚RE' oder der ‚Pauly-Wissowa, in: Mensching: Nugae zur Philologie-Geschichte XIII. Berlin 2003, S. 9–33.

Müller, Helen: Im Zeitalter der Sammelwerke. Friedrich Naumanns Projekt eines „Deutschen Staatslexikons" (1914), in: Rüdiger vom Bruch (Hg.): Friedrich Naumann in seiner Zeit. Berlin et al. 2000, S. 189–207.

Müller, Helen: Wissenschaft und Markt um 1900. Das Verlagsunternehmen Walter de Gruyters im literarischen Feld der Jahrhundertwende. Tübingen 2004 (Studien und Texte zur Sozialgeschichte der deutschen Literatur; 104).

Müller-Wille, Staffan: Carl von Linnés Herbarschrank. Zur epistemischen Funktion eines Sammlungsmöbels, in: Anke le Heesen und Emma C. Spary (Hrsg.): Sammeln als Wissen. Das Sammeln und seine wissenschaftsgeschichtliche Bedeutung. Göttingen 2001, S. 22–38.

Paul, Hermann (Hg.): Grundriss der germanischen Philologie. Erster Band. Strassburg 1891.

Paul, Hermann (Hg.): Grundriss der germanischen Philologie. Zweite verbesserte und vermehrte Auflage. Erster Band. Strassburg 1901.

Sachs, Carl: Vorschlag zu einer Encyclopädie der modernen Philologie, in: Archiv für das Studium der neueren Sprachen und Literaturen 23, 1858, S. 1–8.

Sauer, August: Brief an Bernhard Seuffert in Graz, Prag, 17. Juni 1896, Nachlass Bernhard Seuffert, Staatsarchiv Würzburg.

Schnädelbach, Herbert: Philosophie in Deutschland 1831–1933. Frankfurt a. M. 1983.

Schneider, Ulrich Johannes: Der Aufbau der Wissenswelt. Eine phänotypische Beschreibung enzyklopädischer Literatur, in: Ulrich Johannes Schneider (Hg.): Kulturen des Wissens im 18. Jahrhundert. Berlin et al. 2008, S. 81–100.

Spree, Ulrike: Das Streben nach Wissen. Eine vergleichende Gattungsgeschichte der populären Enzyklopädie in Deutschland und Großbritannien im 19. Jahrhundert. Tübingen 2000 (Communicatio; 24).

Stierle, Karlheinz: Altertumswissenschaftliche Hermeneutik und die Entstehung der Neuphilologie, in: Philologie und Hermeneutik im 19. Jahrhundert. Zur Geschichte und Methodologie der Geisteswissenschaften. Hg. von Helmut Flashaar et al. Göttingen 1979, S. 260–288.

Trübner, Karl J.: Brief an Wilhelm Scherer: Nr. 947 (14. Juli 1886). Nachlass Wilhelm Scherer, Archiv der Berlin-Brandenburgischen Akademie der Wissenschaften.

Trübner, Karl J.: Briefe an Hermann Paul: Nr. 3 (10.6.1885), Nr. 16 (4.6.1888), Nr. 49 (7.11.1889), Nr. 65 (30.6. 1890), Nr. 74 (23.12.1890), Nr. 75 (2.1.1891), Nr. 122 (14.6.1893), Nr. 126 (25. Februar 1894), 127 (8.3.1894), Nr. 285 (2.8.1905). Nachlass Hermann Paul, Universitätsbibliothek München.

Trübner-Verlag: Briefe an Hermann Paul: Nr. 294 (24.10.1907), Nr. 328 (3.10.1910), Nr. 351 (2.9. 1911). Nachlass Hermann Paul, Universitätsbibliothek München.

Wolf, Friedrich August: Darstellung der Altertumswissenschaft nach Begriff, Umfang, Zweck und Wert [1807]. Berlin 1985 (Dokumente der Wissenschaftsgeschichte).

Wolf, Johanna: Kontinuität und Wandel der Philologien. Textarchäologische Studien zur Entstehung der Romanischen Philologie im 19. Jahrhundert. Tübingen 2012 (Romanica Monacensia).

Yeo, Richard: Encyclopaedic knowledge, in: Books and the Sciences in History. Hg. von Marina Frasca-Spada und Nick Jardine. Cambridge 2000, S. 207–224.

Ziesak, Anne-Katrin: Der Verlag Walter de Gruyter 1749–1999. Mit Beiträgen von Hans-Robert Cram, Kurt-Georg Cram und Andreas Terwey. Berlin et al. 1999, S. 165–169.

The 'Empire' Writes Back: Literary Recolonizations in Eighteenth Century France (Prévost, Lesage, Fuzelier/Rameau)

Hendrik Schlieper

Abstract French national literature and philology were created around 1800 out of the spirit of a colonial fantasy related to the *Nouvelle-France*, i.e. those colonial possessions in North America that France had to cede to other great powers, especially Great Britain, during the eighteenth century. Usually, this colonial fantasy and the founding fiction of a restituted geopolitical and cultural hegemony of France are associated with the work of Chateaubriand. Chateaubriand, however, stands in a tradition of literary recolonizations that points back to the early eighteenth century and allows a different reading of the "The Empire Writes Back" formula: As shown in the examples of Prévost, Lesage, Fuzelier, and Rameau, the French 'center' writes back a colonial America as early as the 1730s, and with it an identity-forming 'Empire' that forms the basis for the Romantic justification of a French culture and the constitution of Empire in the concrete sense of the nineteenth century.

1 Colonial Fantasies Around and Before 1800

France's fortunes around 1800 were marked by a double experience of loss: with the successive takeover of almost all its colonies by other great powers, France clearly lost geopolitical importance in the course of the eighteenth century, especially since the Seven Years' War, and with the dissolution of the old European *Respublica*

H. Schlieper (✉)
Institut für Germanistik und Vergleichende Literaturwissenschaft,
Universität Paderborn, Paderborn, Deutschland
e-mail: hendrik.schlieper@upb.de

litteraria as a transnational community of scholars, it simultaneously forfeited its cultural-political supremacy. French Romanticism in general and the founding of a French national literature around and after 1800 in particular can be understood as attempts to compensate for this experience of loss by creating corresponding *grands récits*.[1] A central role is played here by a 'colonial fantasy' of a restituted geopolitical and cultural hegemony of France that is dominantly related to the *Nouvelle-France*, i.e. the former French possessions in North America.[2]

In these contexts, Chateaubriand's work is of paradigmatic value. The repeatedly stated 'founding character' of his work concerns, as the *cycle américain* (*Atala, René, Les Natchez*) emphatically demonstrates, also and especially the 'founding fiction' of an imperial tradition that is to take the place of the traditions that have been lost.[3] The beginning of the prologue of *Atala* makes this tradition exemplarily legible: "La France possédait autrefois dans l'Amérique septentrionale un vaste empire, qui s'étendait depuis le Labrador jusqu'aux Florides, et depuis les rivages de l'Atlantique jusqu'aux lacs les plus reculés du haut Canada."[4] The distance clearly marked here, both spatially and temporally, articulates not only melancholic mourning over the loss of former greatness, but also the desire to reappropriate a lost colonial America and thus to (re)create an identity-forming 'empire'.[5]

It has been shown from various sides that this Chateaubriandian invention of tradition refers back to Rousseau and in particular to the Second *Discours* with its phantasms of origins in the history of humanity and society.[6] Now, Rousseau himself stands in a tradition of thought about the political and cultural pioneering role of France that goes back to the beginning of the eighteenth century. This tradition of thought builds on seventeenth-century models of culture and, in particular, on the model of *la France galante*, which describes the cultural practices of a *civilisation* that is understood to be decidedly 'French' and that productively combines cultural and colonial politics from the very beginning.[7] The both aesthetic and ethical

---

[1] Cf. Bercegol et al. (eds.) 2016, esp. Florence Lotterie's "Introduction" (pp. 7–34) and the contributions collected under the section "L'identification romantique, hypothèques et hypothèses" (pp. 243 sqq.).

[2] Cf. on the concept of 'colonial fantasies' Zantop 1999, who understands this to mean literary fictions that function as "preparatory and accompanying fantasies for colonial action" (p. 17) in the run-up to actual German colonial undertakings. The France of 1800 considered here shows, however, that colonial fantasies do not only unfold their effect prospectively or synchronously, but also retrospectively, and thus promote imperial thinking.

[3] Cf. on the founding character of Chateaubriand exemplarily Grimm 1991, esp. pp. 71 sq. and the overview by Roulin 2016, here esp. pp. 55 sq. on the historical 'place' of the *cycle américain*.

[4] Chateaubriand 2008, p. 67.

[5] Cf. Hoffmann 2019, pp. 270 sqq. ("Le deuil de la (nouvelle) France"), and Counter 2018, who understands the titular term "repatriation" as the "reconstruction of a *patrie* – that is, of a symbolically coherent national community" (p. 286).

[6] Cf. the studies by Jauß 1989 and Fumaroli 1994.

[7] On the model of the *France galante*, see the two key studies by Viala 2008 and 2019; on Rousseau's relationship to the gallant tradition, see in both studies the chapters "Triomphes de l'opéra galant (Campra, Rameau, Rousseau)," pp. 398–406, and "L'héritage galant: abrégé de quelques mœurs d'Ancien Régime," pp. 37 sqq. respectively.

cultural practices of this *civilisation française* produce a sociability of "manieres honnêtes, & complaisantes"[8] that regulates the relationship between the sexes in particular; gallant love contours itself as a reciprocal love that connects the partners through the key concept of *tendresse*, which is conceptualised in the central document of gallantry, the *Carte du Tendre* from Madeleine de Scudéry's novel *Clélie*.[9]

Against the horizon of the general 'crisis of European consciousness',[10] the cultural model of the *France galante* also enters a crisis, insofar as gallantry – now increasingly the object of strategic calculation and 'libertine' manipulation – loses its actual meaning.[11] As a culture-creating ideal, it is thus to be understood as early as the beginning of the eighteenth century and increasingly from the 1730s onwards as the *lieu de mémoire* as which it entered Pierre Nora's historiographical enterprise of the same name.[12] This development was accompanied, or rather supported, by a colonial political upheaval: with the Natchez uprising from 1729, French colonial rule in North America experienced a caesura, which formed the basis for continuing and armed conflicts with the indigenous population and with the British colonial power, which would culminate in the loss of the *Nouvelle-France* sealed by the Peace of Paris in 1763.[13]

Precisely in this context, literary texts emerge that function in a double sense as fictions of re-appropriation: First, under the impact of geopolitical developments, they rewrite an 'America' that has been lost, or is in the process of being lost. In doing so, they allow a different reading of the formula "The Empire Writes Back" coined by Salman Rushdie and conceptualized by Bill Ashcroft, Gareth Griffiths, and Helen Tiffin. It usually denotes a paradigm of counter-discursive writing in which literature of the (formerly) colonized 'periphery' is directed against the 'centre' of the colonial power and thus exhibits, subverts and reverses the centre-periphery hierarchy in its constructivity.[14] If the concept of 'empire' is understood in this classical postcolonial reading from the point of view of the colonies, then the texts from France in the 1730s that are of interest here – and entirely in the sense of

---

[8] Cf. the lemma GALANTE, ANTE in Furetière 1702, p. 984: "[…] GALANT, se dit encore d'un homme qui a l'air du monde; qui est poli, qui tâche à plaire, & particulierement aux Dames, par ses manieres honnêtes, & complaisantes; qui a beaucoup d'esprit, de la delicatesse, de l'enjouëment, des manieres touchantes, aisées, & agreables." The orthography of the original remains unchanged here as in the following cited eighteenth century texts.

[9] Cf. on gallant love or gallantry as 'love ethics' of courtly society Steigerwald 2014.

[10] This in the sense of Hazard 1994 ([1]1935).

[11] This is also referred to in the above-mentioned lemma in Furetière 1702, p. 985: "On dit aussi, qu'on homme est un *galant*; pour dire, qu'il est habile, adroit, dangereux, qu'il éntend bien ses affaires: que c'est un fourbe, un frippon". See also in detail Viala 2008, pp. 36–39 ("'Il se prend en bonne et mauvaise part...'") and pp. 451–455 ("Changements de mots"). Losfeld 2015, p. 256 speaks of a "crisis of sociability of the older type" in France since 1730; cf. in detail also Losfeld 2011, pp. 141 sqq.

[12] Cf. Hepp 1997.

[13] The moment of *rupture* is accordingly the focus of Balvay's 2008 study. See also Havard and Vidal 2014, pp. 292–300 ("Le soulèvement des Natchez").

[14] See in detail Rushdie 1982 and Ashcroft et al. 2002 ([1]1989), in overview also Gymnich 2017.

a historical determination of the position of philology – raise the question of the extent to which the empire develops strategies of 'writing back' in its inner centre, in order to 'write back' territories or to reincorporate them qua fiction. On the other hand, the texts considered in the following evoke, in a gesture of reappropriation, the civilizational cultural practices of *la France galante,* which is conceived as an ideal that is as past as it is restitutable, in order to present France's claim to hegemony as legitimate. This leads to the thesis to be discussed here that the 'founding fiction' – so decisive for French national thought – of a restituted geo- and cultural-political hegemony of France finds its actual justification *before* Chateaubriand and more precisely: in the literature of the 1730s. The greater the spatial and above all temporal distance to the actual real 'possession' of the colonial empire, the more effective the written colonial fantasies become. Accordingly, the efforts of colonial re-actualization during the eighteenth century came to an end with the fall of the *Ancien Régime*, on the one hand, and on the other hand, this very end formed the basis for the founding of a French culture with its own national literature and philology under the sign of Romanticism.

In order to plausibilize this thesis, Prévost's novel *Manon Lescaut*, Lesage's drama *Les Mariages de Canada*, written for the *Théâtre de la Foire,* and the ballet opera *Les Indes galantes*, written by Fuzelier and Rameau, will be considered here as three (intertextually linked) texts that appear in the 1730s in immediate chronological succession (1733, 1734, 1735) and make their respective American spaces readable as heterotopias of the *civilisation française.*[15] These texts are paradigmatic because of the climactic movement that their comparison makes visible. As will be shown below, they bring together the temporal distance from the glorious civilizational past and the telos of reappropriation associated with it with a successively increasing spatial distancing: Thus the protagonists of Prévost's novel are led by their fate to a Louisiana that is ambivalently semanticized as 'exile' and positively related to England as an alternative model of civilization. Lesage's drama, in contrast, decidedly outsources the French model of civilization by bringing onto the stage a new French society in the *retraite* of the Canadian wilderness. Finally, Fuzelier and Rameau's ballet opera takes a further, decisive step by staging the American 'others' as the actual bearers of the *civilisation française*, thus pointing the way to Chateaubriand's *sauvages*, which for their part are to be understood as inventions of a genuine French colonial and cultural fantasy.

---

[15] This in the sense of Michel Foucault's definition of heterotopias as "sortes d'utopies effectivement réalisées dans lesquelles les emplacements réels, tous les autres emplacements réels que l'on peut trouver à l'intérieur de la culture sont à la fois représentés, contestés et inversés"; cf. Foucault 2001, p. 1574.

2 Désert(s): Prévosts *Manon Lescaut*

Prévost's "épisode américain" concluding *Manon Lescaut* is one of the most famous literary representations of eighteenth-century *Nouvelle-France*.[16] In the novel's final pages, the title character meets the fate of those "femmes de mauvaises vie",[17] exiled by France to the American colonies: Convicted of fraud and at the insistence of her lover Des Grieux's father, Manon, part of a "déplorable troupe" (430) of female prisoners, is shipped in Le Havre on a ship bound for Louisiana. However, the young Des Grieux, who has broken with his father, has managed to bribe the wardens so that he can accompany his beloved to America. It has been highlighted by historians that the French deportation policy in the early eighteenth century had two aims in banishing young 'fallen' women who had become conspicuous in the eyes of justice: "L'objectif était double: débarrasser le royaume de ses éléments indésirables et favoriser le peuplement de la Louisiane."[18] On this foil, the fate that befalls Manon and Des Grieux in the French colony of Louisiana can also be understood in two different perspectives.[19]

A first reading initially conveys an undoubtedly chilling image of Louisiana, which is entirely under the sign of banishment (and could hardly have less to do with a 're-appropriation fiction'). Thus the "rivage désiré" (433), the America longed for after a long crossing, turns out to be a veritable *locus horribilis*: "Le pays ne nous offrit rien d'agréable à la première vue. C'étaient des campagnes stériles et inhabitées, où l'on voyait à peine quelques roseaux et quelques arbres dépouillés par le vent. Nulle trace d'hommes ni d'animaux." (Ibid.) Likewise, the vaunted city of "Nouvel Orléans" turns out to be a mere "assemblage de quelques pauvres cabanes" (ibid.), whose inhabitants – all French emigrants (voluntarily and involuntarily) from the mother country – welcome the arrivals "comme des gens descendus du ciel", "comme leurs frères, et comme de chers compagnons qui venaient partager leur misère et leur solitude" (ibid.). A brief period of happy cohabitation between the lovers, who settle in a "misérable cabane, composée de planches et de boue" (434), ends abruptly when the governor of the city asserts his claims on Manon: He can dispose of the deportee ("Manon ayant été envoyée de France pour la colonie, c'était à lui à disposer d'elle", 436), which he uses to marry her off to his nephew Synnelet – "pour la colonie", and i.e. in the spirit of colonial settlement policy. After the enraged Des Grieux fatally wounds Synnelet in what he perceives to be a duel, the lovers have no choice but to flee. Together

---

[16] For an overview, see the account by Eche 2013, pp. 49 sq. All quotations are taken from Pierre Berthiaume's and Jean Sgard's edition of Prévost's novel (Prévost 1978).
[17] On this notion, see Havard and Vidal 2014, pp. 217–220 ("Le destin de Manon Lescaut").
[18] Havard and Vidal 2014, p. 217. See also Berthiaume 2002, p. 17.
[19] The following considerations deliberately read Prévost's text 'affirmatively' with a view to the questions of interest here, without going any further into the strategies of ambiguization that result from the narrative framework of the American episode or of the novel as a whole, which is embedded in the *Mémoires et aventures d'un homme de qualité*, as well as from the Grieux's latently unreliable narration.

with Manon, Des Grieux aims to reach the English colonies in the north, from which they are separated by a desert and mountain landscape that is difficult to traverse. The exhausted Manon dies as soon as they have begun their flight, not two miles from the city. All that remains for Des Grieux is to bury her body in the "campagne couverte de sable" (439) and, "le visage tourné vers le sable" (ibid.), to long for his own death on the grave.

It is now futile to point out that the desert described by Prévost has nothing to do with the actual geographical conditions of Louisiana. Obviously, the novel's 'America' functions as a projection for the protagonists' dashed hopes:[20] When the despairing Des Grieux, in the immediate run-up to their common flight, refers to the surroundings as a "désert" (436), this allows for a correspondingly double reading of the colony as a 'land of desert' and a 'land of being abandoned'. Space and subject become one in the America episode of *Manon Lescaut*; in the internal logic of the novel, the protagonists are *désert(s)*.

In contrast, however, Prévost's text shows traces that point to a second possible reading. What is revealed here is an impetus to 'write back' that Louisiana which, in the immediate temporal context of the novel's creation and publication, threatens to slip out of the colonial power's control. Thus, it is first noticeable that the aforementioned colonial policy of marriage and settlement, as which biopolitics in Foucault's sense is concretized here, is made a subject beyond Manon's fate. In the course of Manon's arrival in Louisiana, Des Grieux's narrative perspective draws attention on how the arriving French women are appraised, sorted, and distributed as human commodities in accordance with the colony's established social order, whose continuation is to be ensured by the arranged marriages.[21] Furthermore (and more importantly), Manon and Des Grieux's forced emigration gives space to a theme that can be described, with Jean Sgard, as "espérance américaine".[22] As mentioned, the two lovers' life together in the colony, even if only for a short time, is marked by fulfilled and happy togetherness, which Des Grieux reflects on retrospectively as follows:

> L'Amérique me parut un lieu de délices après cela. C'est au Nouvel Orléans qu'il faut venir, disais-je souvent à Manon, quand on veut goûter les vraies douceurs de l'amour. C'est ici qu'on s'aime sans intérêt, sans jalousie, sans inconstance. Nos compatriotes y viennent chercher de l'or; ils ne s'imaginent pas que nous y avons trouvé des trésors bien plus estimables. (435)

---

[20] In his study *L'Amérique et le rêve exotique dans la littérature française au XVIIe et au XVIIIe siècle* (Chinard 1970), Gilbert Chinard already elaborates this nexus of the "vérité des sentiments" and the "vérité du paysage" in *Manon Lescaut*, cf. pp. 300 sqq., there also on the historical filiation of Prévost and Chateaubriand. Cf. also the corresponding passages in Pioffet 2002, pp. 77–81.

[21] Cf.: "Nous fûmes d'abord présentés à lui. Il [sc. le Gouverneur] s'entretint longtemps en secret avec le capitaine et revenant ensuite à nous, il considéra, l'une après l'autre, toutes les filles qui étaient arrivées par le vaisseau. [...] Le Gouverneur, les ayant longtemps examinées, fit appeler divers jeunes gens de la ville qui languissaient dans l'attente d'une épouse. Il donna les plus jolies aux principaux, et le reste fut tiré au sort." (433 sq.)

[22] Sgard 1995, pp. 239 sq.

Des Grieux's reference to the "vraies douceurs de l'amour" is revealing because with the "douceurs" a central concept of gallantry is invoked in its actual seventeenth century contour.[23] The love that unites Des Grieux and Manon in their American exile can thus be read as one that invokes the ideal of *gallant,* i.e. disinterested, sincere and tender love, and for a brief moment allows the hope of its realizability to emerge – in order to exhibit the experience of its loss all the more pronouncedly. This loss of gallant love is due to the "intérêt", "jalousie" and "inconstance" mentioned by Des Grieux, bad qualities which are here associated with the figure of the governor, but at the same time can be read as the signature of contemporary society, insofar as they stand for the economic (or more precisely: monetary) and social constraints that have successively eroded the cultural model of *la France galante.*

In *Manon Lescaut,* the threat and ultimate loss of the gallant ideal of love corresponds to a spatial movement of distance. Des Grieux associates his flight with Manon from Nouvel Orléans and thus from the sphere of influence of the governor or the French colonial power in general with "deux espérances" (438). These relate, first, to the civilizational 'taming' of the native 'savages' – "apprivois[er] les sauvages" (ibid.) is the colonial figure of thought articulated by Des Grieux. It is hardly coincidental that Des Grieux refers to these very 'savages', who are supposed to show him and Manon the way of escape through the inhospitable country ("des sauvages pour nous aider à nous conduire", ibid.), as a "ressource" (ibid.), as a 'rescue', but also as a human 'resource' in the colonial economic sense.

Secondly (and more importantly), Des Grieux's hopes are directed towards the northern possessions of the "Anglais qui ont, comme nous, des établissements dans cette partie du Nouveau-Monde" (ibid.), which he tries to reach with Manon. With the English possessions, or with the prospect of the "Anglais pour nous recevoir dans leur habitations" (ibid.), an "espoir d'une nouvelle société" takes shape in *Manon Lescaut,* a civilizing hope that (with the given reservations about such a biographical reading) is fed by Prévost's experiences in England and projected onto the English domain.[24] Logically, this means that Prévost's novel, in this respect following the narrative framework of the *Mémoires et aventures d'un homme de qualité,* makes a renewal of the *civilisation française* according to the civilizational model of England conceivable. To the extent that England becomes readable as a 'better France', contemporary French readers are also made aware of their own "manque de vision coloniale".[25]

---

[23] Cf. Barbafieri 2004.

[24] Cf. Sgard 1995, p. 239.

[25] Côté 2020, p. 403, cf. also further ibid.: "Il y a fort à parier que Prévost [...] voulait rappeler que la France avait négligemment sacrifié aux Anglais sa souveraineté sur le nord de la Nouvelle-France, situation officialisée en 1713 par le traité d'Utrecht."

3 "Contentement passe richesse": Lesage's *Les Mariages de Canada*

At the *Foire Saint-Laurent* in Paris in the summer of 1734, a work by Alain-René Lesage is staged for the first time, which exhibits its reference to the *Nouvelle-France* already in its title – *Les Mariages de Canada* – and, one year after the publication of the single edition of *Manon Lescaut*, refers intertextually to Prévost's novel. The generic affiliation of this work results from the place of performance: as is well known, the term *Théâtre de la Foire* gathers together the forms of popular theatre established at the beginning of the eighteenth century at the Parisian markets (*Foires*) Saint-Laurent and Saint-Germain and, as 'market theatre', joins a long line of tradition of impromptu and spectacle theatre.[26] At the epochal threshold around 1700, the formal peculiarities of this theatre result from a protracted interplay of prohibitions and concessions, which point to a tense relationship with the established theatre institutions – the *Comédie-Française*, the *Comédie-Italienne* and the *Opéra* or *Académie Royale de Musique* – which, however, by no means excludes the possibility that playwrights like Lesage were active in both fields.[27]

Lesage himself discusses these contexts in detail in a "Préface" included in the first volume of an anthology of plays performed at the *Théâtre de la Foire*, which he publishes in collaboration with Jacques-Philippe d'Orneval from 1721 onwards.[28] At the same time, the central generic characteristics of a *pièce de la Foire* can be derived from this text: It is a hybrid dramatic genre – "un ingenieux mêlange de tous les autres [Spectacles] ensemble" – that combines declamation in "prose" and "verse" with dance and, above all, song. The latter concerns popular songs in particular, allowing the audience to sing along. The dramaturgical design of these "Piéces [...] mixtes" corresponds to the distraction-laden performance context of the *Foire*, staging an "action simple", which is mostly constituted by a love subject, partly relies on typified figures and leads to a spectacular finale. This finale, known as a "divertissement", brings together declamation, dance, and song in the form of a satirical "vaudeville", which Lesage defines as an "espéce de Poësie particuliere aux François, [...] & la plus propre de toutes à faire valoir les faillies de l'esprit, à relever le ridicule, à corriger les mœurs".

Lesage plays a decisive role in the development of the *Théâtre de la Foire* – and one that is currently being given a new perspective within the framework of a

---

[26] Cf. Schumacher 2007, p. 1115, and Grewe 1989, specifically on *Les Mariages de Canada* pp. 363–365.

[27] Thus, for example, in 1707, the *Théâtre de la Foire* was banned from presenting spoken dialogue on stage, a ban that was lifted again in 1714; conversely, in 1708, the *Opéra* granted it a concession for the use of song and dance, which was temporarily revoked in 1722; on these contexts and their further development in the 1730s, which are of interest here, cf. Berthiaume 1979, pp. 126 sqq. The relationship of Lesage to the institutionalized theaters and the innovative achievements of his dramatic work are addressed in detail in the study by Groß 2016.

[28] Cf. Lesage and Orneval 1721, s.p. ("Preface"). The quotations of the present passage are taken from this text.

large-scale edition project[29] – in that his work promotes the professionalisation of this theatre, which manifests itself in an increased orientation towards the *text*, which in turn becomes concretely tangible in Lesage's and d'Orneval's anthology project.[30] In addition, Lesage's *pièces* encourage a politicization of the *Théâtre de la Foire* by bringing up urgent socio-political questions– going far beyond the supposedly mere entertainment function.[31] *Les Mariages de Canada*, included in 1737 in the ninth volume of the aforementioned anthology, exemplifies these contexts with particular vividness, as will be shown below.[32]

The plot of *Les Mariages de Canada* is set in Québec City, following the director's opening statement. In 19 scenes, the fates of young French lovers are portrayed who, separated from their respective partners against their will, have ended up in the colony and who, in accordance with the *Mariages* of the title, finally find their way back to each other as couples. From the conversation between Damis and his "valet" Mezzetin that opens the plot, we learn that the former is in search of his mistress Lucile, an "innocente Parisienne" (II, 307). Master and servant are at this point in front of a "grande Maison, où sont logées les personnes que l'on envoye de France en Canada" (I, 303). Boniface, the porter who enters, clarifies what this "maison" is all about:

> Toute fille de Paris
> Ou laide ou jolie,
> Qu'on améne en ce pays
> Pour la Colonie.
> On la fait loger céans;
> Et puis, sans perdre de tems,
> On vous la,
> Talera, lera,
> Lera tala, talera lala,
> On vous la marie. (II, 304)

Boniface's reply is first of all both in content and form – via the vocalises in verses 8–10 – exemplary for the parodistic-comical basic tenor of a *pièce de la Foire*. Beyond this, however, the colonial programme of a marriage and settlement policy "[p]our la Colonie" is recognisable – as in Prévost's work: Young women from France are accommodated in the "Maison" run by a certain Madame Bourdon, who are to be married off to French settlers and thus populate the colony. These "fille[s]" brought to the country (by no means always voluntarily) are, in a sense, the virtuous counterparts of Manon Lescaut and her companions in Prévost's novel, referred to as "filles à la cassette" in allusion to the *cassette* containing their modest possessions to take with them to the colony. These are in the famous lineage of the "filles du roi" – some 800

---

[29] Lesage's *Œuvres complètes* have been published since 2009 in a non-chronological order by Honoré Champion, supervised by Christelle Bahier-Porte and Pierre Brunel (12 vols.). Volumes 3 and 4, currently in preparation and edited by Nathalie Rizzoni, are devoted to Lesage's contributions to the *Théâtre de la Foire*.
[30] Cf. Berthiaume 1979, p. 128.
[31] Cf. on this with regard to the colonial-political contexts Deloffre 1997, pp. 305–323, esp. p. 323.
[32] Cf. Lesage 1737, pp. 299–362, from which all the following quotations are taken.

young women chosen at the behest of Louis XIV and sent to the American colonies between 1663 and 1673 for population purposes – whose identity-forming importance to French colonial policy, invoked in Lesage's play, can hardly be overestimated.[33]

It now turns out that Lucile, whom Damis adores, is staying in the aforementioned "maison" of Madame Bourdon, but she pretends to have been married for six months, as Boniface reports to the horrified Damis with the following verses: "*Lucile, m'a dit le Commis, / Est venue ici de Paris / Avec un appellé Clitandre / Ils disent qu'ils sont sous les lois / Du Dieu d'hymen depuis six mois.*" (VI, 322 sq.) Lucile and the aforementioned Clitandre step in at the right moment and clarify the situation: Like Manon Lescaut and Des Grieux, they have already as a married couple on the crossing, thus escaping the marriage against their will that is pending in Québec. The faithful Lucile thus finds herself united with Damis, while Clitandre can in future indulge in a bachelor existence, which he prefers to marrying a "Belle des mains de la Directrice" Madame Bourdon: "J'aime mieux sur mon ame / Rester toujours Garçon / Que d'avoir une Femme / Marquée à son poinçon" (IX, 334), whereby that "poinçon" refers to the "Directrice's" power of disposal over the young French women and possible partners.

The love story of Damis and Lucile is mirrored by that of the Chevalier Moreri, who meets Damis and Mezzetin in the fourth scene and is identified by the latter as the "fils de Libraire" (IV, 310) of their hometown. It emerges from their conversation that the Chevalier's father has decreed his son's banishment to Québec in order to put an end to his inappropriate love affair with Clarice (cf. "Et pour me séparer de Clarice, il [sc. mon Père] m'a brusquement envoyé dans ce pays-ci", IV, 317 sq.). Compared to the quiet and 'pure' Lucile, this same Clarice is a much livelier, a "fille / Fort sage & fort gentille", a "folle amusante" (IV, 316), whose virtuousness is, however, vouched for by her humble origins – the Chevalier calls her "une orpheline sans bien & sans appui" (ibid., 318). The tragic undertone of this scene is seconded by Mezzetin's following comment:

Les Enfans de famille
Sont envoyés ici i, i, i,
Pour oublier les filles.
L'eau de Missicipi, i, i, i,
C'est un fleuve d'Oubli. (IV, 319)

The servant figure comments here on the – if one takes Lesage's play as a starting point: quite common – social practice of ending mesalliances by banishing children or uninvited children-in-law. In Québec, this fate has befallen not only the Chevalier but also Lucile – brought to Québec at the insistence of Damis's mother (cf. II, 306 sq.) – and Clarice, whom, as it turns out, the Chevalier's "Pére furieux" (XVIII, 356) has banished to the American colony at the same time as his son.

In addition to the happy union with his beloved, another moment offers the Chevalier satisfaction, namely the memory of that "désordre effroyable" which he, in order to avenge himself on the "tyrannie" of his father, has caused in the parental

---

[33] See in detail Havard and Vidal 2014, pp. 214–217, and Côté 2020, p. 394.

library by 'profaning' "les plus célébres Ecrivains [...] sans respect pour aucun Auteur ancien ou moderne", i.e. by tearing out pages from the respective existing works (cf. IV, 312 sq.). Significantly, the central novels of gallantry – Madeleine de Scudéry's "Clélie" and her "grand Cyrus" (IV, 314), written jointly with her brother Georges – also fell victim to this rampage. On the one hand, this account by the Chevalier illustrates the parodic 'high culture' tenor of Lesage's play. On the other hand (and more importantly), it reveals that the Chevalier's (and indeed the other main characters') ideal understanding of love – despite all its destructiveness, which moreover turns out in retrospect to be a "tres-legere blessure" (ibid.) – is fed by these works of reference. This becomes clear at the end of the play: The finally happily united lovers Damis-Lucile and Chevalier Moreri-Clarice are married by Madame Bourdon on the spot. These very acts, performed on stage, are significant insofar as they make the respective relationships concretely readable as gallant love relationships and marriages. Damis and Lucile are brought together as "tendres Epoux / Unis des nœuds les plus doux" (XII, 338). The "amour sincére" (ibid., 339), the sincere but also reciprocal love that underlies their marriage, represents here the positive and, seen in this light, ideal 'civilisational' counterpart to the usual alliances decreed in the colonies. The fact that the Chevalier's marriage to Clarice is also modelled as such a gallant love match is again revealed by the central concept of 'tenderness' in the Chevalier's general request: "Ne nous occupons ici" – in Québec– "que de notre tendresse" (XVIII, 357). This background also explains Lesage's choice of names for his characters, who refer to representatives of the younger generation in Molière's comedies, who are united at the happy end in their decidedly gallant love.[34]

Another reference model of gallantry is outlined in the following verses of Clarice, which she declaims at her joyful reunion with her beloved:

> [...] le Dieu puissant de Cithére
> L'apui des amans malheureux,
> Pour nous venger de votre Pére
> Nous a rejoints ici tous deux. (XVIII, 356 f.)

According to Clarice, the "amans malheureux" in the colony have been able to find happiness again through the work of the god of "Cithére" – Kythera. The reference to Kythera has a special meaning here. Contemporarily (and especially since the exhibition of Watteau's Kythera paintings), Kythera has functioned as a place of longing for a latent past, yet still possible, French ideal of conviviality, in which gallantry, *civilisation* and colonial fantasy are imaginatively brought together. At the same time, the real island of Kythera, located off the Peloponnese, is one of the last remaining Venetian colonies at the time of the creation and performance of

---

[34] The edition of Molière's *Œuvres complètes* (2 vols., Paris: Gallimard 2010) by Georges Forestier for the Bibliothèque de la Pléiade has drawn particular attention to the gallant dimension of Molière's comedies.

Lesage's play, and thus plays a central role in the identity building of the Republic of Venice (and beyond).[35]

This horizon of meaning is invoked in the *Mariages de Canada* when the "Directrice", a representative of the French colonial administration, makes the lowing decree: Far from Québec City, "sur les bords du fleuve Saint Laurent", the young generation, i.e. all five main characters (Damis and Lucile, the Chevalier and Clarice, and the "garçon" Clitandre) are to be married and to found a new French settlement ("demeure") together with those couples whose marriages they have contracted in the past three days (cf. XVIII, 358). Included in this is Mezzetin, who, unsurprisingly, finds himself reunited in Québec with his wife Colombine, whom he left behind in France when he departed – in his turn, he can pursue his "forte envi, iiiiiie" of supporting the French colonial enterprise in Canada ("De demeurer en Canada / Pour renforcer la Coloniiiiie," XVIII, 341). The *divertissement* that concludes Lesage's play is accordingly marked by the lovers' 'embarkation' for this Canadian 'Kythera'. It is made very clear that the new settlement, modelled on Kythera's civilisation, will be characterised by a fulfilment of happiness, which is crystallised in the refrain-like repeated verse "Contentement passe richesse": Where nature offers only the simplest things ("de l'eau claire & du pain"), love in partnership can be fulfilled all the more powerfully ("Un Amant avec sa Maîtresse / Oublîroit le genre humain"), according to Mezzetin. Colombine affirms this with reference to the "liberté toute entière" and the "amour" under the sign of consummate gallant "tendresse" to which they will be able to indulge together in their simple hut ("chaumière") (cf. XIX, 360). The reference of a fellow traveller "Suivis des Ris & des Jeux, / Nous nous divertirons sans cesse" also shows that the future settlement will be filled with contented conviviality.[36]

The example of Kythera, on the other hand, reveals the colonial telos associated with this enterprise, which Colombine brings up:

N'apréhendons pas des Hurons
Les farouches visages:
Ou nous les aprivoiserons,
Par nos plus doux usages;
Ou, plus heureux, nous deviendrons
Peut-être aussi Sauvages. (XIX, 360)[37]

The autochthonous "Hurons", according to Colombine, here taking up an idea already articulated by Des Grieux, are to be tamed under the sign of gallant *douceur* –

---

[35] Cf. on this Dickhaut 2012, on the identity-forming function of the real political colony of Kythera for Venice pp. 27 sqq., on the mythicized Kythera in the literature of the early French Enlightenment esp. pp. 399 sqq. (with some references to the *Théâtre de la Foire*), and Viala 2008, pp. 337 sqq. ("L'embarquement pour Saint-Cloud").

[36] It makes sense to read the Canadian "demeure" imagined by Lesage against the backdrop of the classic study by Mauzi 1994 ([1]1960), and this in particular with a view to the remarks on the concept of *repos* (pp. 330–385), which Mauzi combines with a specifically enlightened concept of sociability, cf.: "Si le rêve du repos exclut le monde, il n'est que très rarement un rêve de solitude […] il n'élimine la société dans son ensemble qu'au profit d'une petite société idéale" (p. 355).

[37] In view of the colonial telos manifested here, I would not follow Berthiaume's interpretation that *Les Mariages de Canada* is a "parodie de la colonisation en Nouvelle-France" (Berthiaume 1979, p. 138). Cf. on this colonial-political approach also Deloffre 1997, p. 323.

or else the new settlers are to become 'savages' themselves, whereby the explicit contouring of the "demeure" leaves no doubt that Colombine has in mind here a 'civilized savagery' of genuine French character. In a clearly utopian cut, Lesage's drama thus spatially outsources the French model of civilization – going far beyond Prévost's idea of England – "loin du monde et du bruit" as a "retraite" in the Canadian wilderness.[38] In this way, Lesage consistently carries out a movement that is already laid out in seventeenth-century gallantry, insofar as, for example, in Madeleine de Scudéry's novellas, gallant sociability consciously finds its actual space far away from the court, which is marked by cabals and intrigues, *tromperie* and *dissimulation*. In Lesage's drama, the departure from the court and, associated with it, from one's own cultural space leads to another continent, but at the same time this movement makes clear that herewith the empire is writing back from its centre by simultaneously consolidating and expanding the boundaries of its possessions imaginatively and with its own means of market theatre.

4 "Nos vainqueurs nous rendent la paix / Partageons leurs plaisirs": Fuzeliers and Rameau's *Les Indes galantes*

If one follows the reporting of the *Mercure galant* with regard to the third and last example to be considered here, then the following takes place in the Parisian *Théâtre Italien* on 10 September 1725:

> Les Comédiens Italiens [...] donnerent sur leur Theatre une nouveauté des plus singulieres. Deux Sauvages venus depuis peu de la Loüisiane, grands & bienfaits, âgéz d'environ 25. ans, danserent trois sortes de danses, ensemble & separément, & d'une maniere à ne pas laisser douter qu'ils n'ayent appris les pas & les fauts qu'ils font, très-loin de Paris.[39]

Among the audience is the composer Jean-Philippe Rameau, whom, according to his own admission, "le chant & la danse de ces Sauvages"[40] inspired to write a harpsichord piece. This piece forms the germ of *Les Indes galantes*, which today receives more attention than almost any other music-dramatic work of the eighteenth century, and this less because of the general boom in early modern music theatre than with a view to the post-colonial reinterpretations that this ballet opera, not coincidentally described as a "hymne à la colonisation", is currently experiencing.[41]

---

[38] This in the sense of the study by Beugnot 1996, on the basis of which the traditional lines of Lesage's colonial vision can be made legible.

[39] *Mercure de France* (September 1725), vol. 2, p. 2274.

[40] Rameau in a letter to Antoine Houdar de la Motte, 25 October 1727, reprinted in the *Mercure de France* (March 1765), p. 39.

[41] Cf. Roussillon 2019, pp. 93–97. Roussillon's reflections refer to Clément Cogitore's highly acclaimed production of *Les Indes galantes* at the Opéra Bastille in Paris (2019/2020 season), which relocates Rameau's ballet opera to the Parisian banlieue and combines it with elements of Krump, a current US street dance whose roots lie in the Afro-American population's revolt against racial discrimination. Cf. also Zitzmann 2019 as well as the production of *Les Indes galantes* in the 2015/2016 season by Sidi Larbi Cherkaoui documented on the website of the Bavarian State Opera Munich.

Les Indes galantes was first performed on 23 August 1735 at the *Académie Royale de Musique* as the product of Rameau's collaboration with the librettist Louis Fuzelier. Fuzelier is best known for his work for the *Théâtre de la Foire*, which explains the striking structural similarities between the libretto of the ballet opera and Lesage's play. Like the *pièce de la Foire*, the *ballet héroïque* – the contemporary name for the ballet opera – is a hybrid genre defined by Louis de Cahusac in his famous *Traité de la danse* as "un composé de plusieurs Actes différens qui représentent chacun une action mêlée de divertissemens, de chant & de danse. Ce sont de jolis *Vateau* […]."[42] Cahusac's definition sheds light on the structure of a *ballet héroïque*, which is divided into several acts, usually called *entrées*, and includes spoken, sung, and danced parts. As a rule, the content of the individual *entrées* is linked by an overarching theme introduced in a prologue. The fact that this is dominantly a love theme measured by gallantry is implied by Cahusac's final designation of the genre as "*vateau*", which refers to the painter Antoine Watteau, who was in the gallant tradition.[43]

In keeping with this interpretation, the prologue of the *Indes galantes*[44] stages the confrontation of Hébé, the goddess of youth, with Bellone, the goddess of war, who summons the "[j]eunesse française, espagnole, italienne et polonaise" (15) – young lovers and Hébé's retinue – to war (cf. 17). In this moment of discord, Cupid descends from heaven with an entire "troupe d'Amours" and is asked by Hébé to take the youth and their "plaisirs" away – "dans les climats lointains" (ibid.), with which a colonial telos already becomes visible at this point. A choral song accompanies the departure of the lovers led by the "Amours": "Traversez les plus vastes mers, / Volez, volez, Amours, volez, volez, / Portez vos armes et vos fers / Sur le plus éloigné rivage." (19)

The focus of the plot on the "differents climats des Indes" (ibid.), with which the prologue concludes, gives rise to the settings of the actions that unfold in the following four *entrées*: Gathered under the term "Indes" are "une île turque de la mer des Indes" (first *entrée*), "un désert du Perou" resp. more precisely: the Peru of the Incas (second *entrée*), Persia with the "jardins du palais d'Ali" (third *entrée*) as well as "une fôret de l'Amérique, voisine des colonies françaises et espagnoles" (fourth *entrée*, cf. the respective introductory stage directions 19, 27, 35 and 41). All four *entrées* are characterized by their own imaginary topography and their own style, whereby for the *entrée américaine* considered in more detail here, that of a "comédie pacifique" is suggested.[45]

If we take the aforementioned introductory stage direction as a starting point, we can locate the scene of the fourth *entrée in* contemporary Louisiana. The time of the

---

[42] Cahusac 1754, vol. 3, pp. 108–109.

[43] On Watteau see in detail Viala 2008, pp. 293 sqq.

[44] Quotations are taken from the edition of the libretto procured by Philippe Beaussant (Rameau and Fuzelier 2019), which is based on Sylvie Bouissou's edition of the score (Rameau 2018).

[45] Cf. Bouissou 2014, p. 368.

action is specified at this point with the addition "où doit se célébrer la cérémonie du Grand Calumet de la Paix" (41). This very pipe of peace is easily read as the text's reference to the Natchez uprising in the area, which is directly connected in time to its creation. At the beginning of the *entrée,* however, the political peace agreement contrasts strikingly with the emotional tensions between the four main characters. Adario, the "commandant" of the "guerriers de la nation sauvage", puts it as follows: "Nos guerriers, par mon ordre unis à nos vainqueurs, / Vont ici de la paix célébrer les douceurs; / Mon cœur, seul dans ces lieux, trouve encore des alarmes" (43). Adario, whose name is an explicit reference to the 'savage' of Lahontan's much-commented travelogue (*Dialogues de Lahontan et d'un sauvage dans l'Amérique*) published in 1704,[46] loves Zima, the "fille du chef de la nation sauvage", for whose favour, however, two other men representing the colonial power rival, namely the Spaniard Don Alvar and the Frenchman Damon. Zima, who is devoted to Adario, turns them both down in the following verses:

> Je ne veux d'un époux ni jaloux ni volage.
> (*à l'Espagnol*) Alvar
> Vous aimez trop,
> (*au Français*) Damon
> Et vous, vous n'aimez pas assez. (44)

She counters the in each case intemperate love of the Europeans with her own sincere "amour sans art" (43, cf. also: "Dans nos fôrets on est sincère", 44). Significantly, this Native American love is now characterized as consummate gallant love in its decidedly French coinage, namely as "l'amour le plus tendre" that binds both partners together in reciprocal "égale ardeur." In the internal logic of the ballet opera, the American 'savages' thus turn out to be true representatives of the *civilisation française*;[47] in other words, the American forests present themselves as their suitable – and i.e. also: colonial-politically to be developed – new habitat.

This is reinforced by the change of heart that the Frenchman Damon (in contrast to his Spanish rival) undergoes in his encounter with Zima and Adario. Realizing that he had followed a false understanding of love, subject to "inconstance" (45), he transforms himself from a libertine seducer into the protector of the Native Americans. That this is, of course, a genuinely colonialist gesture can be seen from the enthusiastic approval put into the mouth of Adario's character: "Nos vainqueurs nous rendent la paix / Partageons leurs plaisirs" (46): Via the libretto, the French 'Empire' rewrites its colonial possessions by occupying, pacifying, and 'writing up' a territory that has hitherto been outside its American possessions ("voisine des colonies françaises") and now flourishes entirely under the sign of French civilizing "plaisirs".

This 'tender' conquest is spectacularly celebrated (and performatively codified) by the concluding *divertissement*, which once again emphatically exhibits the cultural practices of the *civilisation française*. The "Danse du Grand Calumet de la

---

[46] This was already pointed out by Chinard 1970, p. 234. Cf. also Côté 2020, p. 390.
[47] The historical gender perspective is discussed by Meglin 2000, pp. 99–103.

Paix en rondeau" is performed on stage, in which, in addition to the main characters, "Sauvages et Sauvagesses, Françaises en habits d'amazones, Guerriers français" and "Bergers et Bergères de la colonie" (46) also participate. Colonial Louisiana thus presents itself not only as a new Arcadia of the "Bergers et Bergères", but at the same time as a new *Royaume du Tendre* on the other side of the Atlantic, which is populated by the "Françaises en habits d'amazones" – and thus by central identity-forming figures of *la France galante*.[48]

Finally, the formation of the dance as a round dance, "en rondeau", is a decisive detail. On the one hand, this projects a decidedly French choreography onto a cultural practice that can often be found in contemporary travelogues about *Nouvelle-France*.[49] Secondly (and more importantly), this *rondeau* brings a circular movement of French civilizational values onto the stage; the *divertissement* of the *Indes galantes* stages a phenomenon of cultural mobility, which Stephen Greenblatt has defined as "*movements* of peoples, objects, images, and ideas"[50] – albeit with a decisive difference: Greenblatt, and with him today's philology oriented towards cultural studies, understand cultural mobility spatially and dominantly centrifugal, i.e. leading away from the 'centre'. *Les Indes galantes*, on the other hand, present a spatial movement that, on the one hand, refers back centripetally to the culture- and identity-creating 'center' and, on the other hand, is oriented temporally, in that civilizational-gallant values that are perceived as past are reactualized. With this spatio-temporal effect, Fuzelier and Rameau's ballet opera goes a further and decisive step beyond the literary recolonizations of Prévost and Lesage, for it presents the abolition of the ideal 'own' in an American 'other' that has moved into a both spatial and temporal distance and can only be recaptured and made present in this way through art. Thus, in the sign of Enlightenment, a figure of thought of colonial and nationally oriented culture becomes visible, which in logical consequence leads to Chateaubriand's 'founding fiction' of an America, which he makes readable as the ideal space of Christian-French civilization. The double mourning over the loss of the (temporally) past and (spatially) lost consequently forms the basis for the re-emergence of a cultural and social ideal in the "aesthetic experience"[51] that never existed in reality: The loss of France's own colonies and the end of the *Ancien Régime* have the effect of turning previous *lieux de mémoire* into new myths of a founding nation, precisely because they lack empiricism. French national literature and philology thus create themselves out of the spirit of a colonial fantasy by seizing one last time around 1800 on their past civilization in the lost colonies before projecting new (imaginative and real) colonial fantasies onto entirely different territories of the world in order to then participate in the constitution of their 'empire' in the concrete sense of the nineteenth century.

---

[48] Cf. on the role of the Amazon for gallant France DeJean 1991.

[49] On the *rondeau* of the *Indes galantes* and the libretto's intertextual references to contemporary travelogues (Lahontan, Picard, Lafitau, and others), see Savage 1983.

[50] Greenblatt 2010, p. 250.

[51] Cf. Grimm 1991, p. 271 on the "transformation of religious into aesthetic experience" in Chateaubriand.

References

Ashcroft, Bill, Griffiths, Gareth und Tiffin, Helen (eds.): The Empire Writes Back. Theory and Practice in Post-Colonial Literatures. London, New York: Routledge 2002 ([1]1989).
Balvay, Arnaud: La Révolte des Natchez. Paris: Éditions du Félin 2008.
Barbafieri, Carine: Du bon usage de la douceur dans la peinture du héros tragique, in: Marie-Hélène Prat and Pierre Servet (eds.): Le doux aux XVIe et XVIIe siècle. Écriture, esthétique, politique, spiritualité. Lyon: PU de Lyon 2004, pp. 161–176.
Bercegol, Fabienne, Genand, Stéphanie und Lotterie, Florence (eds.): Une ‚période sans nom'. Les années 1780–1820 et la fabrique de l'histoire littéraire. Paris: Classiques Garnier 2016.
Berthiaume, Pierre: Lesage et le spectacle forain, in: Études françaises 15.1–2, 1979, pp. 125–141.
Berthiaume, Pierre: Louisiana, or the Shadow Cast by French Colonial Myth, in: Dalhousie French Studies 58, 2002, pp. 10–25.
Beugnot, Bernard: Le discours de la retraite au XVIIe siècle. Loin du monde et du bruit. Paris: PUF 1996.
Bouissou, Sylvie: Jean-Philippe Rameau. Musicien des Lumières. Paris: Fayard 2014.
Cahusac, Louis de: La danse ancienne et moderne ou Traité historique de la danse, 3 vols. The Hague: Jean Neaulme 1754.
Chateaubriand, François-René de: Atala. Ed. Fabienne Bercegol, in: François-René de Chateaubriand: Œuvres completes, vol. XVI. Paris: Honoré Champion 2008, pp. 65–167.
Chinard, Gilbert: L'Amérique et le rêve exotique dans la littérature française au XVIIe et au XVIIIe siècle. Geneva: Slatkine 1970.
Côté, Sébastien: La mise en fiction de l'Amerique du Nord au XVIIIe siècle, in: Revue d'Histoire littéraire de la France 120.2, 2020, pp. 387–404.
Counter, Andrew J.: A Nation of Foreigners. Chateaubriand and Repatriation, in: Nineteenth-Century French Studies 46.3–4, 2018, pp. 285–306.
DeJean, Joan: Amazones et femmes des lettres: pouvoirs politiques et littéraires à l'âge classique, in: Danielle Haase Dubosc and Éliane Viennot (eds.): Femmes et Pouvoirs sous l'Ancien Régime. Paris: Éditions Rivages 1991, pp. 156–171.
Deloffre, Frédéric: Lesage et la Nouvelle-France, in: Jacques Wagner (ed.): Lesage, écrivain (1695–1735). Amsterdam: Rodopi 1997, pp. 305–323.
Dickhaut, Kirsten: Positives Menschenbild und venezianità. Kythera als Modell einer geselligen Utopie in Literatur und Kunst von der italienischen Renaissance bis zur französischen Aufklärung. Wiesbaden: Harrassowitz 2012.
Eche, Antoine: L'espace américain chez l'abbé Prévost: fiction, voyage et images, in: Georges-Henry Laffont et al. (eds.): L'espace du Nouveau Monde. Mythologies et ancrages territoriaux. Rennes: PU de Rennes 2013, pp. 48–63.
Foucault, Michel: Des espaces autres, in: Michel Foucault: Dits et écrits. 1954–1988. Ed. Daniel Defert and François Ewald, vol. 2. Paris: Gallimard 2001, pp. 1571–1581.
Fumaroli, Marc: Chateaubriand et Rousseau, in: Jean-Claude Berchet (ed.): Chateaubriand. Le Tremblement du temps. Toulouse: PU du Mirail 1994, pp. 201–221.
Furetière, Antoine: Dictionnaire universel, contenant généralement tous les mots françois, 3 vols. The Hague, Rotterdam: Arnoud et Reinier Leers ²1702.
Greenblatt, Stephen: A mobility studies manifesto, in: Stephen Greenblatt (ed.): Cultural Mobility. A Manifesto. Cambridge: Cambridge UP 2010, pp. 250–253.
Grewe, Andrea: Monde renversé – Théâtre renversé. Lesage und das Théâtre de la Foire. Bonn: Romanistischer Verlag 1989.
Grimm, Reinhold R.: Romantisches Christentum. Chateaubriands nachrevolutionäre Apologie der Religion, in: Karl Maurer and Winfried Wehle (eds.): Romantik. Aufbruch zur Moderne. Munich: Fink 1991, pp. 13–72.
Groß, Martina: Querelle, Begräbnis, Wiederkehr. Alain-René Lesage, der Markt und das Theater. Heidelberg: Winter 2016.

Gymnich, Marion: Writing Back, in: Dirk Göttsche, Axel Dunker and Gabriele Dürbeck (eds.): Handbuch Postkolonialismus und Literatur. Stuttgart: Metzler 2017, pp. 235–238.
Havard, Gilles and Vidal, Cécile: Histoire de l'Amérique française. Paris: Flammarion 2014.
Hazard, Paul: La Crise de la conscience européenne. 1680–1715. Paris: Fayard 1994 ([1]1935).
Hepp, Noémi: La galanterie, in: Pierre Nora (ed.): Les Lieux de mémoire, vol. III. Paris: Gallimard 1997, pp. 3677–3710.
Hoffmann, Benjamin: L'Amérique posthume. Réinventions littéraires de l'Amérique à la fin du XVIIIe siècle, Paris: Classiques Garnier 2019.
Jauß, Hans Robert: Mythen des Anfangs: Eine geheime Sehnsucht der Aufklärung, in: Hans Robert Jauß: Studien zum Epochenwandel der ästhetischen Moderne. Frankfurt am Main: Suhrkamp 1989, pp. 23–66.
Lesage, Alain-René and Orneval, Jacques-Philippe (eds.): Le Theâtre de la Foire, ou L'Opera Comique. Contenant les meilleures Pieces qui ont été representées aux Foires de S. Germain & de S. Laurent. Paris: Etienne Ganeau 1721.
Lesage, Alain-René: Les Mariages de Canada. Piece d'un acte. Paris: Pierre Gandouin 1737.
Losfeld, Christophe: Geselligkeit, in: Heinz Thoma (ed.): Handbuch Europäische Aufklärung. Begriffe – Konzepte – Wirkung. Stuttgart, Weimar: Metzler 2015, pp. 252–263.
Losfeld, Christophe: Politesse, morale et construction sociale. Pour une histoire des traités de comportements (1670–1788). Paris: Honoré Champion 2011.
Mauzi, Robert: L'idée du bonheur dans la littérature et la pensée françaises au XVIIIe siècle. Paris: Albin Michel 1994 ([1]1960).
Meglin, Joellen A.: Sauvages, Sex Roles, and Semiotics: Representations of Native Americans in the French Ballet, 1736–1837. Part One, The Eighteenth Century, in: Dance Chronicle 23.2, 2000, pp. 87–132.
Pioffet, Marie Christine: L'espace américain comme figure du désenchantement dans l'œuvre romanesque de l'abbé Prévost, in: Études francophones 17.1, 2002, pp. 77–92.
Prévost, Antoine-François: Histoire du chevalier des Grieux et de Manon Lescaut. Ed. Pierre Berthiaume and Jean Sgard, in: Antoine-François Prévost: Œuvres complètes, vol. 1. Grenoble: PU de Grenoble 1978, pp. 365–440.
Rameau, Jean-Philippe: Les Indes galantes, in: Jean-Philippe Rameau: Opera omnia. Ed. Sylvie Bouissou, Serie IV, vol. 2.7. Kassel: Bärenreiter 2018.
Rameau, Jean Philippe und Fuzelier, Louis: Les Indes galantes. Ed. Philippe Beaussant, in: L'Avant-Scène Opéra 312, 2019, pp. 15–51.
Roulin, Jean-Marie: François-René de Chateaubriand: Migrations and Revolution, in: Paul Hamilton (ed.): The Oxford Handbook of European Romanticism. Oxford: Oxford UP 2016, pp. 52–68.
Roussillon, Marine: Rencontre ou révolution? Sur une version krump des Indes galantes, in: L'Avant-Scène Opéra 312, 2019, pp. 93–97.
Rushdie, Salman: The Empire Writes Back with a Vengeance, in: The Times, 3.7.1982, p. 8.
Savage, Roger: Rameau's American dancers, in: Early Music 11.4, 1983, pp. 441–452.
Schumacher, Horst: Théâtre de la Foire, in: Manfred Brauneck and Gérard Schneilin (eds.): Theaterlexikon, vol. 1. Reinbek bei Hamburg: Rowohlt ^{5}2007, p. 1115.
Sgard, Jean: Prévost et l'espérance américaine, in: Jean Sgard: Vingt études sur Prévost d'Exiles. Grenoble: ELLUG 1995, pp. 239–251.
Steigerwald, Jörn: Galante Liebe, in: Kirsten Dickhaut (ed.): Liebessemantik. Frühneuzeitliche Darstellungen von Liebe in Italien und Frankreich. Wiesbaden: Harrassowitz 2014, pp. 693–757.
Viala, Alain: La France galante. Essai historique sur une catégorie culturelle, de ses origines jusqu'à la Révolution. Paris: PUF 2008.
Viala, Alain: La galanterie. Une mythologie française. Paris: Seuil 2019.
Zantop, Susanne: Kolonialphantasien im vorkolonialen Deutschland (1770–1870). Berlin: ESV 1999.
Zitzmann, Marc: Der Barock erobert die Banlieue, in: FAZ, 29.9.2019.

National Literature – World Literature – Literatures of the World: The Example of French-Language Contemporary Literatures from the Caribbean

Gesine Müller

Abstract Where do contemporary French-language literatures from the Caribbean stand in the field of tension between national literature and world literature? While the concept of Francophonie still had clear ideas of France as the centre and the former colonies as the periphery, a "littérature-monde en français" is now being proclaimed that de-hierarchizes the interpretation of the world, and an archipelization is being propagated in which an island can only be thought of in conjunction with others, i.e. as an archipelago, and the regions are more important than national borders. The example of the Gallimard publishing house shows that the criterion of *literatures of the world* is becoming increasingly important for the publishing industry when selecting Caribbean authors.

To make the literatures of the Caribbean the subject of discussion with regard to the field of tension between national literature and world literature means to deal with a conflict that is central to the current phase of globalization and the international book market: The still strongly continuing tradition of national-philological orientation of publishing programs meets literary traditions that per se point beyond national-philological approaches due to the close interconnection of various former colonial spheres in the Caribbean, as well as canonization instances that increasingly follow global strategies. Literary examples from the French-speaking Caribbean can thus be used not only to pose the question of the future of national-philological perspectives, but also to shed light on crucial aspects of the current world literature debate. For Caribbean literatures have been insufficiently considered as *world literature* in the past; at the same time, they fulfill more

---

G. Müller (✉)
Romanisches Seminar, Universität zu Köln, Köln, Deutschland
e-mail: gesine.mueller@uni-koeln.de

© The Author(s), under exclusive license to Springer-Verlag GmbH, DE, part of Springer Nature 2023
C. Strosetzki (ed.), *200 Years of National Philologies*,
https://doi.org/10.1007/978-3-476-05925-3_6

paradigmatically than almost any other literary tradition of the world the criteria that are applied to the new conceptualization of the term *literatures of the world.*

For a long time, France has attempted to resolve the contradiction between a national philology suggesting territorial integrity and the manifold processes of deterritorialization in worldwide French-language literature, both in philological and publishing programmatic terms, with the simultaneously inclusive and exclusive concept of Francophonie. As is well known, the concept of Francophonie has been subject to sometimes harsh criticism for quite some time: The widely received call "Pour une 'littérature-monde' en français", published in *Le Monde* in 2007, is about a renegotiation of the centre-periphery theme:

> Nous pensons, au contraire: revolution copernicienne. Copernicienne, parce qu'elle révèle ce que le milieu littéraire savait déjà, sans l'admittre: le centre, ce point depuis lequel était supposée rayonner une littérature franco-française n'est plus le centre. [...] le centre [...] est désormais partout, aux quatre coins du monde. Fin de la francophonie. Et naissance d'une littérature-monde en français.[1]

In their critique of Francophonie, the undersigned authors dispute the undiminished validity of colonial spatial orders and "call into question [...] precisely that universality which, in every colonial discourse, is inevitably reduced to the proven boundaries of one's own sphere of power and relegates other cultures to internal or external exile."[2] The authors considered "francophones" do not want to continue being a semi-colonial "variante exotique tout juste tolérée"[3] of French literature. Their concern is rather to open up to a *littérature-monde* that no longer recognizes a distinction between center and periphery.[4] But this is by no means intended to play off "the wide world against the old center,"[5] as Camille de Toledo, for example, emphatically responds to the manifesto:

> We do not have to defend the 'periphery' against the 'centre', but rather with it, to make it implode, starting again from the immoderation, the mixture, the creolity of a Rabelais, from the call to invention in Du Bellay, from the original bastard character of the French language, against its fixation, its classical beauty, its whiteness, its purity.[6]

Markus Messling has pointed out that the notion of *littérature-monde*, which the Manifesto makes strong, emphasizes the worldliness:

---

[1] "Pour une 'littérature monde' en français", in *Le Monde,* 15.3.2007.
[2] Karimi 2009, p. 17. In this context, Karimi refers to Frantz Fanon: "Le monde colonisé est un monde coupé en deux. La ligne de partage, la frontière en est indiquée par les casernes et les postes de police. [...] La zone habitée par les colonisés n'est pas complémentaire de la zone habitée par les colons. Ces deux zones s'opposent, mais non au service d'une unité supérieure. Régis par une logique purement aristotélicienne, elles obéissent au principe d'exclusion réciproque: il n'y a pas de conciliation possible" (Fanon 1961, p. 68 f.).
[3] "Pour une littérature monde en français", in *Le Monde,* 15.3.2007.
[4] Cf. Karimi 2009, p. 17.
[5] Messling 2019, p. 30.
[6] Toledo 2008, p. 83, cited in Messling 2019, p. 30.

> The de-hierarchization of the interpretation of the world should not be conducted here in the form of a historical-cultural model and validity debate, but rather by referring to the reality-describing power of literature. This demand has experienced strong alliances in contemporary French literature, which has identified in it a renewal of the power-critical realist tradition since Rabelais. [...] It is not, therefore, a simple demand for worldliness, but the questioning of a centralist attitude to the world [...] The attitude to the world as a whole has become a problem.[7]

Criticism of a centralist attitude to the world thus concerns not only the idea of a national philology, but also the concept of world literature in its Goethean form. Starting from the observation that the traditional conceptions of world literature can no longer be reconciled with a rapidly changing idea of "world", a lively controversy developed around new conceptions, such as those proposed by Franco Moretti, David Damrosch, Emily Apter or Pascale Casanova. Despite persisting hegemonic implications, most of the leading positions on world literature have attempted to inscribe themselves in the contemporary diagnostic discourses on globalization, which comprehensively call into question the institutional, economic, and cultural hegemony of the Global North vis-à-vis the South. The most recent contributions to the debate now follow this up with the question of the extent to which the concept of world literature has gone too far hand in hand with political and economic globalization dynamics and, as a result, is based, on the one hand, on a far too positive image of a coherent, cosmopolitan world and, on the other, with its focus on cultural circulation, book markets, and literary translation, persists in the reproduction of neo-imperialist cartographies.[8]

What is interesting in this context is the concept of the *literatures of the world*, which is not analytically descriptive but rather programmatic: although it ties in with the 'classical' notion of world literature, it is based on a completely different program. It is about the claim to abolish the division between centre and periphery in literary productions from a global perspective, and thus to think of the genesis of cultural production in transnational constellations. Ottmar Ette emphasizes that the concept of the *literatures of the world* – unlike Goethe's concept of world literature – is not tied back to an exemplary centering function of occidental antiquity or Europe. With the term *literatures of the world*, the old concept of world literature is given a completely new meaning, a meaning that lies unmistakably beyond not only the nation-state, but beyond national literature, even if the latter continues to have extremely important instances of production, reproduction, distribution, and reception at its disposal. According to Ottmar Ette, the *literatures of the world* have lost their sedentariness and have increasingly absorbed nomadic patterns of thought,

---

[7] Messling 2019, p. 30.
[8] On the first point of criticism, cf. Siskind 2019, for example; on the second, see, among others, Emily Apter's critique of world literature concepts such as the "world literatures" associated with Goethe, Pascale Casanova's *République mondiale des Lettres*, or Gayatri C. Spivak's planetary model (Apter 2008). At this point, I cannot delve further into the problematics of the current world literature debate. Cf. for instance my recent monograph (Müller 2022) and the two volumes Müller/Siskind (2019) and Müller/Locane/Loy (2018).

writing and perception that are on the move.[9] The characteristics of the *literatures of the world* include not only inner-literary aspects, such as the staging of multilingualism, of decentering, relational movements and of concrete particularities without universalizing claims, but also extra-literary features, such as a large proportion of non-settled authors or the negation of a European/North American claim to interpretation.[10] In my view, what is important when comparing the two concepts of world *literature* and *literatures of the world* is that they stand for two possibilities of paradigm formation in literary theory and cultural studies. It is therefore not surprising that there is often a great deal of intersection in the selection of primary literary texts. In this respect, Caribbean literatures are privileged to be included in the canon of *literatures of the world,* as they fulfil particularly many of the criteria mentioned. But what about the prestigious categorization as world literature?

In the context of world literary logics and canonization processes, it plays a crucial role if texts do not first have to be translated into what remains the most important language for global circulation processes, English, which is why the English-speaking Caribbean occupies a special position here. Some notable texts that have been successfully canonized in world literature include Derek Walcott's *Omeros,* Edward Kamau Brathwaite's *The Arrivants* (1967–1973), Jean Rhys *Wide Sargasso Sea* (1966), V.S. Naipaul's *The Enigma of Arrival* (1987), Dionne Brand's *In Another Place, Not Here (*1996). While literatures from the English-speaking Caribbean have thus certainly been received as world literature and their characteristics can point the way for concepts of literatures of the world, in the case of the Spanish- and especially the French-speaking Caribbean, a world-literary canonization has occurred only in exceptional cases or not at all. Saint-John Perse, for example, who came from Guadeloupe and was awarded the Nobel Prize for Literature in 1960, can be considered one such exception. His poems (*Eloges* 1911; *Anabase* 1924; *Exile* 1942; *Vents* 1946; *Amers* 1957) are oriented precisely not to the Caribbean reality of life, but to modern French poetry in the tradition of Arthur Rimbaud. Another example would be the Cuban author Alejo Carpentier, whose works belong to a distinct variant of magical realism.[11] Selection filters for a particularly favorable reception of the "literary quality" of Carpentier's work are his connectivity to French surrealism and a specific way of representing reality that stages mythical-magical practices as real and appealed to European audiences as exotic.

While the aforementioned authors were primarily received by a rather specialized readership and in their connectivity to European, especially French, traditions, a group of Francophone writers has, as is well known, established itself worldwide at the latest since the beginning of the 1990s, who can point to a philosophically motivated essayistic oeuvre fed by the context of Caribbean experience and whose

---

[9] Ette 2004, p. 179.

[10] For a more nuanced look at the similarities and differences between world literature and literatures of the world, see Müller 2015, 2017a, b, 2018.

[11] The term 'magic realism', for which Latin American authors later became world famous, goes back to a formulation of his in the preface to his novel *El reino de este mundo* (1949).

literary production is clearly inscribed in the programmatic of the literatures of the world. With their valorization of oral Creole traditions, the authors around Patrick Chamoiseau and Raphaël Confiant from Martinique link the act of rebellion against cultural assimilation, which is an essential element of the literary debate in the Antilles, not to the content but to the aesthetic level. Her concern can be read as a variant of the conceptual implication of multilingualism *in* literary texts, a feature of literatures of the world. More recently, the Martinican Fabienne Kanor, born in 1970, has also inscribed herself in this current with her novel *Humus* (Gallimard 2006). The success of this literary language may have consequences for standard French, for via the path of the major literary prizes – at the latest since Patrick Chamoiseau was awarded the Prix Goncourt for his novel *Texaco* (Gallimard 1992) – texts in French with a Creole-oral flavour are increasingly entering a newly contoured literary canon, which in its traditional form is the basis for written French. Chamoiseau's novel, which can stand paradigmatically for the concept of literatures of the world, is initially set on the outskirts of Martinique's capital, Fort-de-France, where a *banlieue of* improvised housing has grown up on the former site of the Texaco oil company, an illegal neighborhood that is about to be bulldozed. The novel thrives on the voices of a variety of characters who bring Martinique's colonial history to life, mapping the intertwining of African, European, and Asian influences in Martinique.

Other novels by contemporary French-speaking Caribbean authors that have subsequently appeared and that correspond to a large extent to the characteristics of Literatures of the World include, in addition to Chamoiseau's *Un dimanche au cachot* (Gallimard 2007), published two years later, *Adèle et la pacotilleuse* (Gallimard 2005) and *Case à Chine* (Gallimard 2007) by Raphaël Confiant, or *Les Dieux voyagent la nuit* (Éditions du Rocher 2006) by Louis-Philippe Dalembert.[12]

This 1992 award to Chamoiseau, when the prestigious Prix Goncourt went to an author from the Antilles for the first time in just over seventy years,[13] can certainly be considered a key moment in the canonization of literatures of the world in the French-speaking context. A Prix Goncourt did not go to a Caribbean author after that, but the Prix Médicis did, awarded in 2009 to Dany Laferrière, published in Montréal, for *L'enigme du retour,* an event that can again be considered decisive for Caribbean literary production and its international perception. With an external gaze, the novel tells a family story between Haiti and Canada, in which the protagonist, a Haitian writer in exile, returns to Haiti on the occasion of his father's funeral.

Such awards are still exceptional today. But it is interesting to see that the Gallimard publishing house, which initially published Glissant, Confiant and Chamoiseau, has in recent years increasingly represented authors from the Francophone Caribbean, after a long time in which Cuban authors such as Alejo Carpentier were disproportionately represented among the Antillean authors. The

---

[12] For a more detailed analysis of Caribbean contemporary literatures, see Müller 2017a, b.
[13] In 1921, René Maran had last won with the novel *Batouala*, an event that went down in history as the first time that an author declared to be 'black' won a major French literary prize.

volume *Pour une littérature-monde*, which was published by Gallimard in 2007 following the aforementioned appeal "Pour une 'littérature-monde' en français", could perhaps be seen as the initial spark here. Maryse Condé, Édouard Glissant, Fabienne Kanor, Lyonel Trouillot and Dany Laferrière, among others, were involved in this volume, all of them authors from the Francophone Caribbean whose works very strongly represent the criteria of literatures of the world.

What has long been true for literatures of the Anglophone Caribbean can currently also be observed on the French book market, namely that the criterion of *literatures of the world* is becoming increasingly important for the publishing industry in the selection of Caribbean authors. Literary texts that have successfully passed this first selection filter then pass through the instances that are decisive for international canonisation, which continue to be located in particular in the Western world, in our case in France. This finding of an increased international circulation of literatures of the world due to concrete publishing policies is an observation whose systematic investigation is still pending.[14]

The significance of the classical (French) canonization instances, the most important of which are literary prizes, has changed in the course of globalization, as James F. English convincingly points out in his book *Economy of Prestige*. He understands the *economy of prestige* as a global system consisting of many local cultural markets, which until the 1960s was characterised by an (inter)nationalist paradigm. As with sporting competitions, it was about cultural competition between nation states represented by their national artists. In the course of economic and cultural globalization, however, the importance of national cultural fields increasingly declined. In his remarks, English traces a "New Geography of Prestige"[15] that is characterized not by a mere denationalization, but by an even more radical deterritorialization of prestige.[16] Using the example of the Nobel Prize for Literature, he demonstrates a "globalist strategy",[17] "a conscious strategy aimed at honoring writers of *world literature* who could nonetheless and simultaneously be identified with *local* roots or sites of production, and indeed whose place within world literature was a function of their particular relationship to those local roots."[18] The Nobel Prize for Literature was thus intended to represent a literature that could be considered originally global; a world literature whose fields of production and reception could only be traced on a global scale.[19] Nevertheless, some scholars, such as

---

[14] The fact that on the German book market, too, a clear national literary classification is becoming less and less of a prerequisite for inclusion in the publishing programme was recently pointed out by Jo Lendle, publisher of Hanser Verlag, at the *Cologne Talks on World Literature* 2018: "When I look at what we have done at Hanser in recent years and will be doing in the next few years, it is almost exclusively authors who are somewhere in between" (cf. the recording of the panel discussion at https://youtu.be/8_4SoJ-PiH4).

[15] English 2005, p. 264.

[16] English 2005, pp. 264–282.

[17] English 2005, p. 302.

[18] English 2005, p. 303 (emphasis in original).

[19] English 2005, 304.

Gouhua Zhu and Yonghua Tang, see the Nobel Prize in Literature as an expression of cultural hegemony and invoke the end of the Nobel era. By giving preference to works with "transnational and cross-cultural appeal",[20] the prize only reinforces long-outdated philosophical and aesthetic theories of a "universal human nature" and a "common humanity".[21]

The field of tension between national literature – world literature – literatures of the world has become highly dynamic in the course of globalization. The current debate about this appears to be one of the most important philological questions of our time. And the literatures of the Caribbean, especially those of the French-speaking world, can provide information about this. Both at the level of publishing selection and at the level of philological canonization, they are symptomatic of a paradigm shift from world literature in the tradition of Goethe to the literatures of the world.

If one considers literature as a kind of seismograph of epistemic upheavals, then the following example of the project (co-)conceived by the Martinican author Édouard Glissant can perhaps give an indication of a kind of literary production that takes leave of national-literary concepts, but is also located beyond universalist market-conformist world literary logics and is most likely, in the sense of the literatures of the world, always oriented towards the relational connectedness of the diverse and towards peaceful coexistence. This is the book series *Les peuples de l'eau,* edited by Glissant at Éditions du Seuil, which to a certain extent combines theory formation and literary production.[22]

The internationally renowned poet, essayist and cultural theorist Édouard Glissant from Martinique is, among other things, a pioneer of archipelagic thinking, which takes the relational logic of archipelagos as a starting point for redefining global togetherness. In relation to the field of tension between national literature and world literature, it is significant here that an island can never be thought of alone, but always only in conjunction with others, i.e. as an archipelago.

Glissant conceived the book series *Les peuples de l'eau* and the underlying project of a round-the-world voyage together with Patrice Franceschi, the captain of a three-masted sailing vessel: In July 2004, under the auspices of UNESCO, the *Boudeuse* sets out from Corsica with a crew of 24 on board and returns there in June 2007. Twelve expeditions will lead to eight 'peoples on the water', who live on isolated islands, inaccessible river banks or remote coasts and can only be reached by water. Writers and journalists selected by Glissant accompany the scientific team on each of the expeditions and bear witness to the wide scope of this project, which admittedly cannot be measured solely by established standards such as a translation index. These include Régis Debray, Patrick Chamoiseau, J.M.G. Le Clézio, Antonio Tabucchi and André Velter. During the journey, which lasts a total of three years and to which someone new joins every now and then for a few weeks or months, the

---

[20] Zhu/Tang 2018, p. 3.
[21] Zhu/Tang 2018, p. 3.
[22] On the *Völker am Wasser* project, see also Müller 2019.

Yuhup tribe on the Amazon and the Rapa Nui on Easter Island are visited, as well as the Bati on the island of Seram in the Moluccas, the Badjao, a nomadic people in the sea of Celebes, whalers on Lamarela in Indonesia or the Moken in Burma.[23] From Franceschi's documentations, the following (rough) route emerges: Corsica – Colombian Amazon – Easter Island – Tuamotu Archipelago and Marquesas Islands – Futuna – Vanuatu – Sulawesi – Oman.

"Ce qu'on appelle l'aventure est d'abord constitué de temps morts et de més-aventures", writes conflict researcher Gérard Chaliand.[24] In his account, it becomes clear that this journey is not only about other spaces of movement, about other dynamics than those conditioned by package tourism, globalization, or geopolitical power relations, but that the decelerated mode of travel also opens up other spaces of reflection that determine writing.[25] Thus Chaliand's first volume in the series documents in particular the journey itself, the slow approach to Amazonia, always in critical reflection of the expeditionary journeys of earlier centuries, so that exotic/post-exotic patterns of perception by European travellers become a central theme. In doing so, he addresses the background conditions of the project: Franceschi had already embarked on a circumnavigation of the world in 1999–2001 in a junk named *Boudeuse,* which was supposed to repeat Antoine de Bougainville's famous route after 200 years, but he was shipwrecked in the process.[26] For a new attempt, he bought a ship without knowing how his project would be financed and, together with Glissant, conceived the *Völker am Wasser* project.[27]

What kind of (world) literature has now emerged from this project, which approaches the encounter with the Other almost programmatically within archipelagic patterns of thought and movement? In any case, it implies a change of perspective that takes into account the fact that the globe, that the 'real world' consists of 70% oceans, but that only very few authors have narrated from the water – Derek Walcott, together with Le Clézio and some Caribbean authors around Édouard Glissant, may be the exception. J.M.G. Le Clézio's contribution to the series, the cultural reportage *Raga. Approche du continent invisible* (2006) about his journey to the South Pacific, or more precisely to Pentecost Island,[28] makes clear in yet another way how the specific approach of the project can reveal and perhaps also change outdated patterns of perception: "On dit de l'Afrique qu'elle est le continent oublié," writes Le Clézio, "L'Océanie, c'est le continent invisible. Invisible, parce que les voyageurs qui s'ont aventurés la première fois ne l'ont pas aperçue, et parce

---

[23] Chaliand 2006, p. 13.

[24] Chaliand 2006, p. 11.

[25] Cf. Klingler 2009.

[26] Chaliand 2006, p. 23.

[27] On the equipment of the ship, cf. Chaliand 2006, pp. 19–21. The documentaries that Patrice Franceschi made about the circumnavigation and the individual expeditions in a co-production with the broadcaster France 5 convey detailed impressions of the ship and also of the effort it must have taken to make it seaworthy for this purpose.

[28] Raga is the name of the island in the Apma language. It belongs geographically to the New Hebrides archipelago and politically to the Republic of Vanuatu.

que aujourd'hui elle reste un lieu sans reconnaissance internationale, un passage, une absence en quelque sorte".[29] In this opening quotation from *Raga,* two modes of decentering relationalities can already be identified that are significant for the entire project and can take the place of the Eurocentric perspective: On the one hand, there is the perception of Oceania as an archipelagic (and not continental) continent, as an island world in the sense of Ette,[30] and on the other hand, there is the interrelationship with other world regions traditionally perceived as 'peripheral' from Europe, such as Africa.

Glissant himself, no longer able to take on the rigors of such a journey, found ways to encounter the remote world of Easter Island in the South Pacific in both its ordinariness and its concreteness just a few years before his death in February 2011: The volume *La terre magnétique. Les errances de Rapa Nui, l'île de Paques* (2007) he compiled with his wife, who was on site and sent him material. Here Glissant once again emphasizes the importance of the island figure, which in its own logic eludes all too smooth appropriation and interpretation and directly influences the writing process.[31] This again echoes the "archipelagic thinking" that Glissant had already sketched out in 1996 in his *Introduction à une poétique du Divers:*

> What I see today is that the continents are 'archipelagic', at least from the point of view of the outside world. The Americas are becoming archipelagic, they are being formed into regions outside the national borders. I believe that this is a term that needs to be established in its dignity, the term 'region'. Europe is becoming archipelagic. Linguistic regions, cultural regions, beyond the barriers of nations, are islands, but open islands, which is their main condition for survival.[32]

Édouard Glissant's concept of archipelagic thinking is more than a description; it is a program that finds its echo in the concept of the *literatures of the world.* Archipelagic thought is one of the multiplicities to which philologies must open themselves in order to adequately confront relevant contemporary literature.

---

[29] In his review of the volume, Burkhard Müller also emphasizes such a shift in traditional perspectives and the patterns of interpretation associated with them: "Le Clézio does not perceive the island peoples primarily as something threatened, but sees in their exposure the opportunity for friction, for a preferentially active, even revolutionary transformation of what is storming at them from all sides" (Müller 2009).

[30] Ette 2005, p. 137.

[31] Cf. e.g. Glissant 2007, p. 25.

[32] Glissant 1996, p. 44. [Today it seems to me, at least from the outside, that the continents are archipelaginating. The Americas are archipelaginating, transcending national boundaries to form regions. And I think this concept of region must regain its old dignity. Europe, too, is archipelagicizing. Linguistic, cultural regions beyond national boundaries are islands, but open islands, that is the basic condition of their survival].

References

"Literarisches Sextett", Podiumsdiskussion im Rahmen der *Kölner Gespräche zur Weltliteratur 2018*. Teilnehmer: Florian Borchmeyer (Schaubühne Berlin), Andreas Breitenstein (Neue Zürcher Zeitung), Jo Lendle (Hanser Verlag), Sandra Richter (Deutsches Literaturarchiv Marbach), Andreas Rötzer (Matthes & Seitz), Uljana Wolf (Autorin); Moderation: Benjamin Loy. Videodokumentation online unter: https://youtu.be/8_4SoJ-PiH4 (letzter Aufruf 17.02.2020).

"Pour une littérature monde en français", in: *Le Monde,* 15.03.2007 (erstmals veröffentlicht am 03.02.2011). Online unter: https://www.lemonde.fr/livres/article/2007/03/15/des-ecrivains-plaident-pour-un-roman-en-francais-ouvert-sur-le-monde_883572_3260.html (letzter Aufruf 28.01.2020).

Apter, Emily: Untranslatables: A World System, in: New Literary History 39, 3, 2008, Johns Hopkins UP, S. 581–598.

Chaliand, Gérard: Aux confins de l'Eldorado. La Boudeuse en Amazonie. Paris: Éditions du Seuil 2006.

English, James F.: The Economy of Prestige: Prizes, Awards, and the Circulation of Cultural Value. Cambridge, Mass.: Harvard University Press 2005.

Ette, Ottmar: Wege des Wissens. Fünf Thesen zum Weltbewusstsein und den Literaturen der Welt. In: Sabine Hofmann, Monika Wehrheim (Hg.): Lateinamerika. Orte und Ordnungen des Wissens. Festschrift für Birgit Scharlau. Tübingen 2004, S. 169–184.

Ette, Ottmar: Von Inseln, Grenzen und Vektoren. Versuch über die fraktale Inselwelt der Karibik, in: Marianne Braig et al. (Hg.): Grenzen der Macht – Macht der Grenzen. Lateinamerika im globalen Kontext. Frankfurt am Main: Vervuert 2005, S. 135–180.

Fanon, Frantz: Les damnés de la terre. Paris: Maspero 1961.

Glissant, Édouard: La terre magnétique. Les errances de Rapa Nui, l'île de Pâques. Paris: Éditions du Seuil 2007.

Glissant, Édouard: Introduction à une poétique du Divers. Paris: Gallimard 1996.

Karimi, Kian-Harald: *La dernière ressource de notre grandeur.* Die Frankophonie zwischen imperialer Vergangenheit und postkolonialer Zukunft, in: Gesine Müller, Susanne Stemmler (Hg.): Raum – Bewegung – Passage. Postkoloniale frankophone Literaturen. Tübingen: Narr 2009, S. 15–31.

Klingler, Margrit: *Völker am Wasser.* Gespräch mit Manfred Metzner, Deutschlandfunk, 05.01.2009. Online unter: http://www.deutschlandfunk.de/voelker-am-wasser.700.de.html?dram:article_id=83899 (letzter Aufruf 06.06.2018).

Le Clézio, Jean Marie Gustave: Raga. Approche d'un continent invisible. Paris: Éditions du Seuil 2006.

Messling, Markus: Universalität nach dem Universalismus. Über frankophone Literaturen der Gegenwart. Berlin: Matthes & Seitz 2019.

Müller, Burkhard: Korallenkalk und Wassertaufe, in: Süddeutsche Zeitung, 20.06.2009.

Müller, Gesine, Jorge Locane, Benjamin Loy (Hg.): Re-mapping World Literature. Writing, Book Markets and Epistemologies between Latin America and the Global South/Escrituras, mercados y epistemologías entre América Latina y el Sur Global. Berlin, Boston: De Gruyter 2018.

Müller, Gesine: Debating World Literature without the World: Ideas for Materializing Literary Studies based on Examples from Latin American and the Caribbean, in: Gesine Müller, Mariano Siskind (Hg.): World Literature, Cosmopolitanism, Globality: Beyond, Against, Post, Otherwise. Berlin, Boston: De Gruyter 2019, S. 13–31.

Müller, Gesine, Mariano Siskind (Hg.): World Literature, Cosmopolitanism, Globality: Beyond, Against, Post, Otherwise. Berlin, Boston: Der Gruyter 2019.

Müller, Gesine: How Is World Literature Made? The Global Circulations of Latin American Literatures. Berlin, Boston: De Gruyter 2022.

Müller, Gesine: García Márquez zwischen Weltliteratur und Literaturen der Welt, in: Patricia Gwozdz, Markus Lenz (Hg.): Literaturen der Welt. Zugänge, Modelle, Analysen eines Konzepts im Übergang. Heidelberg: Winter 2018, S. 99–124.

Müller, Gesine: Karibische Literaturen zwischen ‚Weltliteratur' und ‚Literaturen der Welt, in: Lendemains XLII, 168 (Dossier "Les Antilles et les littératures du monde", hg. von Ottmar Ette, Gesine Müller), 2017a, S. 73–84.

Müller, Gesine: El debate sobre la literatura mundial y sus dimensiones editoriales: la región del Caribe a modo de ejemplo, in: Revista chilena 96, 2017b, S. 67–85.

Müller, Gesine: ¿Literatura mundial o literaturas mundiales? Un estudio de caso de las letras latinoamericanas en la editorial Suhrkamp, in: Gesine Müller, Dunia Gras Miravet (Hg.): América Latina y la Literatura Mundial: mercado editorial, redes globales y la invención de un continente. Madrid: Vervuert-Iberoamericana (Reihe Nuevos Hispanismos, hg. von Julio Ortega) 2015, S. 81–98.

Siskind, Mariano: Towards a cosmopolitanism of loss: An essay about the end of the world, in: Gesine Müller, Mariano Siskind (Hg.): World Literature, Cosmopolitanism, Globality. Beyond, Against, Post, Otherwise. Berlin: De Gruyter 2019, S. 205–236.

Toledo, Camille de: Visiter le Flurkistan, ou les Illusions de la littérature-monde. Paris: Presses Universitaires de France – PUF 2008.

Zhu, Gouhua, Yonghua Tang: The End of the Nobel Era and the Reconstruction of the World Republic of Letters, in: Comparative Literature and Culture 20, 7, 2018. Online unter: https://docs.lib.purdue.edu/cgi/viewcontent.cgi?article=3329&context=clcweb (letzter Aufruf 18.02.2020).

Transversal Similarities: Philology Beyond Tradition, Influence and Interconnectedness

Albrecht Koschorke

Abstract The contribution is based on the experiences of a German scholar with the research interests of students of non-European origin, specifically from China. In the two exemplary works discussed, German-Chinese comparisons are made that go beyond national-philologically anchored notions of comparability. In one case, it is a matter of observed similarities between the idylls of Salomon Gessner from the eighteenth century on the one hand, and poems by Tao Yuanming from the fourth century B.C.E. on the other. In the other paper, a dissertation, the contemporary Chinese writer Mo Yan is compared with Jean Paul (1763–1825) on the basis of his humorous encyclopedic writing procedures. The works compared in each case are not linked by a common epochal context, nor by recourse to common traditions, nor by relations of influence or entanglement. Nevertheless, similarities cannot be dismissed out of hand. This raises the question of how such transversal similarities can be conceptualized and explained beyond the paradigm of cultural difference.

This post is inspired by two Chinese German studies students, Xioating He and Siqi Li. Ms. He is working on her dissertation, Ms. Li has completed her Bachelor's degree and is now pursuing a Master's degree. Both have chosen their own topics, and both have chosen a comparative perspective. This is a preferred approach, especially by students from the Far East: They look beyond the great geographical and cultural distance for connecting elements, be it on the path of a comparative, or a reception-historical study – or a combination of both.

In the case of the comparative objects chosen here, according to all that is known, a reception-historical connection does not exist. The two students each build a

---

A. Koschorke (✉)
Fachbereich Literatur, Kunst und Medienwissenschaften, Universität Konstanz, Constance, Germany
e-mail: albrecht.koschorke@uni-konstanz.de

bridge between two independent literary products that are completely uninfluenced by each other. Nor is there any question here of a *tertium comparationis*, which is usually used: the texts being compared do not date from the same period. In one case there are two, in the other even twelve centuries between the authors compared. Correspondingly, the proposed topics caused a great deal of initial irritation on my side. In works that operate within a national-philological framework, one usually assumes the unifying effect of a common linguistic-cultural tradition within which the later are in a more or less explicit dialogue with the earlier. Comparative studies stabilize their comparative perspective, insofar as no direct interactions can be demonstrated, by referring to the same set of motifs or to a unifying epochal background. This is possible to the extent that the literatures being compared draw from a shared pool and/or seem to be synchronizable with one another due to their historic periodization. Accordingly, no one will take offence at a comparative study of the French and German Middle Ages or of European Romanticism. (It would be more difficult with the classics.) But how is a methodically controlled comparison to be possible if there is no middle element either on the synchronic or on the diachronic axis? What, then, is the common element that makes the differences significant and thus allows to compare them in a meaningful way in the first place?

From such doubts it becomes apparent how strongly the classical national philologies are dependent on a historicist paradigm that has developed in close entanglement with their genesis in nineteenth-century Europe. This is still true for more recent diffusionist approaches, regardless of whether they work with conventional or digital methods.[1] This historicism inscribed in national philology, like the discipline itself, cannot be completely detached from a container model of culture; it can only deal with phenomena that are 'related' to each other because they are located in a cultural continuum. It has no language for entirely independent parallel developments without the aid of typologies that are believed to have been overcome. The absorption of postcolonial theories in the relevant disciplines has even exacerbated this dilemma, because it leads to a strong emphasis on the cultural bondage of each individual text and trains one to distrust cross-cultural categories as an expression of Western striving for hegemony.

Siqi Li came to me with the intention of taking a closer look at the Swiss idyll poet Salomon Gessner (1730–1788). Gessner stemmed from the patrician class of the city of Zurich, which formed his centre throughout his life, but was drawn to country life. He became famous as a writer of idylls modelled on early modern pastoral poetry, thus joining a genre tradition that goes back to the Greek poet Theocritus in the third century BC. The linguistic-cultural resonance of his poems is accordingly Greek mythology. They are about Daphnis and Phillis, Venus and Pan, flute players in love and singers who, as with Theocritus, challenge each other to competition. Ms. Li, however, had another kindred spirit in mind. Gessner's idylls reminded her of the Chinese poet Tao Yuanming from the fourth century of the Christian era. She therefore wanted to compare the works of Gessner and Tao.

---

[1] Cf. the reflections on the spread of the Western European novel in Moretti 2014, pp. 54–68.

At first glance, there is no relationship whatsoever between the poets. To the best of my knowledge, it is unlikely that a Chinese author such as Tao would have been aware of Greco-Roman bucolics – even if one concedes the possibility that literary imaginaries may have travelled between the Mediterranean and the empires of the Far East along ancient trade routes. As a highly artificial genre anchored in the knowledge horizon of Mediterranean antiquity and largely self-contained through the reuse of standing motifs, bucolic in particular does not seem easily adaptable to other cultural contexts. Conversely, Gessner will hardly ever have heard the name Tao Yuanming in eighteenth century Zurich. A comparison on the basis of an adoption and adaptation is therefore not possible, so that the question of the tertium, the middle axis of comparability, arises again. Which paths lead from a Zurich painter-poet of the Enlightenment period to a learned Chinese civil servant in the confluence of Confucian, Buddhist and Daoist currents, who lived in the warlike period of the Six Dynasties and withdrew from government service to pursue his poetic inclinations in rural seclusion?

At second glance, however, there are astonishing parallels between the works of the two men whose lives were so far apart in time and space.[2] For the European idyll in the wake of Theocritus, to which Gessner follows, coincides in many elements with the garden-and-field poetry of Tao and his successors. Both praise the countryside as a place of retreat from urban life and the world of politics in times of turmoil, alleged moral decay, and shaking of the political order. Thus the preface to Gessner's *Idylls* states:

> Often I tear myself away from the city and flee to lonely places, then the beauty of nature snatches my mind away from all the disgust and all the harsh impressions that have pursued me from the city; completely enraptured, completely moved by its beauty, I am then as happy as a shepherd in the golden age of the world and richer than a king.[3]

Tao Yuanming expresses very similar emotions in his programmatic poem *Returning to the Fields:*

> When I was young, I was out of tune with the herd:
> My only love was for the hills and mountains.
> Unwitting I fell into the Web of the World's dust
> And was not free until my thirtieth year.
> The migrant bird longs for the old wood:
> The fish in the tank thinks of its native pool.
> I had rescued from wildness a patch of the Southern Moor
> And, still rustic, I returned to field and garden.
> My ground covers no more than ten acres:
> My thatched cottage has eight or nine rooms.
> Elms and willows cluster by the eaves:
> Peach trees and plum trees grow before the hall.
> […]
> At gate and courtyard—no murmur of the World's dust:
> In the empty rooms—leisure and deep stillness.

---

[2] This has already been elaborated in published research articles. Cf. Jin 2008, pp. 19–39.
[3] Geßner 1973, p. 15.

Long I lived checked by the bars of a cage:
Now I have turned again to Nature and Freedom.[4]

Just as Gessner refers to the ancient topos of the "golden age of the world", Tao, in his famous fable *The Peach Blossom Spring,* also evokes a time-removed Otherworld.[5] Thus, in their poetry, both devote themselves to a counter-fiction – which, incidentally, is highly reflective – that contains utopian qualities and evokes the happiness and virtue of a contemplative, small-scale life.[6] There are similarities right down to the motifs; according to Ms. Li, the concept of the *locus amoenus* is applicable to both lines of tradition, with tranquil ponds, clear springs, innocent cottage dwellers and other props – even if this *locus amoenus* is botanically different: violets and laurel in the European case, chrysanthemums and peach blossoms in the Chinese.

Can we therefore speak in a transcultural, possibly world-literary perspective of a genre of the idyll that is only expressed in two different variants in China and Europe? How do we generally deal with literary phenomena that arise from their own contexts of origin, have developed independently of one another, and yet exhibit striking similarities? How can such similarities be explained? In the case at hand, a literary sociological argument is offered across conventional epochal divisions. In China, as in Europe, we are dealing with agrarian societies in which agricultural yields lead to surplus production sufficient to support an upper class. This sets in motion processes of hobnobbing and urbanization that create an urban-rural divide. While these processes generate a cultural pull towards the respective centres, they also trigger a counter-movement with a time lag. On top of the broad agrarian population, the second layer of a – often merely seasonal – repopulation of the countryside by wealthy residents of the residences and cities is then laid down. This development is nourished by an imaginative 'understudy' of the rural area, into which anti-court or anti-urban, in both cases in the broadest sense anti-political impulses flow. Iconic for this is the type of private citizen, recurring in poetry and philosophy across the epochs, who retreats to his country house out of weariness of the political intrigues and generally of the compression of social constraints in the administrative centres, be it embittered or liberated, in order to live out for himself and others the often literarised utopia of a meditative, self-sufficient existence in harmony with nature.

Norbert Elias described such romanticizations of rural life as counter-reactions to the process of civilization, and although his theory of civilization revolves around Europe, it does offer points of departure for a cultural comparison that goes beyond this particular continent. However, this quickly leads to generalizations of the kind

---

[4]Yuanming 1919, p. 113.

[5]There is, however, an essential difference: Geßner, like Theocritus, sings of the supposedly idle existence of shepherds, whereas in Tao's rural world work is done.

[6]This is a basic feature of Daoism. Siqi Li cites the image of the ideal society as formulated by Tao Tse, the founder of this doctrine. In one of his poems it says: "Let a country be small, few in number. [...] Good find it the food, comfortable its huts, pretty the garments, cheerful the customs." (Cited in Schwarz 1976. p. 18 f.).

that were characteristic of world-historically oriented sociology around 1900 with its models of cultural stages, but which have since fallen into disrepute. Literary studies, especially if it sympathizes with the paradigm of "untranslatability",[7] currently has little to offer, apart from isolated approaches,[8] which would be equal to the macrosociological grand theories of Max Weber's type in terms of the range of possible explanations. Thus, for the time being, we are confined to individual observations with a low degree of systematization. So far, there are not even any reference works that allow a comparative view beyond the European language area, for example on the lemma 'idyll'.

At first glance, Xiaoting He's project brings together two authors who are closer to each other, but it generates a possibly even greater explanatory effort. The starting point of her study are parallels between the poetics of the German author Jean Paul (1763–1825) and the Chinese contemporary writer Mo Yan (born 1955). As far as I know, Jean Paul has not yet been translated into Chinese, and so it is once again unlikely that the similarities to be demonstrated are based on even remote knowledge. Even more so, the temporal distance between the authors rules out an *entanglement* according to the paradigm currently favored among historians. Subject of the comparative consideration are therefore also here two presumably independent phenomena.[9]

The finding of comparability as such, however, is convincing, as I had to concede in my role as designated supervisor after some initial reluctance. Like Jean Paul, Mo Yan is a humorous writer, and although both the word and the concept of 'humour' raise a number of cross-cultural issues, the similarities in poetic procedure are striking. Both novelists are masters of a lavishly circuitous narrative that chains digression to digression, both are fond of seemingly unmotivated conceits, and both profess this programmatically. Interestingly, they describe the production process of such, as it were, wild florilegias in a similar topic of literary sowing and reaping. Mo Yan defends his tendency to digressions and rule-breaking juxtapositions with the words that he plants "millet after the radish",[10] while Jean Paul regards his ideas as "poetic tulips" that he does not want to weed out because then there would be nothing left of the book.[11] In both cases, this creative arbitrariness is at the same time the subject of self-deprecating commentary, which, behind the most diverse focalizations, repeatedly brings to light the fictional author himself or his doppelgängeric mirror figures. For the basic pattern of works such as the *Flegeljahre* (Jean Paul, 1804) and *Life and Death Are Wearing Me Out* (Mo Yan, 2006), in which the analogies become particularly clear, is the description of life – whereby the popular idea of being able to be reborn as an animal allows Mo Yan even greater possibilities for

---

[7] Cf. Apter 2013.
[8] So with Beecroft 2015.
[9] At most, it is conceivable that Mo Yan could have received Laurence Sterne, who was a model for Jean Paul and whom some Western reviewers of Mo Yan feel reminded of.
[10] Quoted from a chapter of the dissertation in progress by Xiaoting He, whose translation.
[11] Jean Paul 2009, p. 14.

variation than Jean Paul. Often, to further the confusion, the fictional author or editor brought into play bears the name of the real one. From such seemingly autobiographical recursions to one's own author-persona grows another common trait, namely the delight in ironic self-praise, which, however, can turn at any time into parodic denigration of one's own person. The correspondence extends once again to the topicality used. Thus it says – to document one of the parallels pointed out by Mrs. He with her approval also in the wording – in Jean Paul:

> If you knew how little I ask about J.P.F. Richter; an insignificant wretch; but I live in it, in the wretch. [...] All my writing is actually inner self-biography; and all poetry is a description of self-life, for one knows and lives no other life than one's own.[12]

Accordingly with Mo Yan:

> As he lay in the relative comfort of a hard-sleeper cot – relative to a hard-seater, that is – the puffy, balding, beady-eyed, twisted-mouthed, middle-aged writer Mo Yan wasn't sleepy at all. The overhead lights went out as the train carried him into the night, leaving only the dim yellow glare of the floor lights to see by. I know there are many similarities between me and this Mo Yan, but many contradictions as well. I'm a hermit crab, and Mo Yan is the shell I'm occupying. Mo Yan is the raingear, that protects me from storms, a dog hide to ward off the chilled winds, a mask I wear to seduce girls from good families. There are times when I feel that this Mo Yan is a heavy burden, but I can't seem to cast it off, just as a hermit crab cannot rid itself of its shell.[13]

In such again fictionalizing ways, both Jean Paul and Mo Yan make their own narrative process thematic. They love to indulge in self-quotation, drawing attention to intertextual connections with other of their works, or inhibiting the flow of narrative to engage in skirmishes with reviewers (real or fictional). Reader addresses that break through the illusionism of the narrative are also a frequently used device, just as her style of humorous storytelling in general relies heavily on narrative metalepses in the sense of Gérard Genette. It need not be emphasized that the narrator proves to be an extremely unreliable instance.

As with Jean Paul, famous for his box of notes, this excessive narrative in Mo Yan, in love with his own linguisticity and its richness of association, rests on an encyclopedic foundation. Although the Chinese novelist derives his overflowing eloquence from the oral traditions of the peasant world from which he hails, his digressive confusions are also undoubtedly the fruit of a distinctly scriptural-cultural conditioning of the works. Through their overemphasized – and in this way again ironized – orientation towards the readership and the book market, both novelists reveal themselves as freelance writers who are dependent on the commercial success of their products.

As should have emerged from these hints, the similarities here extend far beyond a generic scheme shared by two authors. They can be found right down to the nuances of writing style, without denying the enormous cultural gap between the imaginary worlds produced in this way. Whether the similarities between Jean Paul

---

[12] Jean Paul 2004, p. 113.
[13] Yan 2012, p. 331 f.

and Mo Yan can be approached with a transcultural theory of humour remains to be seen. If what can be read in Jean Paul scholarship on the subject of humour is to apply to Mo Yan, then it could be argued that his novels, which emerged from the collectivism of the Mao era, experiment with strategies of radical subjectivation. But one can also look at the humorous writing style from another angle. The humorist, who indulges in word jokes, in the play of quotations, secondary meanings, and side paths, has an oversized treasure of knowledge at his disposal, which, however, has been torn from its ontological anchorage, as it were, has reached its limit of validity, and as a result has become lexically freely combinable. As far as Jean Paul is concerned, he draws an important part of his semantic resources from the accumulated polyhistorical knowledge of the Baroque, which, precisely because it was already *outdated in* his time, could be used as literary play material. An even more radical epochal break is reflected in Mo Yan's literary works, which are full of supernatural happenings and enigmatic metamorphoses in their own manifestation of magical realism. Mo Yan thus revives a world of folk religious beliefs in rural China that came to an abrupt end with the revolution. But because he is writing not only about an epochal break, but also about a deep epistemological break, it could be assumed that the humorous form of writing lends itself to an art form of speech that is broken in itself.

My knowledge is not sufficient to be able to verify whether the speculation just expressed holds. It is quite possible that this is not the case. However, this mistake would then perhaps not only be attributable to the lack of competence of the author of these lines, but would also be symptomatic of deficits in the discipline he represents. As a result of its basic national-philological character, literary studies has hardly any theoretical instruments at its disposal for dealing with, so to speak, transversal evidence that is not covered by a comparative research design essentially limited to European languages. Accordingly, it reacts helplessly when it comes to combining the study of individual philologies into a global history of literature that can compete with corresponding efforts in the field of historical studies. Such a global history of literature cannot merely be a spatially extended history of interconnections. It must provide models for the fact that comparable causes also produce similar cultural effects independently of one another. The challenge, in other words, is to identify and explain cultural isomorphies. The paradigm of cultural difference, which has shaped the poststructuralist-postcolonial epistemology of the past decades, obscures our view of many similarities between literatures.[14] If one assumes that the number of possible types of society or, on a smaller scale, of basic social situations and conflicts, is limited, then an argument for the multiple invention of certain aesthetic solutions to problems can be derived from this purely in terms of calculation. It may even be possible to attach greater weight to the role of transcultural universals than is usually the case in textual studies. Conversely, this means withdrawing the insistence on cultural specificity that goes hand in hand with the disciplinary history of the national philologies, without therefore immediately

---

[14] In more detail: Koschorke 2015, pp. 35–45. English version: Koschorke 2018, pp. 25–34.

feeding the fear of a relapse into anthropological essentializations that have been overcome. – The challenge would then be to bring together the sensitivity for the individual text developed in the classical philologies with a larger-scale functional history of literature.[15]

References

Apter, Emily: Against World Literature: On the Politics of Untranslatability. London/New York: Verso 2013.
Beecroft, Alexander: An Ecology of World Literature. From Antiquity to the Present Day. London/New York: Verso 2015.
Geßner, Salomon: Idyllen. Kritische Ausgabe. Hg. von E. Theodor Voss. Stuttgart: Reclam 1973.
Jin, Xiuli: Schöne Landschaften. Zu Salomon Gessners Idyllen, in: Literaturstraße. Chinesisch-deutsche Zeitschrift für Sprach- und Literaturwissenschaft. Bd. 9, 2008, p. 19–39.
Koschorke, Albrecht: Ähnlichkeit. Valenzen eines post-postkolonialen Konzepts, in: Anil Bhatti und Dorothee Kimmich (Hg.): Ähnlichkeit. Ein kulturtheoretisches Paradigma. Konstanz: Konstanz University Press, 2015, p. 35–45.
Koschorke, Albrecht: Similarity. Valences of a post-colonial concept, in: Anil Bhatti und Dorothee Kimmich (Hg.): Similarity. A Paradigm for Culture Theory. New Delhi: Tulika Book 2018, p. 25–34.
Moretti, Franco: Conjectures on World Literature, in: New Left review 1/4, 2014, p. 54–68.
Paul, Jean: Merkblatt 1818, in: Helmut Pfotenhauer (Hg.): Jean Paul, Lebensbeschreibung. Veröffentlichte und nachgelassene autobiographische Schriften. München/Wien: Carl Hanser Verlag, 2004.
Paul, Jean: Hesperus oder 45 Hundsposttage. Eine Biographie, in: Barbara Hunfeld (Hg.): Jean Paul, Werke. Historisch-Kritische Ausgabe. Bd. I. Tübingen: Niemeyer, 2009.
Schwarz, Ernst: Chrysanthemenim Spiegel. Klassische chinesische Dichtungen. Berlin: Aufbau-Verlag 1976.
Twellmann, Marcus: Gattungsgeschichte als transnationale Funktionsgeschichte literarisch-sozialer Institutionen. Ein Problemaufriss mit Blick auf den Bildungsroman, in: DVjs 94, 2020, p. 385–415.
Yan, Mo: The Republic of Wine. New York: Simon & Schuster 2012
Yuanming, Tao: Returning to the Fields. In: A Hundred and Seventy Chinese Poems. Translated by Arthur Waley. New York: A. Knopf 1919, p. 113

---

[15] Cf. as an approach in this direction: Twellmann 2020, pp. 385–415.

Social Traumas and the Literary Canon: Reflections on the Function of Literary Education for Intercultural Competence Using the Example of *El olvido que seremos* by Héctor Abad Faciolince

Frank Reiser

Abstract This article explores the question of the extent to which literary canons still play or should play a role in grammar school foreign language teaching, which is quantitatively the most important field of activity for foreign language philologists. In relevant framework papers, such traditional educational content or even literary experience as an end in itself tend to recede into the background today, in favour of a usage of literature as a medium of (inter)cultural or regional insights. A text that lends itself particularly well to the latter, since it addresses several sociocultural key aspects of Spanish language teaching in grammar schools, is Héctor Abad Faciolince's *El olvido que seremos* (2006). A closer analysis shows, however, that the contemporary historical and socio-critical level of the text also and especially functions essentially through diverse references to the literary and artistic canon. The case study thus provides evidence that even under the premises of today's general educational goals and beyond philological specialization, an orientation knowledge of transnational canons can be useful.

The question of the usefulness of literature is as old as literature itself, and it is also at the centre of current debates. It can be understood in terms of the communication of knowledge beyond the sciences in the modern, especially STEM-influenced sense, as a source of knowledge of the world,[1] knowledge of life or even knowledge about survival as well as meta-knowledge about life discourses (according to the

---

[1] Klinkert 2010.

F. Reiser (✉)
Romanisches Seminar der Universität, Universität Freiburg, Freiburg, Deutschland
e-mail: frank.reiser@romanistik.uni-freiburg.de

deliberately ambiguous term *ÜberLebenswissen* suggested by Ottmar Ette).[2] Following this, one can reject an all too simple meaning of 'utility' and 'world knowledge' *au premier degré* and foreground 'possibility knowledge': alternative worlds in the fictional space of literature that train our sense of possibility and thus our world-modelling competence; in an intercultural sense, the confrontation with alternative world-knowledge of fiction becomes relevant, in the form of the literary 'interplay of the potential to irritate, to challenge familiar notions of self and world' that helps the reader to gain 'an awareness of heterogeneity and a tolerance of ambiguity';[3] in a very fundamental sense, Hans Ulrich Gumbrecht's call for a re-aestheticization of literary studies, which focuses on the factor of presence (the auratic in the sense of Benjamin's essay on the *The Work of Art in the Age of Mechanical Reproduction*[4]) and experience, could probably be seen as a form of the latter,[5] in opposition to the focus on knowledge in the narrower, declarative sense and on ethical imperatives, albeit with the *potential for irritation* inherent in *aesthetic* experience (as the etymology already indicates), which, by questioning what is believed to be certain, cannot be entirely denied an ethical effect on life outside literature.

No matter how one wants to weigh these positions against each other or connect them: in order to determine the position of literary studies, it might be considered a sensible premise to think large, to "not lift the 'treasure' alone", as Ottmar Ette puts it, "but [...] to make it democratically available to as broad a section of the population as possible"[6] and not to belong to the apocalyptics who indulge in the ivory tower of supposedly 'pure' scholarship, thereby committing those 'deadly sins' that Ralf Junkerjürgen recently catalogued.[7] And the area that comes into consideration in this sense as the *débouché* of literary studies, as domain of (self-)justification and as point of orientation, is grammar school teaching: historically, it is most closely connected with philology – to this day, not without reason, the best-known association of grammar school teachers in Germany is called *Deutscher Philologenverband* –, since literature was regarded as the perfect expression of both language and culture and at the same time as the guarantor of the educational level that the *Gymnasium* was supposed to impart in the eyes of the educated middle-class, and even if since then the weights have shifted between the subjects and within them again in the focal points, and social exclusivity of the institution, where it still exists, is now regarded as a problem, the *Gymnasium* remains the professional goal for the vast majority of philology students and not without reason the orientation point for

---

[2] Ette 2004, 2005, 2010.
[3] Bracker 2015, p. 14, p. 32.
[4] Benjamin 1980, pp. 471–508.
[5] Gumbrecht 2010.
[6] Ette 2017, p. 255.
[7] Junkerjürgen 2018, pp. 63–81. In the given context, these would include above all no. 1, "Literary studies striving for autonomy", and no. 3, "Secondary literature replacing primary literature". See also Ette 2004, p. 255: "There is no doubt that the humanities must take a stand outside their own campus, their own playing field."

philological curricula under the sign of coherence and professional orientation.[8] The need to take this more into account in debates about the function of literature and the role of the humanities was pointed out not least by Andreas Kablitz in a highly regarded public contribution in 2014.[9]

In order to approach the question posed in the present volume about the status of the national philologies and the significance of traditional cultural contents such as literary canons for intercultural competence, we can therefore, according to the above premises, suppose to gain insights in particular from concrete framework specifications for grammar school foreign language teaching. Let us do this exemplarily for the subject Spanish.

A cursory glance through the current German education plans for upper secondary level shows only isolated references to the literary canon, and these with an accent on the early modern period that is at least surprising, given the target group. Bavaria, for example, stipulates "representative examples of texts from the siglo de oro" without explicitly naming works,[10] Saxony dares to name the *Quixote,* which, as we may assume, is also primarily meant in the Bavarian framework paper, but curiously under the heading "taller de teatro".[11] Hesse delegates the canon question to external consecration authorities with reference to the Nobel Prize and the *premio Cervantes*, but also mentions García Márquez, Alejo Carpentier and Pablo Neruda by name.[12] Schleswig-Holstein and Thuringia tend to focus more on the visual arts and cinema with regard to the artistic canon in Spanish lessons.[13] Much more frequently, however, than the literary canon and the at least implied treatment of literature as a object *sui generis*, literary texts appear as transitive objects, i.e. as 'vehicles' for insights into the societies of the target countries and a comparative and critical view of the pupils' own culture with the aim of fostering intercultural-communicative competence. Thus, the Bavarian papers state: "The pupils [...] look at the Spanish-

---

[8] Cf. for example the thematic issue "PädagogInnenbildung Neu: Auf dem Weg zu Professionalisierung und Kompetenzorientierung?" of the journal *Quo vadis Romania? Zeitschrift für eine aktuelle Romanistik*, 44, 2014/15.

[9] Kablitz 2014: "Literature is a case of particularly complex language use. The insights that can be gained into its structure through the analysis of its use in literature are not the least of the yields of its study. It is so above all with regard to that relevant institution which still represents a highly significant, indeed probably the most important 'field of application' of the humanities, even if recent debates have woefully neglected its importance: the secondary school. Raising awareness of their significance for our community and highlighting the eminent importance of the humanities for school education is an urgent and undoubtedly neglected task of these humanities themselves".

[10] Lehrplanauszug aus dem Fachlehrplan für Klasse 11 Spanisch (Gym), as of 19.09.2020, ch. "Sp 11 5: Themengebiete", pp. 8–9.

[11] Lehrplan Gymnasium Spanisch, as of August 2019, Jahrgangsstufen 11/12 – Grundkurs dreistündig, Lernbereich 3: Texte und Themenbereiche/Wahlbereich 5: "Taller de teatro", p. 51.

[12] Kerncurriculum gymnasiale Oberstufe Spanisch, as of 2016, ch. A3.3 "Kurshalbjahre und Themenfelder", p. 39.

[13] Schleswig-Holstein, Lehrplan für die Sekundarstufe II Gymnasium Spanisch, as of 2002, ch. 4.4 "Themen", p. 45; Thuringia, Lehrplan für den Erwerb der allgemeinen Hochschulreife Spanisch, fortgeführte FS, as of 2011, ch. 4.2 "Zentrale Inhalte", p. 83.

speaking world and their own world from different regional and social perspectives, including notably through the critical examination of the literary and artistic works of the target culture, draw comparisons and thereby critically question their own prejudices and stereotypes towards other cultures and persons as well as their own values",[14] and later, in a similar way, they are supposed to "reflect on social developments of the target culture in the past when encountering more complex authentic texts and documents, including notably from the fields of literature, film, art, and media".[15] In Bremen, the topic is "The individual and society in the mirror of literature, art and media", with exemplary reference to García Lorca.[16] In Hesse, literature serves two heteronomous goals at the same time, because it appears there in the context of the main topic "Latinoamérica ayer y hoy", there the sub-topic "Desigualdad social y económica" and "Derechos humanos", where, however, in the specification a turn is made towards communicative competence: "In dealing with the issues described, above all receptive and language-mediating competences for the development and transfer of literary texts and authentic materials are essential".[17] Highlighting, as do the Hessian regulations, the aspects of social inequality and human rights in Latin American civilisation units is quite widespread, often unsurprisingly with reference to the context of dictatorial heritage; for example in Baden-Württemberg,[18] Bavaria,[19] Bremen,[20] Lower Saxony,[21] Saxony-Anhalt and Schleswig-Holstein.[22] Berlin and Brandenburg focus on "Current Social, Political and Economic [...] Conflicts in Latin America", "Political and Social Commitment" and "Life Courses in Spain and Latin America".[23]

---

[14] Lehrplanauszug aus dem Fachlehrplan für Klasse 11 Spanisch (Gym), as of 19.09.2020, ch. "Sp 11 2: Interkulturelle Kompetenzen", pp. 5–6.

[15] Lehrplanauszug aus dem Fachlehrplan für Klasse 12 Spanisch (Gym), as of 19.09.2020, ch. "Sp 12 2: Interkulturelle Kompetenzen", p. 5.

[16] Bildungsplan für die gymnasiale Oberstufe Spanisch (neu aufgenommene Fremdsprache), as of 2015, ch. 2 "Themen und Inhalte", p. 8.

[17] Hessen, Kerncurriculum gymnasiale Oberstufe Spanisch, as of 2016, ch. A3.3 "Kurshalbjahre und Themen-felder", p. 38.

[18] "Violence in political conflicts" (Baden-Württemberg, Bildungsplan für Spanisch als dritte Fremdsprache [Profilfach], as of 2016, Klassen 11/12, ch. 3.2.1. "Soziokulturelles Orientierungswissen/Themen", p. 26).

[19] "memoria histórica" with reference to dictatorships (Bayern, Lehrplanauszug aus dem Fachlehrplan für Klasse 12 Spanisch [Gym], as of 19.09.2020, ch. "Sp 12: Sprechen", pp. 2–8).

[20] "Hispanoamérica – los derechos humanos" (Bremen, Bildungsplan für die gymnasiale Oberstufe Spanisch [neu aufgenommene Fremdsprache], as of 2015, ch. 2 "Themen und Inhalte", p. 8); but mentioned here as a non-obligatory topic suggestion.

[21] "dictaduras [...] Hispanoamérica / derechos humanos" (Kerncurriculum für das Gymnasium – gymnasiale Oberstufe Spanisch, as of 2011, ch. 4 "Themenfelder", p. 38).

[22] "From dictatorship to democracy" (Saxony-Anhalt, Fachlehrplan Gymnasium Spanisch, as of 01.07.2019, ch. 5, "Kommunikative Inhalte und soziokulturelles Orientierungswissen", p. 36; identical regulation for Schleswig-Holstein, Lehrplan für die Sekundarstufe II Gymnasium Spanisch, as of 2002, ch. 4.4 "Themen", p. 41).

[23] Berlin, Rahmenlehrplan für den Unterricht in der gymnasialen Oberstufe Spanisch, as of 01.08.2017, ch. 4. "Kompetenzentwicklung und Inhalte in den Kurshalbjahren", p. 32.

Leaving aside the question of the weighting of aesthetic (in a sense 'intransitive') literary experience in the curricula, which is certainly important but not at issue here, let us accept the functionalisation and partial subordination of literature to heteronomous competence goals and, in the sense of a case study, take a closer look at a literary text that fits in this regard. I propose here the autobiography-autofiction[24] *El olvido que seremos* by Héctor Abad Faciolince, published in 2006, in which the author recounts his childhood and youth in Medellín, but above all, and inseparably from it, provides a portrait of his father Héctor Abad Gómez, the medical professor, social physician, and human rights activist who was very well known in Colombia and beyond and who was shot dead on the open street by a state-ordered hit squad in 1987. The text – widely received in translations internationally, awarded prizes and filmed in 2015 under the title *Carta a una sombra* – not only corresponds exactly to the thematic triad of conflicts, social commitment and life courses in Latin America defined for grammar schools in Berlin and Brandenburg, as cited above, but also opens up a cultural studies perspective on violence, hegemonic processes of meaning-making and, above all, memory and cultures of remembrance beyond traditional regional insights, as already indicated by the title, a title whose scepticism the text itself contradicts performatively in an interesting way by emphatically setting up a monument to the author's father. The father-son relationship, highlighted by the text as truly exceptional, does not remain on the level of the individual case – be it seen as happy or tragic, depending on the perspective or phase –, but also stands as an example for a fundamental political problem, as the author himself emphasizes: "Hay miles y miles de padres asesinados en este país tan fértil para la muerte. Pero es un caso especial, sin duda, y para mí el más triste. Además reúne y resume muchísimas de las muertes injustas que hemos padecido aquí."[25] Not only the circumstances of his death, but also the prominence of Héctor Abad Gómez as president of the *Comité de Derechos Humanos de Antioquia*, founder of the *Escuela Nacional de Salud Pública*, and today namesake of the superordinate faculty, give the text a supra-individual dimension, even in the parts that are (auto)biographical in the strictest sense: for the author, remembering his youth means, essentially, remembering and commemorating his father, and that, in turn, addresses a moral stance of the individual within fields of social conflict.[26] Thus Abad Faciolince describes the conflicts in the microcosm of his family as reflections of the social macrocosm, which in turn is not only to be understood synchronously, but for its part is located within supra-temporal and transnational oppositions: colonialism, (national) Catholicism vs. the Enlightenment – the third section of the book is entitled "Guerras de religión y antídoto ilustrado" (OS 79 et seq.) – as

---

[24] On the question of genre mixing, cf. González Molina 2014, p. 4.
[25] Abad Faciolince 2017, p. 296 (hereinafter cited as OS).
[26] On the intertwining of individual and collective perspectives, Vanegas Vásquez 2015, p. 96 summarises: "En el texto se juega una doble respuesta a la realidad del país: por un lado, configura la experiencia individual-íntima del sujeto narrador, pero al mismo tiempo esta presencia narrativa evoca un devenir histórico, por supuesto colectivo, de la violencia sociopolítica colombiana"; cf. also González Molina 2014, p. 15.

well as, as it were as synthesis of both, the "Gran Misión" as a "Reconquista Católica de América" (OS 73) pushed by Francoist Spain, with the prefix *Re-* in double meaning of the reconquest against the supposedly atheistic or/and communist liberalism on the one hand and the *renewed Conquista* of Latin America by Europe on the other hand. *El olvido que seremos* thus combines autobiographical with communicative and cultural memory in the sense of Jan and Aleida Assmann,[27] and even explicitly reflects this transition at the end of the text.[28]

If in *El olvido que seremos* the social, political and ideological problems with all their relevance for knowledge of Colombia in particular and Latin America in general, understanding of cultural processes and democracy building, represent one of the clearly dominant thematic levels, what is the role of literature, literary communication, literary canons? What schemata and points of reference does literature provide in the context of the representation of social problems? A first aspect has already been mentioned: Literature as a carrier of memory. In view of the prominence of Héctor Abad Gómez and the existing public media of remembrance dedicated to his person, a text like *El olvido que seremos* as a pure memory cue is not necessary in itself; the added value consists, on the one hand, of course, in the son's perspective – combining the public with the private and subjective vision – and, on the other hand, in a form of 'intertextual' memory, as the title already indicates: It is the first verse of a sonnet, which Abad Faciolince is convinced is a work by Jorge Luis Borges, and which he (incorrectly) remembers as being titled 'Epitaph', which is printed in full in the text (OS 279–80) and, with its almost neo-baroque vanitas scenario, stands in striking contradiction to Abad Faciolince's explicitly and implicitly stated intention to set up a textual monument to his father. Despite this textual tension, at second glance the poem nevertheless proves to be a memorial text on an

---

[27] Cf. for example Assmann 1992, pp. 29–86.

[28] "Aunque puedo creerlo, no quiero imaginar el momento doloroso en que también las personas que más quiero – hijos, mujer, amigos, parientes – dejarán de existir, que será el momento en que yo dejaré de vivir, como recuerdo vívido de alguien, definitivamente. [...] Si las palabras transmiten en parte nuestras ideas, nuestros recuerdos y nuestros pensamientos [...], si las palabras trazan un mapa aproximado de nuestra mente, buena parte de mi memoria se ha trasladado a este libro, y como todos los hombres somos hermanos, en cierto sentido, porque lo que pensamos y decimos se parece, porque nuestra manera de sentir es casi idéntica, espero tener en ustedes, lectores, unos aliados, unos cómplices, capaces de resonar con las mismas cuerdas en esa caja oscura del alma, tan parecida en todos, que es la mente que comparte nuestra especie. [...] Y si mis recuerdos entran en armonía con algunos de ustedes, y si lo que yo he sentido (y dejaré de sentir) es comprensible e identificable con algo que ustedes también sienten o han sentido, entonces este olvido que seremos puede postergarse por un instante más, en el fugaz reverberar de sus neuronas, gracias a los ojos, pocos o muchos, que alguna vez se detengan en estas letras" (OS 318–19). Regardless of how one wishes to judge the hermeneutic optimism of presupposing, on the one hand, the "transmission" of memory into writing and, on the other, in the reader the "same strings" and a "similar soul" as a guarantor of understanding, the passage thematizes the transition from autobiographical to communicative memory through the act of narration in itself and to cultural memory through conservation in a widely received and adapted literary text; its binding, formalized and group-related status that is essential for entering the domain of cultural memory will depend on the further canonization of the text – also and especially as *school reading*.

indexical level, for a copy of the text was in the father's pocket when he was murdered and still bore the bloody traces of the attack; moreover, the father had copied the sonnet by hand that day, which, through an act of symbolic appropriation, makes it his testament and his *own* epitaph, more precisely: *One half* of a *double* epitaph – again intertwining individual with collective levels – because along with the sonnet in the bag was a copy of the publicly circulating death list on which Héctor Abad Gómez was included with many other government critics and activists (OS 286). Incidentally, like the poem, this list also enters the text *El olvido que seremos* as a citation in a sense, as the names of others killed appear repeatedly within the narrative discourse (e.g. OS 285, 305). With regard to the question of literary canonization, it is now interesting to note here that Héctor Abad Faciolince not only understandably attaches importance to the sonnet as such, but also to the clarification of its (disputed) authorship, to which he in turn devotes most of his 2010 book *Traiciones de la memoria*. If it is possible to attribute the epitaph sonnet found with his father's body to Jorge Luis Borges, then the father participates through his symbolic co-authorship (medially as a copyist and in a brutal-physical sense as a signer[29]) in the canonical and thus memory-guaranteeing status of the Argentine writer, who, for his part, is associated through his narratives – one may think here in particular of *Funes el memorioso* – with the ambivalence of remembering and forgetting that, as we have seen, also characterizes *El olvido que seremos*.[30]

If the title of the book already traces the programmatic theme of memory and legacy back to literary references in the complex way presented, this is no less true for the characterization of Héctor Abad Gómez as a *father figure*, which is particularly significant with regard to the autobiographical dimension of the text, where the canonical references clearly are used negatively in terms of counter-models. These include, first of all, Shakespeare's Hamlet and his father, who appears to him as a ghost after his murder, in a superimposition of subjective-internal and objective-external figure, as is in a certain sense also peculiar to Héctor Abad Gómez in his double role as the son's subjective object of memory and the object of the official *memoria histórica*, but with the difference that Abad Faciolince rejects – or literary sublimates – the principle of retaliation:

> Han pasado casi veinte años desde que lo mataron, y durante estos veinte años, cada mes, cada semana, yo he sentido que tenía el deber ineludible, no digo de vengar su muerte, pero sí, al menos, de contarla. No puedo decir que su fantasma se me haya aparecido por las noches, como el fantasma del padre de Hamlet, a pedirme que vengue su monstruoso y ter-

---

[29] "el epitafio de Borges copiado de su puño y letra, salpicado de sangre" (OS 286).

[30] It should be noted in passing that the textual criticism done in search for the authorship of the sonnet, which is the subject of *Traiciones de la memoria* and involves numerous Borges specialists, is an exciting example of interdiscursive feedback effects between literature and literary studies: An intertextual reference in one literary text (*El olvido que seremos*) to another literary text (the sonnet), for whose efficacy the author function (*fonction-auteur*) is so important that a writer undertakes literary studies research, which he reports in a recent literary text (*Traiciones de la memoria*). For a determination of the position of the discipline of literary studies, it is – despite complicated epistomological questions related to it – not a point of view to be underestimated: its implication in its object itself.

rible asesinato. Mi papá nos enseñó a evitar la venganza. Las pocas veces que he soñado con él, en esas fantasmales imágenes de la memoria y de la fantasía que se nos aparecen mientras dormimos, nuestras conversaciones han sido más plácidas que angustiadas, y en todo caso llenas de ese cariño físico que siempre nos tuvimos. No hemos soñado el uno con el otro para pedir venganza, sino para abrazarnos. (OS 295)

What is important here is that the principle of retribution in *El olvido que seremos* is not situated solely at the individual or family level, but is the core and motor of the violence in political conflicts that make up the core of the book in terms of social criticism and contemporary history.

The more structural reference is to Kafka's *Letter to the father*, and this in a twofold dialogical[31] manner. First, in Abad Faciolince, it is not the son but the father who speaks in a letter (OS 297 et seq.). The letter to the son, quoted in full in the text, is recontextualized here as source within a portrait addressed to a wider public, as a plea for individual freedom over social constraints, and as a neostoicist-like warning against striving for dominance.[32] In a second, autoreferential step, it appears implicitly[33] and explicitly[34] as a communicative counterpart to the text *El olvido que seremos* itself, which thus becomes – once again in total contradiction to Kafka – a *(reply) letter to the father* or "carta a una sombra". The reference to Kafka's letter thereby foregrounds *ex negativo* two social concerns: the rejection of patriarchal repression in the microcosm of the familial as well as in the macrocosm of the socio-political sphere and the encouragement to take a public stand as an intellectual. Both converge in the detailed account that the author devotes, in an autobiographical manner, to the development and promotion of his writing vocation, in which his father assumes the decisive role of mentor and motivator.[35] One of the central episodes here is the time spent together in Mexico City (OS 224 et seq.), which brings the son into contact with intellectuals, but above all offers him the freedom for extensive Proust readings, which in retrospect become the context and model for his self-discovery as a writer (OS 228–29); significantly, this phase, as the autobiographical narrator emphasizes, goes hand in hand with a distancing from the

---

[31] In describing the intertextual relationship, I make use of the categories proposed by Manfred Pfister (1985).

[32] Among the many other literary references of *El olvido que seremos*, which cannot be commented on further in the present sketchy analysis, neostoicist ethics definitely forms a figure of relevance with Jorge Manrique, Montaigne and Antonio Machado (OS 271 et seq.; 13; 296).

[33] "Aquí estoy de regreso, escribiendo sobre él *desde donde él me escribía* [...]" (OS 299, my italics).

[34] "Cuando, muchos años más tarde, leí la *Carta al padre* de Kafka, yo pensé que podría escribir esa misma carta, pero al revés, con puros antónimos y situaciones opuestas" (OS 28).

[35] Cf. Vanegas Vásquez 2015, p. 102: "Es interesante que a lo largo de todo el relato el narrador-autor configure la presencia del papá, la memoria que guarda de él, como causa y efecto de su devenir en el mundo de las letras. La formulación literaria del padre [...] se proyecta como instancia de autorreflexión para recordar que detrás de toda la existencia propia hay siempre un libro. La forma como Abad Faciolince organiza el pasado a través de la escritura configura una realidad donde se combina el impacto intelectual de los libros con la experiencia emocional, reconoce que asociada a cada escena de lectura está el padre como mentor y motivador."

father, which signifies precisely a lack of paternal control. In autobiographical retrospect, however, a much earlier phase appears as the actual origin of authorship, namely the early childhood discovery of writing in a purely material sense, without any commitment to semantics:

> [C]elebraba, en mi escritura, hasta los garabatos sin sentido, y me enseñó muy despacio la manera en que las letras representaban los sonidos, para que mis errores iniciales no produjeran risa. Yo aprendí, gracias a su paciencia, todo el abecedario, los números y los signos de puntuación en su máquina de escribir. Tal vez por eso un teclado – mucho más que un lápiz o un bolígrafo – es para mí la representación más fidedigna de la escritura. Esa manera de ir hundiendo sonidos, como en un piano, para convertir las ideas en letras y en palabras, me pareció desde el principio – y me sigue pareciendo – una de las magias más extraordinarias del mundo. (OS 24)

It is no coincidence that one of the most famous modern writers' autobiographies appears here as an intertext, namely Sartre's *Les mots*, where, although in a much more patriarchally controlled environment, precisely this almost pre-linguistic, cultic encounter with the written media becomes the origin of the literary vocation: Abad Faciolince's text refers via Sartre to the concept of *engagement* as well as the figure of the intellectual, i.e. the bearer of critical intervention in the social and political sphere, consecrated by literary or scholarly achievement and thereby independent of party politics.[36] And indeed, there is a clear connection from that depicted 'act of birth' to the social statement through *El olvido que seremos* itself, which, as Reyes Albarracín points out, would not be possible at all without that writerly consecration: "A diferencia de un alto porcentaje de víctimas que están condenadas a un silenciamiento sistemático, Héctor Abad Faciolince es un sobreviviente excepcional, pues su reconocimiento público como escritor e intelectual garantiza precisamente la posibilidad de relatar su versión frente a la muerte de su padre, planteando en distintos escenarios los debates que considere necesarios."[37] In accordance with the symbiosis between father and son that is the leitmotif in *El olvido que seremos*, there is also a relevant intertextual reference in an analogous way for the father as *intellectuel*. It appears in a newspaper article by Héctor Abad Gómez, quoted extensively again in the text, in which the latter condemns torture by the military and, invoking the leading members of the government, makes several accusations introduced with the anaphoric phrase "Yo acuso" (OS 250–51): it is an echo of that famous open letter entitled *J'accuse*, written by Émile Zola and published on 13 January 1898 in *L'Aurore* and in parallel as a poster and pamphlet, with which he used the means of scandalization[38] not only to prevent the government, military, and judiciary from liquidating the Dreyfus affair as quietly as possible, but also to trigger further public partisanship that constituted the *intellectuels* as a specific group

---

[36] For a summary of this complex model, which was developed in France but has developed an international impact, see Jurt 2000.

[37] Reyes Albarracín 2010, p. 26 (footnote).

[38] Scandalisation also appears selectively as an effective moment in *El olvido que seremos* (e.g. OS 310–11), but this cannot be explored in depth here; on the structure and function of the scandal, see Gelz et al. 2014.

for the first time.[39] Héctor Abad Gómez's article, and especially its inclusion and embedding in the son's literary text, amounts to a statement about the status of the father, the ethical commitment of the educated elite, and the state of development of Colombian society. Incidentally, the concept of the intellectual is matched by the fact that the father was not authorized to speak on the basis of literary consecration, but of academic authority – and that, as the son interestingly reconstructs elsewhere, he did not initially adhere to any particular political party or ideology, but was only discursively constructed as a 'leftist' by his detractors and only then inwardly assumed this position, convinced by subsequent readings.[40]

In the connection that emerges here between resistance to dominant anti-liberal positions and artistic reception, another literary and cinematic reference plays a role. In chapter 37, the narrator recalls the great importance his father attached to Visconti's screen adaption of Thomas Mann's *Death in Venice*, both personally and with regard to his then seventeen-year-old son:

> [D]os veces me llevó mi papá a ver una película, *Muerte en Venecia*, de Luchino Visconti, ese bellísimo film basado en una novela corta de Thomas Mann en el que un hombre en el declinar de sus días [...] siente que al mismo tiempo se exalta y sucumbe ante la belleza absoluta representada por la figura de un muchacho polaco, Tadzio. Dice Mann que él no quiso representar la belleza en una muchacha, sino en un joven, para que los lectores no creyeran que esa admiración era puramente sexual, de simple atracción de cuerpos. Lo que el protagonista, Gustav von Aschenbach, sentía, era algo más, y también algo menos: el enamoramiento de un cuerpo casi abstracto, la personificación de un ideal, digámoslo así, platónico, representado en la belleza andrógina de un adolescente. Yo estaba demasiado metido en mi propio mundo cuando mi papá insistió en que viéramos la película por tercera vez, quizá al darse cuenta de que yo no había sido capaz de percibir su sentido más hondo y más oculto.
>
> En una carta que me escribió en el año 75 [...] decía lo siguiente: "Para mí, paulatinamente, se me va haciendo cada vez más evidente que lo que más admiro es la belleza. [...] Estoy seguro de que me aceptarás la invitación de que veamos juntos esta tarde *Muerte en Venecia*, de Visconti. La primera vez que la vi sólo me impresionó la forma. La última vez entendí su esencia, su fondo. Lo comentaremos esta noche".
>
> Fuimos a verla otra vez, esa tarde, pero no la comentamos esa noche, quizá porque había algo que yo no quería entender a mis diecisiete años. Creo que sólo un decenio más tarde, después de su muerte, y al escarbar en sus cajones llegué a comprender bien lo que mi papá quería que yo viera cuando me llevó a repetir *Muerte en Venecia*. (OS 265–266)

Whatever, from the narrator's point of view, the "sentido más hondo y más oculto" is, which he was unable to understand as an adolescent – Chapter 37 remains vague

---

[39] Cf. Jurt 2000, pp. 108–109.

[40] "Un político muy importante, Cipriano Restrepo Jaramillo, había dicho en el Club Unión – el más exclusivo de Medellín – que Abad Gómez era el marxista mejor estructurado de la ciudad, y un peligroso izquierdista al que había que cortarle las alas para que no volara. Mi papá se había formado en una escuela pragmática norteamericana (en la Universidad de Minnesota), no había leído nunca a Marx y confundía a Hegel con Engels. Por saber bien de qué lo estaban acusando, resolvió leerlos, y no todo le pareció descabellado: en parte, y poco a poco a lo largo de su vida, se convirtió en algo parecido al luchador izquierdista que lo acusaban de ser" (OS 55).

in its answer and rather follows the figure of paralepsis by announcing, both literally and figuratively, the opening of a drawer, whose contents the readers do not get to see at all in the end – in any case, in the context of *El olvido que seremos* and the social problems it addresses, the emphasis on *Death in Venice* has a dual function.

On the one hand, there is the reference to the topic of homosexuality, which, although the quoted passage refers to Thomas Mann's intention to tone down this dimension in his novella, is nevertheless clearly prominent in the film version in the way Gustav von Aschenbach, embodied by Dirk Bogarde, reacts to the boy, and of course outside fiction in the person of the director Luchino Visconti. In Abad Faciolince's text, it represents one of the fields of social conflict in which the father defends liberal positions against the prevailing repression:[41] when the son turns to the father with the agonizing fear of being homosexual, the father responds with a plea (which, as in other passages, can almost be read as a thesis-like insertion) for the free development of the individual and against dissimulation, which – in contrast to homosexuality itself – represents the real evil (OS 164).

On the other hand, *Death in Venice,* as explicitly emphasized in the passage quoted above from the point of view of both Thomas Mann and Héctor Abad Gómez, represents an aestheticist stance that focuses on the artistic artefact and does not transcend it towards concepts, theses, or ideologies. That this position is not merely a side note to his father's conception of art, which may appear as a curious contradiction or counterweight to his social commitment, but rather a political statement in the context of *El olvido que seremos*, is evident elsewhere in his reading of the Bible, when in conversation with his son he weighs the New and Old Testaments against each other in their *literary* quality.[42] This application of non-religious criteria to the Bible is consequently placed in the immediate context of a broader examination of the crimes committed by the church (OS 90–91) and in the indirect context of the already mentioned *Gran Misión*, the prevailing anti-liberal Catholic rollback in Colombia; it is thus (more subtly) part of the already mentioned

---

[41] "La expresión del afecto entre hombres entraba en el terreno de la cursilería o de la maricada, y sólo estaban permitidas las grandes palmadas y los madrazas, como la mayor muestra cariño" (OS 38); accentuated, this aspect is found in the description of the milieu of the Opus Dei boys' school, officially hostile to sexuality in an almost manic way, but at the same time permeated by the padres' hypocritical homoerotic desire: "Y creo que sus [sc. of padre Mario] mañanas y tardes consistían en el deleite vicario e inconfesable de asistir una tras otra, como en una larga sesión de pornografía oral, a las minuciosas confesiones de nuestra irreprimible sed de sexo. El padre Mario quería siempre detalles, más detalles, con quién y cuántas veces y con cuál de las manos y a qué horas y en dónde, y uno le notaba que esas revelaciones, aunque las condenara de palabra, le atraían de una manera enfermiza, tenaz, y que su insistencia en el interrogatorio lo único que revelaba era su ansia por explorarlas" (OS 97).

[42] "el Nuevo Testamento era mucho menos buen libro que el Antiguo, literariamente hablando" (OS 91).

"antídoto ilustrado", which gives its heading to the third section of the book.[43] That the father's anticlerical position is political is made clear not only by the fact that the cardinal in charge, after the assassination, refuses to offer the victim a funeral mass, thus siding with the murderers, but also by the fact that the narrator interprets this situation as an actualization of the very canonical theme in Western literary history that exemplarily combines religious and political revolt: Antigone.[44]

After this sketchy reading, let us return to our initial question. *El olvido que seremos* is evidently a highly transitive text that cannot be read without reference to the social and political conflicts specific to this Latin-American region, thus to the very knowledge educational curricula for Spanish classes prescribe as obligatory in the interest of intercultural competence. The text not only offers a narrative and individualized or fictionalized treatment of these problems, but also *arises* directly from them insofar as a (personally experienced, but at the same time exemplary) murder is the trigger and reason for its functionalization as a medium of remembrance in the context of *memoria histórica*; even in the parts that are autobiographical in the narrower sense, it remains committed to this perspective, because the author's childhood and youth took place in the context of these social tensions. The analysis has clearly shown, however, that the social and political issues and conflicts here are linked to a variety of canonical literary intertexts that are far more than a simple autobiographical reflection of the privileged educated bourgeois home into which the author was born: In *El olvido que seremos*, literature provides schemata for understanding and categories for judging social and political conflicts in Colombia,[45] facilitates the understanding of others that is central to ethical behavior,[46]

---

[43] An interesting point, which can only be briefly touched upon here, is that the narrator's portrayal of the father in turn postfigures Christian schemata in the sense of a religious counter-text, for example when the father returns and appears to the child as the sole saviour from a cesspool of sin ("el papá que volvía [...] a rescatarme de ese mundo sórdido de rosarios, enfermedades, pecados, faldas y sotanas, de rezos, espíritus, fantasmas y superstición [...] ahí venía mi salvador, mi verdadero Salvador", OS 128), he, in clear allusion to mystical scenarios, illuminates the son with his light in the midst of complete darkness ("yo vivía azotado por un vendaval contradictorio, aunque mi verdadero héroe, secreto y vencedor, era ese nocturno caballero solitario que con paciencia de profesor y amor de padre me lo aclaraba todo con la luz de su inteligencia, al amparo de la oscuridad", OS 88–89) or the son extends the actually binary relationship son-father to the Trinity by signing with "Héctor Abad III" and thus symbolically ascribing to the father – according to his often emphasized spiritual function as a guide – the role also of the Holy Spirit: "Héctor Abad III, porque tú vales por dos" (OS 12) – or "dios", as we would, in a way, not be mistaken to read here.

[44] "El cardenal, con su orden despiadada, parecía pronunciar las palabras con que Creonte quiso dejar insepulto al hermano de Antígona: 'Nunca el enemigo, ni después de muerto, es amigo'. Y mi tío, el hermano de mi papá, parecía decir las palabras de Antígona, la hermana de Polinices: 'No he nacido para compartir odio, sino amor'" (OS 204).

[45] In this context, Teresa García Díaz speaks of literature as a register and of a symbiosis between life and literary imagination: "La literatura comparte junto con la historia su relevancia como registro. [...] Por ello, en la novela hay una simbiosis entre experiencia vital e imaginación" (García Díaz 2013, p. 213).

[46] The narrator formulates this thought explicitly: "La compasión es, en buena medida, una cualidad de la imaginación: consiste en la capacidad de ponerse en el lugar del otro, de imaginarse lo que sentiríamos en caso de estar padeciendo una situación análoga. Siempre me ha parecido que los despiadados carecen de imaginación literaria – esa capacidad que nos dan las grandes novelas de meternos en la piel de otros [...]" (OS 210).

and in this sense constitutes indispensable life knowledge. Without an understanding of the references, even readers with a focus on literary mimesis of social realities will miss central insights and theses of the text and its embedding in a culturally and historically overarching context. I admit that the results of an isolated case study such as the present one cannot be transferred without further ado to readings and learning objectives in general; however, the text studied certainly has a certain informative value simply because of its broad (also international and media) reception and its own incipient canonization.[47] On this basis, the question of whether knowledge about cultural canon can serve intercultural competence will tend to be answered in the affirmative, if we take into account that – as the example examined also shows – a canon that is appropriate in this sense cannot be confined to national boundaries. Philology today, especially in the context of globalization, may no longer be defined by an educated bourgeoisie and its pedagogical priorities, as was still the case in the nineteenth century, but this does not mean that its main field of activity, schools, with the competency goals specified there, would no longer require orientation knowledge in the field of literary history and (transnational) canon and, above all, the ability to relate this to new issues, even if they are, at first glance, beyond the sphere of literature.

References

Abad Faciolince, Héctor: El olvido que seremos. Barcelona: Alfaguara 2017.
Abad Faciolince, Héctor: Brief an einen Schatten (transl. by Sabine Giersberg). Berlin: Berenberg 2009.
Assmann, Jan: Das kulturelle Gedächtnis. Schrift, Erinnerung und politische Identität in frühen Hochkulturen. München: Beck 1992.
Baden-Württemberg, Bildungsplan für Spanisch als dritte Fremdsprache [Profilfach], Stand 2016, Klassen 11/12.
Bayern, Lehrplanauszug aus dem Fachlehrplan für Klasse 12 Spanisch [Gym], Stand 19.09.2020.
Benjamin, Walter: Das Kunstwerk im Zeitalter seiner technischen Reproduzierbarkeit, in: Walter Benjamin, Gesammelte Schriften, vol. I, Werkausgabe Band 2, Rolf Tiedemann & Hermann Schweppenhäuser (Eds.). Frankfurt/Main: Suhrkamp 1980, pp. 471–508.
Berlin, Rahmenlehrplan für den Unterricht in der gymnasialen Oberstufe Spanisch, Stand 01.08.2017.
Bracker, Elisabeth: Fremdsprachliche Literaturdidaktik. Plädoyer für die Realisierung bildender Erfahrungsräume im Unterricht. Wiesbaden: Springer 2015.
Bremen, Bildungsplan für die gymnasiale Oberstufe Spanisch [neu aufgenommene Fremdsprache], Stand 2015.
Ette, Ottmar: Die Aufgabe der Philologie. Berlin: Kadmos 2004 (ÜberLebenswissen, 1).
Ette, Ottmar: ZwischenWeltenSchreiben: Literaturen ohne festen Wohnsitz. Berlin: Kadmos 2005.
Ette, Ottmar: ZusammenLebensWissen: List, Last und Lust literarischer Konvivenz im globalen Maßstab. Berlin: Kadmos 2010.

---

[47] On the reception of *El olvido que seremos*, see González Molina 2014, p. 3 (footnotes 2 and 3).

Ette, Ottmar: Romanistik in Bewegung oder Für eine transareale Literaturwissenschaft, in: Julian Drews et al. (Eds.): Romanistik in Bewegung. Aufgaben und Ziele einer Philologie im Wandel. Berlin: Kadmos 2017, pp. 237–258.

García Díaz, Teresa: Las heridas de la memoria: Héctor Abad Faciolince, in: Visitas al patio, 7, 2013, pp. 203–219.

Gelz, Andreas, Hüser, Dietmar, & Ruß-Sattar, Sabine (Eds.): Skandale zwischen Moderne und Postmoderne. Interdisziplinäre Perspektiven auf Formen gesellschaftlicher Transgression. Berlin: De Gruyter 2014.

González Molina, Óscar Javier: Una poética de la memoria y el olvido en *Traiciones de la memoria* y *El olvido que seremos* de Héctor Abad Faciolince, in: Badebec, 6, 03.2014, pp. 1–21.

Gumbrecht, Hans Ulrich: Diesseits der Hermeneutik. Die Produktion von Präsenz. Frankfurt/Main: Suhrkamp 2010.

Junkerjürgen, Ralf: Neun Todsünden romanistischer Literaturwissenschaft. Ein Erfahrungsbericht, in: HeLix, 11, 2018, pp. 63–81.

Jurt, Joseph: ‚Les intellectuels': ein französisches Modell, in: Sven Hanuschek, Therese Hörnigk, & Christine Malende (Eds.): Schriftsteller als Intellektuelle. Berlin: De Gruyter 2000, pp. 103–134.

Kablitz, Andreas: Der Systemfehler der Geisteswissenschaften, in: Frankfurter Allgemeine Zeitung, 31.12.2014, N4.

Hessen, Kerncurriculum für das Gymnasium – gymnasiale Oberstufe Spanisch, Stand 2011.

Klinkert, Thomas: Epistemologische Fiktionen. Zur Interferenz von Literatur und Wissenschaft seit der Aufklärung. Berlin: De Gruyter 2010.

PädagogInnenbildung Neu: Auf dem Weg zu Professionalisierung und Kompetenzorientierung? [Themenheft], in: Quo vadis Romania? Zeitschrift für eine aktuelle Romanistik, 44, 2014/15.

Pfister, Manfred: Konzepte der Intertextualität, in: Ulrich Broich & Manfred Pfister (Eds.): Intertextualität. Formen, Funktionen, anglistische Fallstudien. Berlin: De Gruyter 1985, pp. 1–30.

Reyes Albarracín, Fredy Leonardo: *El olvido que seremos* y *Mi confesión:* testimonio, memoria e historia, in: Comunicación y Ciudadanía, 4 (julio–diciembre), 2010, pp. 24–30.

Sachsen-Anhalt, Fachlehrplan Gymnasium Spanisch, Stand 01.07.2019.

Schleswig-Holstein, Lehrplan für die Sekundarstufe II Gymnasium Spanisch, Stand 2002.

Vanegas Vásquez, Orfa Kelita: Lecturas del ‚yo escritor' en *El olvido que seremos* y *Traiciones de la memoria*, in: Visitas al patio, 09.2015, pp. 95–105.

"What do you read, my lord?": Purposes and Potential of English Literary Studies

Roland Weidle

Abstract Based on the question of the relationship between "deep reading" and "skim reading", this article explores the question of which techniques, contents and competences can be promoted and taught in the context of a literary studies programme in English. It outlines a number of techniques, contents and competences that students can or should acquire in the course of their studies in literary studies in English. These include the techniques of deep reading and skim reading as well as self-expression in academic exchange. After a brief presentation of the most important "educational contents" (Dehn et al., Lesesozialisation, Literaturunterricht und Leseförderung in der Schule, in: Bodo Franzmann et al. (Ed.): Handbuch Lesen. Baltmannsweiler: Schneider Verlag Hohengehren 2001, pp. 568–637, 2001), five central competences are outlined on the basis of selected examples of English literature (and above all from Shakespeare's plays), which can be fostered and developed in the examination of English literature in the context of an English studies programme.

In her 2018 book *Reader, Come Home: The Reading Brain in a Digital World,* the US neuroscientist Maryanne Wolf refers to recent studies that have shown that a new type of reading has emerged in the course of digitization, "skimming"[1] or

---

[1] Wolf Reader 2018a, p. 76. Wolf refers to the work of Ziming Liu 2006, 2012, Naomi Baron 2015, Andrew Piper 2012, David Ulin 2010, Mangen and Weel 2015, and Mangen and Weel 2016.

"skim reading",[2] translated roughly as "fleeting" or "cursory" reading. This is a procedure in which we first read the first line of a text, then only focus on selected passages, before slowing down again at the end and taking in whole sentences. This all leads to the result that we can faster absorb larger amounts of information and data, however, at a high price: we do not allow ourselves time for the critical examination of the data and thereby neglect the development of some of "our most important intellectual and affective processes",[3] which are promoted by "deep reading", namely: "internalized knowledge, analogical reasoning, and inference; perspective-taking and empathy; critical analysis and the generation of insight".[4] Wolf describes what happens in the brain during reading and identifies the same processes as in science:

> Getting to the truth of things – whether in science, in life, or in text – requires observation, hypotheses, and predictions based on inference and deduction, testing and evaluation, interpretation and conclusion, and when possible, new proof of these conclusions through their replication.[5]

The question "What do you read?", quoted in my title and addressed to Hamlet by the royal advisor Polonius, therefore needs to be extended accordingly: "What and *how* do you read?". However, I do not want to join the ranks of those who lament the "increasing endangerment of reading"[6] that can be found in many places, but rather take Wolf's plea for "deep reading" as an opportunity to raise the question of the contents, tasks and possibilities of literary studies in general, and of English studies in particular, and in doing so to focus on the important "intellectual and affective processes" mentioned by Wolf that can be promoted by reading or studying.

1 Study of English

But let's take a look first at the contents and goals of an English Studies programme as practiced at many German universities, using the English Department at the Ruhr-Universität Bochum as an example. According to the study guide made available online, the English Bachelor's programme at the Ruhr-Universität is intended to

---

[2] Wolf 2018b Skim Reading.
[3] Wolf 2018b Skim Reading.
[4] Wolf 2018b Skim Reading.
[5] Wolf 2018b Reader, p. 58.
[6] "zunehmende[…] Gefährdung des Lesens" (Dehn et al. 2001, p. 569). In recent years, several empirical studies on learning behaviour with digital and analog texts have been published. The majority of them conclude that learning success "in terms of speed of processing, text recall, and reading comprehension" (Singer and Alexander 2017, p. 156) is lower when reading digital texts than print texts due to various factors. See also Mangen et al. 2013, Wallis 2010, Ophir et al. 2009, Levine et al. 2007, Kerr and Symons 2006. For a more detailed review of these studies, see Singer and Alexander 2017.

lead to a scientifically founded insight into the language, literature and culture of Great Britain, the USA and/or, to a limited extent, other English-speaking countries. At the same time, the degree programme should lead to an active command of the contemporary English language, both written and spoken, as well as to the ability to understand varieties of English. At the same time, the course of study is clearly oriented towards professional fields and areas of social application. Taking into account the requirements and changes in the professional world, the programme should provide students with the necessary specialized knowledge, abilities, skills and methods in such a way that enables them to carry out scientific work, to critically classify and transfer scientific findings. The programme also aims to impart interdisciplinary qualifications such as communication skills or argumentation and cooperation skills.[7]

In addition to mastering the language, dealing with the literature and culture of the English-speaking world and a practical orientation towards "areas of social application", students should therefore be enabled to critically classify and transfer scientific findings and be trained in their "communication skills" and "cooperation skills". The standard period of study is six semesters,[8] which are divided into a basic phase (1st year) and an advanced phase (2nd and 3rd year). In the compulsory basic modules, the foundations are laid in the areas of language and text production, literary and cultural studies and linguistics.[9] In the advanced phase, students can focus on these areas within a given framework. Students *must* take at least one module in literary *or* cultural studies[10] and *may* take a maximum of two modules in these areas. While in most cases students are required to write term papers in seminars, exercises and lectures usually conclude with a test (often in *multiple choice*-format) or an examination. The programme is completed with a 30-minute oral examination on two topics as well as the writing of a Bachelor's thesis of approximately thirty pages, unless this is written in the second subject.[11] Students thus take at least one,[12] in the best case seven courses[13] in literary or cultural studies.[14] So how is it possible to teach or develop specific techniques, contents and competences within such a limited framework?

---

[7] Englisches Seminar 2016, p. 2; translation from German: R. W.

[8] Englisches Seminar 2016, p. 3.

[9] These are: in the module "Language and Text Production" the courses "Grammar" and "Academic Skills", in the module "Literature and Cultural Studies" the courses "Introduction to Literary Studies" and "Introduction to Cultural Studies", and in the module "Linguistics" the courses "English Sound and Sound Systems" and "Introduction to Linguistics" (cf. Englisches Seminar 2016, pp. 6–7).

[10] Consisting of a lecture, an exercise ("Übung") and a seminar.

[11] The Bachelor's programme at the Ruhr-Universität is a double degree programme.

[12] The compulsory exercise "Introduction to Literary Studies" in the basic module.

[13] The compulsory introduction to literary studies in the basic module as well as two modules in literary studies, each consisting of three courses in the advanced module.

[14] At English departments at other German universities the situation is comparable due to the Bologna Process initiated at the end of the 1990s.

2 Techniques

The most important technique to be acquired and used in a course of study is that of reading correctly. This refers to a technique that goes beyond the acquisition of written language and the sub-processes of meaning extraction on the word, sentence and text level outlined by Ursula Christmann and Norbert Groeben;[15] rather, it understands reading in the sense of Mechthild Dehn "as an extension of literal practices, as the incipient development of literary competence, and finally as being able to apply that which is read in problem solving."[16] Beyond this, however, proper reading requires a knowledge of what texts one can or must read and how. Since the 1970s, this technique has been subsumed under the skill of "metacognition," which includes not only "knowing what one knows,"[17] but also "controlling and directing cognitive activity".[18] That is, in addition to *deep reading,* it is also necessary to use the technique of *skim reading* in a meaningful way in literary studies, but on the condition that one knows which technique to use with which texts and in which learning situations. The English philosopher, statesman and co-founder of modern empirical science, Sir Francis Bacon (1561–1626), described this ability to apply different reading techniques in his essay "Of Studies" as follows:

> Read not to contradict and confute; nor to believe and take for granted; nor to find talk and discourse; but to weigh and consider. Some books are to be tasted, others to be swallowed, and some few to be chewed and digested; that is, some books are to be read only in parts; others to be read, but not curiously; and some few to be read wholly, and with diligence and attention. Some books also may be read by deputy, and extracts made of them by others […].[19]

In addition to correct reading, 'correct' thinking is also required. Of course, this does not refer to the content, but to the way in which thoughts can be structured. The student can already learn this in the first English rhetoric, Thomas Wilson's *Arte of Rhetorique* (1553), which follows the classical five stages of *inventio, dispositio, elocutio, memoria* and *actio* in describing the elaboration and presentation of a lecture. Students can try this out for themselves in course presentations and in seminar discussions, but also in oral and written examinations.

Another fundamental set of techniques in this context concerns self-presentation as a participant in scientific exchange. This applies not only to structural elements of a presentation or paper, but also to aspects such as voice projection, intonation, posture, gestures and facial expressions, as well as communication in general. For example, Hamlet's advice to the actors "Nor do not saw the air too much with your

---

[15] Christmann and Groeben 2001, p. 148.

[16] „als Erweiterung literaler Praktiken, als beginnende Entfaltung literarischer Kompetenz und schließlich für das ‚Erlesen'des Geschriebenen als Problemlösen"(Dehn et al. 2001, p. 572).

[17] "Wissen über das eigene Wissen" (Christmann and Groeben 2001, p. 199).

[18] "die Kontrolle und Steuerung der kognitiven Aktivität"(Christmann and Groeben 2001, p. 199).

[19] Bacon 2008b, p. 439.

hand, thus, but use all gently"[20] can be integrated into teaching through appropriate exercises.

Finally, the core business of literary work should be pointed out: the analysis and interpretation of texts. Theories and methods of text analysis and interpretation as tools of literary studies need to be taught and practiced as of the very first course.

3 Contents

In addition to these basic techniques, which the student can acquire within the framework of a course in literary studies, I consider the teaching of essential "educational content"[21] necessary within the limited framework of a Bachelor's course in English studies.

Although the notion of a canon has become problematic in recent decades, a rudimentary knowledge of central epochs, genres and discourses is indispensable in literary studies. The study of English literature should give students the opportunity to gain an overview of the literary and cultural history of the English or Anglophone world and to develop a historical awareness of the historicity of literature. Although this is only possible to a limited extent within the framework of the Bachelor's programme, courses such as lectures can provide an initial overview of the most important epochs, while seminars and exercises can focus and enlarge on specific topics. The latter teaching formats can offer initial 'islands of knowledge' to awaken an interest in students to discover further 'islands' and to establish connections between them.

Starting from this, the next step is to broaden the perspective to the European context. Looking beyond the boundaries of a national literature can sharpen the view for common roots, similarities but also differences. The study of English literature thus contributes to the development of an awareness of European cultural history. For many of the central cultural and literary events and developments can only be understood in a wider European context, such as the export of sonnet culture from Italy, the rise of commercial theatre in the late sixteenth century, Henry VIII's break with Rome, and the emergence of a middle-class consciousness in sixteenth-century England.

Ultimately, the aim is to raise awareness of the literariness and poeticity of English literature. Students should be given the opportunity to examine the characteristics, the role but also the various functions ascribed to literature in English and British cultures. Thus, early modern English drama had a different status and different functions than the sentimental plays of the eighteenth century, and the poems of Wordsworth and Coleridge need to be understood as deliberate counter-designs to

---

[20] Shakespeare 1997.
[21] I follow Dehn et al. 2001 here in distinguishing between techniques and "text indexing skills" ("Texterschließungskompetenz[en]", p. 599) on the one hand and "educational content" ("Bildungsinhalt", ibid.) on the other.

the classicist poetics of Alexander Pope and John Dryden and their underlying conception of society.

4 Competences

Through the knowledge and techniques acquired, students are able to develop competences that go beyond the interests of a purely English literary studies perspective. These are cultural, hermeneutic, epistemological but also ethical competences, which can be summarized in the broadest sense as skills of 'understanding the world'.[22] Some of these competences will be briefly outlined below, using the example of the academic study of Shakespeare. In doing so, the competences are deliberately reduced to somewhat simplified and even bold terms in order to draw attention to their central functions.

4.1 Decoding

The world is a system of signs, a text to be deciphered. This applies not only to literature, but also to the understanding of actions and people in everday life. In order to decipher the contexts of meaning in the real world, certain interpretive skills and the ability to identify relevant signals in the first place are required. How can I correctly interpret the behaviour of people, correctly decode the signals received and participate in successful communication?

The success and failure of human interaction occupies a central position in Shakespeare's plays. Unlike in ancient drama, the characters do not fail because they try to evade their predestined future, but because they cannot read or interpret the world (and, moreover, themselves) correctly. This becomes particularly evident in the historical dramas, which focus on weak ruler figures such as Henry VI and Richard II, who exhibit considerable deficiencies both in interpreting and staging the world and themselves.[23] In these plays Shakespeare ensures that the audience always has an edge of knowledge and can thus compare the perspectives of characters with varying degrees of interpretive knowledge with their own knowledge. For Bertrand Evans, this "superior awareness"[24] is *the* formative feature of Shakespeare's

---

[22] Cf. the objectives of literature teaching listed by Dehn et al. 2001, among which the authors include the promotion of the "joy of reading" ("Freude am Lesen", 598) and of "imagination and creativity" ("Imagination und Kreativität, 599) as well as the teaching of "literary education" ("literarische[...] Bildung", ibid.) and of "text comprehension skills" ("Texterschließungskompetenz", 598), and also the ability to deal "with one's own person" ("mit der eigenen Person", 600) and "basic anthropological questions" ("anthropologischen Grundfragen", ibid.).

[23] For Henry VI, see Weidle 2002, pp. 201–206; for Richard II, see Weidle 2002, pp. 230–38.

[24] Evans 1960, passim, especially pp. vii–xi.

dramas. In Shakespeare, then, the spectators always adopt a double perspective in which they grasp everything "with parted eye",[25] that is, the events are perceived simultaneously from different points of view.[26] Thus, in engaging with Shakespeare and adopting this dual perspective, students sharpen their own interpretive skills, as these differences between characters must be deciphered through careful analysis and interpretation. Shakespeare's dramas thus serve a similar function to novels, about which Patrica Waugh writes:

> Novels provide training too in practical reasoning skills; in thinking beyond linear models of causality that reduce human and social processes to mechanical systems or discrete causes. That the real world is complex, messy and interconnected, self-interpreting and indeterminate; that it is always more than the sum of its parts, renders any single or linear model of causality grossly inadequate as the vehicle for explaining its emergent behaviours. [...] at the level of negotiating a storyline, novels offer a 'workout' for both linear and more complex kinds of thinking, requiring the exercise of hypothesis revision, inference, abduction, close observation, pattern recognition and the 'looping' effect of language and values.[27]

4.2 Perspective Taking

In her analysis of the 'therapeutic'[28] functions of the novel, Waugh also attributes to this genre the quality of "perspective taking",[29] a quality Martha C. Nussbaum describes as follows:

> Why novels and not histories or biographies? My central subject is the ability to imagine what it is like to live the life of another person who might, given changes in circumstance, be oneself or one of one's loved ones. [...] Literature focuses on the possible, inviting its readers to wonder about themselves. Aristotle is correct. Unlike most historical works, literary works typically invite their readers to put themselves in the place of people of many different kinds and to take on their experiences. In their very mode of address to their imagined reader, they convey the sense that there are links of possibility, at least on a very general level, between the characters and the reader.[30]

The competence of decoding to be acquired through the reading and analysis of literature therefore goes hand in hand with, or rather requires, the willingness to engage with other voices and to be able to adopt other perspectives, skills that are

---

[25] *A Midsummer Night's Dream* IV.1.186.

[26] The above quotation from *A Midsummer Night's Dream* reads in full: "Methinks I see these things with parted eye, / When everything seems *double*." (IV.1.186–87; emphasis R. W.).

[27] Waugh 2015, p. 43. Unlike Waugh, who attributes this 'workout' function exclusively to fictional narrative literature, I see precisely in the "multimedial nature of dramatic text presentation" (Pfister 1993, p. 7) and the physical mode of presentation a special suitability of theatre to train the ability of "close observation".

[28] Cf. the title of the cited article, "The Novel as Therapy."

[29] Waugh 2015, p. 44.

[30] Nussbaum 1995, p. 5.

indispensable in responsible social interaction. An example from the tragedy *King Lear* will illustrate this.

In a scene at the beginning of the drama (I.2), the old Duke of Gloucester first appears and attributes the alleged misconduct of his son Edgar to the recent solar and lunar eclipses: "These late eclipses in the sun and moon portend no good to us. [...] Love cools, friendship falls off, brothers divide; in cities, mutinies; in countries, discord; in palaces, treason; and the bond cracked 'twixt son and father."[31] He thus gives expression to the medieval belief in a geocentric universe, characterized by correspondence relations between microcosm and macrocosm. This Ptolemaic cosmology is also known as the "Elizabethan world view".[32]

As soon as Gloucester steps off the stage, however, the bastard son Edmund, who has previously slandered Edgar to his father, calls this belief nonsensical:

> This is the excellent foppery of the world, that, when we are sick in fortune, often the surfeit of our own behavior, we make guilty of our disasters the sun, the moon, and the stars; as if we were villains by necessity; fools by heavenly compulsion; knaves, thieves, and treachers, by spherical predominance [...].[33]

Here, then, students are confronted in immediate succession with two opposing world views, which they must relate to the cultural context of the early modern period as a threshold period, to their own knowledge, but also to the speakers' perspectives. On the one hand, being placed in the literary tradition of the vice figure, Edmund is clearly set up as the play's villain, but on the other hand, Edmund is also the mouthpiece of a philosophy that seems to most of us today a good deal more reasonable than that of his father. This dialogical structure requires from the students the willingness, but also the ability, to adopt other perspectives and to critically engage with them.

4.3 Questioning

Decoding and adopting other or multiple perspectives enable and encourage students to question assumptions, statements, and expectations, both about the world and about themselves. Again, what Waugh says for novels applies to literature in general, and Shakespeare's dramas in particular:

> In reading fiction, through the entanglement with recognitions, identifications, challenges to our confirmation biases, we arrive at ourselves expanded through an encounter with the new and strange. We are made to review and therefore become more acquainted with our own expectations and wider assumptions, our own interpretative stance.[34]

---

[31] *King Lear* I.2.96–101.
[32] Cf. Tillyard 1988.
[33] *King Lear* I.2.109–14.
[34] Waugh 2015, p. 37.

The critical and sceptical attitude to be developed applies not only to attitudes and assumptions concerning one's own person, but also to the available sources of information in general. Especially in today's digital age, in which there is an overabundance of easily accessible information, it is important to critically question its content and origin and to correlate statements and their content with speaker instances and pragmatic contexts. In Shakespeare criticism, this aspect plays an important role whenever attempts are made to extract Shakespeare's view from the various character perspectives.[35] Ulysses' famous ordo-speech in *Troilus and Cressida*, for example, is often understood as Shakespeare's commitment to the Elizabethan worldview already mentioned. In the speech, the Greek commander attributes the lack of success over the Trojans to the absence in his own camp of that order which constitutes and holds together the universe as a whole. "[N]eglection of degree" and "envious fever" between superiors and subordinates have led to "pale and bloodless emulation."[36] Taken in isolation, this is indeed an affirmation of Ptolemaic cosmology based on hierarchies and correspondences, however, as the drama progresses, it is Ulysses himself who actively promotes this rivalry within his camp (particularly among Achilles and Ajax) in order to achieve his goals and who thus acts contrary to his own beliefs. Ulysses' statement can thus, after careful analysis, be identified as only lip service, as a narrative that does not reflect Shakespeare's opinion, but serves primarily to characterize the Greek military leader as a manipulative strategist.

4.4 Disenchanting

In a next step, questioning can be followed by rationalization and disenchantment in the sense of Max Weber. In his famous lecture "Science as a Profession", Weber named as the most important characteristic of the process of intellectualization the knowledge and the belief "that in principle there are no mysterious incalculable powers [...] that one can rather *control* all things – in principle – by *calculation*. But that means: the disenchantment of the world".[37] Students should therefore learn to trust in the power of their intellect and in a rational approach to the phenomena of the world in order to deconstruct, and thereby to resist hegemonic metanarratives.

---

[35] Ekbert Faas (1986, p. xiii) warns in this context: "Needless to say, no dramatis persona, not even the speaker of the Sonnets, should be identified with Shakespeare." Cf. also Weidle 2013, pp. 261–64.

[36] *Troilus and Cressida* I.3.127, 133, 134. René Girard sees in this "mimetic desire" (Girard 2004, passim) a basic dramaturgical principle of Shakespeare.

[37] Weber 1994, p. 9.

4.5 Enduring

The acquisition of the aforementioned competences of decoding, perspective taking, questioning and disenchanting entails breaking with familiar patterns and ideas, as well as contradictions and uncertainties that must be endured and accepted. The desire for clear answers, simple solutions, ultimate certainty and closure can thereby rarely be satisfied. Shakespeare's plays exemplify this openness. Even in his comedies, long referred to as "happy comedies,"[38] Shakespeare raises questions and doubts, often as part of the supposed "happy ending,"[39] that irritate and disturb: What future, for example, are couples like Demetrius and Helena in *A Midsummer Night's Dream* and Benedict and Beatrice in *Much Ado About Nothing* faced with? Only by means of a magic juice can Demetrius be made to fall in love with the formerly despised Helena. Beatrice and Benedict are paired off against their will, even though the former insists that she does not love Benedict at all.[40] Shakespeare's dramas resist unequivocal classifications and readings, we constantly oscillate between different perspectives, and conflicts are only temporarily resolved.[41] In most cases, as in our own lives, we are denied simple solutions and answers to complex questions.

4.6 Empathizing

The last competence to be mentioned results primarily from perspective taking and is perhaps the most important skill to train: the ability to empathize. The English philosopher Adam Smith defined empathy (still called *sympathy* in the eighteenth century) as follows:

> By the imagination we place ourselves in his ["our brother's"] situation, we conceive ourselves enduring all the same torments, we enter as it were into his body, and become in

---

[38] Cf. Wilson 1962.

[39] All comedies end with at least one wedding: two in *Much Ado About Nothing* and *Twelfth Night*, three in *A Midsummer Night's Dream,* and as many as four in *As You Like It* and *Measure for Measure*. *Love's Labour's Lost* is the only exception, as here four marriages are merely promised after the passing of a year.

[40] "Ben.: Do not you love me? / Beatr.: Why no, no more than reason." (*Much Ado About Nothing* V.4.73–74); "Ben.: Then you do not love me? / Beatr.: No, truly, but in friendly recompense." (V.4.82–83).

[41] Especially the so-called problem plays *All's Well that Ends Well, Troilus and Cressida* and *Measure for Measure* are characterized by ambiguous moral value systems. Cf. also those characters in the comedies who end up humiliated or excluded from society or who voluntarily separate themselves from society, such as Malvolio in *Twelfth Night,* Falstaff in *The Merry Wives of Windsor,* Don John in *Much Ado About Nothing* and Jaques in *As You Like It.*

some measure the same person with him, and thence form some idea of his sensations, and even feel something which, though weaker in degree, is not altogether unlike them.[42]

For Smith, *sympathy,* the ability (and desire) to empathize with others, is the basic building block of ethical action and, above all, an active process that requires the use of imagination. The reading and study of literary texts require, activate, and train the use of imagination and thus provide students with an opportunity to rehearse the interactional process of empathy in their engagement with fictional worlds. Again, what is true for novels can also be applied to literary texts in general:

> Novels [...] in general construct and speak to an implicit reader who shares with the characters certain hopes, fears, and general human concerns, and who for that reason is able to form bonds of identification and sympathy with them, but who is also situated elsewhere and needs to be informed about the concrete situation of the characters. [...] This play back and forth between the general and the concrete is, I claim, built into the very structure of the genre, in its mode of address to its readers. In this way, the novel constructs a paradigm of a style of ethical reasoning that is context-specific without being relativistic, in which we get potentially universalizable conrete prescriptions by bringing a general idea of human flourishing to bear on a concrete situation, which we are invited to enter through the imagination.[43]

For Maryanne Wolf, quoted at the beginning of this article, this ability to take on the perspective and feelings of another is thus not only trained when reading novels, but is also "one of the most profound, insufficiently heralded contributions of the deep-reading processes".[44] The act of *deep reading,* according to Wolf, is

> a special place in which human beings are freed from themselves to pass over to others and, in so doing, learn what it means to be another person with aspirations, doubts, and emotions that they might otherwise never have known.[45]

Deep, close reading, especially of fictional literature, thus constitutes a kind of "moral laboratory"[46] in which the reader's brain is encouraged to actively simulate the consciousness of other (even if only fictional) characters, including those characters with whom one would not normally establish a relationship. Reading fictional stories thus allows the reader to experience "what it truly means to be another person".[47]

If, in the course of their literary studies, students are encouraged and trained to deal with stories and fictional lives, then this is also a form of ethical instruction, in the course of which moral responsibility and the formation of a "fellow-feeling"[48]

---

[42] Smith 1976, I.i.1, p. 9. Cf. also: "His agonies, when they are thus brought home to ourselves, when we have thus adopted and made them our own, begin at last to affect us, and we then tremble and shudder at the thought of what he feels" (ibid.).
[43] Nussbaum 1995, pp. 7–8.
[44] Wolf 2018a Reader, p. 42.
[45] Wolf 2018a Reader, p. 43.
[46] Cf. the title of Hakemulder 2000.
[47] Wolf 2018a Reader, pp. 52–53.
[48] Smith 1976, I.1.1, p. 10.

can be tested and promoted by adopting other perspectives.[49] This would then also honour Bacon's understanding of a science that serves the "advantage and benefit of mankind".[50]

References

Alexander, Patricia A. and Lauren M. Singer: Reading Across Mediums. Effects of Reading Digital and Print Texts on Comprehension and Calibration, in: The Journal of Experimental Education 85.1, 2017, pp. 155–72.

Bacon, Francis: The Advancement of Learning (1605), in: Brian Vickers (Ed.): The Major Works including New Atlantis and the Essays. Oxford: Oxford UP 2008a, pp. 120–299.

Bacon, Francis: The Essays or Counsels Civil and Moral (1625), in: Brian Vickers (Ed.): The Major Works including New Atlantis and the Essays. Oxford: Oxford UP 2008b, pp. 341–456.

Baron, Naomi S.: Words Onscreen. The Fate of Reading in a Digital World. Oxford: Oxford UP 2015.

Christmann, Ursula und Norbert Groeben: Psychologie des Lesens, in: Bodo Franzmann et al. (Ed.): Handbuch Lesen. Baltmannsweiler: Schneider Verlag Hohengehren 2001, pp. 145–223.

Dehn, Mechthild et al.: Lesesozialisation, Literaturunterricht und Leseförderung in der Schule, in: Bodo Franzmann et al. (Ed.): Handbuch Lesen. Baltmannsweiler: Schneider Verlag Hohengehren 2001, pp. 568–637.

Englisches Seminar der Ruhr-Universitaet Bochum: Informationen zum B.A.-Studiengang Anglistik/Amerikanistik. Bochum: RUB 01.10.2016, http://www.es.rub.de/studyguides.html, accessed 20.02.2020.

Evans, Bertrand: Shakespeare's Comedies. Oxford: Oxford UP 1960.

Faas, Ekbert: Shakespeare's Poetics. Cambridge: Cambridge UP 1986.

Girard, René: A Theatre of Envy. South Bend, Indiana: St. Augustine's Press 2004.

Hakemulder, Frank: The Moral Laboratory. Experiments Examining the Effects of Reading Literature on Social Perception and Moral Self-Concept. Amsterdam: John Benjamins Publishing Company 2000.

Kerr, Matthew A. and Sonya E. Symons: Computerized Presentation of Texts. Effects on Children's Reading of Informational Material, in: Reading and Writing 19.1, 2006, pp. 1–19.

Konrath, Sara H. et al.: Changes in Dispositional Empathy in American College Students over Time. A Meta-Analysis, in: Personality and Social Psychology Review, 15.2, Mai 2011, pp. 180–98.

Levine, Laura E. et al: Electronic Media Use, Reading, and Academic Distractibility in College Youth, in: CyberPsychology & Behaviour 10.4, 2007, pp. 560–66.

Liu, Ziming: Digital Reading, in: Chinese Journal of Library and Information Science 5.1, 2012, pp. 85–94.

Liu, Ziming: Reading Behaviour in the Digital Environment. Changes in Reading Behaviour over the Past Ten Years, in: Journal of Documentation 61.6, 2006, pp. 700–12.

Mangen, Anne, and Adriaan van der Weel: The Evolution of Reading in the Age of Digitisation. An Integrative Framework for Reading Research, in: Literacy 50.3, September 2016, pp. 116–24.

---

[49] That this is necessary is shown by studies on declining empathy among young people over the last twenty years. Cf. Konrath et al. 2011 and Wolf 2018a Reader, p. 50.

[50] For Bacon, "the last or furthest end of knowledge […] is to give a true account of their [men's] gift of reason, to the benefit and the use of men" (Bacon 2008a Advancement, p. 147).

Mangen, Anne, and Adriaan van der Weel: Why Don't We Read Hypertext Novels?, in: Convergence. The International Journal of Research into New Media Technologies 23.2, May 2015, pp. 166–81.
Mangen, Anne et al.: Reading Linear Texts on Paper Versus Computer Screen. Effects on Reading Comprehension, in: International Journal of Educational Research 58, 2013, pp. 61–68.
Nussbaum, Martha: Poetic Justice. The Literary Imagination and Public Life. Boston: Beacon Press, 1995.
Ophir, Eyal et al.: Cognitive Control in Media Multitaskers, in: Proceedings of the National Academy of Sciences 106.37, 2009, pp. 15583–87.
Piper, Andrew: Books Was There. Reading in Electronic Times. Chicago: University of Chicago Press 2012.
Pfister, Manfred: The Theory and Analysis of Drama. Cambridge: Cambridge UP 1993.
Shakespeare, William: The Norton Shakespeare. Based on the Oxford Edition. Ed. by Stephen Greenblatt et al., New York: Norton 1997.
Smith, Adam: The Theory of Moral Sentiments. 1759. Ed. by D. D. Raphael and A. L. Macfie, Indianapolis: Liberty Fund 1976.
Tillyard, Eustace Mandeville Wetenhall: The Elizabethan World Picture. 1943. London: Penguin 1988.
Ulin, David L.: The Lost Art of Reading. Why Books Matter in a Distracted Time. Seattle, WA: Sasquatch Books 2010.
Wallis, Claudia.: The Impacts of Media Multitasking on Children's Learning and Development. Report from a Research Seminar. New York: Joan Ganz Cooney Center at Sesame Workshop 2010.
Waugh, Patricia: The Novel as Therapy. Ministrations of Voice in an Age of Risk, in: Journal of the British Academy 3, 2015, pp. 35–68.
Weber, Max: Wissenschaft als Beruf 1917/19, in: Wolfgang J. Mommsen and Wolfgang Schluchter (Ed.): Studienausgabe der Max Weber-Gesamtausgabe, vol. I/17. Tübingen: J. C. B. Mohr 1994, pp. 1–23.
Weidle, Roland: Shakespeares dramaturgische Perspektive. Die theatrale Grammatik Erving Goffmans als Modell strategischer Interaktion in den Komödien und Historien. Heidelberg: Winter 2002.
Weidle, Roland: Zur Rekonstruktion von ‚Shakespeares' immanenter theatraler Poetik. Probleme und Auswege – aufgezeigt an *Hamlet,* in: Valeska von Rosen et al. (Ed.): Poiesis. Praktiken der Kreativität in den Künsten der Frühen Neuzeit. Zürich: diaphanes 2013, pp. 257–71.
Wilson, John Dover: Shakespeare's Happy Comedies. London: Faber & Faber 1962.
Wolf, Maryanne: Reader, Come Home. The Reading Brain in a Digital World. New York: HarperCollins 2018a.
Profound, in: The Guardian, 25. August 2018b, https://www.theguardian.com/commentisfree/2018/aug/25/skim-reading-new-normal-maryanne-wolf, accessed 20.02.2020.

Systems Theory Reflections on the Relationship Between Literature and Society: With a Case Study on Elio Vittorini

Thomas Klinkert

Abstract This article centers on an analysis of Elio Vittorini's novel *Le donne di Messina* (1949, 1964). The novel recounts a new beginning in a country destroyed by fascism and war. The story of an abandoned village that is repopulated and restored by strangers initially appears as a utopia of a society without private property. But this utopia proves fragile as, on the one hand, the former proprietors reclaim ownership and, on the other, a former fascist lives among the villagers. In addition to the story and its ideological significance, Vittorini also showcases the narrative process, resulting in reflexive refractions, ambivalences and uncertainties. The present textual analysis is framed by system-theoretical considerations on the connections between literature and society. In particular, it addresses Luhmann's concept of symbolically generalized communication media and interprets fictionality as such a medium. Systems theory is employed heuristically to gain a perspective on Vittorini's novel and the tensions and contradictions manifest in it between utopia and reality, between literary autonomy and political engagement. Finally, against this background, some theses on the place of literary studies in the present are developed and put forth.

1 Introduction

The aim of this article is twofold. First, following Niklas Luhmann, some fundamental considerations are made about the connections between literature and society. Society is described in systems theory as being based on communication. In this context, a central function is performed by symbolically generalized

T. Klinkert (✉)
Romanisches Seminar, Universität Zürich, Zürich, Switzerland
e-mail: thomas.klinkert@uzh.ch

communication media, which increase the probability of success of writing-based communication, in particular. Inspired by but going beyond Luhmann, I advance the thesis that, like money, love, power and truth, fictionality also can be regarded as a symbolically generalized medium of communication. This delineates the status of literature (or poetry) as a system already becoming differentiated from philosophy and historiography in antiquity. Furthermore, it is shown that, in the context of the functionally differentiated society emerging in modernity, the criterion of literary autonomy comes into conflict with the writer's claim to political or moral commitment. This conflict is then examined with reference to the Italian author Elio Vittorini. His novel *Le donne di Messina* is, on the one hand, a text that narrates the origin and genesis of society, in the form of a thought experiment, and reflects the constitutive role of narration in the process of society's formation. On the other hand, it is an example of the strong divergence between political partisanship and formal literary experimentation. The idealistic-utopian dimension of the re-emergence of a society after the destruction caused by war and fascism is not merely subverted at the level of plot, for instance by representatives of the old order reasserting their claims to ownership. Also and above all, it is reflexively refracted at the level of narrative mediation, and its mimetic truth called into question. By making the narrative process itself the object of narration, Vittorini reveals the limits of what can be objectively mediated and known. At the same time, he shows that the emergence of society and narrative (fluctuating between factuality and fiction) are inextricably linked. The case study of Vittorini is followed by a brief concluding reflection on the current status of literary studies.

2 Systems Theory: Society as Communication

Social systems are founded by means of communication. From a systems theory perspective, communication is the operation "that performs the autopoiesis of the system and thus demarcates a system from its environment."[1] Autopoiesis means that a system produces itself the operations necessary for its functioning. "The system produces itself. Not only does it produce its own structures, just as certain computers can develop programs for themselves, but it is also autonomous at the level of operations."[2] Communication does rely on the participation of mental systems, it would not even be possible without them, but it is a genuinely social operation because (a) it cannot be attributed to any single mental system alone, but is an interaction between at least two systems, a 'sender' and a 'receiver,' and because (b) it is impossible for the mental systems involved to know each other's state from

---

[1] Luhmann 1998, vol. I, p. 81.
[2] Luhmann 2003, p. 110. – For an application of the autopoiesis concept in literary studies, see Klinkert 2011.

within. Mental states can only be attributed to the other in the form of "operational fictions"[3] and participate in the social activity of communication to that extent.

Communication as the "smallest possible unit of a social system"[4] consists of three components: information, utterance and understanding.[5] It enables subsequent communicative acts. In other words, communication arises from and is always embedded in communication, it is "autopoietic insofar as it can only be generated in a recursive connection with other communications, i.e. only in a network in the reproduction of which each individual communication itself participates".[6] A communication is completed by understanding; indeed, a successful act of communication can only be said to exist once understanding has taken place: "Only understanding retroactively generates communication."[7] Communication is time-bound and situation-bound: This applies to the act of utterance as well as to the act of understanding and the related act of information acquisition. If one understands information to be a "surprising selection from amongst several possibilities,"[8] then this presupposes a comparison with expectations that can only be described and understood in the respective situational context and depending on the participants involved. Therefore, communication cannot simply be conceived of as a mechanical transmission, information "cannot be gained purely passively as a logical consequence of signals received from the environment".[9] Rather, it presupposes the active participation of the receiver, his interests, his expectations, which guide him in the selection of information.

In view of this, successful communication is a highly contingent and thus improbable event. For, even if – which is by no means self-evident – the recipient of a communication understands it and selects the relevant information, (s)he is in principle free to accept or reject the proposal of meaning or communication associated with the communication. Social systems thus require means for their functioning that reduce the improbability of successful communication. Luhmann speaks, in this context, of symbolically generalized communication media. Their function is to "make the acceptance of a communication expectable in cases where rejection is probable."[10] These communication media are *symbolic* in that they are self-reflexive and co-signify their own sign function, that is, they highlight the unity of the signifier and signified. "Symbolization thus expresses – thereby permitting it to be treated in communication – that in the difference [between the signifier and signified] there lies a unity and that what is separated belongs together, so that the signifier can be

---

[3] Luhmann 1998, vol. I, p. 82.
[4] Luhmann 1998, vol. I, p. 82.
[5] Luhmann 1998, vol. I, p. 72.
[6] Luhmann 1998, vol. I, p. 82 f.
[7] Luhmann 1998, vol. I, p. 72.
[8] Luhmann 1998, vol. I, p. 71.
[9] Luhmann 1998, vol. I, p. 71.
[10] Luhmann 1998, vol. I, p. 316.

used to stand for the signified (and not only: to indicate the signified) [...]."[11] In this sense, to take an example from the functional system of the economy, money acts as a stand-in for prices and goods, and does so independently of its material value; money is a symbolic medium of communication that bridges the difference between the signifier (coin, note, bank statement) and the signified (value, price) through the unity it symbolizes, thereby making the acceptance of improbable communications (exchange of goods) probable. *Generalized,* these media must be because they must be appropriate for different situations. With money one can buy not only food, but also vehicles, household appliances, medical treatment or works of art, in short: all kinds of goods or services.

Further symbolically generalized communication media discussed by Luhmann are truth, power and love. The medium of truth is particularly important in the present context. Luhmann understands it not as a characteristic of statements in their relation to extra-linguistic reality, but as "a medium of emergence of improbable communication".[12] Luhmann situates the origin of truth as a symbolically generalized medium of communication in connection with the emergence of the Greek alphabetic script in antiquity, based on media-historical studies by Eric A. Havelock, Jack Goody and Ian Watt.[13] A problem following from the generalization of written communication that emerged at that time is the separation of the act of utterance from the act of reception, and the consequent growing improbability of communication success. The binary opposition true vs. false as a schematism to be applied in written communication – Luhmann speaks of binary coding – reduces the number of possible reactions to a text to exactly two, which constitutes a simplification and thus increases the probability of communication succeeding.

Around the same time, as Wolfgang Rösler has shown, an awareness of fictionality emerged in ancient Greece.[14] As Rösler demonstrates, this phenomenon also arises as a consequence of the invention of alphabetic writing. In terms of media history, it can be said that the general dissemination of writing results, on the one hand, in an accumulation of knowledge and, on the other, in the perception of differences between the present and the past, and thus in the emergence of an awareness of historical change. In the process, a gradual differentiation of the fields of philosophy, historiography and poetry occurs. While philosophy and historiography are subject to a coding of true/false, poetry holds a special status, insofar as it is conceded to be exempt from this binary coding: this is a manifestation of the awareness of fictionality.

Inspired by Luhmann, I would like to describe fiction – complementary to truth – as a symbolically generalized medium of communication.[15] Fiction is characterized by the fact that the opposition true vs. false is bracketed, i.e. that an uncertainty

---

[11] Luhmann 1998, vol. I, p. 319.

[12] Luhmann 1992, p. 173.

[13] Cf. Havelock 1963, Goody/Watt 1968.

[14] Rösler 1980.

[15] For a more detailed explanation of this connection, I refer to Klinkert 2010, pp. 21–38.

arises as to whether this opposition is valid or not. This uncertainty stems from the complex interplay between the situation of utterance *(énonciation)* and the uttered *(énoncé)*; at the level of the *énoncé,* the opposition retains its validity, but in the relationship between *énonciation* and *énoncé,* it is suspended. The narrator of a novel or the speaker of a poem does not have to provide evidence for the statements (s)he makes; (s)he is allowed to relate invented content as though it were true, without being held liable for 'false statements,' that is, without being guilty of lying. While the discourses of philosophy and historiography are binary coded according to the opposition true/false, poetic discourse is subject to this coding and yet simultaneously suspends it. It *can* therefore contain statements of truth, but *does not have to,* and through this double coding becomes free for a different way of dealing with the matters of the world.

This entails consequences for the relationship between literature and society. Literature as a socially institutionalized field of fiction can represent social conditions mimetically or realistically, i.e. in a way that makes them appear reality-conforming.[16] This means that the same laws apply in a literary world that also exist in the reality we are familiar with (and not, for example, that, as in Dante's *Commedia,* a living person may enter the realm of the dead, or that, as in the Grimm Brothers' *Children's and Household Tales,* animals can speak), that principles such as causality, probability, necessity are respected, and so on. The mimetic dimension can manifest in various ways: abstractly, through the representation of social values and norms (marriage rules, virtues, moral principles such as honor, bravery, loyalty, etc.), or concretely, in the representation of characters and the relationships that exist between them (partnership, family, community, institutions, etc.), as well as in spatial and temporal conditions that form the background (geographical location, socio-cultural conditions, lifeworld, etc.). However, the functioning of the mimetic illusion is based on a habit of overlooking whose mode of operation can be easily understood if one thinks of the significance of the camera in the feature film.

---

[16] This is not the place to enter into a detailed discussion of the concept of realism. A few basic remarks must therefore suffice. One can distinguish two basic meanings in literary studies usage. On the one hand, *realism* is used as a transhistorical stylistic term. A representation is close to reality or conforms to reality, it refrains from stylization and exaggeration – the work is termed realistic. On the other hand, *realism* is used to denote the nineteenth century novel by such authors as Balzac, Stendhal, Flaubert, Maupassant, Zola, Manzoni, Verga, Dickens, George Eliot, Dostoevsky, Tolstoy, Stifter, Fontane etc. In this sense, realism is used as a period term, so it is actually inconsistent with the transhistorical stylistic concept. Erich Auerbach attempted to reconcile the two meanings of the term *realism*. According to him, the realist novel of the nineteenth century can be described as a departure from the classicist doctrine of stylistic levels: "By making random persons of everyday life, in their dependence on contemporary circumstances, the subjects of serious, problematic, even tragic representation, Stendhal and Balzac broke the classical rule of the distinction of stylistic levels, according to which the everyday and the practically real were allowed a place in literature only within the framework of a low or middle style, that is, either as grotesquely comic or as pleasant, light, colorful and elegant entertainment. They thus completed a development that had been in preparation for a long time [...] – and they paved the way for modern realism, which has since unfolded in ever richer forms, in keeping with the continuously changing and expanding reality of our life." (Auerbach 1982 [1946], p. 515).

As a spectator in the cinema, of course one knows in principle that the images projected onto the screen were taken by a camera and hence do not depict reality, but are part of a staging, a simulation of reality. And yet, one tends to forget this knowledge, at least temporarily, since the camera itself cannot normally be seen. Just as the camera can show us people and things in situations in which no observer is normally present (such as in love scenes or when someone is alone at home – or, to give a less banal example, in the case of a parallel montage, which shows two spatially separate but simultaneous actions, which could not possibly be seen simultaneously by one and the same observer in the lifeworld), a novel will, for instance, gloss over the fact that the protagonist's thoughts, emotions, and motivations can only be communicated because the narrator does not have to account for how (s)he acquired the knowledge in question. Ultimately based on invention, the narrator's omniscience with regard to what (s)he narrates is an indicator of fictionality.[17] The fact that, as the reader of a novel, one can become an observer of the normally unobservable is thus due to the fictionality of literary discourse. If, according to Luhmann, art is the visualization of the unobservable,[18] then it is based in a very fundamental way on fictionality.[19] The latter is thus constitutive for mimetic literature to exist at all, and in order to create and plausibilize the mimetic illusion, it must simultaneously make itself invisible. Thus the apparent closeness of mimetic literature to reality proves to be a product of literary fiction.

3 *Le donne di Messina* by Elio Vittorini Between Social Utopia and Narrative Autoreferentiality

Now, there are literary texts that showcase this very mechanism by making what is generally hidden in mimetic literature, i.e. fictionality, the object of representation. In the second part of this study, one such case will be considered. It is the novel *Le donne di Messina* by the Italian writer Elio Vittorini (1908–1966). This novel is of twofold interest in the present context. Firstly, it is self-reflexive, in that it not only tells a mimetic story of the origins of a society, but also takes the telling of the story into account, thus revealing some of the fundamental problems of the mimetic representation of society. Secondly, this novel manifests a conflict between two claims

---

[17] The omniscience of the narrator may be limited in the case of internal or external focalization, but this does not mean that it is thereby eliminated. When, for example, Flaubert's narrator communicates the wishes and desires of Emma Bovary in a perspectival connection to the perceptual horizon of his protagonist, this is no less a manifestation of omniscience on the part of the narrator than in the novels of Balzac, who as a rule makes no such perspectival restrictions.

[18] Cf. Luhmann 1995, p. 227, where it is said that the function of art is to "include something that is in principle incommunicable, namely perception, in the communication context of society".

[19] Luhmann 1995, p. 229: "The work of art thus establishes its own reality, which differs from ordinary reality. It simultaneously constitutes […] a reality that is by definition imaginary or fictional."

of the modern writer: the claim to socio-political engagement and that of creating works that are part of the autonomous system of literature that has emerged in modernity. Both dimensions can be described from the perspective of systems theory.

The fundamental contradiction between moral-ethical partisanship and formal literary experimentation is explained by the conditions of the functionally differentiated society of modernity, which is characterized by social subsystems specialized to perform different functions. According to Luhmann, the function of science is to produce truth, the function of economics is to provide for the distribution of scarce goods, the function of politics is to make binding decisions, the function of the legal system is to regulate normative expectations, the function of religion is to deal with contingency, and the function of art is to make the unobservable visible. According to this view, each social functional system is responsible for exactly one function that can only be fulfilled within it and through its efficacy. For example, politics cannot create jobs. It can only make decisions that create environmental conditions favorable to the economic system, which, in turn, enable the exchange of goods to increase within it, thereby creating jobs. If we look at art, we find that, by producing certain forms, it enables processes of perception which the viewers may experience as interesting, exciting, exhilarating, alienating, and so on. Therefore, the genuine inherent duty of artists within the art system is to develop innovative forms that facilitate such deautomatized perception processes. By contrast, such dimensions as morality, politics or engagement are, from this perspective, foreign to art. An artist can, of course, hold political convictions, (s)he can espouse certain ethical-moral principles, adhere to them in his or her private life, but also as a public figure, advocate or support them. But (s)he cannot, in the proper sense, inscribe these views, attitudes and convictions in works of art, since it is not the function of art to propagate such principles or to ensure their observance.[20]

This conflict has characterized modern art and literature since the eighteenth century. As is well known, certain works of art created since that time have become the subject of bitter disputes and have caused scandal, like Goethe's *Werther* (1774), which ends with the morally offensive suicide of the protagonist. Other famous examples include Flaubert's *Madame Bovary* (1857), Baudelaire's *Les Fleurs du Mal* (1857), and Barbey d'Aurevilly's *Les Diaboliques* (1874), which were put on trial in France for allegedly offending public morals and decency. As late as the twentieth century, books such as *Ulysses* by James Joyce (1922) and *Lady Chatterley's Lover* by D. H. Lawrence (1928) were banned for obscenity. André

---

[20] Vittorini himself addressed the problematic relationship between engagement and autonomy: "*L'arte 'engagé'...* [sic] *La letteratura 'engagé'...* [sic] Io nego che uno scrittore (o un pittore, un musicista) possa impegnarsi a lavorare in un senso piuttosto che in un altro, e poi averne qualche risultato valido. Uno sforzo velleitario, da parte sua, non coinvolge, al piú, che il suo intelletto e non fa che accentuare il lato 'intellettualistico' della sua arte (...). Ma c'è un engagement 'naturale' che agisce in lui al di fuori della sua volontà. Gli viene dall'esperienza collettiva di cui egli è spontaneo portatore, e costituisce, segreta in lui stesso, l'elemento principale della sua attività." (Vittorini 1957, p. 306. This is a reprint of an article published in August 1948 in the journal *Rencontres Internationales de Genève*, entitled "Un 'engagement' naturale". The omissions are Vittorini's.)

Gide coined the saying, "C'est avec les beaux sentiments qu'on fait de la mauvaise littérature."[21] This sums up the core problem. The artistic quality of a literary work does not depend on extraneous aspects, such as moral attitudes, political commitment, or other "beaux sentiments," but solely on features specific to literature (forms of representation, modes of writing, language, etc.). Art is autonomous in the age of modernity, and this autonomy manifests, among other things, in the fact that works of art may violate extra-artistic principles.

In the course of this general trend of modernism, the experience of fascism and the Second World War in Europe, and particularly in Italy, was conducive to reflections on the relationship between artistic autonomy and political-moral commitment under aggravated conditions. Elio Vittorini is a particularly instructive example of this. The conflictual relationship between commitment and experimentation is reflected in his entire œuvre. It is well known that Vittorini himself had initially been a supporter of the official ideology during the fascist period.[22] He was a member of the fascist party and belonged to the left-wing fascists who sympathized with communism, as was reflected, for example, in his novel *Il garofano rosso* (written 1933–1935). His increasing distance and detachment from fascism then manifested in *Conversazione in Sicilia* (1938–1941, originally entitled *Nome e lagrime*). Here, the critical attitude towards the fascist regime finds expression, among other things, in a general sense of dejection that the first-person narrator suffers from and that he attributes to the conditions of the times. Time and again he speaks of lost humanity, subtly suggesting that this feeling of forlornness is due to concrete political circumstances such as the Spanish Civil War and the international isolation of Fascist Italy. The two fascist fellow passengers on the train 'Coi Baffi' and 'Senza Baffi' also become the targets of veiled criticism. While in this novel the author's anti-fascist stance could be read between the lines, as it were, due to the fascist censorship that prevailed during the writing of the novel, the novel *Uomini e no,* published in 1945, i.e. after the end of fascism and the war, displays clear partisanship in favor of the Resistenza and against the fascist regime. The stark dichotomy between humans and non-humans, already clearly marked in the title, is however then qualified in the text. For, here it becomes apparent that there are humans on the side of the fascists as well, and that, conversely, the Resistenza fighters must also perform inhumane acts in order to achieve their goals. The manicheism suggested in the title is thus not maintained by the text itself. In the post-war years, Vittorini's literary production stalls. Apart from the publication of *Le donne di Messina* (1949 and, in a revised version, in 1964), his presence in the public sphere is now limited to that of a cultural journalist and critical intellectual, an editor of magazines (*Il Politecnico,* 1945–1947, *Il Menabò,* 1959–1967, together with Italo Calvino) and the book series "Gettoni" published by Einaudi. He also publishes his *Diario in pubblico* in 1957. In the 1950s he is still working on the novel *Le città del mondo,* which is left unfinished and published posthumously. His late work, beginning with *Le donne di*

---

[21] Diary entry of September 2, 1940 (Gide 1952, p. 618).
[22] Cf. Raffaelli 2014, esp. pp. 5–16.

Messina, revolves around the conflictual relationship between autonomy and heteronomy, between engagement and a literature governed by its own laws.[23]

This must be situated against the background of Italian post-war literature. The uniqueness of this literature was described in detail by Italo Calvino in a text from 1964. It is the author's preface to his novel *Il sentiero dei nidi di ragno,* first published in 1947. According to Calvino, the period at the end of the war was characterized by collective storytelling. All people had shared a common horizon of experience, they had experienced the war, fascist oppression, the liberation struggle of the partisans at first hand and were animated by the urge to speak and tell about it. Neorealism, the artistic movement of the immediate post-war period that produced short stories, novels and films, was the direct result of this urge to tell stories. Everywhere in the lifeworld of the time – whether on the train, waiting in shops or eating in public dining halls – people made use of their regained freedom and told each other about their experiences: "ci muovevamo in un multicolore universo di storie."[24]

Vittorini's novel *Le donne di Messina* (1949; 1964) can be cited as an excellent example of this analysis by Calvino. The novel, in fact, takes place in the immediate post-war period and its plot is mediated by a collective and polyphonic narrative process. Italy has been destroyed and bombarded, towns and villages lie in ruins, and with great effort and privations, everyday life gradually revives. Vittorini lets the action of his novel – which generally recounts a new beginning after the war and specifically portrays the emergence of a new society in a single village – begin on the road and on trains criss-crossing Italy. After the standstill brought about by the war, the very nomadic travel activity that allowed Italy to become a unitary state in the first place now resumes. In the words of the narrator:

> Ricominciò il grande andirivieni di popolo per via del quale l'Italia è un paese solo invece di migliaia di paesi; fu nella primavera del '45, fu quell'estate; ed ora cresce in questo '46, e continua a crescere, di settentrionali e meridionali che cercano sistemazione, di reduci che cercano, di ex deportati che cercano, di partigiani che cercano, di brava gente e di non brava gente che cerca qualcosa...[25]

In the midst of this general movement of countless people journeying through their war-torn country, it happens that a number of individuals end up in a destroyed and abandoned village near Bologna and settle there.[26] This sequence of events begins

---

[23] "[…] il lavoro di Vittorini (dagli anni del 'Politecnico' alla stazione dei 'Gettoni' e poi fin dentro le pagine fascinose del 'Menabò' e le folgorazioni critiche de *Le due tensioni*) fu dominato dal medesimo interrogativo: che cosa può fare la letteratura per uscire dall'autoreferenzialità senza consegnarsi a una eteronomia penitenziale, quale può essere, in altri termini, il contributo specifico dello scrittore per promuovere il riscatto dell'umanità offesa." (Catalano 2013, p. 145.) On engagement in Vittorini and Calvino, see also Burns 2000.

[24] Calvino 1991, p. 1186. – On the emergence of neorealism from lifeworld communication contexts, see Corti 1978, pp. 31–39.

[25] Vittorini 1974, p. 7.

[26] The exact location of the village, situated in the northern Apennines, remains indeterminate. Thus, one of the characters in Chapter VII suggests that the lights of Bologna can be seen from the village, to which someone replies: 'Siamo per questo anche dalle parti di Ancona, se cento chilometri in più o in meno non contano nulla' (Vittorini 1974, p. 22).

in Chapter IV of the novel, triggered when a truck breaks down, as a result of which the first people happen upon the abandoned village nearby.

The appropriation of the ruined village by newcomers, whom chance has led there, is the central plot of the novel. This plot is narrated in an unusual manner. In addition to the village plot, a travel story is told, first collectively, then individually. This travel story centers on Uncle Agrippa, an elderly man who has been searching for his missing daughter for years and is therefore continually traversing Italy by train. He is already well known among the travelers and tells them about his daughter who has become involved with soldiers, but in whose virtue he continues to trust and that he hopes to find again one day. Agrippa encounters, among others, a character named Carlo il Calvo, who, as we learn in Chapter XXVII, has firsthand knowledge of the village in which the main action is set. The novel's overarching narrator, for his part, is situated on the train as a witness. Hence, the text constructs a narrative situation based on witnessing: People meet by chance on trains, tell each other stories based in part on firsthand observation and testimony, and quite literally transport these stories, the train being a means of public transport. In addition to eyewitness accounts of the village, there is another source, a *registro,* first mentioned in Chapter XXI. In this source, the villagers have recorded their daily experiences, as though in a diary. An additional source, as is common in the *verismo* novel, is the chorus of voices of the villagers themselves, who have their say, for example, in chapters XLIV to XLVII. In this way, a polyphonic narrative situation takes shape. What is narrated is communicated through different sources, levels of mediation and voices, in a multi-perspectival and polyphonic manner. This corresponds well to that universe of stories of which Italo Calvino speaks in his 1964 preface. Italian society in the immediate post-war period is presented by Vittorini as a universe of stories and overlapping narrative processes.

The village story at its center is linked to fundamental ethical, political and economic questions. On the one hand, the text thus aims to renew the conventional narrative structure in an avant-garde fashion, and to make the narrative process itself the center of focus. On the other hand, it tells the story of a precarious utopia.[27] In the development of the village by its various inhabitants, it is shown in many ways that they can only succeed together. For example, Carlo il Calvo reports that the villagers jointly own property, not out of ideological conviction, but by necessity:

> Lui può ridere all'idea che sia per un principio. Essi non hanno princìpi, né forse sapevano che possono esistere dei princìpi. Solo hanno capito che non restava loro da scegliere. O avere le cose in comune, e lavorare a vantaggio comune; o rinunciare a star lì e tornare al viaggio avanti e indietro, al vagabondaggio, al bracciantato d'una settimana in un posto e una settimana in un altro posto, alla borsa nera la più spicciola, al piccolo ladrocinio.[28]

The people living in the village are like "gypsies" ("zingari"), says Carlo il Calvo in conversation with Uncle Agrippa, and "gypsies," he asserts, have no principles after all. They act according to the dictates of necessity:

---

[27] De Michelis 2017, p. 41 speaks of "l'utopia autarchica delle *Donne di Messina*".
[28] Vittorini 1974, p. 103.

È stata la semplice necessità, "e non quello che si dice", a far lavorare quegli zingari col criterio delle cose messe in comune. Perché se uno o due più furbi si fossero resi padroni non sarebbero mai riusciti a tenere gli altri là, nelle condizioni in cui erano. Dovunque oggi ci si trova a dover ricominciare dal nulla, non avendo compensi immediati, avendo anche pericoli e stenti, non c'è da far altro che mettere in comune.[29]

The new beginning of economic and social cooperation after destruction presupposes that people deal with each other in solidarity and on an equal footing. The passage quoted is reminiscent of Rousseau's thought, since Rousseau famously declared the invention of property to be the greatest sin in the history of mankind.[30] According to Carlo il Calvo's account, under the conditions prevailing in the village, a new society is founded without property and thus without inequality. This would be, if it actually worked, the realization of a utopia.[31]

However, the story of the village shows that the utopia is doomed to fail. There are two reasons for this. One is the fact that former inhabitants of the village reclaim ownership, and the other is that one of the most active and committed new inhabitants of the village is a former fascist. This is Faccia Cattiva, one of the novel's protagonists, who is romantically involved with Siracusa, presumably the missing daughter of Uncle Agrippa. Faccia Cattiva, whose real name is Ventura, is a complex and ambivalent character. This is already evident in his relationship with Siracusa. The first scene in which the two are depicted is an attempted rape, though Siracusa succeeds in defending herself and calls Ventura a fascist.[32] Only later on does it become clear that this designation is not merely a verbal counter-aggression, which would be understandable given the circumstances, but is actually indicative of Ventura's past. In Chapter LIX, Carlo il Calvo reports of Ventura, whom he has known for a long time, that the latter had been a particularly brave fascist officer who, however, made two mistakes after his internment in an Allied prison camp:

"Solo che ha commesso una sciocchezza" dice. "Se ne stava al sicuro nel campo prigionieri degli Alleati… Lì i partigiani non potevano toccarlo. E lui invece n'è scappato, il giugno o maggio dell'anno scorso, perdendo con ciò il beneficio della protezione e poi quello del condono che tanti che c'erano ne hanno avuto. E non gli è bastato" soggiunge. "C'è una sciocchezza più grave che ha commesso. Non gli è bastato di essere diventato un latitante, un clandestino, e ha commesso la sciocchezza più grave di mettersi con un branco di disperati che sono tutt'altro di com'è lui, e di abbracciare una causa ch'è tutto il contrario della sua, sicché i nemici che aveva li ha conservati e quelli che gli erano amici invece li ha perduti…"[33]

---

[29] Vittorini 1974, p. 104.

[30] Rousseau 1964, p. 164.

[31] The attempt to establish a propertyless society must, of course, also be viewed against the background of communism, which Vittorini endorsed for a time, before the break between him and the chairman of the PCI, Palmiro Togliatti, occurred in 1951.

[32] Vittorini 1974, pp. 39–42.

[33] Vittorini 1974, p. 244.

Following Lotman, Ventura has performed an eventful spatial shift,[34] as he has moved from the side of the fascist military to that of the clandestine villagers, thereby making new enemies, namely those who want to uphold the former distribution of property. Among them is Carlo il Calvo himself, who comes to the village as a representative of the land registry office and attempts to reconcile the interests of the old and new inhabitants. This is the subject of chapter LIV. The attempt to establish a utopian, propertyless society, in which Ventura's commitment plays a crucial role, thus appears to be endangered from within. For, Ventura is a complex figure, simultaneously good and evil, and the management of the purportedly derelict village collides with older property rights, as recorded in the land registry. The various private and public dimensions of this story are so contradictory and intertwined that there can be no good resolution.

This holds true as the story of the village takes its course. The utopia of a village community without private property is already doomed to fail by virtue of the broader socio-economic framework surrounding the village, which stands in clear opposition to the utopian vision. Chapter LXXVI raises the issue of the low economic return that the subsistence economy of such a village community, a cooperative, yields:

> Voi avete impiegato ottocentomila ore di energia per rattoppare quattro case, rimediare qualche metro di diga, rimettere in sesto un paio di rogge e ripulire dalle mine alcune centinaia di ettari di terreno... Un risultato economico piuttosto mediocre, dovete convenirne, pur contando che avete anche arato e seminato e raccolto...[35]

Under favorable external conditions, a labor-intensive subsistence economy can at best meet its own needs ("il fabbisogno per voi stessi").[36] In order to make a profit, one would have to sell what one has produced at an inflated price, that would not be competitive in the marketplace. In the globalized market of goods and commodities, one must adapt to the conditions prevailing there and can only produce those goods which one is able to sell. In line with these considerations, the epilogue of the novel reveals that the capitalist economic order ultimately prevails and conditions in the village 'normalize'. Carlo il Calvo, who had offered a contract to the villagers on behalf of the land registry, says in Chapter LXXIX that order has been restored ("l'ordine è stato ristabilito, il diritto della proprietà è stato ristabilito").[37] Thus, he has fulfilled his official function. But, at the same time, he states that he personally holds a different view. He himself had not wanted to bring about this state of affairs. Rather, he had executed the wishes of his clients, whose main interest presumably consisted in skimming off profits: "Loro è l'afflusso in tasca che vogliono."[38]

The experiment of building a society without property has thus failed. What remains, however, is the option to remember and recount it. This becomes very clear

---

[34] Lotman 1972, p. 332.
[35] Vittorini 1974, p. 339.
[36] Vittorini 1974, p. 339.
[37] Vittorini 1974, p. 355.
[38] Vittorini 1974, p. 355.

in chapter LXXX, where years later, Uncle Agrippa and Carlo il Calvo, still traveling through Italy by train, look back on the beginnings of the village and regretfully conclude that the utopia has failed. Here the temporal distance is already inscribed in the narrative process itself:[39]

> Il discorso si ripete, lasciato, ripreso; e accade che lo zio Agrippa dica "peccato", accade che anche il signor Carlo dica "peccato"; accade cioè che il discorso abbia una digressione del tipo stesso che aveva nel '46 quando alle volte si viaggiava al buio tra piccoli punti di fuoco che si accendevano e si spegnevano, si ravvivavano e si offuscavano.
> Era più che altro il signor Carlo che allora parlava.
> Diceva di loro che toglievano le mine, eccetera, eccetera: "uomini, donne, bambini". E diceva che commettevano un abuso, che non erano in regola, che pressappoco rubavano. Ma diceva anche che erano molto bravi, che la cosa che facevano era di per sé positiva, e che il sistema che avevano adottato risultava logico e in fondo il migliore possibile nelle circostanze e condizioni in cui si trovavano.
> Ora lo zio Agrippa glielo ricorda. Dicevate questo. Dicevate quello. È lui che ora parla di più, nella digressione che si apre tra nebbia e nebbia lungo la campagna che dio sa cosa può sembrare di importante anche così di nebbia fino a che non si arriva in bocca a una qualunque città, sotto a una tettoia di stazione. Questo. Quello. "L'apprezzavate."[40]

The narrative process on the train, which has been foregrounded throughout the novel, here becomes self-reflexive with regard to its own history. Uncle Agrippa and Carlo il Calvo recall together the story of their encounters on the train and the associated narratives of the village. The ambivalent role of Carlo il Calvo is now also highlighted. He had, after all, been an active figure as well as a witness and narrator, and, as Uncle Agrippa now makes clear to him, on the one hand represented the old property relations, but on the other hand, as narrator, reported on the experiment with approval and enthusiasm. This fundamental ambivalence, represented by the internal narrator Carlo il Calvo, concerns the entire text. Looking back once more now, we can observe that in some passages the uncertainty of what is reported by the narrator becomes apparent. I would like to cite a few examples of this:

> Il treno dal quale Carlo il Calvo ha indicato le alture passa ai piedi del villaggio, uscendo da una galleria ed entrando in un'altra, alle cinque del mattino.
> Ma ho idea che quando Carlo il Calvo ha indicato le alture sia stato più presto o più tardi; non si è usciti, in quel momento, da nessuna galleria, né si è entrati in nessun'altra; e può darsi che le alture indicate non siano le stesse su un pendìo delle quali sorge il villaggio; o che siano le stesse però vedute in un'altra prospettiva di solitudini, da più a nord o da più a sud.[41]

---

[39] This new perspective is also due to the fact that Vittorini fundamentally revised the second part of the novel for the second edition in 1964: "Divisa in due parti, essa [the 1964 revision] è da considerare, rispetto all'originaria, solo corretta e riordinata nella prima metà e invece riscritta, e anche ripensata, nella seconda." (Vittorini 1974, p. 2) Cf. Fabre 2012, pp. 73–82, esp. p. 75: "La riscrittura si configura allora come una correzione rispetto all'immagine consolatoria di un fuori dalla storia e il piccolo gruppo vi viene 'ridimensionato', attraverso il confonto [sic] con un processo storico percepito come ineluttabile."
[40] Vittorini 1974, pp. 358–359.
[41] Vittorini 1974, pp. 55–56.

The uncertainty signaled in this passage with regard to the localization of the primary plot setting is a consequence of the mobility of the train. The fact that the primary fictional narrative situation is conceived as a serialized set of encounters of the same characters on trains can be understood as an epistemological metaphor. All forms of narrative are based on situations of observation, on perspectives and on the perceptual limitations, ambiguities, and uncertainties they entail. The discrepancy between the immobility of a setting such as the village and the mobility of the train, which dissolves the space into a series of shifting perspectives, is a clear allusion to the impossibility of adopting a definitive perspective on what is being narrated. Carlo il Calvo is the primary witness to the action, and he moves to and fro between the setting of the village, as the site of the action, and the train, as the site of the narrative. Now add to this the fact that the actual narrator of the text is not Carlo il Calvo, but an anonymous traveler who is also present on the train. This actual narrator designates himself programmatically, at the beginning of the text, as a train traveler with changing identities. He is an Apulian, Milanese, Ligurian or Emilian, each traveling for different reasons. In a sense, then, the narrator is an Everyman who, as he travels by train, happens to witness the conversations in which Carlo il Calvo and Uncle Agrippa exchange ideas and tell the story of the village. In chapter XVI, it becomes clear that the narrator is present on the train along with Carlo il Calvo and Uncle Agrippa:

> Un vetro è abbassato, ma di qui non si vede nulla, non c'è stazione. Anche dall'altra parte è abbassato un vetro, e anche di là non si vede che il lungo fronte del treno con vetri che si abbassano come il mio e gente che si affaccia com'io mi sono affacciato.[42]

As one of many anonymous fellow travelers, the narrator is thus present on the train. Yet, much remains unclear in this regard, especially the questions of how often the superordinate narrator travels together with Uncle Agrippa and Carlo il Calvo and where he obtained the register of the village from which he quotes, as well as the question of how he obtained knowledge of the monologues of the various villagers.[43] Perhaps this narrative situation can be interpreted as telling, *pars pro toto*, a possible history of Italy after 1945 through the story of the village, and to mean that the mediating agency of this narrative is a collective one. The mass of anonymous Italians traveling on the trains becomes the narrator of its own history. The aforementioned uncertainty is repeatedly evident in the text, in which, as has already been shown, narration is multi-perspectival. At one point, different media too (oral and written) are confronted with each other.

> Dalle testimonianze orali sembrerebbe che qui fosse entrato in scena Faccia Cattiva, ma è più plausibile supporre, sulla traccia del *Registro,* che si sia avuto prima tutto un giorno in

---

[42] Vittorini 1974, p. 47.

[43] In chapter III, the narrator refers to the character who will later be called "zio Agrippa" as "mio consanguineo, quasi come mia madre per me, fratello di lei, e figlio della mia nonna" (Vittorini 1974, p. 8). However, he immediately adds the following: "Ma voglio sia chiaro ch'egli è solo uno di tanti, solo tipico di gente e gente, nulla di speciale" (Vittorini 1974, p. 8). It is, thus, not about "zio Agrippa" as an individual, but as a paradigmatic figure of the traveling Italian, just as the narrator also describes himself as an interchangeable element of the paradigm 'Italian': "Io sono pugliese […]. O sono milanese […]. O sono un ligure […]" (Vittorini 1974, pp. 3–4).

cui Fischio si intrattenne a parlare molto seriamente con Ventura, ed entrambi si intrattennero con altri, e interrogarono l'Antonia.[44]

With such references to divergent versions of the story, the text raises a fundamental doubt as to the truth and unambiguity of this story, thus shattering the mimetic illusion. The whole complex narrative arrangement, the experimental superimposition of various mediating processes, inserts itself, as it were, in front of the story to be told, rendering its plot, as well as its interpretability, not to mention its veracity and authenticity, fundamentally uncertain. Narration as such, on the other hand, becomes the second, equally important subject of the novel. The novel not only tells the story of a social experiment, but also and simultaneously tells the story of a narrative experiment. The intent of this narrative experiment is not only the communication of verified facts. Rather, it is also concerned with atmospheres, interpretations, the connection between the authenticated and the invented, the superimposition of history, which takes place in the here and now, and its mythical substratum. It is hence a manifestation of fictionality as undecidability with regard to the opposition true/false. This is exemplified by the title of the novel *Le donne di Messina*. In chapter XVIII, one of the men of the village says to one of the women, who is from Messina, that the women of Messina are accustomed to rebuilding demolished houses. The woman from Messina does not understand why the man thinks that this is customary in her city, whereupon the man explains that there is a song to this effect, which he then quotes in fragments. In this conversation, the encounter between reality and the mythically exaggerated past, as it is sedimented in the aforementioned song, becomes very clear. The woman, who is in fact from Messina, has no personal memory of the reconstruction of her city after an earthquake. That there have been such situations in the past is culturally transmitted through the fragmentarily recollected song, which speaks of the reconstruction activities of the *donne di Messina*. The fact that the text signals precisely this passage in its title clearly indicates the conception of reality with which it operates. What is at issue, here, is not the mere registration of the factual, but rather the complex intermingling of the factual and the imaginary, which manifests upon numerous occasions in the subjective perspectives and narrative acts.[45]

4 Conclusions

In conclusion, I would like to draw some inferences from the above regarding the relevance of national philological literary studies for our present time:

1. Literature is a functional domain of society that enables society to describe itself, by availing itself of the symbolically generalized communication medium of 'fictionality'.

---

[44] Vittorini 1974, p. 90.

[45] The encounter and overlapping of the factual and the imaginary is of fundamental importance to Vittorini; cf. Klinkert 2001.

2. A theoretical foundation is needed to describe and analyze literature adequately. The Luhmannian systems theory, chosen as a point of reference here, is of particular relevance because, on the one hand, it views society, at its core, as a sum of communications and, on the other, it provides a framework for describing the status of art and literature as social systems.
3. Also indispensable for the description and analysis of literature are components of traditional philology, such as knowledge of national languages and cultures, of canonization processes, as well as philologically precise, textual analysis in the spirit of a hermeneutics that enables the individual texts to speak to us in their rich complexity.
4. Significant advances in insight can result when, as has been endeavored here, general principles and theorems of systems theory are related to a concrete individual case, which, in turn, contains elements of a theoretical description of the connection between literature and society. The achievement of systems theory then consists in making the theory-shaped components of the individual text visible in their analytical potential. Systems theory is thus an instrument that enables analytical observation and sharpening.
5. Under no circumstances should the present attempt be understood to encourage indiscriminately applying a "super-theory,"[46] immune to criticism through a claim to absolute validity (and thus 'always right') to a particular object, merely in order to be confirmed by it. This would be a tautological and therefore wholly dispensable enterprise. Rather, it should have become apparent that I tend to make use of theory in the mode of *bricolage,* i.e. to borrow from it certain elements that seem suitable to my subject area and then to adjust them in such a way that they allow the specificity of that subject area to be better and more sharply discerned. Furthermore, it should be emphasized that the selection and perspectivization of theory elements is always already conducted in view of the subject area of literature, and they are thereby 'infected' by literature, so to speak. In this sense, the use of theory for the analysis of literature is not a one-sided relation, but a reciprocal one.

References

Auerbach, Erich: Mimesis. Dargestellte Wirklichkeit in der abendländischen Literatur [1946]. Bern, München: Francke 1982, 7th ed.
Burns, Jennifer: Telling Tales about 'Impegno': Commitment and Hindsight in Vittorini and Calvino, in: The Modern Language Review 95, 4, 2000, pp. 992–1006.
Calvino, Italo: Prefazione 1964 al *Sentiero dei nidi di ragno,* in: Romanzi e racconti. Claudio Milanini (ed.). Vol. I. Milano: Mondadori 1991, pp. 1185–1204.
Catalano, Ettore: Il radicalismo di Elio Vittorini. Dall'estremismo corporativo alle tensioni utopiche, in: Ettore Catalano: Strategie di scrittura nella letteratura italiana. Bari: Progedit 2013, pp. 141–147.

---

[46] Cf. Hempfer 2002.

Corti, Maria: Il viaggio testuale. Le ideologie e le strutture semiotiche. Torino: Einaudi 1978.
de Michelis, Cesare: L'ostinata modernità di Vittorini, in: La modernità letteraria 10, 2017, pp. 41–50.
Fabre, Marie: L'ultimo Vittorini e la 'verità industriale'. Dal 'Menabò' alle *Donne di Messina* (1964), in: Levia Gravia 14, 2012, pp. 59–82.
Gide, André: Poésie, Journal, Souvenirs. Paris, Gallimard 1952, vol. II.
Goody, Jack/Watt, Ian: The Consequences of Literacy, in: Jack Goody (ed.): Literacy in Traditional Societies. Cambridge: Cambridge University Press 1968, pp. 27–68.
Havelock, Eric A.: Preface to Plato. Cambridge/Mass., London: Harvard University Press 1963.
Hempfer, Klaus W.: Schwierigkeiten mit einer 'Supertheorie': Bemerkungen zur Systemtheorie Luhmanns und deren Übertragbarkeit auf die Literaturwissenschaft [1990], in: Klaus W. Hempfer: Grundlagen der Textinterpretation. Stefan Hartung (ed.). Stuttgart: Steiner 2002, pp. 211–229.
Klinkert, Thomas: Sizilien als 'città universale del genere umano'. Zum Verhältnis von Mythos und Geschichte in Elio Vittorinis *Le città del mondo,* in: Gudrun Held, Peter Kuon, Rainer Zaiser, with the collaboration of Monika Neuhofer (ed.): Sprache und Stadt – Stadt und Literatur. Tübingen: Stauffenburg 2001, pp. 263–289.
Klinkert, Thomas: Epistemologische Fiktionen. Zur Interferenz von Literatur und Wissenschaft seit der Aufklärung. Berlin, New York: de Gruyter 2010.
Klinkert, Thomas: Autopoiesis – Chrétien de Troyes, in: Niels Werber (Hg.): Systemtheoretische Literaturwissenschaft. Begriffe – Methoden – Anwendungen. Berlin, New York: de Gruyter 2011, pp. 59–76.
Lotman, Jurij M.: Die Struktur literarischer Texte. Rolf-Dietrich Keil (transl.). München: Fink 1972.
Luhmann, Niklas: Die Wissenschaft der Gesellschaft [1990]. Frankfurt am Main: Suhrkamp 1992.
Luhmann, Niklas: Die Kunst der Gesellschaft. Frankfurt am Main: Suhrkamp 1995.
Luhmann, Niklas: Die Gesellschaft der Gesellschaft [1997]. 2 vol. Frankfurt am Main: Suhrkamp 1998.
Luhmann, Niklas: Einführung in die Systemtheorie [2002]. Dirk Baecker (ed.). Darmstadt: Wissenschaftliche Buchgesellschaft 2003.
Raffaelli, Massimo: I fascisti di sinistra e altri scritti sulla prosa. Torino: Aragno 2014.
Rösler, Wolfgang: Die Entdeckung der Fiktionalität in der Antike, in: Poetica 12, 1980, pp. 283–319.
Rousseau, Jean-Jacques: Discours sur l'origine et les fondemens de l'inégalité parmi les hommes, in: Œuvres complètes. Bernard Gagnebin, Marcel Raymond (ed.). Vol. III. Paris: Gallimard 1964, pp. 109–237.
Vittorini, Elio: Le donne di Messina, in: Le opere narrative. Maria Corti (ed.). Vol. II. Milano: Mondadori 1974, pp. 1–370.
Vittorini, Elio: Diario in pubblico, Milano: Bompiani 1957.

Theory Instead of 'Belesenheit'? Undergraduate Studies of German Literature After 1968

Jochen Strobel

Abstract If 'Belesenheit' (being widely read) is considered today to be a bourgeois ideal that has long since become anachronistic, this contribution, which argues in terms of discourse theory and praxeology, traces the obsolescence of this virtue in the context of the 1968 movement, specifically in the early history of the then newly established undergraduate course in literary studies. In order to achieve wholeness in a unity of (theoretical) discourse and life practice, the organizers of the entry courses and the authors of the new introductory textbooks leave behind a systematic and far-reaching reading practice in favor of a theory-based reading of individual texts now designated as exemplary, which are admittedly still largely taken from the canon. Primary text reading now has exclusively heuristic value, and often runs only via text excerpts. In the final analysis, the new undergraduate studies – such as the Marburg model – are concerned with the theoretically founded practice of life, no longer with 'education' for the 'gifted' or with an autonomously conceived world of 'poetry'. The paradigm shift is also evident in the explosion of introductory literature for undergraduate study. Unlike Karl Otto Conrady's canon-and-education transitional product of 1966, the sometimes decade-long successful introductions of the 1970s open up to the telos of 'theory and method' and a culture of chunk reading. The question of the (self-)purpose of primary text reading, meanwhile, returns in canon debates, such as around 2000.

J. Strobel (✉)
Germanistik und Kunstwissenschaften, Philipps-Universität Marburg, Marburg, Deutschland
e-mail: jochen.strobel@uni-marburg.de

© The Author(s), under exclusive license to Springer-Verlag GmbH, DE, part of Springer Nature 2023
C. Strosetzki (ed.), *200 Years of National Philologies*,
https://doi.org/10.1007/978-3-476-05925-3_11

156   J. Strobel

1 'Belesenheit'

To throw 'Belesenheit' (Being Widely Read) into the pot as a virtue around 2020, as the Viennese philosopher Konrad Paul Liessmann has done in his book *Bildung als Provokation (Education as Provocation),* at first seems backward-looking, since the term can serve as a synonym for the equally obsolete, at any rate little-used 'Gelehrsamkeit' (erudition). Liessmann's attack on the competence orientation in school German lessons makes him, as an alternative to the mere ability to act, recall a status of personality formation achieved or to be achieved by means of education, precisely the specifically literary Belesenheit, which he is admittedly only able to define with difficulty or perhaps better: to encircle in paraphrasing. Thus it is a collection of catchwords that contribute to the approximation of the term: "advanced educational aspiration"; "a close relationship to very specific books and texts"; intensive reading of literary (and also, for example, philosophical) texts; more than mere "text indexing competence"; the "aspiration to a certain quantity"; the ability to relate different of the many texts read to one another.[1] The literary scholar is referred to as the type of the Belesenheits-Pro – the last mentioned characteristic just works towards it. However, Liessmann associates Belesenheit with the absence of concrete utility.[2] Belesenheit is a goal to be achieved only alinearly and unplanned, the "sum of manifold reading experiences that have left their mark on a person's life".[3] The path to this goal becomes only conditionally transparent by means of the criteria mentioned: what and how much must be read, and how exactly, so that finally the "close relationship" occurs? Are the acquisition of competence and the possession of education actually mutually exclusive?

The vagueness of the concept and the possible results of following it are bound to provoke contradiction; this is undoubtedly the aim of Liessmann's polemic. In an article in the daily newspaper *Der Standard,* an interrupting German teacher dares to doubt that being Widely read is actually of no use in real life, as does Liessmann's retreat into the old bourgeois 'high culture'.[4] In the meantime, Liessmann himself does not hesitate to introduce Belesenheit as a cultural-critical ideal of the past, about whose revival he himself might have doubts.

In the nineteenth century and far beyond, Belesenheit was the explicit or implicit goal of educated middle-class reading practice – the fact that it was considered desirable was certainly a consequence of discursive constraints, but even then it could not be normatively planned. Literary reading was considered the "royal road to aesthetic experience"; intensive *and* extensive reading were equally on the agenda. The method was "a professional-systematic working through of texts", an "intellectualized form of reading".[5] The educated person had to receive literature

---

[1] Liessmann 2017, p. 16 f.
[2] Ibid., p. 17.
[3] Ibid., p. 23.
[4] Cf. Skrivanek 2017.
[5] Schneider 2018, p. 73 f.

like a grammar school or university professor. The presuppositional richness of comprehending reading 'difficult' texts such as those of the Romantic period suggests "a comprehensive literary education"[6] to the point of aporia: to be able to read (and understand) texts, one always had to have read many texts. Far from a curriculum, literary education revealed itself to be a high ridge whose initial grounds could not be specified, but on which intellectual activity could be miraculously fused with aesthetic sensibility.

Of course, the student of literature was expected to read widely. A slow loss of attractiveness of the social project 'Bildungsbürgertum' is certainly suitable as a crude explanation for the fact that a concept 'Belesenheit' does not play a major role in the present. This essay, which argues discourse-theoretically and praxeologically, tries to find clues for the obsolescence of the concept around and shortly after 1968. It would be too simplistic to argue that 'the sixty-eighters' destroyed this bourgeois ideal in an iconoclastic manner. Rather, the argument is to be made not so much on the basis of the well-researched history of events and along the ideological and philosophical themes of the time, but along the traces of academic practice. The analysis of the interweaving of discourses and practices in the seminar necessarily contributes to a history of the sciences and their institutions; for this purpose, for example, study regulations, lecture notes, seminar protocols and also textbooks are to be consulted. According to the sociologist Andreas Reckwitz, practices are considered to be "socially regulated, typified, routinized form[s] of physical behavior",[7] which indispensably includes participation in seminars as well as refusal to participate and behavior in the seminar, such as the formation of hierarchies. In this context, practice and discourse are to be understood as correlated. It is undecidable whether "culture can be analysed primarily at the level of discourses (or texts or symbol sequences) or at the level of (physically anchored) routinised social practices".[8] For his study of "left-alternative lifes" from 1970 onwards – the period that is also of interest here – historian Sven Reichardt has paid the utmost attention to "the extent to which the revolutionary ideas of the historical actors were linked to the practice of life".[9] Here one should think above all of the how and the what of university readings, of arguing out as a social interaction typical of the time, in contrast, for example, to the silent reading of the bourgeois tradition. Part of the left-alternative habitus and lifestyle is "Ganzheitlichkeit",[10] if possible the avoidance of a balancing act between discourse and life practice; in the 1970s and early 1980s, theoretical analysis increasingly took a back seat to practical implementation.[11] Such a development could only be demonstrated for German literary studies, for example, by means of a large-scale empirical study.

---

[6] Ibid., p. 75.
[7] Reckwitz 2006, p. 36; see also Kasper and Strobel 2016.
[8] Reckwitz 2004, p. 15.
[9] Reichardt ² 2014, p. 15.
[10] Ibid., p. 55.
[11] Cf. ibid.

The main sources of this contribution will be introductory textbooks in (Modern German) Literary Studies (chapter "The 'Empire' Writes Back: Literary Recolonizations in Eighteenth Century France (Prévost, Lesage, Fuzelier/Rameau)") as well as plans for the then new undergraduate curriculum and its implementation in teaching (chapter "On the Transformation of Philological Knowledge Orders and Information Stores at the Turn of the Nineteenth and Twentieth Centuries: Developments and Causes"; both mainly on the basis of the example of Marburg), insofar as the wordlessness of annotated lecture notes can be at all guiding. First of all, however, and primarily on the basis of Wolfgang Kayser's book *Das sprachliche Kunstwerk (The Linguistic Work of Art) recte* 1948[12], which went through nine editions in the 1960s, the implications of literary reading practice in times of the methodological paradigm of 'work immanence' will be discussed (chapter "Cervantes, Camões and the Elementary/Basic Elements of the Spanish Language: The Functions of Knowledge About the Iberoromania in Nineteenth-Century Germany"). This will be followed by a focus on the theoretical reading that was crucial for the student movement and, subsequently, for 'left-wing' university teaching (chapter "On Why the Modern Philologies Were Included in the University Canon of Subjects in the Nineteenth Century").

In this context, the results should be anticipated that reading procedures in the sense of the already mentioned 'must *have* read' have hardly been addressed since 1968, that despite certain expansions in teaching, the canon from Lessing to modernity continues to be valid, but primary texts to be read are basically attributed exemplary character. In the perception of the students, they are individual pieces, not elements of a library to be explored conceived as a continuum. The field of tension between immersion[13] and distancing, which is given for every reading of fictional or literary texts, is switched to a dominance of distancing in favour of theory: theory is regarded as an incentive to reflect on social reality and thus one's own life practice, while the reading of literary texts takes on the function of perceiving conditions of former social reality in relation to one's own in a propaedeutic way. Reading without a purpose or serving a mere personality ideal of 'education' no longer has a place here, even if the teachers of the 1970s are aware that literature builds on literature, that knowing intertextual relationships is basically inescapable for literary scholars. The 68ers, who turned away from broad reading in favour of the principles of exemplarity and mere heuristics in the teaching of primary text reading, had an easy time of it, since in their school days and studies of the 1950s and 1960s they had still become acquainted with that fund of literary tradition from which they could repel, but which those born later began to lack more and more.

In the course of a process of scientification that had already begun in the postwar period, those literary scholars who seemed to be "rather [...] called to the service of art" then began in the course of the 1960s – quite contrary to their intention – to

---

[12] Cf. Kayser [14] 1969.
[13] Cf. basically: Ryan 1992.

curtail the credibility of their subject.[14] Klaus-Michael Bogdal, for example, quotes Rainer Gruenter, a full professor in 1964, that education is "something highly private, individual; it can neither be taught nor ascertained in examinations, and the conditions under which it arises are so varied that it can neither be awakened nor fostered by regulated recommendations or public grants."[15] And yet, it might be added, it was considered the basis of literary study.

2 'Poetry' as an Autonomous World?

Wolfgang Kayser's highly successful book, which was recommended to students in the 1950s (and according to the number of copies: far beyond) as the "Bible of Germanists",[16] certainly bears the traits of a transitional phenomenon. The book pays homage to the immanence of the work, praises, with Dilthey, poetry as an experience; the book is still very much attached to the paradigm of the author, whom an adept of *universitas* has to trace.[17] At the same time, Kayser reveals a pioneering interest in the structures of the work of art; he begins to work in terms of narrative theory[18] and presents himself as a comparatist in the texts analyzed, many excerpts of which are included in the volume. He presents himself as both theory-friendly and pragmatic in that he intends to "demonstrate to the reader [...] how to handle the theoretical tools."[19] Although teachers and introductions to literary studies alike may have chafed against Kayser since the early 1970s, they are indebted to him.

In contrast to his successors, however, Kayser already states in his preface to the explanation of his world-literary approach "that the forces which form the linguistic structure of poetry as well as its form are almost everywhere the same, and that genuine Belesenheit deepens the understanding of the individual work in a wide field."[20] The primacy of a hermeneutics immanent to the work or poetry is thus named. If commonalities and analogies of the individual phenomena of holistically conceived 'poetry' were universal, then one would not need to know so many as Kayser demands. Rather, it seems that universally applicable experiential knowledge is acquired through many individual experiences; thus, only many readings in their sum constitute Belesenheit. Hundreds of quoted and interpreted texts and text excerpts (preferably from the lyrical genres) initially serve as examples and evidence, but in view of what has been quoted they point to the necessity of knowing all these texts in their entirety as well. Kayser does not reveal how this is to be

---

[14] Cf. Bogdal 2002, p. 59, quote ibid.
[15] Gruenter 1964, quoted in Bogdal 2002, p. 59.
[16] Dittmann 2018.
[17] Cf. for example Kayser [14] 1969, p. 189.
[18] Cf. Schönert 2013, pp. 128–132.
[19] Kayser [14] 1969, p. 6.
[20] Ibid.

accomplished; the "great and difficult art of reading correctly" already means: interpreting correctly.[21] The high art of examining style – and here Kayser remains far away in the pre-theoretical field – he describes with intersubjectively hardly comprehensible emotional states such as "intuition", "sensing", "awe", "enthusiasm"[22] and finally with the creativity of the interpreter: an independent interpretation is "a complete new beginning in the most possible impartiality"[23] as a leap out of the system of method-guided work instructions. With Dilthey as a guarantor of the experiential character of both the production and reception of the work of art, Kayser's concept of literary-scientific practice can flaunt a closeness to life. This connection, however, is entirely tied to the myth of talent as a possible criterion for exclusion: the person to whom a work of art appears dusty and to whom it remains inaccessible can simply be denied talent.

The latter plays the key role in Kayser's conception of a science of poetry that operates with immanence of work. His assertions that the study of literature presupposes a dual talent, a theoretical talent and a talent for the subject matter, which expresses itself "as enthusiasm", proved untenable; the latter "usually outweighs [...] theoretical interest", is often "a symptom of artistic receptivity" and "at the same time a sign of its own latent creative power".[24] This provides a very traditionally creative-aesthetic-sounding answer to the riddle of Belesenheit, the reference to the ineffable and unlearnable, yet productive, of that which is acquired on the basis of talent. There is no mention of the blessings of domestic educational capital (and economic capital). As early as 1968, Jost Hermand had only scorn and derision left for "the more or less subtle immersion in the work of art as a work of art" (with Kayser or Emil Staiger as his guarantors); the "gesture of reverence" demanded of the (academic) reader was no longer acceptable – for political reasons.[25]

Yet the emotional rupture that the scientification of literary reading in a science of 'modern' literature signified was already far in the past. Wilhelm Scherer had already prescribed "rule-governed distancing"[26] to his students, had established a dichotomy between pleasurable 'normal reading' and interpretive reading, if not justified, then at least transferred it into university practice as a literary scholar. In 1889, three years after Scherer's death, Julius Hart quoted one of Scherer's students who had lived this dichotomy: '[A]s a student, I read poetic works with great relish; today I read a work by Goethe or the most insignificant, without knowing what I am reading, unconcerned with its content, its poetic beauties, quite indifferent to them. I see only words, commas, dots."[27]

---

[21] Ibid., p. 11.
[22] Ibid., p. 329.
[23] Ibid., p. 328.
[24] Ibid., p. 11.
[25] Hermand 1968, pp. 149 and 153.
[26] Klausnitzer 2011, p. 45.
[27] Hart 1889, p. 31 f. The quotation is also found in Klausnitzer, ibid.

However, the question arises as to whether the reading practices played off against each other here are tenable in view of the findings of reader research in cognitive science, which came to the conclusion that in the reading of fictional texts cognitive as well as emotional processes (such as empathy or identification with characters) collide with the formation of mental models,[28] and that biological *and* cultural factors play a role in the mental genesis of textual meaning.[29] Certainly, immersive reading can be relegated in favour of predominantly cognitive processes – this is more or less in line with the demands of a scientised literary science – but the remnants of identificatory reading can probably not be tamed.

3 Theory

From the sit-ins of the student movement to the terror of the Red Army Fraction (RAF), the practice of the 68ers – a term quite broadly defined here, including even the most radical offshoots – was based on theory. In his book *Der lange Sommer der Theorie (The Long Summer of Theory)*, which systematically develops this connection using the example of the Merve publishers Peter Gente and Heidi Paris, Philipp Felsch draws attention to the groundbreaking effect of Theodor W. Adorno's book of aphorisms *Minima Moralia* as early as the 1950s. This perhaps first 'theory book' was not only suitable for Gente as a "vade mecum":[30] in terms of form, it is kept in the tradition of moralistics and early Romanticism and is consequently close to literature, at the same time suitable to replace extensive educated bourgeois literary reading and yet to satisfy the reading addiction once acquired.[31] It was no coincidence that Adorno was *the* guarantor of the 68ers, since he stood for a distancing with his critical view of the cultural heritage after the break with civilization.[32] This included reading the classics.

Yet discursivization or scientification did not automatically mean disillusionment. In the heyday of '68ers', according to Silvio Vietta, despite all the "anti-bourgeoisie", there was an "aesthetic attitude to life" that at least gave contemporary pop-cultural and pop-literary currents a chance.[33] However, literary life in general, and by no means university literary studies in particular, already marked a trend towards the de-autonomization of literature – and this is where a revision of the canon at the university came in.[34]

---

[28] Cf. Schreier 2007, pp. 197 and 200.

[29] Cf. Brosch 2018, p. 425.

[30] Felsch ² 2018, p. 28.

[31] Cf. Felsch's motto: "'We are obsessed readers.' Heidi Paris […] & Peter Gente." (Felsch ² 2018, p. 5.)

[32] Cf. ibid., p. 33.

[33] Vietta 2009, p. 236.

[34] Cf. ibid.

Louis Althusser's notion of a "theoretical practice"[35] gets to the heart of the fact that the increasing enthusiasm for theory was never self-sufficient, but was always oriented towards proximity to life, a "theory of practice", to quote Pierre Bourdieu. While the revolutionary expectations of 1968 may have faded, the academic reform that lasted well into the 1970s, with its reorientation in the humanities towards a discussion of theory, was always intended to be close to life. The debates in the lecture hall were intended to have an impact on the lives of those involved.[36] With 'theory', authors and texts had found their way into the humanities seminar that were imported from other fields,[37] that were intended to irritate and ultimately change the lives of both teachers and students. Thus, if studies were to be given 'immediate relevance to society', then this included, especially after 1970, an 'increasingly strong commitment to Marxist theories *or instructions for action*'.[38]

For the new German studies, this meant in concrete terms conducting a discussion of methods that has not been concluded to this day, in the midst of which it was diagnosed as early as 1971 that soon after 1945, one had "settled into a 'pluralism of methods'" instead of discussing "methods and goals".[39] Translating theory into disciplinary 'methods' concretized the scientific impetus of the time. The following generations of students were then confronted with a defilee of methods; they were less political and did not have "the same elitist education or the same ideological motivation as the students of the late sixties",[40] i.e. they were presumably less well read. For them – unlike for their lecturers – the balancing act between literary reading and the acquisition of methodological competence was also less tangible.

4 The New Undergraduate Studies and Its Practices

In the first half of the 1970s, the '(Mid-level faculty) in particular[41] attempted to drive forward the process of restructuring the subject and institutions by establishing an undergraduate course. This is basically no more than a special case of the routine try-and-error process that has characterized the university for centuries. The subject of German Studies has undoubtedly gained from the innovations of the time through procedures and facilities that became established quite quickly, such as tutorials, collaborative work and collective authorship, papers, alternation between

---

[35] Cf. Felsch ² 2018, p. 70.

[36] If seminars in literary studies today are heavily weighted towards the present and address topics that engage with the life problems of the students being courted, this is an indirect consequence of the replacement of inner-literary topics (authors, genres, epochs, styles, etc.) with socially relevant ones.

[37] Cf. Culler 2002, p. 12 f.

[38] Hermand 1994, pp. 159 and 160. emphasis in the last quotation from J.S.

[39] Heller and Hüppauf 1971, p. 1.

[40] Hermand 1994, p. 174.

[41] On phases of subject history in the context of the student movement, cf. Schönert 2008.

plenary and small groups, method-guided discussion, de-hierarchization in social interaction, in short: "experimentation with new forms of academic teaching"[42] and continues to profit from them today.[43] This should be emphasized at the outset.

Now a double canon relativization began to spread, because the binding nature of the literary canon decreased and at the same time no canonical specialized knowledge was established, as far as methods and contents of the basic studies were reflected in introductory textbooks. Jörg Schönert has elicited similarities and differences; it is difficult to draw generally valid conclusions, for example, from the fact that genre theory is sometimes included and sometimes not, that metrics and rhetoric are dealt with or not, that the round of methods is sometimes longer and sometimes shorter.[44] But if one correlate of the now rising debate culture is "the dwindling integration of the practice of German studies into an 'educated' public", then this certainly has to do with reciprocal expectations, e.g. with the prejudice of the literary scholars' knowledge, who now apparently shone above all with their knowledge of theory. The compulsion for socio-political relevance of German studies content also had a rapid impact on the teaching of German in schools, as can be seen, for example, in the debate about the Hessian framework guidelines of 1973, which even reached the "Spiegel".[45]

The 'practice' of the 68ers after 1968 was, among other things, that of the humanities seminar. At the time, the Philipps-Universität Marburg was one of the 'red' universities, along with the FU Berlin and the University of Frankfurt, but this was largely limited to the initiatives from sociology and political science (with the widely influential Wolfgang Abendroth and his circle of students[46]). But even the new generation of German scholars who were able to establish themselves professionally in the course of the 1970s probably saw themselves largely as politically left-wing.[47]

The Marburg "Plan of Undergraduate Studies for Modern German Literature (Draft)", presented by the "Basic Study Colloquium of the Basic Group for German Studies" in April 1973, set the goal of the study reform to "combine intellectual with sensual experience of changes in one's own collective and individual political and private practice".[48] For all the scientification, sensual experiences are demanded in the consummation or better: at the end of the academic procedures, whereas they

---

[42] Herrmann 2009, p. 246.

[43] This relates to the prehistory since the early 1960s, but German studies has also benefited through the "wider waves of the student movement." (Ibid., p. 246.)

[44] Cf. Schönert 2013, pp. 141–145.

[45] Cf. Schönert 2008; on the 1973 debate, cf. N.N. 1973a.

[46] Cf. Peter 2014.

[47] There is still no standard work on 'Marburg 1968'; as far as I can see, Marburg German Studies around and after 1968 has not yet been researched. I would like to express my sincere thanks to Prof. Dr. Günter Giesenfeld, a contemporary witness, for providing me with a copy of the basic study plan cited here, as well as for numerous conversations. He is co-author of the plan of undergraduate studies.

[48] N.N.: Basic Study Plan 1973b, p. 7.

had hitherto stood at the root as an aesthetic sensation up to the enthusiasm for reading. This must be taken into account, otherwise the programme of the basic studies would be too soberly Marxist: The political qualification of the students to be acquired in the course of study is justified by their class interest in the context of teacher training – the study of German studies is thus perspectivized on the fact that the capitalist state articulates its interest in domination, among other things, in employing teachers who contribute to the maintenance of the political status quo. Among other things, making the future "pedagogical intelligentsia"[49] aware of this is the task of the undergraduate studies; the political work of the students is to be promoted. The link between the "training areas"[50] school and university is a tutorial – and this instrument, which has since been discarded, seems particularly forward-looking from today's point of view – whose tasks are "both reflection on school training and preparation for future practice in the university field".[51] Whatever one thinks of the political orientation of the teaching – it was certainly sensible to "clarify or create the motivational basis for a career-related study of German".[52] A "correction and expansion of the acquired knowledge and skills in dealing with literature in view of the fact that literary studies can only be understood as a part of a comprehensive social science",[53] probably excluded an apolitical, autonomous, i.e. "only" literary reading in favour of exemplary interpretative work with a political vanishing point. No wonder that the "juxtaposition of work-immanent and materialistic method"[54] and thus an interweaving of form and content analysis becomes a topic. Mere 'reading' here would mean remaining on the "empirical plane".[55] In place of the obligatory nature of broad reading (and thus of the access, perhaps experienced rather passively, to an available library of 'works' considered valuable, which the reader can only master through strict selection), there is intensive access to individual texts that can be selected almost at will, whose social conditionality, as well as that of the readers and scholars, is now the focus. The concrete procedures are subject to relativization; the main thing is that they remain rationally controllable. Now every student is allowed to become productive, to produce his or her own "products", "essays", which are set in relation to the primary text: "The various possibilities of dealing with the complex of themes are thematised as exemplary approaches to a literary product and their epistemological value is set in relation to its statement".[56]

---

[49] Ibid., p. 5.
[50] Ibid., p. 8.
[51] Ibid., p. 9.
[52] Ibid.
[53] Ibid., p. 9.
[54] Ibid., p. 10.
[55] Ibid.
[56] Ibid.

The text as a 'product' – "literature as specific human labour"[57] – is an individual case within the framework of its production conditions, and likewise the act of reception objectified in the paper is an individual case within the framework of the student's (socially conditioned) prior knowledge. Students and teachers are now committed to these individual readings. At the same time, "the specific character of the subject matter"[58] must not be neglected, i.e. despite everything, the special features that distinguish a novel from a document must be explored. Instead of mere 'reading', there is "distanced study of texts",[59] instead of "the usual variety of literature on offer, a limited number of texts, which can then, however, be discussed intensively".[60] The imperative of intensity, of the 'depth' of study moves from primary contact with the source to reflection.

If one looks at the annotated course catalogues of the Department 9 "Modern German Literature and Art Studies" offered since the winter semester 1972/73, one is immediately struck by the thematic conventionality of many courses oriented to the paradigms author, epoch, genre, in addition to a rich interdisciplinary or comparative programme (literature, music, visual arts). However, the political perspective can occasionally be seen in the titles ("Concept and function of literature in the bourgeois struggle for emancipation of the 18th century"[61]). Seminar topics on the literature of the women's movement, on mass media, or specifically on photography as a means of communication were undoubtedly innovative. For a project seminar on "Literature in the First World War", knowledge of primary texts is not assumed (those dealt with in the seminar remain unnamed), on the other hand, it is stated: "An indispensable prerequisite is the study of Lenin's 'Imperialism as the Highest Stage of Capitalism' and his essays on the causes and character of the war published after 4 August 1914."[62]

The Vormärz plays a major role that cannot be overlooked; the Marburg Institute soon took the initiative for a historical-critical Büchner edition, which was completed in 2013. In the summer semester of 1973, a four-hour project seminar on the topic of "Literature and Society of the German Vormärz"[63] was offered, which consisted of a plenary for all as well as four thematically very different seminars and clearly served to expand the canon or to form a counter-canon. The twofold perspectivization is clear from the title. Literary-political expressions of the oppressed classes, for example in the medium of the pamphlet, the "Neue Rheinische Zeitung" directed by Marx, texts by Heine and Börne as well as texts by Feuerbach, Ruge, Engels and Marx form the spectrum that articulates the principles of the exemplary and the counter-canonical. Except for the selection of Heine's texts (as a political

---

[57] Department 9 1972/73, p. 11b.
[58] N. N.: Basic study plan 1973b, p. 14.
[59] Ibid., p. 19.
[60] Ibid., p. 20.
[61] Department 9 1972/73, p. 10.
[62] Ibid., p. 12.
[63] Department 9 1973, pp. 14–16.

agitator, to be sure), what was offered did not belong to what had been read in German studies up to that point. It is also noticeable that actual theory seminars – unlike those offered since the turn to postmodernism in the 1980s – were hardly offered: Theory was the basis of *all* seminars.

Thus, new topics may have been added to the usual ones (Grimmelshausen; drama theory; Goethe's *Elective Affinities,* etc.): it is not so much a departure from the university canon that characterizes the course of study, but rather the consecutive orientation of the courses, which aim to 'pick up' the student in his or her respective social situation, and their theoretical orientation. The graduate courses in Hamburg, for example, was the responsibility of the professors, unlike the undergraduate studies[64] – this dichotomy is not evident in Marburg, where a generational change took place soon after 1970 and most of the mid-level staff were 'transferred' to professorial employment. But also in Hamburg (as at about the same time at many other West German universities[65]), multi-part entry courses with a considerable theoretical emphasis were offered from 1971 onwards.[66]

5 Introductory Textbooks

The student finds orientation for action (not just knowledge to be reproduced!) in textbooks; introductory books convey not only content but also "values, attitudes, working techniques".[67] With the undergraduate studies, the flood of introductory literature also swelled in literary studies – practical introductions to the study of 'German philology', however, had already been published around 1900.[68] If textbooks on literary studies are generally caught between the conflicting demands of conveying "*categorical knowledge* and *aesthetic experience*",[69] one of their tasks should be to describe in more detail the relationship between the procedures of reading sources and the scientific achievements in knowledge that build on them. The basic study plan and the course catalogue had emphasized the dominance of the latter with a more or less expandable fund of sources; now it is to be expected that the textbook intended for first-year students will proceed more systematically and explicitly. It must transfer the idea of the Marburg reform group, for example, to make students aware of the biographical and epistemic break between school and university at the beginning of their studies, to the level of content and procedures to be taught. The introductions of the 1970s stand at the beginning of a chain of

---

[64] Cf. Schönert 2008.
[65] Cf. Müller-Solger 1972; Schönert 2005.
[66] Cf. Schönert et al. 2010.
[67] Martus and Spoerhase 2013, p. 25. So too Schönert 2013: the introductory books showed that and how the academic reform was to bring about a "further development" of the philologies "in their subject areas and procedures" (Schönert 2013, p. 125).
[68] Cf. Sittig 2013.
[69] Klausnitzer 2011, p. 29.

textbook publications in literary studies that continues to this day and which, since Bologna, have taken up the cause of "increasingly acquiring competencies".[70] One would think that this would include 'proper' reading.

The early 1970s can be seen as an era of experimentation with different introductory formats, which in turn also respond to publishing strategies (not to be discussed here). Examples of textbook formats that seek to avoid the dilemma of aesthetic experience and scholarly knowledge are, on the one hand, the reader, the anthology with a particular didactic objective that is fed by text excerpts worth reading, and, on the other hand, the introduction to methods, which, for example in a historically conceived sequence, breaks theory down into literary methods and postulates selectivity (as well as begins to guide the student towards a decision in favor of his or her own method-guided work). An example of the former format, situated between textbook and university reader and at the same time appealing to the widest circle of readers, might be the *Klassenbuch,* co-published by Hans Magnus Enzensberger in 1972 in the "Sammlung Luchterhand", a *reading book on the class struggles in Germany,* which brings together reading pieces by canonical and counter-canonical authors (in the first volume, among others, Schubart, Bürger, Moritz, Campe, Forster, Büchner, Hoffmann von Fallersleben and Bettine von Arnim).[71] The equally successful volume *Methoden der Literaturwissenschaft (Methods of Literary Studies)* by Manon Maren-Grisebach, published in the new UTB paperback series, can serve as an example of the opposite model, method explication.[72] What could appear to be a proof of methodological pluralism is basically a history of theoretical appropriation processes in German studies from positivism to structuralism, not a textbook on the basis of which a course of study could have been organized. If *here* the trimmed source excerpt is simply presented, *then* the literary text is completely lost sight of.

Even if the introductory book presents itself as a written introductory course from the new undergraduate studies, the literary text is often only present as a snippet, as an example sentence. The fact that this rather linguistic procedure is not used by chance is shown, for example, by Jürgen Link's 1974 volume *Basic concepts of literary studies,* which takes the conceptuality of work in the humanities as radically as possible and breaks the subject down into its terms. The result is not an encyclopaedia, but a workbook with many concrete tasks for the reader.[73] Due to the structuralist approach, many textual examples are *not* taken from literature, and thus refer to the subject matter of further study a little in advance.

A total of four once prominent introductions should be considered here in a little more detail.[74]

---

[70] Sittig and Standke 2013, p. 8.

[71] Cf. Enzensberger et al. [9] 1983.

[72] Cf. Maren-Grisebach [9] 1985.

[73] Cf. Link [3] 1985.

[74] Schönert gives *this* canon in 2013, together with Kayser [14] 1969 (with Schönert also basic information on the volume concepts and their authors), but without Schulte-Sasse/Werner [4] 1986. This volume should not be omitted here, since its semiotic-structuralist orientation may have represented the most successful paradigm beyond Marxism and social history.

Karl Otto Conrady's *Introduction to Modern German Literary Studies*, first published in paperback in 1966 in "Rowohlts deutscher Enzyklopädie", is still far removed from a didactically planned structure; it is a book that introduces the subject and its study at a high level. The volume bears witness to the extent to which, long before 1968, the content and aims of the student movement were put on the agenda by already established protagonists. Conrady, who is still known today for daring to bring up the National Socialist past of his own generation of teachers at the Munich Germanists' Congress in 1966, opposes a university that breeds "authority-obsessed learners and mechanical memorizers" in favour of a "self-activation" of the students through tutorials, among other things.[75] According to its self-image, a surrogate for the disoriented freshmen at the mass university, it is a plea for self-study, not yet an actual textbook. In this it resembles Kayser's standard work, which itself was still located in the vicinity of literary writing, despite its completely different structure. Conrady defines the subject in terms of its structures and areas of responsibility, its history and the course of study it has spawned. He does not shy away from addressing precisely the actual study and its practice, thus in a separate chapter the "practice of reading and learning".[76] Both the individual requirements for study and the what and how of primary text reading are negotiated. At the beginning there is the elitist argument of professional aptitude and the unwavering reading practice associated with it, which the author invokes with disarming frankness. Similar to Kayser, then, the innate and the emotionally expressive are emphasized and made, as it were, the touchstone for the reading freshman. An "elementary enjoyment of literature" is written into his or her specifications, as it were: "[W]hoever could perhaps even live without literature should not choose this course of study."[77] Arguments for exclusion, which the following generation of lecturers probably rightly associated with social background rather than 'talent', are absolutised by Conrady ("one becomes a philologist through incessant reading"[78]) and also projected back onto the student's previous life: "Anyone who comes to university and wants to study literary studies must already have read a lot, otherwise he will always be left behind."[79] To this radicalism, which conveys to many freshmen that it is long and always too late for their studies, is added a 20-page reading list with a "basic stock [sic] of literature that the student should, in my opinion, have become acquainted with in his studies and before."[80] Having worked through the list, which counts hundreds of texts, is thus basically only the prerequisite for the student to enter the *inner circle of* the subject. Shortly before 1968, Conrady, himself a reformer, once again pronounces the credo of literary studies, which is concerned with the immanence of the work: Belesenheit – but he already demands this under

---

[75] Conrady 1966, p. 10.
[76] Cf. ibid., pp. 91–96.
[77] Ibid., p. 78.
[78] Ibid.
[79] Ibid.
[80] Ibid., p. 113, for the list cf. pp. 114–133.

Theory Instead of 'Belesenheit'? Undergraduate Studies of German... 169

reformist auspices as an exclusion criterion at the mass university and as a catalogue of measures that leads not to education but to examinability.[81]

On the plus side, Conrady is willing to teach the techniques of systematic, intensive and extensive reading in detail. The goal is unmistakably: "sufficient knowledge of the literatures of many times and many authors".[82]

All subsequent introductions stand out from this high sense of entitlement, which may have been similar with Kayser, but is not conveyed so drastically; they want to serve rather than patronize or diagnose. To accuse students in doubt of their ignorance and lack of talent no longer fitted into a time in which one already looked back wistfully on "literary education", according to the Göttingen Ordinarius Walther Killy in 1970, i.e. already shortly after the 'revolt' and even before the reform: it had become "dubious as the core of a 'general education' – that deceptive humanistic hope; even more dubious is literature as a mass subject."[83]

The introduction from 1972, written by Dieter Breuer and others, which emerged from the Aachener Undergraduate Studies and its "work paper[s]",[84] belonged to this period. Despite its conception as a workbook, from today's perspective it is somewhat deterringly theory-heavy and didactically ill-conceived, including long, complexly concept-heavy sections of text.[85] Primary texts are more than ever used as examples; Karl Arnold Kortum's comic verse epic *Life, opinions and deeds of Hieronimus Jobs the candidate*, which is quoted in excerpts and with accompanying texts, serves as an example for detailed textual analysis. The detailed ideology-critical introduction, like the Marburg Undergraduate Studies Paper, turns against the automatism of German teacher training, which up to now has aimed at "access to poetry"[86] in its qualitatively highest and autonomously conceivable forms. Rather between the lines the epistemic break has taken place: In a review of earlier times, the behavior of the former bourgeois students who "participated in the literary and artistic life of their hometowns, read a lot, and attended the theater with beautiful regularity" is evaluated highly critically.[87] What is caricatured here as misconduct had to be corrected in the entry courses.[88]

In contrast to this volume, the 1976 *Introduction to Modern German Literary Studies* by Dieter Gutzen, Norbert Oellers, and Jürgen H. Petersen is still successful

---

[81] The fact that Hans Grimm's völkisch bestseller *Volk ohne Raum* appears in the list is particularly disconcerting (cf. ibid., p. 128).

[82] Ibid., p. 92.

[83] Killy 1970.

[84] Stroszeck 1972, p. 11.

[85] Schönert nevertheless still recognizes the proximity to Kayser, albeit with a de-ontologizing tendency: cf. Schönert 2013, p. 138.

[86] Schmidt 1972, p. 19.

[87] Ibid., p. 24.

[88] This is also provided for in the Munich undergraduate studies plan: "reader analysis" is practiced "as a prerequisite for text analysis"; thus, "the identification processes that take place during reading are to be demonstrated in order to enable a conscious determination of interests and goals (related to studies and profession)". (Grimminger et al. 1972, p. 115.)

today and has been published in many editions; unlike all the other introductions analyzed here, it already lacked the component of higher education policy.[89] Still, or again in a certain continuity to Kayser, the volume conveys study contents such as text interpretation (in a scholarly continuation of techniques also conveyed by Kayser, among others) or methodology.[90] The latter contains mostly canonical texts, often in the form of excerpts, as well as work assignments, following the pattern of school German textbooks. Thus the primary literary text gains in visibility, but also in exemplariness. The student liked to feel reminded of his school books and read texts in order to solve tasks on them. In this way, the high methodological and political demands of the academic reform had been scaled down to a presumably practicable level, albeit with the effect of the schooling that is still much lamented today. This volume also emerged from the undergraduate studies, namely the Bonn one, which makes the rubrication as "workbook" plausible. Now, however, *after* the academic reform, the authors are concerned that the students should always use the volume in connection with literary texts, "and not only with those reproduced here, but also with those of their own choice", always with the "principle of close reference to literature".[91] Tentatively, the ideal of Belesenheit, which in the meantime has disappeared, is mentioned in the preface.

The volume by Jochen Schulte-Sasse and Renate Werner, published in 1977, is again a script for overcrowded entry courses, and at the same time an introduction that has been reprinted several times. Still quite reform-minded, but already afflicted with the experiences of the first years of reform, it sets itself the noble goal of not only theorizing (on a semiotic basis), but also of introducing "basic features of literary thinking and working" and thus establishing "the connection between theory and practice that is indispensable especially for beginners".[92] Although, logically in the sense of a course, literary categories are in the foreground and literary texts are in turn introduced as exemplary objects of analysis, the volume professes the learning objective, which is also comprehensible from today's point of view, of "developing aesthetic sensitivity on the basis of artistically valuable texts".[93] This remains a desideratum; fortunately, this goal is not linked to talent, but to university work. In any case, however, both authors militantly distance themselves from a purely emotional reduction of the process of understanding as "empathy" à la Staiger, Kayser and others.[94] The signal is: the reading process cannot remain on a purely emotional level. And: after all, reading as a practice is reflected upon; the solution is then once again found in contextualization. There is still an interest in the constitution of meaning in reading, which remains an understanding reading and must be scientifically 'enriched' in a semiotic way with a knowledge of text structures and contexts.

---

[89] Cf. Gutzen et al. 1976a.
[90] Cf. Schönert 2013, p. 139.
[91] Gutzen et al. 1976b, p. 7.
[92] Schulte-Sasse and Werner ⁴1986, p. 9.
[93] Ibid., p. 12.
[94] Cf. Ibid., pp. 28–30.

With the exception of a novel by Eugenie Marlitt, which is recommended for reading as a whole, the volume works largely with canonical textual examples from Hebel to Benn and Brecht. The balancing act between aesthetically sensitive reading and contextually bound analysis remains unclear. Remarkably, aesthetic sensibility remains largely tied to products of the high ridge.

6 Review and Outlook

Among the practices of literary studies, reading primary texts has not been highly regarded since the 1970s, since it is something pre-theoretical, pre-methodical, a virtue of cultural self-production of the bourgeoisie, according to the tenor at the time. In the introductory literature for prospective Germanists, the how and the how much of reading is no longer answered, or only answered shamefully and cautiously. In particular, the creative content of this practice is suspect to the authors of basic curricula and introductory textbooks; this is shifted to the creative handling of theory in the act of interpretation (or at least the act of producing one's own, method-guided texts).

But also the introductory books and modules continued to diversify over the decades, whether this concerned the differentiation of methods, internationality, accelerated innovativeness or the awareness of the contingency of each concept.[95]

For the period around 1968, "canon destruction"[96] or "questioning of the previous literary canon"[97] is stated. This should be put into perspective a little on the basis of the sources examined: A reading canon in the sense of an implicit corpus of literary texts worth reading has continued to be practiced in German studies at all times, sometimes expanded, sometimes reduced. The claim to broad reading that stood on its own or promoted 'education' was, on the other hand, clearly abandoned or at most only hintingly reproduced; of epistemological and methodological interest was above all the intensive, understanding reading of the individual text to be analysed according to the rules of the art. Only *the turns that* can be associated with terms such as 'discourse analysis' and 'cultural studies' moved away from the paradigm of the individual text and its (contextual) understanding in general from the 1980s onwards; the reformers of the 1970s still wanted to make individual, complete texts (which they now no longer called 'works') the basis of their work. Exceptions tend to confirm the rule here. The evidence of the introductory textbook, however, which reprints literary texts in portions, may have had a mentality-changing effect here and increasingly discouraged students from undergoing the laborious task of reading whole texts. This is not at all contradicted by the fact that, with the social history of literature in the 1970s, traits of a reintegration of the canon

---

[95] Cf. Kaulen 2002, pp. 1019–1021.
[96] Erhart 1998, p. 108.
[97] Hermand 1994, p. 146.

can be recorded again, just as the canon returned as a research topic around 2000[98] and as a reading list with recommendations. Conrady's reading plan celebrated a happy reign in 1994 as the Reclam reading list.[99]

Among the more recent introductory textbooks that have ventured into the subject of reading, Ralf Klausnitzer's 2004 volume is particularly noteworthy. In a chapter of his own, the author not only evokes the importance of reading for all further practices of the discipline in the narrower sense, he calls for a double reading, the first course of which takes into account a 'natural', meaning-giving as well as emotional-aesthetic, reading process: "In a first encounter with the text, it is almost indispensable to read [...] in order to entertain oneself, to make experiences or to get excited about particular forms of language design. Going beyond fascination, however, it is then necessary to ask about procedures and techniques that trigger these effects."[100]

Klausnitzer thus revises the myth of non-identificatory reading as the sole duty of the literary scholar, with which the author of this essay was also maltreated in his studies at the end of the 1980s. But sensitive suggestions like Klausnitzer's remain rather the exception. The Bologna Process has produced reading modules that guarantee, but also demand, a protected space of intensive and extensive primary text reading throughout the course of study, and end this phase with a module examination. Here, too, it is not taught *how to* read, but in view of an examination regulation, reading is at least demanded to a modest extent.[101]

Not in the exclusion, but in the relativizing devaluation of the 'trivial', i.e. the entertaining, do the representatives of the immanence of the work, the 68ers and the present-day propagators of a long-lost 'Belesenheit' à la Liessmann meet. But reading as a cultural technique, and especially the reading of extensive and complex texts, 'educates' at all times and should be useful to everyone beyond the hours of reading. This insight has only been conveyed by recent reader research, which has been able to close a gap in the world view of all those for whom reading was much more about the *what* than *the how*. The Stavanger Declaration on the Future of Reading (E-READ), published in January 2019, appears modest yet revolutionary, stemming from an EU research project on the impact of digitalisation on reading. Paper, according to the 130-plus reading researchers, will remain "the preferred reading medium for single longer texts [...] when it comes to deeper understanding of texts and retention."[102] Now, the specificity of literary reading is just *not* mentioned here anymore, but the *how* and *the what for* made one sit up and take notice: "Reading long texts is invaluable for a number of cognitive benefits such as

---

[98] Cf. v. Heydebrand 1998.
[99] Cf. reading list 1994.
[100] Klausnitzer 2004, p. 216.
[101] One example is the Marburg M.A. programme "German Literature. Text – Culture – Media", which replaced the previous M.A. "German Literature" in the winter semester 2020/2021.
[102] E-READ: On the Future of Reading 2019.

concentration, vocabulary-building, and memory."[103] Among the research group's recommendations is the development of strategies for students "to use so that they can succeed in deep reading and higher-order reading processes on digital devices."[104] This also names the tasks of a future Literary studies, for which Belesenheit can thus be a virtue and not just an end in itself.

References

Bogdal, Klaus-Michael: Wissenskanon und Kanonwissen. Literaturwissenschaftliche Standardwerke in Zeiten disziplinären Umbruchs, in: Heinz-Ludwig Arnold (Hg.): Literarische Kanonbildung. München: edition text + kritik 2002, S. 55–89.
Brosch, Renate: Lesen aus Sicht der Kognitionswissenschaften, in: Alexander Honold und Rolf Parr (Hg.): Grundthemen der Literaturwissenschaft: Lesen. Berlin/Boston: de Gruyter 2018, S. 425–441.
Conrady, Karl Otto: Einführung in die Neuere deutsche Literaturwissenschaft. Rowohlt: Reinbek 1966.
Culler, Jonathan: Literaturtheorie. Eine kurze Einführung. Stuttgart: Reclam 2002.
Dittmann, Ulrich: ‚1968', das Institut für Deutsche Philologie und Walter Müller-Seidel. Erinnerungen eines ehemaligen Assistenten an der Universität München, in: literaturkritik. de, Juli 2018. (https://literaturkritik.de/1968-das-institut-fuer-deutsche-philologie-und-walter-mueller-seidel,24694.html; 10.4.2020)
Enzensberger, Hans Magnus/Nitsche, Rainer/Roehler, Klaus (Hg.): Klassenbuch 1. Ein Lesebuch zu den Klassenkämpfen in Deutschland 1756–1850. Darmstadt/Neuwied: Luchterhand ^{9}1983 [zuerst 1972].
Erhart, Walter: Kanonisierungsbedarf und Kanonisierung in der deutschen Literaturwissenschaft (1945–1995), in: Renate von Heydebrand (Hg.): Kanon Macht Kultur. Theoretische, historische und soziale Aspekte ästhetischer Kanonbildungen. Stuttgart/Weimar: Metzler 1998, S. 97–121.
Fachbereich 9 Neuere deutsche Literatur- und Kunstwissenschaften: Lehrveranstaltungen im Wintersemester 1972/73. Marburg/L.: Philipps-Universität [1972]. [Masch.]
Fachbereich 9 Neuere deutsche Literatur- und Kunstwissenschaften: Lehrveranstaltungen im Sommersemester 1973. Marburg/L.: Philipps-Universität [1973]. [Masch.]
Felsch, Philipp: Der lange Sommer der Theorie. Geschichte einer Revolte 1960–1990. Frankfurt a. M.: Fischer Taschenbuch ^{2}2018.
Grimminger, Rolf/Ortmann, Christa/Solms, Wilhelm: Einführungen in eine subjektbezogene Literaturwissenschaft, in: Hermann Müller-Solger (Hg.): Einführung in das Studium der Literaturwissenschaft. Modelle der Praxis. Tübingen: Niemeyer 1972, S. 113–151.
Gruenter, Rainer: Die Zukunft unserer Bildungsanstalten, in: Gert Kalow (Hg.): Sind wir noch das Volk der Dichter und Denker? 14 Antworten. Reinbek: Rowohlt 1964, S. 117 f.
Gutzen, Dieter/Oellers, Norbert/Petersen, Jürgen H.: Einführung in die neuere deutsche Literaturwissenschaft. Ein Arbeitsbuch. Berlin: Erich Schmidt 1976a.
Gutzen, Dieter/Oellers, Norbert/Petersen, Jürgen H.: Vorwort, in: Dieter Gutzen/Norbert Oellers/ Jürgen H. Petersen: Einführung in die neuere deutsche Literaturwissenschaft. Ein Arbeitsbuch. Berlin: Erich Schmidt 1976b, S. 7 f.
Hart, Julius: Eine schein-empirische Poetik, in: Kritisches Jahrbuch 1, 1889, S. 29–39.

---

[103] Ibid.
[104] Ibid.

Heller, Albert und Hüppauf, Bernd: Einleitung, in: Jürgen Hauff/Albrecht Heller/Bernd Hüppauf/ Lothar Köhn/Klaus-Peter Philippi: Methodendiskussion. Arbeitsbuch zur Literaturwissenschaft. Band I. Frankfurt a. M.: Athenäum 1971, S. 1–27.

Hermand, Jost: Synthetisches Interpretieren. Zur Methodik der Literaturwissenschaft. München: Nymphenburger 1968.

Hermand, Jost: Geschichte der Germanistik. Reinbek: Rowohlt Taschenbuch 1994.

Herrmann, Hans Peter: Wie sinnvoll reden über ,1968 und die Germanistik'?, in: Gerhard Kaiser und Jens Saadhoff (Hg.): Spiele um Grenzen. Germanistik zwischen Weimarer und Berliner Republik. Heidelberg: Synchron 2009, S. 243–260.

Heydebrand, Renate von (Hg.): Kanon Macht Kultur. Theoretische, historische und soziale Aspekte ästhetischer Kanonbildungen. Stuttgart/Weimar: Metzler 1998.

Kasper, Norman und Strobel, Jochen: Zugänge zur historischen Romantik im Spannungs- und Synthesefeld von Diskurs und Praxis. Einleitung, in: Norman Kasper und Jochen Strobel (Hg.): Praxis und Diskurs der Romantik 1800–1900. Paderborn: Schöningh 2016, S. 7–21.

Kaulen, Heinrich: Die Literaturwissenschaft im „Methodenkarussell" – ratlos?, in: Hartmut Kugler (Hg.): www.germanistik2001.de. Bd. 2. Bielefeld: Aisthesis 2002, S. 1017–1034.

Kayser, Wolfgang: Das sprachliche Kunstwerk. Eine Einführung in die Literaturwissenschaft. Bern/München: Francke [14]1969.

Killy, Walther: Wozu eigentlich Literaturwissenschaft? Plädoyer für eine vorläufige und bescheidene Germanistik, in: Die Zeit 8, 1970. (https://www.zeit.de/1970/08/wozu-eigentlich-literaturwissenschaft/komplettansicht; 13.4.2020)

Klausnitzer, Ralf: Literaturwissenschaft. Begriffe – Verfahren – Arbeitstechniken. Berlin/New York: de Gruyter 2004.

Klausnitzer, Ralf: Unter Druck. Kategoriale Erkenntnis und ästhetische Erfahrung in Lehrwerken, in: Zeitschrift für Germanistik N. F. 21, 2011, S. 25–51.

Liessmann, Konrad Paul: Bildung als Provokation. Wien: Zsolnay 2017.

Link, Jürgen: Literaturwissenschaftliche Grundbegriffe. Eine programmierte Einführung auf strukturalistischer Basis. München: Fink [3]1985 [zuerst 1974].

Maren-Grisebach, Manon: Methoden der Literaturwissenschaft. Tübingen: Francke [9]1985 [zuerst 1970].

Martus, Steffen und Spoerhase, Carlos: Eine praxeologische Perspektive auf ,Einführungen', in: Claudius Sittig und Jan Standke (Hg.): Literaturwissenschaftliche Lehrbuchkultur. Zu Geschichte und Gegenwart germanistischer Bildungsmedien. Würzburg: Königshausen & Neumann 2013, S. 25–39.

Müller-Solger, Hermann (Hg.): Einführung in das Studium der Literaturwissenschaft. Modelle der Praxis. Tübingen: Niemeyer 1972.

N.N.: Defizit Deutsch, in: Der Spiegel vom 3.12.1973a, S. 74–78. (https://www.spiegel.de/spiegel/print/d-41840134.html; 11.4.2020). https://www.spiegel.de/politik/defizit-deutsch-a-b21277f9-0002-0001-0000-000041840134?context=issue (2.8.2021)

N.N.: Grundstudienplan Neuere deutsche Literatur (Entwurf). Vorgelegt vom Grundstudiencolloquium der Basisgruppe Germanistik. Marburg 1973b. [Masch.]

Peter, Lothar: Marx an die Uni. Die „Marburger Schule". Geschichte, Probleme, Akteure. Köln: PapyRossa 2014.

Reckwitz, Andreas: Die Kontingenzperspektive der ,Kultur'. Kulturbegriffe, Kulturtheorien und das kulturwissenschaftliche Forschungsprogramm, in: Friedrich Jaeger und Jörn Rüsen (Hg.): Handbuch der Kulturwissenschaften. Bd. 1: Themen und Tendenzen. Stuttgart/Weimar: Metzler 2004, S. 1–20.

Reckwitz, Andreas: Das hybride Subjekt. Eine Theorie der Subjektkulturen von der bügerlichen Moderne bis zur Postmoderne. Weilerswist: Velbrück 2006.

Reichardt, Sven: Authentizität und Gemeinschaft. Linksalternatives Leben in den siebziger und frühen achtziger Jahren. Berlin: Suhrkamp [2]2014.

Ryan, Marie-Laure: Possible worlds, artificial intelligence, and narrative theory. Bloomington: Indiana Univ. Press 1992.

Schmidt, Peter: Studienmotivation und Studienmodell, in: Dieter Breuer/Paul Hocks/Helmut Schanze/Peter Schmidt/Franz Günter Sieveke/Hauke Stroszeck (Hg.): Literaturwissenschaft. Eine Einführung für Germanisten. Frankfurt a. M./Berlin/Wien: Ullstein 1972, S. 16–34.

Schneider, Jost: Geschichte und Sozialgeschichte des Lesens und der Lesekulturen, in: Alexander Honold und Rolf Parr (Hg.): Grundthemen der Literaturwissenschaft: Lesen. Berlin/Boston: de Gruyter 2018, S. 29–98.

Schönert, Jörg: Die erste Dokumentation zur Reform des literaturwissenschaftlichen Grundstudiums: „Modelle der Praxis" von 1972, in: Gst.Litwiss Portal, 31.3.2005. (http://fheh.org/wp-content/uploads/2016/07/schoenertmodelle.pdf; 11.4.2020)

Schönert, Jörg: Versäumte Lektionen? 1968 und die Germanistik der BRD in ihrer Reformphase 1965–1975, in: literaturkritik.de, August 2008. (https://literaturkritik.de/id/12169; 11.4.2020)

Schönert, Jörg/Lange, Tanja/Schernus, Wilhelm: Pilotstudie „Zur Entwicklungsgeschichte des germanistisch-literaturwissenschaftlichen Grundstudiums an der Universität Hamburg (1970–2009)" [2010] (http://fheh.org/wp-content/uploads/2016/07/schoenertpilotstudie.pdf; 11.4.2020)

Schönert, Jörg: Zur ‚ersten Generation' von ‚Einführungen in die Literaturwissenschaft', in: Claudius Sittig und Jan Standke (Hg.): Literaturwissenschaftliche Lehrbuchkultur. Zu Geschichte und Gegenwart germanistischer Bildungsmedien. Würzburg: Königshausen & Neumann 2013, S. 123–145.

Schreier, Margrit: Textwirkungen, in: Thomas Anz (Hg.): Handbuch Literaturwissenschaft. Bd. 1: Gegenstände und Grundbegriffe. Stuttgart/Weimar: Metzler 2007, S. 193–202.

Schulte-Sasse, Jochen und Werner, Renate: Einführung in die Literaturwissenschaft. München: Fink [4]1986.

Sittig, Claudius: ‚Wie studiert man deutsche Philologie?' Praxiorientierte Einführungen in das Studium der Germanistik um 1900, in: Claudius Sittig und Jan Standke (Hg.): Literaturwissenschaftliche Lehrbuchkultur. Zu Geschichte und Gegenwart germanistischer Bildungsmedien. Würzburg: Königshausen & Neumann 2013, S. 99–121.

Skrivanek, Thomas: Kulturkampf um die Belesenheit. Ja, wir brauchen Literaturunterricht. Aber warum alles, was nicht Hochkultur oder humanistische Bildung ist, für minderwertig erklären? In: Der Standard vom 19.9.2017. (https://www.derstandard.de/story/2000064231729/kulturkampf-um-die-belesenheit; 10.4.2020)

Stroszeck, Hauke: Statt eines Vorworts, in: Dieter Breuer u. a. (Hg.): Literaturwissenschaft. Eine Einführung für Germanisten. Frankfurt a. M./Berlin/Wien: Ullstein 1972, S. 5–15.

Vietta, Silvio: 1968, Kritische Theorie und die Moderne. Denkfehler, Illusionen – Modernisierungsschübe, in: Gerhard Kaiser und Jens Saadhoff (Hg.): Spiele um Grenzen. Germanistik zwischen Weimarer und Berliner Republik. Heidelberg: Synchron 2009, S. 209–242.

E-READ: Stavanger-Erklärung: Zur Zukunft des Lesens, in: Frankfurter allgemeine Zeitung vom 22.1.2019. (https://www.faz.net/aktuell/feuilleton/buecher/themen/stavanger-erklaerung-von-e-read-zur-zukunft-des-lesens-16000793-p2.html; 12.4.2020)

Leitkultur: The Need for Commentary in Modern Society and the Lifeworld

Christian Bermes

Abstract The article addresses the question of the respective national philology as part of culture and then deals with the discussions about Leitkultur. After a look at Gehlen's understanding of commentary literature as a moment of modern art and the phenomenological explication of the lifeworld, it becomes clear that the culture of Leitkultur cannot simply be reduced to commentary on the lifeworld nor to the lifeworld itself. Rather, the theme of Leitkultur is revealed in the reflection on the intertwining of lifeworld and commentary – such a reflection is not independent of the discussions on the function and role of national philologies.

1 The Questionabilty of the Leitkultur Debate

The status and significance of national philologies refer in at least three respects to the discussions about a or the 'Leitkultur'. First, national philologies are candidates that promise information about what can be understood as a Leitkultur. In this sense, the respective national philology would be the *object of* the Leitkultur, as it were the thing to which one could point when searching for the or a Leitkultur. Secondly, the respective texts assigned to a national philology can be understood as media in which relevant things for a Leitkultur are negotiated. In this second sense, national philologies would articulate the *content of* this or that Leitkultur. And third, and finally, reflection on the criteria that identify a philology as a national philology

---

C. Bermes (✉)
Institut für Philosophie, Universität Koblenz Landau,
Landau, Deutschland
e-mail: bermes@uni-landau.de

© The Author(s), under exclusive license to Springer-Verlag GmbH, DE, part of Springer Nature 2023
C. Strosetzki (ed.), *200 Years of National Philologies*,
https://doi.org/10.1007/978-3-476-05925-3_12

could be understood to mean that such reflection is also relevant to the determination of a Leitkultur in a broader sense. The work on national philology would then be a work on the *standards of* Leitkultur.

Furthermore, the question of the *function of* the Leitkultur also arises. Let us recall the discussions that took place about 20 years ago following the reflections and suggestions of Bassam Tibi. What remains in the collective memory is the tense state of the discussion in the politically interested public and the feature pages. It was by no means easy to articulate an objective position in these sometimes heated and prejudiced times. Today the smoke has cleared, as can be seen, among other things, from Thea Dorn's recent inclusion of the following sentences in her book *Deutsch, nicht dumpf. Ein Leitfaden für aufgeklärte Patrioten (A Guide for Enlightened Patriots)*: "As a society, precisely because we want to remain an open, diverse, 'colourful' society, must we not also look for something that unites us, despite all our differences? But how can we hope for something that unites us if we outlaw what is binding?"[1]

Nevertheless, even in times of a now cooled-down discussion about the Leitkultur, the impression is becoming more and more solidified that one can actually only choose between two positions of an alternative: namely between either more or less manifest customs on the one hand or the constitutional legal order on the other hand. Many will want to refer to the Constitution (Grundgesetz) as the unifying and binding factor, some will cite traditions to illustrate the Leitkultur.

This alternative, however, which is certainly pointedly formulated here, but which certainly hits a striking strand of the discussions, is admittedly highly questionable. And this for a simple reason: the question of the Leitkultur does not seem to be a question that can be answered by a decision for or against one of these options. The core of the question about the Leitkultur is rather documented in the fact that modern societies are in need of commentary (*kommentarbedürftig*) and understand themselves out of this need for commentary (*Kommentarbedürftigkeit*). The debate about the Leitkultur is a specific expression of such a need for commentary and thus of a society under the conditions of modernity. It is therefore not beyond modern society, nor does it fall behind it, but it is a feature of it.

Modernity (including all past and future postmodernisms) is distinguished by the fact that it cannot exist without continuous commentary. This is also evident earlier in the twentieth century in a wide variety of debates – recall only the following formative disputes: The discussion about the value freedom or neutrality thesis between Weber and Spranger; the positivism dispute in sociology in the 1960s between Adorno and Habermas on the one side and Popper and Albert on the other; or the historians' dispute of the 1980s. One could also recall other controversies: for example, the polemic about the distinction between two cultures (following C.P. Snow) or the discussions of the 1980s about the Just War.

If one sees the current discussion about Leitkultur in this light, i.e. if it is placed in the debates of the twentieth century and at the same time related to the need for

---

[1] Dorn 2018, p. 54.

commentary in modern societies, then the current discussion presents itself in a new light. On the one hand, there is nothing unusual about it, because modern societies communicate and stage their self-image in this way; on the other hand, the current debate draws attention to the blind spot of modern society by making the limits of ongoing commentary an issue. The need for commentary in modern societies always refers to its unquestioned precondition – the lifeworld as the point of reference for commentary.

If one continues to understand the debate about the Leitkultur in the sense of a diagnosis of the times, that is, in the sense that it expresses a crisis phenomenon, then this can be marked more clearly in the correlation of the need for commentary and the lifeworld – at least if one understands the concept of the lifeworld in the classical sense used by Husserl as a rehabilitation of the doxa, the opinion. For then the debates about Leitkultur would reveal the highly interesting crisis experience of the present, that commentaries as interpretations (of culture) and opinions as statements (of culture) drift apart. The perpetual self-commentary of modern society no longer seems to find any resistance in opinions.

2 The Need for Comment by the Company

With *Zeit-Bilder*, which fascinated not only Adorno, Arnold Gehlen offers an option for understanding modern art of the early twentieth century – especially that of Klee and Kandinsky – both historically and systematically. However, the analyses can also be read as a set for describing modern society. For it is not only modern art – according to Gehlen's topos and punchline – that has become 'in need of comment' (*kommentarbedürftig*), but also modern society.

Gehlen turns to painting "under the *guiding idea of pictorial rationality*".[2] The question of the subjects plays just as little a role in this perspective as "the stylistic-historical concepts of art history" can be used as guidelines for the investigation. Rather, Gehlen attempts to understand the changes from idealistic to realistic art and from the latter to abstract painting in terms of the sociology of art. In the alternation of "pictorial forms" between idealistic and realistic art and between realistic art and abstract painting, Gehlen traces the logic of pictorial rationality. If idealistic art – for example religious painting – is distinguished by "visualization",[3] which "always presupposes connotations, i.e. what is known in advance and brought along mentally", "which it lifts into contemplation", realistic art is distinguished by "recognition". "In this is expressed a turning of the interest of time to the existing, the present, and the repeatable; this is the pictorial form of modern times since the Renaissance and the epoch of discoveries." The arts "no longer have an institutional mission; they become private and democratic, settling into the immediacy of the

---

[2] Gehlen 2016, p. 15.
[3] Gehlen 2016, p. 16 f.

given." Realist art, an art of bourgeois society, is replaced in a radical new beginning, or rather broken up by abstract painting. With this, nature "has come out of sight", also "the primary motif" is deleted, the picture appears as irrational, "and the question arises where the conceptuality attached to our view has migrated to: to the commentary literature, which must be regarded precisely as a component of this art".[4]

This is not the place to unfold Gehlen's sociology of art in its entirety, which, beyond this threefold structure, is distinguished by finesse, a wealth of knowledge, and subtlety. Crucial to understanding it in our context is the determination of the need for commentary in modern art, which is already inherent in the topos of a *peinture conceptuelle*. The aesthetic experience, in which perception and concept originally appear as intertwined, becomes fragile in modernity. The concept migrates, as it were, from aesthetic experience into the aesthetic-conceptual commentary. This in turn does not simply stand beyond the work of art, it itself becomes part of the work of art. "This entire literature," the commentary literature of modern art, "*thus belongs to the essence of the thing itself,* it is for internal reasons a substantial component of art."[5]

What tasks does such an understood commentary literature face in the field of modern aesthetics? Gehlen elaborates on this in a number of ways, three aspects of which may be singled out: First, commentaries must "justify the claim to sovereignty of modern painting, because it no longer leans on a given nature or on given worlds of ideas." Secondly, the commentaries have to explain the principles of the new aesthetic procedures. And since modern society no longer makes its own demands on art, the artists themselves must face their own (challenges). Then the commentaries have "an informational and propagandistic function in the relationship between artist and audience".[6]

The need for commentary in modern art can also be read as a need for commentary in modern society. Society has become fragile, it has lost its center and assures itself of its foundations in its own commentary. This has to justify the significance of modern society, which can no longer lean on anything except its own commentary. The debate about the Leitkultur thus appears as a self-commentary of modernity, which, however, reflects its own limit: the Lebenswelt (Lifeworld).

3 The Resistance of the Lifeworld

If the concept of the lifeworld is used today in the feuilleton or in political debates, then it is no longer recognizable that a philosophical problem of the first order is associated with the concept. And one suspects a fortiori no longer that Husserl, in

---

[4] Gehlen 2016, p. 18.
[5] Gehlen 2016, p. 231.
[6] Gehlen 2016, p. 74.

the 1930s, tied the fate of all philosophy and of European culture to this concept. Barely one hundred years after Husserl's reflections on the lifeworld, one might almost suspect, the situation has reversed: no longer is the lifeworld to be made strong in the face of a positivist worldview; rather, the lifeworld must be protected from its own rhetoric.

In contemporary and colloquial uses of the term, 'lifeworld' is mostly understood as an everydayness that individual subjects have a grip on, permeate and dominate. The contemporary rhetoric of the lifeworld is distinguished by the fact that, in contrast to, say, the orders of law, politics, education, or other structures of sociality, the *lifeworld* is conceived as a *free space of agency* with a rather high degree of arbitrariness for individual subjects. In the lifeworld, according to one of the contemporary semantic keynotes, things can be sovereignly regulated by the lifeworld player that have always been regulated elsewhere or are regulated by something else. This explains the popular compilations for book titles and workshops such as 'Law and Lifeworld', 'Media and Lifeworld', 'Economy and Lifeworld', 'Politics and Lifeworld' or 'School and Lifeworld'.

Secondly, the semantic aura of the term as it is used today also includes something that could perhaps be described as an *idyll of the living world.* One feels comfortable in one's living room of supposedly private sensual impressions and does not want to be disturbed in it. It is this somewhat solipsistic idea that also surrounds the lifeworld concept and is also expressed in the fact that one should only not get too close to the lifeworld of the other in order not to irritate it – and oneself.

Thirdly, there is something that can be described as the *complacency of the lifeworld.* It consists in the fact that in contemporary usages it is not infrequently assumed without much thought that the lifeworld is completely transparent and clear for the subjects acting in it. In contrast, the structures of society are confused; the only thing that is clear is the familiarity of the lifeworld. Even if one were to assume that the lifeworld means something like customs and practices, which necessarily always lie behind human action and cognition, this does not mean that such customs and practices are always transparent. For they lie at the back of action, not before everyone's eyes.

For all the difficulties of interpreting Husserl's idea of the lifeworld, which one may well have, it is clear that *such modern lifeworld prejudices have little to do with phenomenology..*[7] Husserl, who introduced the term into phenomenology and who gave the concept of the 'lifeworld' an unparalleled career boost in philosophical discussion with his *Krisis writing*, rather associates the term with a contrary intuition.[8] If one wants to think at all in terms of the dichotomy of 'freely negotiable' and 'not freely regulable' just mentioned, then for Husserl the term lifeworld tends to indicate a sphere that is not easily manipulable, that cannot be shaped or controlled at will. While social systems such as those of law can certainly be changed, this is not so easily possible with the practices of the lifeworld. And if aspects of

---

[7] Bermes 2017a.
[8] Bermes 2017b.

sensuality are to be associated with the lifeworld, they are in no way negotiated in Husserl as private impressions of an isolated and shielded ego. Subjective experience here does not mean a retreat into a private interiority. And also the complacency of the supposedly transparent life-world turns out to be a misunderstood utopia in Husserl. For Husserl's lifeworld is distinguished less by a transparency comparable to that of the sciences than by resistance, as is the case, for example, with opinions, the sphere of doxa. In this sense, the explication of the lifeworld leads to an archaeology of doxa.

This Husserlian idea of a justification of the doxa,[9] the opinions that sustain human life, that give human life form and shape, is an idea that Heidegger also took up. In his Marburg lecture from the summer semester of 1924, which Heidegger gave under the title *Grundbegriffe der Aristotelischen Philosophie (Basic Concepts of Aristotelian Philosophy)*, he explicitly addresses the opinion (doxa). He points out that it is necessary to understand the concept of opinion if one is to understand what the "fundamental phenomenon of everydayness"[10] means. For doxa "is the way in which life knows about itself."[11] The fundamental role of opinion could hardly be expressed more clearly.

Whoever possesses an opinion, Heidegger explains, *has it, he does not seek it*. This is understandable if opinion is understood in the sense of 'having a view'. For one does not seek a view, one always already has it. And with a view a position is taken which always allows for other positions. From this starting point, the phenomenological description opens up further features of the concept of opinion: namely, opinions can then be understood as *statements in* which not only the 'view of something' is expressed, but also the *position on something (the position)* and *the position towards oneself (the attitude)*. It is thus inherent in the concept of opinion that both the content of the opinion and the bearer of an opinion and his position as well as his attitude play a role.

Opinions further open up a structure of *reciprocity*. The concept of opinion is associated with a space of reciprocal relations between people. Opinions are thus not simply subjectively arbitrary, but always refer to the horizon of others (and other opinions). Part of the concept of opinion, according to reciprocity, is that others also have opinions, which do not always have to be the same. Opinions thus open up an understanding of the world. Every opinion is open to opinions that others may also have. One can stand up for an opinion alone, but always within the horizon of other opinions.

Opinions, moreover, are subject *to revision*. Again, it is in the concept of opinion that opinions express varying degrees of resistance or rigidity, but are not irrevocable. What is interesting, of course, is the different ways in which opinions are revised. For in most cases an opinion is not theoretically refuted, but in practical

---

[9] Husserl 1985, p. 44.
[10] Heidegger 2002, p. 136.
[11] Heidegger 2002, p. 138.

contexts an opinion can become 'obsolete' or 'lose its function', so to speak, and a new opinion can take its place.

Equally important, opinions are not simple representations or ideas. It is perfectly possible to ascribe ideas or mental representations to non-human living beings, but 'opinions' can only be where the world of humans is expressed in opinions. Humans, it can be pointedly said, can be described as those living beings who have opinions and deal with opinions. Conceptual representations or ideas can also come to other living beings, but humans understand themselves and the world through opinions.

4 The Culture of the Leitkultur

If in modern art the concept has migrated out of aesthetic experience into commentary, it can also be said that in modernity the concept has migrated out of social experience into commentary. But the culture of the leading culture is then neither simply the commentary nor the lifeworld, understood as the resistance of the doxa against which the commentary rubs. This would only lead to the popular dichotomies – for example, between tradition and law – that have shaped and continue to shape the Leitkultur debate. The subject of Leitkultur, in contrast, is the reflection on the mutual intertwining of the two. And one could give such a twist to the concept of culture par excellence. For comments without opinions are empty and opinions without comments are blind. The idea of national philology does not fail because of this entanglement, it is rather an expression of it.

References

Bermes, Christian: Die Lebenswelt, in: Sebastian Luft und Maren Wehrle (Hg.): Husserl-Handbuch. Leben – Werk – Wirkung. Stuttgart: Metzler 2017a, S. 230–236.
Bermes, Christian: Die Krisis der europäischen Wissenschaften und die transzendentale Phänomenologie (Husserl), in: Sebastian Luft und Maren Wehrle (Hg.): Husserl-Handbuch. Leben – Werk – Wirkung. Stuttgart: Metzler 2017b, S. 97–104.
Dorn, Thea: deutsch, nicht dumpf. Ein Leitfaden für aufgeklärte Patrioten. München: Albrecht Knaus 2018.
Gehlen, Arnold: Zeit-Bilder. Zur Soziologie und Ästhetik der modernen Malerei (1960/1986). Hg. von Karl-Siegbert Rehberg. Frankfurt a. M.: Klostermann 2016, Gesamtausgabe, 9.
Heidegger, Martin: Grundbegriffe der aristotelischen Philosophie (1924). Hg. von Mark Michalski. Frankfurt a. M.: Klostermann 2002, Gesamtausgabe, 18.
Husserl, Edmund: Erfahrung und Urteil. Untersuchungen zur Genealogie der Logik. Hamburg: Meiner 1985, 6. Aufl.

Approaches to Interculturality and Decolonization in German Studies in Southern Africa

Gesa Singer

Abstract The history of German as a subject in Southern Africa goes back to later phases of colonisation by European settlers and has been marked by many upheavals. The academic orientation of studies at universities is still oriented towards European standards today, although since the end of apartheid the need for more representation of African thematic complexes and perspectives has also been taken into account institutionally. Despite the dwindling importance of German in schools, university German studies has become well established and internationally oriented. Recently, approaches to interculturality and decolonisation of German studies can be discerned in the academic landscape in Southern Africa. Professional qualification and the training of students' discursive skills are desiderata that are to be addressed by approaches to interculturality and decolonisation in research and teaching.

1 Intercultural from the Beginning?

Although the discussion about the differences and especially the hierarchization of German studies at home and abroad[1] nowadays seems partly obsolete in view of the diverse spheres of influence and modernization impulses in both spheres, one could make the claim that the intercultural is inherent in German studies abroad anyway. Seeking one's own in the foreign or the foreign in one's own is thus a heuristic

---

[1] On this, see Strosetzki in the preface to this volume: "Zentrum und Peripherie".

G. Singer (✉)
School of Languages and Literatures, German Section, University of Cape Town, Cape Town, South Africa
e-mail: Gesa.Singer@t-online.de

© The Author(s), under exclusive license to Springer-Verlag GmbH, DE, part of Springer Nature 2023
C. Strosetzki (ed.), *200 Years of National Philologies*,
https://doi.org/10.1007/978-3-476-05925-3_13

category that 'naturally' underlies the study of German language and literature outside German-speaking countries; whether this process takes place implicitly as 'appropriation', 'cultural contrast' or explicitly as 'inter- or transcultural'. Thus, this also applies to the African context:

> "From its inception, the practice of German studies in teaching and research in the African context has been oriented in such a way as to be intercultural. Its intercultural aspects constitute self-learning through foreign learning, cultural exchange, intercultural hermeneutics and communication, and foreign understanding."[2]

However, it is important to be aware that (especially in the past decades) 'German Studies' in Southern Africa (at least in South Africa and Namibia; Mozambique, on the other hand, has a Portuguese influence due to its own colonial history) were also and primarily attended by native speakers of German: "Namibia and South Africa are the only two countries on the African continent that have significant German minorities and accordingly offer not only German as a foreign language, but also German as a mother tongue."[3]

2 History

A cursory look at some phases in the history of the subject will illustrate the mix of circumstances that have led to its present state, especially in South Africa. "German has always been a foreign language in South Africa throughout its history – even in the 'Dutch period'. The numerically quite high proportion of German-speaking settlers in the Cape did not change this."[4] Although German played a certain role among the European settlers of the seventeenth century, its influence in education was marginal for a long time because of the dominance of Afrikaans and English in the Cape. However, the later and fractured establishment of the subject in the school sector[5] towards the middle of the nineteenth century and finally in the twentieth century at universities[6] was oriented towards high European standards:

> German studies at 'English' universities, if one can generalise somewhat, was thus characterised by high academic standards, which were always oriented towards international stan-

---

[2] Demanou 2020, p. 130.
[3] Augart 2012, p. 10.
[4] Pakendorf 2016, p. 83.
[5] According to Pakendorf 2016, p. 84, "[...] German was offered as a school subject for the first time in 1830. Firstly, these tentative beginnings were limited to the greater Cape Town area; in the hinterland there were no state schools for a long time, teaching here remained the responsibility of the church and often also of mostly poorly educated private teachers [...]".
[6] Cf. Pakendorf 2016, p. 84: "In the 19th century, with few interruptions, German was taught continuously at schools in the Cape Colony and was also offered at the University of the Cape of Good Hope, founded in 1873." Cf. also on the numerical development Kußler 2001; Augart 2012; and on the content of Malzan 2018.

dards. At the same time, however, few of its representatives – most of whom came from Europe or felt European after all – seem to have been remotely interested in local issues or problems and, moreover, were hardly prepared to make concessions to South African students who had no or only an imperfect command of German.[7]

3 Significance, Curricula and Literatures

3.1 Past

Apartheid, which defined half the twentieth century, eventually brought about drastic changes in education. While in times of apartheid the preoccupation with everything that did not come from South Africa was of interest, after its end there arose the need to deal with oneself and to valorise African heritage. This was accompanied by structural changes that were intended to take account of the changed sociopolitical conditions:

> Following initial efforts by the ANC government in the aftermath of the 1994 political change, the restructuring of South Africa's university landscape was pursued with vigour between 2001 and 2004. This involved attempts to eliminate the segregation and inequality created by apartheid legislation from existing universities organised along racial lines and discriminatory policies through mergers and regrouping, which also led to renaming in some cases.[8]

To this day, however, German also ekes out an existence as one of the other foreign languages alongside, for example, French, Spanish and Chinese, and in the course of job cuts and cost-cutting measures, as well as the accompanying institutional dissolution of departments, it has often been merged with other foreign languages in 'schools'. Although for several decades graduates of German schools made up the lion's share of German students and at least some of them also had German as a family language, the proportion of students for whom German is a foreign language is increasing overall (but to varying degrees at different universities).

> Until the 1970s, curricula for German in the Bachelor's programme were structured similarly at all universities, in that language acquisition preceded the actual study, either because one had a school degree in the subject, or because one acquired the language in an intensive course, the so-called German Special. Curricula for the course of study were consistently based on those offered by German universities and were thus literature-oriented. The first year of study was devoted to the history of literature, and the second year included an introduction to the history of the language as well as Middle High German, in addition to the literature of the 19th century. Finally, the third year of study covered the literature of the Middle Ages, the Classics and the literature of the 20th century. In addition, advanced language courses were offered in all years. When new professors were hired in the mid-1970s

---

[7] Pakendorf 2019, p. 88; "It should be emphasized here that throughout the period up to 1990, despite various alleged or real attempts at reform on the part of the government of the day, the economy and political rule were firmly in the hands of the white minority." (Pakendorf 2016, p. 86).

[8] von Malzan 2014, p. 10.

due to a change of generations, the curricula changed. On the one hand, one wanted to adapt to new developments in German studies in Germany, and on the other hand, the educational landscape began to change with the uprising of the students in Soweto in 1976, so that Middle High German was removed from the curricula.[9]

To this day, the programmes reflect an orientation of teaching (and research) towards literary studies as the supreme discipline, which has grown historically:

However, with the traditional focus on German literary history with an emphasis on the nineteenth and twentieth centuries established, according to Neville[10]

> [...] German literature is not necessarily able to empower or equip South African students in the contemporary discourses of the South African context, because the knowledge gained through this literature is probably not directly transferable to their context. [...] This literary focus area cannot be focused on explaining Germany to South African students, but should encourage critical engagement. Emphasis is therefore placed on "cultural studies viewpoints"[11], i.e. the ability to navigate through culture and language. However, this often requires a new determination of the choice of literature, as has been done in several German departments in South Africa.[12]

Zappen-Thomson (2000) reported on approaches to intercultural German teaching in Namibia's multicultural environment, according to which teaching, especially in primary and secondary education, is often contrastive rather than intercultural.

3.2 Present and Future

Meanwhile, German studies worldwide has incorporated intercultural aspects as well as the study of authors with migrant backgrounds into its curriculum, and this is also reflected in the programmes of some German departments in Southern Africa. That the.

The fact that the study of multi-ethnic Germany and Germany as a country of migration is a welcome surprise for some students, as they may tend to assume a homogeneous German social structure due to their socialisation or school education, is one of the learner-centred and motivational aspects that contemporary didactics should make use of. This offers more discursive potential when dealing with literature against the background of complex social conditions and can also act as motivation in the efforts to achieve understanding (in the target language!) about individual sensitivities and problem situations by dealing with the (fictional) life situations of the protagonists.

In particular, the thematisation of linguistic identity and the limits of multilingualism, which is one of the core themes of intercultural literature, can stimulate students to reflect, especially as it affects multilingualism itself in many cases and

---

[9] Maltzan 2018, p. 103.
[10] Neville 2020, p. 77.
[11] Laurien 2006, 443.
[12] Neville 2020, p. 77.

the promotion of multilingualism[13] is also one of the priority goals of South African educational policy.

Another point of contact for a cultural studies-oriented study of literature can be found in the exploration of Afro-German identities, which also refer to discourses conducted in the course of decolonization and anti-racism, and it is palpable,

> [...] why Afro-German identities should be a current focus of discussion and study. According to the current discourse on refugees and foreigners in Germany, a study of Afro-German identities is important because it radically challenges the concept of a mono-ethnic Germany. Meanwhile, Afro-Germans are a part of Germany's history -they were an often ignored minority in the last centuries[14]

Contemporary intercultural readings – contrastive, discursive and complementary to the established canon – thus also form the precondition and necessity for the critical analysis of now common concepts such as difference and hybridity.[15]

The adherence to the classical canon of readings as well as traditional methods of interpretation

> [...] is potentially problematic, however, as German society is not a static entity. Most importantly, literature written by minorities in Germany could develop a broad understanding of Germany in students and support the ability to navigate between different perspectives. Migration literature has long been established in the professional literature as a supplement to DaF instruction with the goal of emphasizing and presenting the complexity of Germany.[16]

An expansion of the canon therefore proves to be unavoidable. In addition to the established canon, it is worthwhile – especially in the postgraduate programme – to read cultural studies texts that also deal critically with (post)colonialism and racism.[17]

> In the narrative texts of W.O. von Horn, Sir John Retcliffe, Karl May, August Niemann and also Wilhelm Raabe, the course is set for the perception of South Africa in German-language literature; this differs from the rest of the discourse on Africa because an already

---

[13] South Africa has 11 official languages.
[14] Neville 2020, p. 80.
[15] Cf. Neville's recourse to Homi Bhaba: "The fact that Afro-German literature often cannot simply be pinned down to one genre or textual form reflects Bhabha's postcolonial understanding of transitions. According to Bhabha, "we are in the moment of transition" (Bhabha 2000, p. 1). Given this, it seems reasonable to see Afro-German literature as part of this moment. Transitions are defined as points "where space and time intersect, creating complex configurations of difference and identity, past and present, inside and outside, inclusion and exclusion" (Bhabha 2000, p. 1). This quote points to the interstices opened up by these crossings, which are "characterized by the overlapping and de-placement (displacement) of areas of difference" (Bhabha 2000, p. 2)." (Neville 2020, p. 84). In addition, it may also be worthwhile to engage with aspects of the postmigrant (El-Tayeb 2016; Foroutan 2018).
[16] Neville 2020, p. 85.
[17] In the Honours Programme at UCT 2021/22, for example, a critical comparative reading of Gerhard Seyfried: 'Herero' (2003) and Uwe Timm: 'Morenga' (1978), which address the genocide of the Herero, as well as Wilhem Raabe's 'Abu Telfan' (1867) and 'Stopfkuchen' (1891) and its complex (re)interpretation of colonial ideology is planned.

colonized country is depicted here [...]. In South Africa, the German adventurer, discoverer and conqueror does not encounter a wilderness given over to the experience, the thirst for knowledge and the exploitation of the European [...].[18]

Parodic, provocative and counterfactual texts could also be integrated into such a process of deciphering and deconstructing, and the means of irony could be discussed at the same time.[19]

The selection of topics with both local and global relevance is one of the most exciting areas:

Because of the social problems in South Africa, which are historical as well as sometimes cultural and often have an impact on young people in the country, exposure to literature in a foreign language may provide a space to discuss issues that may still be taboo in the family or even in the larger cultural space.[20]

However, linguistic possibilities and hurdles must also be taken into account, since not all universities, such as Stellenbosch University in the Western Cape, have a large group of students enrolled for whom German (along with Afrikaans, for example) is a family language, and especially since the demand for and, above all, the supply of German at schools has declined in recent years.[21]

Sadikou (2020) proposes the combination of multilingualism, intertextuality and translation in order to make German studies as a whole more internationalized

The common denominator of these three areas – multilingualism, intertextuality as well as translation – is that students of German Studies can acquire multi-perspective views. It is precisely in this multiperspectivity, which students can acquire through concentrated readings of canonical texts such as Heinrich Heine, Goethe, Novalis, or, concerning the new generation, Ilija Trojanow, Navid Kermani or Sherko Fatah, that an incommensurable added value for the interculturality of German Studies lies.[22]

While in my experience students intuitively bring up thematic aspects around identity, alterity and stereotypes and belonging or non-belonging even without prior theoretical knowledge in the field of intercultural literature when dealing with texts by, for example, Abbas Khider, Emine Sevgi Özdamar, Feridun Zaimoglu etc., it is worth taking a closer look at which specific aspects are particularly virulent when working with students in Southern Africa.

---

[18] Ullrich 2019, p. 60.

[19] Cf. Kpao Sarè 2019, p. 85): "Often the aim of fiction alternative-history writing is to portray a better social or world political alternative. The centre of power constructed in the films and novels examined here is not located where one would expect it to be, namely in the centre, in the North, in the Occident or in Europe, but conversely in peripheral Africa. Through counterfactual representation, they thus offer an opportunity to observe more thoroughly and factually the issue of immigration or migration and related constellations of problems."

[20] Thorpe 2014, p. 36.

[21] In the past, English was occasionally used as the language of the seminar in literature classes in order to avoid the linguistic pitfalls. However, in my opinion, this approach does not lead to the desired immersive contact with German in all subject areas.

[22] Sadikou 2020, p. 29.

According to Mühr, 'belonging' appears to be particularly fruitful as a category of analysis when dealing with German-language literature in Southern Africa, since it can be shown that "[...] in the context of both colonial and postcolonial literature, the description of social location by means of the category of belonging is more appropriate than descriptive procedures of the experience of foreignness or categories of the social-psychological discourse of identity."[23]

In this context, I think it is particularly appealing if the composition of the group is heterogeneous and (exchange) students from other countries, with heterogeneous and multilingual language requirements, as well as with their own experiences and viewpoints, can also contribute something to the multiperspectivity of the analysis. In times of the pandemic, such intercultural encounters are also producible by means of technology and are increasingly integrated into contemporary teaching.

4 Academic Cooperation and Further Development

The continuity of SAGV (German Studies Association in Southern Africa) and now cooperation and joint conferences with GAS (German Studies in Sub-Saharan Africa) are among the academic achievements that promise further academic expansion of the subject in the region.

Labour Market Connectivity
While the academic side of the subject continues to prosper despite severe restrictions, hegemonic as well as (post)colonial structures and asymmetries are still clearly noticeable on the student side, which expressed themselves with violent reactions in the 'Fees must fall' movement, among others.[24]

The high youth unemployment rate in South Africa, for example, as well as the almost obvious lack of alternatives to a degree course in comparison to the almost non-existent vocational training opportunities, make it obvious to consider possible vocational orientations of a German degree course:

> German Studies in Southern Africa is still predominantly oriented towards literary studies, although at most universities it is now more of a language course programme with literary studies modules than German Studies. There are hardly any practice-oriented courses of study, and only some universities offer courses leading to professional qualifications, mainly in the fields of translation and DAF didactics. [...] Courses of study in which German can be taken as an elective subject, thus usually enriching a concrete career goal with a language competence, come closer to the idea of a professional qualification through the language German [...] Summing up now, there are tendencies towards professional orientation and professional qualification, but German departments in Southern Africa – as in other countries – have to deal with a greater practical orientation through appropriate

---

[23] Mühr 2020, p. 187.
[24] Cf. https://uni.de/redaktion/fees-must-fall; https://en.wikipedia.org/wiki/FeesMustFall.

courses of study or modules and the various application aspects of international German studies and strive for professionalisation in their discipline.[25]

While German Studies at the University of Namibia strives for practical relevance through the inclusion of modules on German as a language in business and tourism, as well as a postgraduate programme leading to a translator's diploma,[26] South African German Studies departments, at least in the Western Cape, have traditionally been more linguistic-literary. "South African universities often find it very cumbersome to introduce new courses or launch new programmes, although interdisciplinary collaboration, especially in research, is increasingly taking place."[27]

An essential component for the academic qualification of graduates as well as the long-term consolidation of the subject, on the other hand, is also the staffing policy at universities, which is increasingly oriented towards aspects of equality, whereby (at first glance absurdly) the category of race and nationality is once again brought into the conversation and under changed auspices.

> A challenge for all departments would now be to recruit more (South) African lecturers when further positions open up. This would open up career prospects for current students to be employed as German lecturers at a university in the country after completing their studies or doctorate. On the part of the governments in Namibia and South Africa, the pressure to employ local and, above all, black academics is increasing; the hurdles for foreign academics to obtain a work permit in South Africa are becoming ever higher, as experienced by the German departments in Windhoek, Bellville, Zululand and Johannesburg. If the restructuring of universities outlined at the beginning of this article continues, the proportion of white students, who currently make up the majority of all learners of German in South Africa, will gradually shrink.[28]

A high degree of transparency, quality development and commitment is therefore necessary in order to do justice to the numerous particularities, needs and problems facing German Studies in Southern Africa.

> The practice of German studies as an intercultural science in Africa is confronted with considerable difficulties. On the one hand, the cultural exchange it promotes is conditioned by power relations. [...] On the other hand, interculturally oriented German studies in Africa is primarily aimed at producing academics and DaF teachers, because its practice in teaching and research does not equip students with sufficient material to be efficiently employed in other socio-professional fields in society.[29]

While in Namibia the prospect of remaining in the teaching profession and in the tourism industry were constant prospects,[30] such study destinations are less attractive to South African students (also because of the low pay).

---

[25] Augart 2014, p. 234.
[26] Zappen-Thomson 2014.
[27] Thorpe 2014, p. 30.
[28] Annas 2003: p. 106.
[29] Demanou 2020, p. 130.
[30] Cf. Shilongo 2017.

5 Didactic Perspectives

What demands and perspectives can be derived from all this? Demands for a supplementation of the programme content, for example?

> The teaching of German Studies in the African context should be oriented towards the students' professional perspectives and opportunities within society. This can be made possible by developing transversal knowledge on the basis of the seminar content. By this I mean the totality of specialist knowledge that is useful in the business world: IT knowledge, dealing with the Internet, writing techniques, etc.[31]

While some of these can be considered prerequisites of the degree, others have areas of overlap with other subjects and needs for propaedeutic courses arise.

In addition to the linguistic, cultural and analytical knowledge acquired in a German degree course, it is not least the communicative, discursive and (self-)reflexive skills and soft skills tested and refined during the degree course that can have a positive effect on career orientation and qualification.[32] These should also be upgraded in the administrative field, especially since they form the basis for interdisciplinary and effective work, and create a counterweight to 'output'-oriented structures that still predominantly shape school socialisation.

German Studies departments in Southern Africa not only strive to participate in global discourses, but also to enrich them with their own expertise and perspectives and to enable their graduates to do likewise.

References

Annas, Rolf: Deutsch an Universitäten im südlichen Afrika. Zur Entwicklung des Fachs seit 2003, in: Acta Germanica, Bd. 44. Frankfurt am Main: Stellenbosch 2016, S. 105–118.
Augart, Julia: (Süd)afrikanische Germanistik–Zur Positionierung und Professionalisierung der Germanistik im südlichen Afrika. DOI: eDUSA7.1: 7–22. 2012. [letzter Besuch: 14.02.2021].
Augart, Julia: Deutsch Akademischer Austauschdienst (DAAD): Deutsch für den Beruf? Zur Professionalisierung in den Curricula im südlichen Afrika, in: Deutsche Sprache und Kultur im afrikanischen Kontext. Beiträge der DAAD-Germanistentagung 2012 mit Partnerländern in der Region Subsahara-Afrika. Göttingen: Wallstein 2014, S. 225–234.
Bhabha, Homi, K: Die Verortung der Kultur (2000, Englisch: The location of culture 1994, Übersetzt von M. Schiffmann und J.Freudl). Stauffenburg Verlag, Tübingen.
Demanou, René: Germanistik in Afrika im Spannungsverhältnis von Interkulturalität und Beschäftigungsfähigkeit, in: Nicole Colin et al. (Hg.): Germanistik – eine interkulturelle Wissenschaft?, Synchron Publishers, Heidelberg 2020, S. 123–131.
El-Tayeb, Fatima: Undeutsch. Die Konstruktion des Anderen in der postmigrantischen Gesellschaft. Bielefeld: Transcript Verlag 2016.
Foroutan, Naika 2018: Die postmigrantische Perspektive. Aushandlungsprozesse in pluralen Gesellschaften. In: Marc Hill und Erol Yildiz (Hg.): Erfahrungen – Ideen – Reflexionen, 2018. Open access Triedere.pdf, S. 15–27. [letzter Besuch: 14.01.2021]

---

[31] Demanou 2020, p. 130.
[32] Singer 2020.

Kpao Sarè, Constant: Afrika-Paradies. Eine alternativgeschichtliche Gestaltung der Migration nach Afrika in ausgewählten anderssprachigen Filmen und Romanen, in: Carlotta von Maltzan et al. (Hg.): Grenzen und Migration: Afrika und Europa. (Jahrbuch für Internationale Germanistik, Bd. 134) Bern: Peter Lang u. a. 2019, S. 73–87.

Kußler, Rainer: Deutschunterricht und Germanistikstudium in Südafrika, in: Gerhard Helbig, et al. (Hg.): Deutsch als Fremdsprache. Ein internationales Handbuch. 2. Halbband. Berlin / New York: De Gruyter 2001, S. 1609–1619.

Laurien, Ingrid: Das Fach ‚Deutsch' an Universitäten im ‚Neuen Südafrika'. Eine Legitimation für Europa? In: Info DaF, Nr. 5, 2006, S. 438–445.

Mühr, Stephan: Apartheid und Zugehörigkeit. Zugehörigkeit als Analysekategorie kolonialer und postkolonialer Literatur am Bespiel Namibias, in: Claus Altmayer et al. (Hg.): Zugehörigkeiten. Ansätze und Perspektive in Germanistik und Deutsch als Fremd- und Zweitsprache. Tübingen: Stauffenberg Verlag 2020, S. 175–190.

Neville, Daniella: Zur Relevanz der Afro-Deutschen Literatur im südafrikanischen DaF-Kontext. In: eDUSA 15, 2020-74-96, 2020. https://www.sagv.org.za/wp-content/uploads/2020/10/eDUSA-gesamt-2020_-Final.pdf [letzter Besuch: 14.02.2021].

Pakendorf, Gunther: Zur Geschichte des Germanistenverbands im Südlichen Afrika(SAGV) im sozialpolitischen Kontext, in: Acta Germanica, 44, 2016, S. 82–104. http://www.sagverband.co.za/wp-content/uploads/2019/02/german_v44_a22.pdf [letzter Besuch: 14.02.2021].

Sadikou, Nadjib: Interkulturelle Germanistik. Überlegungen zur Internationalität des Faches, in: Nicole Colin et al. (Hg.): Germanistik – eine interkulturelle Wissenschaft?, Heidelberg: Synchron Publishers, 2020, S. 21–30.

Shilongo, Shoosha: Warum studiert man Deutsch in Namibia? Eine Untersuchung zum Deutschstudium an der University of Namibia, in: eDUSA (Deutschunterricht im südlichen Afrika), Jahrgang 11/1 2017, S. 28–45. https://www.sagv.org.za/wp-content/uploads/2019/edusa/eDUSA-gesamt-2017.pdf [letzter Besuch: 14.02.2021].

Singer, Gesa: Internationalisierung der Germanistik durch interkulturelle Didaktik. In: Nicole Colin et al. (Hg.): Germanistik – eine interkulturelle Wissenschaft?, in: Heidelberg: Synchron Publishers 2020, S. 43–49.

Thorpe, Kathleen: Auswahlkriterien für literarische Texte im DaF-Unterricht in Südafrika, in: Deutsch Akademischer Austauschdienst (DAAD) (Hg.): Deutsche Sprache und Kultur im afrikanischen Kontext. Beiträge der DAAD-Germanistentagung 2012 mit Partnerländern in der Region Subsahara-Afrika. Göttingen: Wallstein 2014.

Maltzan, Carlotta von: Zum Wert von ‚Kultur' und Literatur im Fremdsprachenunterricht: Beispiel Südafrika, in: Altmayer, Claus et al. (Hg.): Literatur in Deutsch als Fremdsprache und internationaler Germanistik. Konzepte, Themen und Forschungsperspektiven. Bd. 3. Tübingen: Stauffenburg 2014, S. 97–106.

Maltzan, Carlotta von: Deutsch im Kontext der südafrikanischen Bildungspolitik und der Ruf nach Dekolonisierung, in: Jahrbuch für Internationale Germanistik. Jahrgang L/Heft 1. Berlin 2018, S. 99–110. https://www.researchgate.net/publication/269963696_Sprachenpolitik_und_die_Rolle_der_Fremdsprachen_Deutsch_in_Sudafrika [letzter Besuch: 14.02.2021].

Ullrich, Heiko: Figurentypologie als ethnographisches Analyseinstrument. Die Darstellung Südafrikas in der deutschen Literatur von 1850–1890, in: Wilhelm Amann et al. (Hg.): Zeitschrift für interkulturelle Germanistik. 10. Jahrgang, Heft 1. Bielefeld: Transcript Verlag 2019, S. 59–80

Zappen-Thomson, Marianne: Interkulturelles Lernen und Lehren in einer multikulturellen Gesellschaft: Deutsch als Fremdsprache in Namibia. Göttingen: Klaus Hess Verlag 2000.

Zappen-Thomson, Marianne: Genau so, aber doch ganz anders. Die deutsche Sprache in Namibia, in: Jacob Emmanuel Mabe (Hg.): Warum lernt und lehrt man Deutsch in Afrika? Autobiographische Ansichten und didaktische Erfahrungen. Festschrift zu Ehren von Anton Wilhelm Amo. Nordhausen: Verlag Traugott Bautz GmbH 2014, S. 53–64.

Romanistics as a Passion: Narratives from the Recent History of the Discipline

Klaus-Dieter Ertler

Abstract Since the upheaval of the late 1960s, the profile of Romance philology has changed significantly. To take stock of this more recent development, autobiographical reports published under the title "Romance Philology as Passion" are used to generate an overall picture that allows an adequate approach to the subject, which is still all too vivid and changeable due to its historical proximity. In the reports analysed here, two thematic areas dominate, concerning careers as well as networks and institutions. These are, on the one hand, the historically conceived paradigm shifts that emanated from the '68 movement. The other is the confessional contexts of career formation. The references to religious structures in the development process of Romance scholars are numerous and manifest themselves above all in the bipolarity between Protestantism and Catholicism, which, against the specific background of Romance cultures, results in a series of dazzling configurations.

With its numerous interconnections and ramifications, the subject of Romance Studies is one of the most dazzling fields of research in contemporary intellectual history, characterized by cultural diversity. Emerging on the one hand as a product of German-speaking Romanticism and nation-state in the first half of the nineteenth century and institutionalized for the first time in the context of the founding of the study of Romance languages (1836) at the University of Bonn by Friedrich Diez, and on the other hand challenged by philological traditions and developments in the respective Romance cultures, the subject has maintained this basic tension until today. The question arises as to whether it is precisely this seemingly paradoxically skewed situation that has given the subject its unique selling point, which on the one hand still distinguishes it today, but on the other hand – especially against the

---

K.-D. Ertler (✉)
Institut für Romanistik, Universität Graz, Graz, Österreich
e-mail: klaus.ertler@uni-graz.at

© The Author(s), under exclusive license to Springer-Verlag GmbH, DE, part of Springer Nature 2023
C. Strosetzki (ed.), *200 Years of National Philologies*,
https://doi.org/10.1007/978-3-476-05925-3_14

background of more recent developments in research-oriented differentiation – seems to weaken it. As a guiding difference, this opposing structure has been able to persist to the present day – not least for pragmatic reasons of university funding – if one considers that most professorships in German-speaking countries – with the exception of Switzerland – are advertised less according to single-language, i.e. national-philological criteria, but rather following a rather broad Romance Studies profile.

If we take a look at the last decades of the history of the discipline, the profile of Romance Philology has become considerably more complex since the upheaval of the late 1960s.[1] To take stock of this more recent development, we have decided to use autobiographical accounts to sketch an overall picture that allows an adequate approach to the subject, which is still all too vivid and changeable due to its historical proximity.[2]

The basis for this was the "Autobiographical History" entitled "Romanistik als Passion. Sternstunden der neueren Fachgeschichte", which is available in seven volumes. 156 texts from the pens of emeritus or retired colleagues provide an insight into the recent development of the subject, whereby most of the reports were written by the authors themselves, while a few reports were written as part of an interview or as an obituary by close relatives or acquaintances.[3]

Thus our first volume, published in June 2007, was mostly well received by scholars.[4] The detailed analysis by Frank-Rutger Hausmann in *Romanische Forschungen* provided a first analytical stocktaking of the texts.[5] In addition, the subject-historical topic was included in the conception of the subsequent Romance Studies Conference, which was organized by Paul Geyer in Bonn in 2009 under the motto "Romance Studies – Profession and Vocation". Shortly before that, the self-image of the subject was discussed in detail in the *journal Romanische Forschungen*[6] among Romance scholars.

With the theme "Romance Studies in Dialogue", the Romance Studies Conference 2011 in Berlin also continued the idea of bringing linguistics, literature and cultural

---

[1] *The Romanistenlexikon (Dictionary of Romance Studies)* compiled by Frank-Rutger Hausmann in recent years, a list of Romance scholars who have worked in or come from the German-speaking world, has proved to be extremely prominent.

[2] It should be recalled that the specialist history of Romance studies – apart from the pioneering work of Frank-Rutger Hausmann, Hans Ulrich Gumbrecht, Ottmar Ette and others – has also been represented by colleagues in Graz. With the processing of the Hugo Schuchardt Archive in the 1980s by Klaus Lichem, Michaela Wolf and later Bernhard Hurch, as well as our relevant work on Ulrich Schulz-Buschhaus and his function as an architect of Romance Studies between 1968 and 2000, a significant contribution was made to the development of this branch of research. Cf. for example the databases Hurch and Ertler.

[3] Some autobiographical narratives were subsequently developed into a book of their own. Cf. for example Siebenmann 2011, Röseberg 2018 or Schober 2011.

[4] Ertler 2007.

[5] Hausmann 2008, pp. 50–58.

[6] Cf. Behrens 2008, pp. 329–337 – Ertler 2008, pp. 338–343 – Geyer 2008, pp. 344–349 – Lüsebrink 2008, pp. 350–355 – Mecke 2008, pp. 356–363 – Neumann 2008, pp. 364–369.

studies closer together again, not only methodologically and in terms of content, but also via the path of generational exchange, and from this to promote not only philology in the narrower sense, but also the development of a newer type of cultural studies.

Romance Studies as Passion also inscribed itself in this context.[7] Frank-Rutger Hausmann again wrote a substantial review for it.[8] At the 2013 Romance Studies Conference in Würzburg, Karlheinz Stierle gave a keynote address on the topic of "Romance Studies as Passion, as Science and as Mission" and showed very clearly in his presentation that some of the energies behind research have a special function for the subject of Romance Studies in particular. According to him, Romance cultures not only provide a wide range of research fields, but can also prove to be extremely attractive in the run-up to careers. Moreover, it becomes clear in his remarks – as is also underlined by the individual contributions to the seven volumes[9] on *Romance Studies as Passion* – that the function of individual mediators can sometimes play an essential role in the early awakening of interest in the subject.[10]

According to anthropologically constant elements, the elements of career development can be well observed in the reports and usually clearly structured into adjuvants and opponents. The traced path usually leads from childhood and youth experiences, school years, studies, relevant experiences abroad, dissertation, habilitation, professorship and retirement. For the older generation, the war and post-war experiences with the corresponding ideological profiling play an important role, while for the younger representatives of Romance Studies, the upheaval of the 1960s is in the foreground. It is noticeable that the path to Romance Studies and the later internal orientation is often closely linked to these vectors. This also includes the confessional orientation, whose experience of self and foreignness in the German-speaking as well as Romance context leads to fundamental decisions of the future researcher's personality.

It is easy to understand that autobiography as a genre presents a challenge to any researcher. Pascal's dictum "le moi est haïssable", which Klaus Heitmann[11] cites as a possible hurdle in his report from Heidelberg, may resonate in some "narratives", but it could not nip the invested narrative potential of the Romance representatives in the bud. Nevertheless, one should not underestimate the risk of discrediting of any kind associated with the "storytelling" of career development, since the careers were usually not always about royal roads leading to a professorship, but often about paths tangled in the thicket of institutions, which could sometimes even lead

---

[7] Ertler 2011.
[8] Cf. Hausmann 2012, pp. 63–65.
[9] From the third volume onwards, students of prominent colleagues also write about teachers such as Karlheinz Barck, Eugenio Coseriu, Harri Meier, Gerhard Rohlfs, Brigitte Schlieben-Lange and Mario Wandruszka. This is an idea launched by Jens Lüdtke and Hans-Martin Gauger. Cf. Ertler 2014. Cf. also the review of this volume by Hausmann 2015, pp. 72–76.
[10] See also the reviews of the fourth volume (Ertler 2015) by Hausmann 2017, pp. 221–226 and by Schiller (q.v.).
[11] Heitmann 2018, p. 113.

across mined terrain of difficult departments or faculties. As the appointments in general showed, the three factors of "ability", "diligence" and "luck" often took on important functions.

The charm of the individual narratives lies precisely in this difficult challenge to the representatives of the discipline to draw a personal arc over the great moments of their careers and thus to locate themselves in the quicksand of the history of the discipline with anecdotal sprinklings.

If one interprets the 156 narratives with the criteria of Franco Moretti's "distant reading", networks that at first glance remain invisible come to the fore. Starting from a few research personalities, the subject of Romance Studies has become more broadly differentiated in the post-war period, whereby the focus – perhaps due to the proximity to France – tended to be in the south-west German universities. However, Munich, Berlin and other university locations also played a leading role during this period.

As far as the more recent historical development of the subject is concerned, several paradigmatic upheavals can be identified in the relevant decades of the post-war period, three of which may be highlighted here. A central landmark is to be found in the 1968 movement, which can be seen not least as a symptom of the way in which the culture of remembrance was dealt with after 1945 and which gave rise to broad cross-cultural areas of discourse.

In this context, the traditional Romance philology with its focus on Old French text corpora and a holistic conception of language and literature – linked to the structures of the full university – lost its effectiveness. A further turning point became apparent at the end of the 1980s, when the projects of modernism came to an end with the collapse of the Soviet Union and the later merger of the two German states, and were given a new theoretical and pragmatic configuration, which went hand in hand with the triumph of information technology. With the associated post-modernism, there was a renewed differentiation of Romance Studies practice, so that hitherto marginal structures moved to the centre and peripheries of Romance cultures, such as African Lusitanian Studies or the Canadian Francophonie, were given greater attention.

A third milestone could be identified towards the end of the 1990s with the university and curricula reforms triggered by the Bologna Process, which profoundly modified teaching and research practices and brought the subject under new self-explanatory pressure through interdisciplinary links with other subjects, especially pedagogy and didactics. The fact that the humanities as a whole gradually came under pressure in the context of recent social developments of economy and social relevance did not always have a positive effect on the new forms of the subject of Romance Studies. However, one should not underestimate their viability in times of new technical forms of communication, since the study and teaching of Romance languages, literatures, cultures, didactics, etc. will assume a central supply function for the development of knowledge in the future.

1 Narratives on the 1968 Movement

The generations speaking here were generally shaped not only by the post-war events, but mostly also by the effects of the 1968 movement, which were perceived differently depending on personal experience and attitude and were to continue to have an impact for a long time. They became one of the central themes of autobiographical accounts. The accompanying changes in methodology and theory, as well as the splitting of Romance philology into literary and linguistic studies, shaped the discursivism of the period. But the newly established universities and the professorships associated with them were also reflected in the overall profile presented.

In the collection, Jürgen Grimm dealt most extensively with the paradigm shift of the '68 movement:

> Although I was no longer a youngster at that time, the '68 riots had a strong influence on me. In this respect, my sympathy for a literary sociological method by no means 'fell from the sky', but corresponded to the spirit of the times, or at least a certain spirit of the times. The spirit of the student riots of 1968 has long been water under the bridge. But it was followed by an awakening that continues to have an effect today. While the world of literature and the humanities had been methodologically characterised by a few precisely describable models up to that point, the need for the scientification of teaching and research, which was powerfully articulated in the context of the 68 riots, triggered a veritable explosion of (literary) scientific paradigms. In the radicality of their positions, they called into question old familiar certainties and made conventional methodology appear obsolete.[12]

Karl Kohut puts it in a similar way when he underlines the positive effects of the upheaval on his subject as well as on his career:

> "In the 68s, a fundamental change in Romance studies finally took place, the consequences of which can still be felt today. Literary studies appeared as a "soft" science whose raison d'être was by no means proven. Hence came the attempts to support it by other, "harder" sciences, such as linguistics, psychology or sociology. The ensuing discussion of methods continues to this day (one need only look at the various introductions to the Romance Studies subfields), and methods threaten to eclipse literature as such. In the years that followed, other outside currents came to dominate our (and not only our) subject periodically, the latest of which, for the time being, is the debate on postcolonialism. In 1974, before the end of my two-year term as dean, I received a call to the newly founded comprehensive university in Duisburg [...]. North Rhine-Westphalia had founded five comprehensive universities in the early 1970s and was considered by us young professors to be the academic state of the future."[13]

For Jürgen Meisel, the 68ers brought a welcome change in university structures:

> I therefore cannot understand the nostalgic sympathy for the Ordinary University that is cultivated by representatives of my generation and older. As beneficiaries of the system, they only remember positive aspects, whereas they only remember the excesses and excesses of the '1968' student movement. However, the reforms and democratisation of the university that this triggered were overdue, even if the price of bureaucratisation and com-

---

[12] Grimm 2007, p. 180 f.
[13] Kohut 2007, p. 273.

mittee torment had to be paid. I, for one, would not have wanted to work at the 'good old' university, nor would I have been able to.[14]

From a peripheral perspective, Adelheid Schuhmann outlines the development in northern Germany:

> At the time, Kiel was a relatively small university away from the large university centres such as Berlin, Hamburg or Frankfurt, where the student unrest of the 1968s developed, and was largely spared major actions by protesting and striking students. Nevertheless, the general politicization of the student body also reached Kiel University and, especially in the humanities subjects, students increasingly demanded greater consideration of social and historical references and the removal of taboos about the recent German past. This not inconsiderably changed the traditional orientation of German and Romance studies towards the classics of literature and prepared the rise of regional studies and regional studies in the 1970s up to cultural studies in the 1990s.[15]

Klaus Heitmann followed the events with moderate sympathy:

> In the years of my return to Marburg, things were stormy in terms of university politics. The university was a focal point of the left-wing student revolt, which also severely affected Romance colleagues. I was not one of them. On the contrary, I sympathized with the critics of the system for long stretches, at least with the more moderate among them, notwithstanding my good relations with conservative colleagues. [...] Occasionally I ask myself whether I might not be able to pass for an old 68er.[16]

Karl Maurer, for his part, did not chalk up the experience to anything negative either:

> The events of 1968 in Bochum were relatively peaceful, although of course time-consuming and exhausting. I soon became the preferred candidate of the Trotskyist-dominated student council for the upcoming election of the rector, and its members had confidence in me despite my political views, which differed from their own. [...] Also as dean in the revolutionary year 1968/69 I enjoyed an unshakeable student goodwill. [...].[17]

Friedrich Wolfzettel characterizes the events as a kind of catharsis or preparation for a new departure:

> But we were also, in a way, the last post-war generation, who, at the end of our studies, with the events surrounding Benno Ohnesorg and the beginnings of the 1968 movement, were abruptly thrust into a hitherto unknown, ideologically shaped university reality and had to reflect on ourselves.[18]

Nor did the events in Munich leave the orientation of the discipline unscathed, as Wulf Oesterreicher points out with no small sense of corporate identity:

> The Institute for Romance Philology, with the special feature since 1968 of a separate Institute for Italian Philology (in fact, however, only literary studies and language practice), which today only nominally exists, offered the entire Romance Studies spectrum, i.e. not only the major Romance languages French, Spanish and Italian, but also Romanian and

---

[14] Meisel 2018, p. 245.
[15] Schuhmann 2011, p. 394.
[16] Heitmann 2018, p. 119.
[17] Maurer 2018, p. 223 f.
[18] Wolfzettel 2014, p. 387.

Portuguese, above all also with its Brazilian expression. Catalan, Occitan and Romansh were also taught regularly. The numerous professors 'exported' from Munich [...] testify to the presence of Munich Romance Studies.[19]

For Volker Roloff it was

> in Munich Romance Studies in the 1960s [...] it was customary to work on topics that were as traditional as possible – a dissertation on a living author, for example, was hardly conceivable, and medieval literature was a focus of teaching and research. Despite my sympathy for the 68ers, who also changed the university scene in Munich, I enjoyed attending the seminars on medieval literature [...], especially events on Arthurian epic, perhaps also because here the adventures and escapades, the sudden, dangerous departures that seem to violate the norms of courtly society, create the tension. [...] Only later did it become clear to me how much, for example, Sartre's theory of games (and the corresponding scenarios in *Les jeux sont faits* or *Huis clos*), Erving Goffman's *theory of the role-playing games of everyday life,* Guy Debord's *La société du spectacle* and the experiments of the Surrealists corresponded to the zeitgeist of 1968 – and from there also inspired my own studies of theatre and later also of theatricality and spectatorship in various media.[20]

"University life in Tübingen, including at the Romance Seminar, was," according to Harald Weydt,

> largely shaped by the student movement. The '68 movement was in full swing. On the one hand, I [Weydt] was open-minded and thought it was overdue that the rule of professors and full professors was broken up; on the other hand, I had an anti-communist past: I had experienced so much inhumanity and authoritarianism in the GDR that it was impossible for me – if I wanted to remain at peace with myself – to march behind red flags and adopt the slogans. [...] Quite noteworthy for the situation at the Romance Seminar during the "student unrest" was the attitude of Coseriu; he was managing director at the time. Students came to his lecture and demanded time to read statements and discuss them with the plenum. Coseriu matter-of-factly asked back how much time they needed and explained to them that at most he could cede five minutes to that; he had a lot of material. In political discussions he asked them in a friendly and collegial tone whether they had read the following important Marxist writings (from Marx and Hegel to Stalin articles); when they answered in the negative, he emphasized: "But you absolutely have to read that!"[21]

Wolfgang Drost reports on his contribution to the restructuring of Romance Studies in the wake of political events:

> In Stuttgart, I had the task of setting up the literary studies department of Romance philology. It was an exhausting and exciting time. I have particularly fond memories of the work in progress that I initiated, in which we younger people had lively discussions in the evenings. A controversy arose in the faculty over an assistantship, and I was 'dismissed' late in the evening by the chairman of the Mittelbau meeting after a lively exchange of words, not without a point. My direct manner had an unexpected effect: representatives of the Mittelbau surprisingly accepted me as their candidate in a department meeting without having asked me beforehand: thus I became dean. It was the aftermath of May 68, which I had experienced as an assistant in Tübingen in long nocturnal meetings.[22]

---

[19] Oesterreicher 2014, p. 200.
[20] Roloff 2015, p. 288 f.
[21] Weydt 2015, p. 434/437.
[22] Drost 2014, p. 101.

The linguist Christoph Schwarze, who worked in Kiel from 1970 and moved to Constance in 1975, is in favour of the new structures, especially the Constance model of subject agglutination:

> After the reform in the Romance Seminar was completed, I had ideal working conditions, especially because the linguists located in the various seminars began to regard linguistics as a discipline and strove to overcome their own isolation in the philologies. Cooperation with linguistic German studies [...] was particularly close.[23]
>
> - Moreover, the spirit of optimism of the first years in Kiel had meanwhile faded, a sharper demarcation between single-language and general linguistics was becoming apparent, and linguistic colleagues from the philologies were increasingly withdrawing back into their seminars. In Constance, on the other hand, there was a department of linguistics based on the idea of a fundamental disciplinary unity of all linguistic subjects. For me, the professorship in Constance was the best I could expect in the German-speaking world.[24]

Walter Bruno Berg, however, takes a critical view of the situation in Heidelberg:

> At the Romance Studies Department, the political fractures ran parallel to the disciplinary boundaries. For the 68ers, Marxist-inspired sociology of literature, which Erich Köhler had represented with the charisma of a founding father, stood for subject-historical "progress". Linguistics, on the other hand, represented in particular by the renowned lexicographers Kurt Baldinger and Bodo Müller, looked to the past with its three dictionary projects on Old French, Old Spanish and Old Provençal. As rector of the University of Heidelberg during the crucial months from March 1968 to July 1969, Baldinger had also outed himself – in the view of the 'left' – as a 'conservative'. Köhler's appointment to the vacant Friedrich post in tranquil Freiburg left a 'void' in this situation in several respects. He had not wanted to take on the role of helmsman on a sinking ship.[25]

Clearly negative words can be found, for example, from Barbara Wehr, who did not want to understand the political excesses:

> I perceived the political unrest after 1968 primarily as disruptions in the course of teaching. Various left-wing groups blew up the lectures. I explain the fact that I missed out on important political content by the fact that I did not like the language in which the theses were proclaimed, a kind of "party Chinese".[26]

Gerhard Penzkofer also focuses on the political language and expresses himself in an overly negative way:

> Probably the Red Cells and their colleagues nevertheless represent the spirit of optimism of the early 70s that accompanied the student movement. [...] At the same time, without suspecting it, they are a mirror and distorted image of the conservative Bavarian Catholic society they fight against: authoritarian, infallible in the name of Marxism, fundamentalist – with capital as a narrow basis of interpretation -, dominantly textual, and, of course, male: in the leadership ranks one looks for women in vain.[27]

---

[23] Schwarze 2014, p. 306.
[24] Schwarze 2014, p. 309.
[25] Berg 2015, p. 38.
[26] Weir 2015, p. 391.
[27] Penzkofer 2018, p. 291.

Klaus Bochmann emphasises that the '68 movement also left deep traces in the university system in the GDR and provided the impetus for the restructuring of the faculties and their distribution of subjects:

> The 3rd university reform set in motion in the GDR in 1968 provided for the dissolution of the philological institutes and the formation of large institutes or sections that were to concentrate on priority tasks. In this centralization there seemed to be no room for smaller subjects, especially in Leipzig, where linguists and literary scholars would now be represented separately, some in the German Studies / Literary Studies Section (the 'National Philology' was the only one not to be torn apart!), the others in the Theoretical and Applied Linguistics Section (the "TAS") [...] I had campaigned for the preservation of the unity of linguistics and literary studies, but the reformers supported by the Berlin Ministry were stronger than we 'conservatives'.[28]

At the Austrian Institutes of Romance Studies, the '68 movement did not seem to bring any blatant cuts for the time being, but in the following years it flowed all the more clearly into the university structures, especially with regard to the parity between professors, mid-level staff and students in the committees. One consequence of this development was the establishment of the new University of Klagenfurt, to which Ulrich Schulz-Buschhaus was appointed and from which Ulrich Wandruszka reports:

> I went after all and [...] have not regretted the decision to this day, even though I missed and disliked many things about this young university. I disliked the excessive politicization and ideologization of the university, which at that time was still called the University of Educational Sciences, whose spirit seemed to me in part like a late rehash of the '68 movement. Only now this was no longer carried by left-wing anarchic students, but by definitely placed and pragmatized or fighting for their pragmatization long-serving mid-level faculty members.[29]

Hans Goebl underlines these experiences:

> At first, for someone who had become accustomed to German customs – which, moreover, in Bavaria bore only a few traces of the '68 hype – the one-third parity found here was new and took some getting used to. This provided for the participation of three clearly defined curiae (professors, non-professorial staff, students) in all university-political decisions, which manifested itself in votes. This was (of course) associated with a massive politicization – always in the sense of the cited curiae – of the most important decision-making procedures at all levels of the university.[30]

On the whole, the events of the 1968 movement brought about a difficult and time-consuming phase for most of the contributors, which was accompanied by a sometimes strenuous relearning process, but on the other hand it can be concluded that this questioning of the traditional university and also social model resulted in new structures and fields of work. The founding of reform universities such as those in North Rhine-Westphalia or Klagenfurt also resulted in professorships with new orientations and research traditions. However, the tradition-conscious philologically motivated marriage between linguistics and literary studies was thus divorced.

---

[28] Bochmann 2014, p. 43.
[29] Wandruszka 2015, p. 381.
[30] Goebl 2015, p. 115.

2 Narratives on the Connection Between Philology and Confessional Practice

2.1 Judaism

In the narratives, the connection between philological practice and confessional orientation also becomes evident. Thus, the Jewish religion tends to occupy a place in the past, against the background of which one's own historical positioning is perceived – often with mixed feelings. On the one hand, it enables a critical examination of the then still current processing of history; on the other hand, it is filled with new life – especially during visits to France by the prospective Romance scholars. It also gives rise to the development of specific fields of work within Romance philology. The thematization of the Jewish denomination also led to ideological distortions in Romance philology in connection with the processing of the recent past after the Second World War.

An example of such a linkage is found in the report of the Munich Romance scholar Heinrich Bihler on the development of his field of research:

> However, I was then fascinated by modern research into the styles of language and literature. In German-language Romance studies, it was not only Leo Spitzer (1887–1960), but above all the Vossler student Helmut Hatzfeld (1892–1979), who for six decades in countless studies had investigated the stylistic elements in individual texts, in entire works and epochs of Spanish, French and Italian, occasionally also German and Anglo-Saxon literatures on the basis of his unusually broad educational horizon – still an old-style polymath.[31]

In addition, Bihler comments in detail on the tragic fate of both Jewish scholars in corresponding footnotes. In his case, however, this basic attitude does not lead later – as should often be the case – to a blanket endorsement of the 68er movement, quite the contrary.

The cultural self-location of young German-speaking students in France could act like a catharsis immediately after the war. The micro-narrative of Dietrich Briesemeister, who was able to draw his conclusions early on from the reaction of the French environment, may serve as an example:

> When I went to Paris again for three months in the summer of 1953, I was given an address while looking for accommodation. The landlady accepted me as a lodging guest. [...] When I answered that I was German, the door crashed into the lock. I was completely disturbed. When my eyes fell once more on the brass plate on the doorbell, I realized the reason for the rebuff: Cohen is a Jewish family name. A hard lesson in history and regional studies, and again the shame of being from Germany.[32]

The presence of the Jewish denomination in the accounts either remains confined to the past or, in the case of experiences abroad – especially in France – acts as a problematic foreign experience that is usually experienced as a purification in relation to

---

[31] Bihler 2007, p. 18.
[32] Briesemeister 2007, p. 34.

one's own history. The subject of Judaism is therefore often approached with a particular sensitivity, since there was no significant Jewish offspring within German-language post-war Romance Studies and the relevant philology attempted to compensate for this barrenness by reading the writings of Auerbach, Spitzer, Hatzfeld and others.

2.2 Protestantism

What remains exceedingly vivid in the narratives, however, is the positioning with regard to the two dominant denominations and their effects on philology: both the Protestant and the Catholic tradition preoccupy the budding Romanists of the post-war period, especially since they were dealing with a field of research that was primarily supported by Catholic ethics, even though the generally religion-critical 1968 movement was to push this topic into the background. Nevertheless, the question repeatedly arises as to whether a Protestant-directed reading of a counter-Reformation text constellation – as, for example, in Spanish literature – could be adequately applied at all, or whether – conversely – as a reading "against the grain" in the sense of Lucien Goldmann and his reception of the Jansenist authors Pascal or Racine – only with different signs – it might not even be more productive than other approaches.

Eberhard Geisler explicitly addresses this connection between textual work and confessional background in his account of his life:

> I enjoyed a Protestant, pietistic upbringing. The Holy Scripture was in the center, finally Scripture in general. From this tradition I inherited that I am receptive to weight of meaning and can approach things with some seriousness. Such an upbringing is a shackle from which I had to gradually free myself, but it can nevertheless enable me to develop a highly sensitive Geiger counter for what can move texts in their innermost being.[33]

Christoph Schwarze's confessional orientation also provided him with basic philological patterns in childhood: "I encountered the linguistically foreign at an early age. Growing up in a Protestant home, I intensively studied the linguistically antiquated Luther Bible and learned many tropical hymns, whose mostly baroque language was obscure to me in places."[34]

Sebastian Neumeister sums up the cultural mishmash in a similar way:

> I was allowed to make this painful experience when I was admitted to the illustrious circle of the German-British Calderón Colloquia on the basis of my habilitation thesis. Here, for decades, the two arch-Catholic dioscuri Alexander Augustinus Parker and Hans Flasche ruled with mild severity. If it was in itself a misunderstanding for them to want to make statements about Calderón as a non-Catholic, then the limit of the permissible was clearly crossed when I dared in 1975 at the "Cuarto Coloquio Anglogermano Hacia Calderón" to criticize Alexander A. Parker's contribution in the discussion. Embarrassed silence was the

---

[33] Geisler 2018, p. 77.
[34] Black 2014, p. 293.

result, similar to that which violations of *political correctness* trigger today, followed by being labeled a pariah for the rest of the meeting.[35]

It is also of interest here that the British branch of Baroque studies defined itself as Catholic and seemed to exclude Protestant views.

Manfred Tietz, who as a baptized Evangelical-Lutheran studied the Spanish Baroque for decades, follows this line of argument and provides an expressive explanatory pattern:

> Through the Bamberg situation [...] I was also very directly confronted with the ideological background of the so specific German Calderón enthusiasm, which – if not its roots – at least receives essential impulses from German Catholicism, which not only in the 19th century succeeded in proving its own 'cultural capacity', questioned by the German Protestants, by means of Catholic Spain and its great cultural achievements.[36]

Whatever one might think of this, the Protestant upbringing, with its accurate reading of the Bible and the textual understanding associated with it, may also have been particularly fruitful for the formation of modern philology, especially philology in the Romance field. Annegret Bollée goes so far as to link the Romance networks of her generation to the Protestant tradition, recognizing this very constellation for a woman's acceptance by the guild: "It has never been difficult for me, because in my generation, born in 1937, the women who had the best chance of becoming a professor were those whose father was already a professor, who were Protestant, and who were the oldest siblings and had younger brothers."[37] Observing Romance philology from a confessional perspective thus exposes a fruitful tension. It was precisely in linguistic research on Creole that this could be drawn upon: "The Catholics, by the way, didn't go along with it at the time. Translating the Bible into Creole was completely unthinkable. They've since gone along with it, but at the time it was far too revolutionary. It was still 1974, where I spent two months in the Seychelles."[38]

As the telling examples of Calderón's reception in literary studies and the famous Creole Bible translations in linguistics underline, confessional affiliation plays no small role in Romance philology in the post-war period, a role to which numerous other representatives also profess: Jürgen Grimm, for example, emphasizes that the "moral climate of his parental home was Protestant-Prussian",[39] Wolf-Dieter Lange had a "deeply Protestant" teacher "with whom [the students] read the *Confessiones* (in the original, of course) in small circles,"[40] Ludwig Schauwecker recalls in his biography that "the foreign Protestants [in Spain] were not subjected to any pressures",[41] and Uwe Dethloff that his family "were tolerated more badly than well

---

[35] Neumeister 2007, p. 410 f.
[36] Tietz 2011, p. 482.
[37] Bollee 2011, p. 42.
[38] Bollee 2011, p. 34.
[39] Grimm 2007, p. 142.
[40] Lange 2007, p. 309.
[41] Schauwecker 2014, p. 268.

by the locals as Protestant refugees from the East".[42] Jens Lüdtke felt "too Protestant to hear the [blasphemous] without shuddering",[43] and Monika Walter relates that "no one in her Protestant conservative-minded family dreamed of socialism".[44] Hans Goebl's "father came from circles that could be described as "bourgeois" for generations and also bequeathed [him] the affiliation with the Lutheran denomination, which [he] had already experienced in a very conscious way as a child in Austria, which in the 1950s was still staunchly Catholic or militantly counter-Reformation.[45]

As the numerous examples show, evangelical socialization seemed to play an important function in the career formation of German-speaking Romance scholars during the postwar period. If one follows the relevant narratives, one can not only discern a subtle line of connection between Bible reading and later philological practice, but also a kind of scholarly – perhaps also secularized – seriousness in the engagement with the "Other" from the mostly Catholic Romania. However one may interpret these functions, the confessional location plays a role in the career pictures of Protestant Romance scholars that should not be underestimated.

2.3 Catholicism

The Catholic dimension manifests itself in the narratives under somewhat different auspices. Basically, the Bible reading with its philological propaedeutics is not in the foreground in adolescence, but the question of a priestly career. As a special characteristic, an intensive Latin instruction could possibly be mentioned. Furthermore, one can observe a tendency – at least as far as the childhood and adolescence of the contributors are concerned – towards stronger references to a peasant, ideal world, whose world view is characterized by joie de vivre and happiness. The southern German and Austrian regions as well as the Rhineland with its carnival have a formative effect here. When Dirk Hoeges sees in his Rhenish-speaking dean "a jovial, fun-loving man and Catholic with a face that always reminded [him] of a commode saint"[46] or Hans Otto Dill classifies his Hispanophone friend as "Catholic and ceremonious",[47] this corresponds to the common stereotypical external perspective. Moreover, stronger connections to Hispanic studies and its institutions can also be observed, which – as in Neuschäfer's case – could even lead to conversion to Catholicism.[48] From time to time, the narratives also mention the

---

[42] Dethloff 2015, p. 82.
[43] Lüdtke 2014, p. 88.
[44] Walter 2018, p. 450.
[45] Goebl 2015, p. 101.
[46] Hoeges 2018, p. 138 f.
[47] Dill 2007, p. 57.
[48] Cf. Neuschäfer 2007.

opening of the Catholic Church through John XXIII's Second Vatican Council (1962–1965) as a positive phenomenon.

In Helmut Feldmann's narrative, a tendency towards an idealizing view of the world is explicitly expressed:

> "My mother came from a down-to-earth, peasant family in a village that at least had a chapel and a school. The pride of the family was an uncle who had become a Catholic priest. My mother modeled my upbringing on this example and hoped that I, too, would find my way into a clerical office."[49] In Hans-Martin Gauger's case, the specifically Catholic attitude toward life is conveyed through the gentle landscapes of the Southwest: "I come from pretty deep southwestern Germany. My hometown is the Upper Swabian Saulgau, today Bad Saulgau. But I was born in Freudenstadt, in 1935 [...] This gently hilly region [...had] been Austrian. So denominationally it is very closed Catholic."[50]

For Johannes Hösle, who also came from Upper Swabia, this code of values formed the basis of his experience, even though he tries to distance himself from a possible priesthood: "I had only vague ideas and plans regarding my professional future, but the thought of a future life as a Catholic clergyman was, apart from periodic fits of occasional self-deception, rather oppressive for me."[51] Winfried Engler also set his sights on the priesthood in his youth in Saulgau: "As the son of a craftsman, I was the first Engler in this Catholic family to graduate from high school and go to university, but, in what is repeatedly recorded in analogous biographies as a family dream(a), to become a priest, not a theologian. Seen in this light, the Romanist is the renegade."[52]

As one of the few women in the field, Rita Schober also comments in her confession on its connection with the socialist experiment: "I was – brought up strictly Catholic in my youth – a "believer" accustomed to following "commandments" and believed that it was possible, with the experiment of socialism, to create a better and peaceful world."[53]

Joseph Jurt refers not only to the rural character of his surroundings, but also to the associated institution of a denominational boarding school:

> During my primary school years, I had always lived in a Swiss-German village, but had already come into contact with relatives who lived in another language area. At the age of thirteen I started grammar school in a Catholic boarding school. Here the focus was now on Latin – eight years without interruption.[54]

In this context, the old languages also pointed the way for Walter Bruno Berg: "Influenced by the milieu Catholicism of the Adenauer era – which in the imagination of my early youth paradoxically coincided with my father's strict

---

[49] Feldmann 2007, p. 65 f.
[50] Gauger 2007, p. 143.
[51] Hösle 2007, p. 201 f.
[52] Engler 2014, p. 115.
[53] Schober 2011, p. 374.
[54] Jurt 2007, p. 232.

anti-fascism – I was enrolled in the humanistic, classical language grammar school in Bergisch Gladbach in 1954 at the request of my parents."[55]

Wolf-Dieter Lange found his way to the Romance world precisely through his interest in the Catholic world and his reading of Curtius:

> Perhaps this circumstance also made it [Curtius' *European Literature and the Latin Middle Ages*] so attractive, so magical as the gateway to a world yet to be opened up, namely that of the Romance languages, which in their relationship to Latin seemed to me like a secular variant of apostolic succession – I was at the time [...] intensively occupied with Catholicism.[56]

And Hans-Jörg Neuschäfer also found a new denomination in his Spanish environment: "the [...] language [of his wife], her friends, her widely ramified family reaching through all social and political shades; the liberal spirit of the Institución libre de enseñanza that prevailed at her home; the complex world of Catholicism, which I later joined, and in which it began to bubble critically as early as the 1950s."[57]

Even among the Catholic-socialized young Romance scholars, relevant institutions usually played a central role in career formation. Thus, one can trace above all references to Catholic universities in general and to Spanish and Latin American or universities in particular, whereby especially German-language Hispanic Studies and with its tendency towards single-philological development within the framework of Romance Studies achieved a special position. Karl Kohut explains this tendency with the attractiveness of Latin American universities:

> "That in the result most of the partners were Catholic universities had less to do with a "network of Catholic universities" (such a network exists, by the way, on the level of higher education policy), but with the circumstance that numerous Catholic universities in Latin America (in contrast to Germany) enjoy a high reputation, even if this is certainly not true for all of them."[58] Numerous Latin Americanists followed this network, as for example Jürgen von Stackelberg, who in 1973 worked at the Catholic University of Valparaíso, "which is not more Catholic than other universities."[59]

It is noticeable, however, that the connections to Catholic universities sometimes led to a need for justification, as Karl Kohut underlines with regard to his appointment in 1982 to the Catholic University of Eichstätt, where, by the way, it was no coincidence that a Latin American focus had developed:

> The reaction of my colleagues, in Duisburg or outside, was clearly negative. The friendliest variant was derision: Bavaria? Catholic university? The laughter intensified. Others reacted with incomprehension, to still others (though few) contact broke off. The price for accepting the call to Eichstätt was a scientific isolation that lasted several years, but was limited to Germany.[60]

---

[55] Berg 2015, p. 29.
[56] Lange 2007, p. 310.
[57] Neuschäfer 2007, p. 449.
[58] Kohut 2007, p. 277.
[59] Stackelberg 2007, p. 614.
[60] Kohut 2007, p. 276.

The discourse of justification goes even further with Klaus Pörtl, who, after his positive experiences at the Catholic University of Pamplona, undertakes a vindication of Opus Dei:

> Many false and, unfortunately, defamatory things have been said about Opus Dei, and especially about Opus Dei universities, probably because of decades of unobjective reporting. I have had enough professional contact with members and friends of Opus Dei to be able to say that the scare stories that are often spread are not true. Certainly, many – not all! – of the employees are devout Catholics faithful to the Pope, the so-called numerarii vow celibacy and live in communities of this Catholic lay order.[61]

Of course, the intensified exchange with the Catholic institutions also applies to the representatives of Italian philology.

The autobiographical narratives of emeritus or retired professors of Romance studies comment on the development of the subject from a personal perspective and thus make a valuable contribution to the "autobiographical history" of Romance philology. Women are almost absent in the first phase, entering the circle of Romance scholars with the appointments around 1968. Two themes dominate the reports, concerning careers as well as networks and institutions. These are, on the one hand, the historically conceived paradigm shifts that started with the 1968 movement and were reflected in the separation of literary and linguistic studies, in the establishment of new Romance studies fields in cultural, regional and media studies such as didactics, etc., in the development of new methods and, above all, in the founding of new universities – reform universities. The end of the 1980s, with the collapse of the Soviet Union and the merging of the FRG and the GDR, as well as the general spread of information technology, also had an impact. Finally, the Bologna Process and the orientation of the universities towards strictly market-oriented ones in the late nineties have also been perceived as an indicator, whereby we would like to cite the career of Ulrich Schulz-Buschhaus as an example for this bracket between 1968 and 2000.

The second thematic area of the narratives concerns the confessional contexts of career formations. References to religious structures in the process of becoming a Romanist are numerous and manifest themselves primarily in the bipolarity between Protestantism and Catholicism, resulting in dazzling configurations against the specific background of Romanist cultures. The Jewish denomination is often referred to, although it plays no role in the career formation of the younger generations.

As the individual narratives have shown, Romance Studies as a passion can be read both in terms of the Romantic tradition, underlining the ideational merits of the subject, and negatively in terms of globalisation, where the danger of unravelling the subject against the backdrop of other philologies may be seen as a problem. However the next careers may develop, attention should be paid to the competences of a further respectful treatment of Romance languages, literatures and cultures in the original.

---

[61] Pörtl 2007, p. 477.

References

Behrens, Rudolf: Romanistische Vorsicht. Anmerkungen zu einer Positionsdebatte, in: Romanische(n) Forschungen 120/3, 2008, S. 329–337.
Berg, Walter Bruno: Alte und Neue Welten der Romanistik, in: Klaus-Dieter Ertler (Hg.): Romanistik als Passion. Sternstunden der neueren Fachgeschichte IV. Münster: Lit Verlag 2015, S. 25–51.
Bihler, Heinrich: Mein Leben als Romanist, in: Klaus-Dieter Ertler (Hg.): Romanistik als Passion. Sternstunden der neueren Fachgeschichte. Münster: Lit Verlag 2007, S. 15–27.
Bochmann, Klaus: ... das Bedürfnis nach dem ganz Anderen, in: Klaus-Dieter Ertler (Hg.): Romanistik als Passion. Sternstunden der neueren Fachgeschichte III. Münster: Lit Verlag 2014, S. 31–67.
Bollee, Annegret: Linguistik unter Palmen, in: Klaus-Dieter Ertler (Hg.): Romanistik als Passion. Sternstunden der neueren Fachgeschichte II. Münster: Lit Verlag 2011, S. 15–46.
Briesemeister, Dietrich: Bilder aus meinen romanistischen Lern-, Lehr- und Wanderjahren, in: Klaus-Dieter Ertler (Hg.): Romanistik als Passion. Sternstunden der neueren Fachgeschichte. Münster: Lit Verlag 2007, S. 29–48.
Dethloff, Uwe: Mein steter Weg von Ost nach West, in: Klaus-Dieter Ertler (Hg.): Romanistik als Passion. Sternstunden der neueren Fachgeschichte IV. Münster: Lit Verlag 2015, S. 79–98.
Dill, Hans-Otto: Von der Ostsee an die Karibik oder die Vita eines ostwestlichen Philologen, in: Klaus-Dieter Ertler (Hg.): Romanistik als Passion. Sternstunden der neueren Fachgeschichte. Münster: Lit Verlag 2007, S. 51–63.
Drost, Wolfgang: Geteilte Liebe: Romanistik und Kunstgeschichte, in: Klaus-Dieter Ertler (Hg.): Romanistik als Passion. Sternstunden der neueren Fachgeschichte III. Münster: Lit Verlag 2014, S. 95–108.
Engler, Winfried: ...allons voir si..., in: Klaus-Dieter Ertler (Hg.): Romanistik als Passion. Sternstunden der neueren Fachgeschichte III. Münster: Lit Verlag 2014, S. 109–123.
Ertler, Klaus-Dieter (Hg.): Romanistik als Passion. Sternstunden der neueren Fachgeschichte. Münster: Lit Verlag 2007.
Ertler, Klaus-Dieter (Hg.): Romanistik als Passion. Sternstunden der neueren Fachgeschichte II. Münster: Lit Verlag 2011.
Ertler, Klaus-Dieter (Hg.): Romanistik als Passion. Sternstunden der neueren Fachgeschichte III. Münster: Lit Verlag 2014.
Ertler, Klaus-Dieter (Hg.): Romanistik als Passion. Sternstunden der neueren Fachgeschichte IV. Münster: Lit Verlag 2015.
Ertler, Klaus-Dieter (Hg.): Romanistik als Passion. Sternstunden der neueren Fachgeschichte V. Münster: Lit Verlag 2018.
Ertler, Klaus-Dieter, Werner Helmich (Hg.): Ulrich Schulz-Buschhaus. Das Aufsatzwerk. URL: http://gams.uni-graz.at/usb (06.11.2019).
Ertler, Klaus-Dieter: Romanistik – Selbstverständnis und Zukunftsperspektiven, in: Romanische(n) Forschungen 120/3, 2008, S. 338–343.
Ertler, Klaus-Dieter (Hg.): Romanistik als Passion. Sternstunden der neueren Fachgeschichte VI. Münster: Lit 2020a.
Ertler, Klaus-Dieter (Hg.): Romanistik als Passion. Sternstunden der neueren Fachgeschichte VII. Münster: Lit 2020b.
Feldmann, Helmut: Mein Leben als „Seiteneinsteiger" in die Romanische Philologie, in: Klaus-Dieter Ertler (Hg.): Romanistik als Passion. Sternstunden der neueren Fachgeschichte. Münster: Lit 2007, S. 65–81.
Gauger, Mans-Martin: Mein Weg in die romanische Sprachwissenschaft, in: Klaus-Dieter Ertler (Hg.): Romanistik als Passion. Sternstunden der neueren Fachgeschichte. Münster: Lit Verlag 2007, S. 143–171.
Geisler, Eberhard: Brouillon für eine Biographie, in: Klaus-Dieter Ertler (Hg.): Romanistik als Passion. Sternstunden der neueren Fachgeschichte V. Münster: Lit Verlag 2018, S. 73–95.

Geyer, Paul: Romanistik als europäische Kulturwissenschaft, in: Romanische(n) Forschungen 120/3, 2008, S. 344–349.
Goebl, Hans: Romanistik: ciència i passió, in: Klaus-Dieter Ertler (Hg.): Romanistik als Passion. Sternstunden der neueren Fachgeschichte IV. Münster: Lit Verlag 2015, S. 99–127.
Grimm, Jürgen: Alles Theater – Rollenspiele, in: Klaus-Dieter Ertler (Hg.): Romanistik als Passion. Sternstunden der neueren Fachgeschichte. Münster: Lit Verlag 2007, S. 173–189.
Hausmann, Frank-Rutger: Romanistenlexikon. URL: http://blog.romanischestudien.de/romanistenlexikon (06.11.2019).
Hausmann, Frank-Rutger: Romanistik als Passion, in: Romanische Forschungen 120/1, 2008, S. 50–58.
Hausmann, Frank-Rutger: Romanistik als Passion, in: Romanische Forschungen 124/1, 2012, S. 63–65.
Hausmann, Frank-Rutger: Romanistik als Passion, in: Romanische Forschungen 127/1, 2015, S. 72–76.
Hausmann, Frank-Rutger: Romanistik als Passion, in: Romanische Forschungen 129/2, 2017, S. 221–226.
Heitmann, Klaus: Bekenntnisse und Erkenntnisse eines akademischen Einzelgängers, in: Klaus-Dieter Ertler (Hg.): Romanistik als Passion. Sternstunden der neueren Fachgeschichte V. Münster: Lit Verlag 2018, S. 111–128.
Hoeges, Dirk: Eine Reise an den Ufern von Lethe und Memnosyne, in: Klaus-Dieter Ertler (Hg.): Romanistik als Passion. Sternstunden der Fachgeschichte V. Münster: Lit Verlag 2018, S. 129–155.
Hösle, Johannes: Ouvertüre eine Romanistenlaufbahn, in: Klaus-Dieter Ertler (Hg.): Romanistik als Passion. Sternstunden der neueren Fachgeschichte. Münster: Lit Verlag 2007, S. 201–213.
Hurch, Bernhard: Hugo Schuchardt Archiv. Graz 2019 URL: http://schuchardt.uni-graz.at/korrespondenz/briefe/briefsuche (06.11.2019).
Jurt, Joseph: „Rien ne se fait sans un petit peu d'enthousiasme" (Voltaire), in: Klaus-Dieter Ertler (Hg.): Romanistik als Passion. Sternstunden der neueren Fachgeschichte. Münster: Lit Verlag 2007, S. 231–246.
Kohut, Karl: Lebenslauf, in: Klaus-Dieter Ertler (Hg.): Romanistik als Passion. Sternstunden der neueren Fachgeschichte. Münster: Lit Verlag 2007, S. 265–285.
Lange, Wolf-Dieter: Markierungen und Begegnungen. Eine empfindsame Reise durch die Welt der Romania, in: Klaus-Dieter Ertler (Hg.): Romanistik als Passion. Sternstunden der neueren Fachgeschichte. Münster: Lit Verlag 2007, S. 307–326.
Lüdtke, Jens: Eugenio Coseriu (1921–2002), in: Klaus-Dieter Ertler (Hg.): Romanistik als Passion. Sternstunden der neueren Fachgeschichte III. Münster: Lit Verlag 2014, S. 69–94.
Lüsebrink, Hans-Jürgen: Postmoderne Herausforderungen. Die deutsche Romanistik in Zeiten von Berufsbezogenheit und Internationalisierung, in: Romanische Forschungen 120/3, 2008, S. 350–355.
Maurer, Karl: Die Begegnung mit der Romania als Sternstunde eines Philologen, in: Klaus-Dieter Ertler (Hg.): Romanistik als Passion. Sternstunden der neueren Fachgeschichte V. Münster: Lit Verlag 2018, S. 203–229.
Mecke, Jochen: Kleine Apologie der Romanistik, in: Romanische Forschungen 120/3, 2008, S. 356–363.
Meisel, Jürgen M.: Romanistische Linguistik als Passion, in: Klaus-Dieter Ertler (Hg.): Romanistik als Passion. Sternstunden der neueren Fachgeschichte V. Münster: Lit Verlag 2018, S. 231–263.
Neumann, Martin: Romanistik als Passion?, in: Romanische Forschungen 120/3, 2008, S. 364–369.
Neumeister, Sebastian: Nostalgische Ansichten eines Literaten II: Protokoll eines Niedergangs, in: Klaus-Dieter Ertler (Hg.): Romanistik als Passion. Sternstunden der neueren Fachgeschichte. Münster: Lit Verlag 2007, S. 403–422.
Neuschäfer, Hans-Jörg: Érase que se era, in: Klaus-Dieter Ertler (Hg.): Romanistik als Passion. Sternstunden der neueren Fachgeschichte. Münster: Lit Verlag 2007, S. 425–440.

Oesterreicher, Wulf: Wie wird einer wie ich Romanist, in: Klaus-Dieter Ertler (Hg.): Romanistik als Passion. Sternstunden der neueren Fachgeschichte III. Münster: Lit Verlag 2014, S. 175–212.

Penzkofer, Gerhard: Wie man Romanist werden kann, in: Klaus-Dieter Ertler (Hg.): Romanistik als Passion. Sternstunden der neueren Fachgeschichte V. Münster: Lit Verlag 2018, S. 287–310.

Pörtl, Klaus: Werdegang eines Iberoromanisten, in: Klaus-Dieter Ertler (Hg.): Romanistik als Passion. Sternstunden der neueren Fachgeschichte. Münster: Lit 2007, S. 471–497.

Roloff, Volker: Romanistische Stationen und Abenteuer, in: Klaus-Dieter Ertler (Hg.): Romanistik als Passion. Sternstunden der neueren Fachgeschichte IV. Münster: Lit Verlag 2015, S. 285–297.

Röseberg, Dorothée (Hg.): Rita Schober – Vita. Eine Nachlese. Tübingen: Narr 2018.

Schauwecker, Ludwig: Wie einer zum Romanisten wurde, in: Klaus-Dieter Ertler (Hg.): Romanistik als Passion. Sternstunden der neueren Fachgeschichte III. Münster: Lit Verlag 2014, S. 265–289.

Schiller, Annette: Informationsmittel: digitales Rezensionsorgan für Bibliothek und Wissenschaft (s. a.), http://ifb.bsz-bw.de/bsz414704266rez-1.pdf [zuletzt konsultiert am 15.11.2019].

Schober, Rita: Vom Aufbau der Romanistik an der Humboldt-Universität in schwieriger Zeit, in: Klaus-Dieter Ertler (Hg.): Romanistik als Passion. Sternstunden der neueren Fachgeschichte II. Münster: Lit Verlag 2011, S. 339–389.

Schuhmann, Adelheid: Eine romanistische Karriere mit Hindernissen, in: Klaus-Dieter Ertler (Hg.): Romanistik als Passion. Sternstunden der neueren Fachgeschichte II. Münster: Lit Verlag 2011, S. 391–407.

Schwarze, Christoph: Autobiographische Notizen, in: Klaus-Dieter Ertler (Hg.): Romanistik als Passion. Sternstunden der neueren Fachgeschichte III. Münster: Lit Verlag 2014, S. 291–315.

Siebenmann, Gustav: Romania – Hispania – América. Fragmente einer Autobiografie. Münster: Lit Verlag 2011.

Stackelberg, Jürgen von: *Prima la musica, poi le parole*. Erlebte Romania und gelebte Romanistik, in: Klaus-Dieter Ertler (Hg.): Romanistik als Passion. Sternstunden der neueren Fachgeschichte. Münster: Lit Verlag 2007, S. 603–618.

Tietz, Manfred: Hispanistische Autobiographie, in: Klaus-Dieter Ertler (Hg.): Romanistik als Passion. Sternstunden der neueren Fachgeschichte II. Münster: Lit Verlag 2011, S. 463–502.

Walter, Monika: Mein doppelter Zufluchtsort, in: Klaus-Dieter Ertler (Hg.): Romanistik als Passion. Sternstunden der neueren Fachgeschichte V. Münster: Lit Verlag 2018, S. 447–469.

Wandruszka, Ulrich: Sternstunden der Romanistik, in: Klaus-Dieter Ertler (Hg.): Romanistik als Passion. Sternstunden der neueren Fachgeschichte IV. Münster: Lit Verlag 2015, S. 361–386.

Wehr, Barbara: Selbstbeschreibung als Romanistin, in: Klaus-Dieter Ertler (Hg.): Romanistik als Passion. Sternstunden der neueren Fachgeschichte IV. Münster: Lit Verlag 2015, S. 387–402.

Weydt, Harald: Romanistik von außen, in: Klaus-Dieter Ertler (Hg.): Romanistik als Passion. Sternstunden der neueren Fachgeschichte IV. Münster: Lit Verlag 2015, S. 423–452.

Wolfzettel, Friedrich: König Artus, in: Klaus-Dieter Ertler (Hg.): Romanistik als Passion. Sternstunden der neueren Fachgeschichte III. Münster: Lit Verlag 2014, S. 371–398.

On the Beginning and End of the Science of the German Language and Literature in Germany

Lothar Bluhm

Abstract Following the current crisis speech, the question of the meaning, tasks and function of the humanities and cultural studies in society will be taken up and discussed in terms of the history of science, focusing on the field of the science of German language and literature. To this end, the beginnings of early German philology some 200 years ago and its functional contexts will be examined in order to subsequently transfer the observations to our time. The necessity of a paradigm shift and a fundamental reorientation of educational policy and organization becomes clear due to the dissolution of the current subject-disciplinary structure at schools and in university teacher training.

1 On the Talk of the Beginning and End of the Humanities and Cultural Studies

Whoever speaks of the beginning and end of a science assumes a series of basic assumptions that are insinuated as set, but can also be disputed. These include the assertion of a fixable uniformity of the knowledge system, but also the assumption of the episodic nature of science, and others. Last but not least, the statement is underpinned by the pattern of retrospection, which at the same time usually means, or at least suggests, that the observer obviously imagines himself to be at the end of what he is talking about.

Thus, when describing the alleged episodic nature, it is obvious to look first at this – presumed – end, or at what is signaled as this end: At the beginning of 2019,

L. Bluhm (✉)
Neuere deutsche Literatur- und Kulturwissenschaft, Universität Koblenz Landau, Landau, Deutschland
e-mail: bluhm@uni-landau.de

© The Author(s), under exclusive license to Springer-Verlag GmbH, DE, part of Springer Nature 2023
C. Strosetzki (ed.), *200 Years of National Philologies*,
https://doi.org/10.1007/978-3-476-05925-3_15

with a view to the much-cited crisis of the contemporary humanities and cultural studies, one read in the headline of a science-critical article in *Zeit online* the call: "Tear down the ivory tower!".[1] Comparable voices calling for the end of the humanities and cultural studies, stating, lamenting or otherwise commenting on it, have been encountered in the journalistic discourse of recent years in a variety of ways – and not only there. The end of the humanities and cultural studies and, in a narrower sense, of the science of German language and literature, of German studies in Germany, has often been invoked; the talk is a topos of modern academic reflection on this subject and is actually as old as the subject itself. Nevertheless, it is not without meaning at the present time. On the contrary, it signals that, in the course of the cyclical history of crisis that accompanies the development of modernity as a matter of course, a state has evidently again been reached in which a renewed analysis of performance and function and a redefinition have become necessary. In other words, talk of a crisis responds to an assessment that has become entrenched in social discourse, according to which the branch of science in question is no longer sufficiently capable of fulfilling the tasks and functions assigned to it by society. The reasons for the assertion of such a malaise can be manifold, for example that science actually no longer has its tasks in view or that the societal tasks themselves have changed without science having sufficiently taken this change into account in its range of services.

And indeed, after the major debates about the social status of the humanities and cultural studies in the late 1960s and the mid-1990s, as well as the many smaller and larger statements since then, there seems to be a renewed urgency to the question. The question of the meaning and profile of the humanities and cultural studies and their task in present and future society has long since become a kind of 'white elephant' in a multitude of social debates. At the same time, we can currently observe a condensation of this kind of crisis speech within the framework of a variety of other discourses critical of society, politics and culture. In the process, these have attained a fundamentality that was alien to earlier crisis discussions. Against the background of more recent and most recent political and social developments – for example, the return of nationalisms that were thought to have been forgotten, fears of globalisation or the so-called 'refugee crisis' – what is now at stake is nothing less than the very existence of contemporary democracy and the liberal democratic culture that sustains it. Those who have eyes to see and ears to hear recognise the process of erosion in which societies find themselves here, as in many other places, and the dangers to the continued existence of contemporary civilisation. The discussion about the functions and achievements of a present as well as a future humanities and cultural studies must be located within the horizon of this field of discourse.

While talking of an end to the humanities and cultural studies, and a narrower sense to the science of German language and literature, there is an essentially wish for a redefinition of its tasks and a call for self-reflection that points to the future. Thus the current call for an end to the humanities and cultural studies – as is usually

---

[1] Hayer 2019.

the case with talk of an end – is at the same time the question of a new beginning. This is also evident in the *Zeit online* article from February 2019 cited at the beginning, whose critique is briefly taken up again here as an exemplary voice. The essayist's call for a demolition of the 'ivory tower' is avowedly a "plea for more interference". The complaint is ignited by the current state of the humanities and cultural studies and their, as it is called, "eremitic existence": "The intellectual is dead," the author points out, "at least in public discussions." Referring to the French philosopher and sociologist Geoffroy de Lagasnerie, Hayer focuses on the "self-imposed neutrality imperative" of contemporary humanities and cultural studies in matters of public debate and social controversy. He complains about the self-sufficiency of the "passive observer role", that science retreats "Biedermeier-like (and certainly also a little complacent) into the apolitical" and takes refuge in the "working off of niche topics that are far removed from reality". Emphasis is placed on the "impression of arbitrariness" that results from a "massive overproduction of studies and articles whose significance for social discourse is hardly discussed". The survival guarantee of the current humanities and cultural studies and their sub-disciplines is essentially only their link with "teacher training", i.e. with the function of being responsible as university disciplines for teacher training and the subject-specific scientific and subject-didactic equipment of the corresponding school subjects.[2]

Hayer's contribution is a cultural-critical essay, not a comprehensive scientific discussion. Accordingly, his plea with a view to future development is also rather narrow and related to the personal rather than the structural dimension. He sees the problems less in the humanities and cultural studies themselves than in the actors representing them: "There is only a lack," he sums up, "of courageous persons in the humanities who are not afraid to go public." In addition to the "stronger scientific flanking of socially relevant discourses" already called for by de Lagasnerie, however, "interfering [...] should be the motto of the hour: in newspapers, talk shows, social networks, and even at demonstrations," he writes. The goal should be to "preserve or reclaim cultural and linguistic spaces" that are endangered or have been lost, and to "take counter-positions" in social disputes where necessary.[3]

The public discussion on the matter is controversial. And so, of course, the cited article has not remained without backlash. In May, the student magazine of the Zeit publishing house, *Zeit Campus,* published an appeal "Away from the Cliché", which celebrates "German Studies as big and strong, popular and lively" and dismisses the crisis speech as "grumbling public opinion" and "bogus discussion brought in from outside". The "pressure to justify" that German studies and the other humanities are under must "stop".[4]

The discussion will not be continued or even attempted to be decided here. Rather, following the recent crisis speech, the question of the meaning, tasks and

---

[2] Hayer 2019.
[3] Hayer 2019.
[4] Herbold 2019.

function of the humanities and cultural studies in society will be taken up and discussed in terms of the history of science, focusing on the field of the science of German language and literature. In a first step, we will look at the beginnings of early German philology about 200 years ago and their functional context, in order to then transfer the core questions to our time and the future tasks, as they now seem to be indicated or structurally emerging, and to discuss them at least briefly. Nevertheless, the look ahead cannot and should not attempt more than an outline.

2 On the Genesis of the Science of German Language and Literature

Anyone looking back to the beginnings of early German philology some 200 years ago follows – consciously or unconsciously – a self-mythification of the actors of the time and their hagiography by a student body, which was accompanied by the capping of traditions in a complex process of concealing, forgetting and discrediting previous achievements. This was as true of the manifold German studies of the earlier scholarly culture as it was of many translational, editorial, and even grammatical achievements.[5] With reservations, this also applies to the model of classical studies and, in the narrower sense, classical philology, to which the early German philologists in the first half of the nineteenth century were committed to a high degree, both methodologically and conceptually. In this context, the assertion of a new beginning may be regarded as something thoroughly typical of the time, as a sign of modernity, and as what is perhaps truly new at its core. "The literary epoch in which I was born," wrote Goethe, who is still held in high esteem as a new beginning, "developed from the preceding epoch through contradiction.[6]

Particularly in an earlier history of scholarship, a certain narrowing of the beginning of early German philology liked to shorten it in terms of event history. Depending on the accent, individual memory-cultural points of reference were and occasionally still are fixed: For the subsequent disciplinary history of memory, for example, the "Germanist[s] primal experience" of his first encounter with Johann Jakob Bodmer's *Proben der alten schwäbischen Poesie des dreyzehnten Jahrhunderts (Samples of Old Swabian Poetry of the Thirteenth Century) of* 1748 in the library of the revered teacher Friedrich Carl von Savigny on a "summer day of the year 1803" was very powerful: "i remember," wrote the elder Grimm brother, "entering from the door on the wall to the right hand at the very back there was also a quartant, Bodmer's collection of the minnelieder, which i seized and opened for the first time [...], that filled me with a sense of my own [...]."[7] Other events that were readily valorized as a kind of Germanist 'Urereignis' were, from the point of view of

---

[5] See comprehensively Bluhm 1997, esp. p. 67 ff.
[6] Goethe 1982, p. 258.
[7] Grimm 1864, p. 115.

medieval reception history, the publication of Ludwig Tieck's 'newly edited' *Minnelieder aus dem Schwäbischen Zeitalter* of 1803 or Friedrich Heinrich von der Hagen's 'Erneuung' *Der Nibelungen Lied* of 1807, among edition-historical Georg Friedrich Benecke's and Carl Lachmann's Iwein edition of 1827, and in general Lachmann's critical text editions, above all Wolfram von Eschenbach's complete edition of 1833, if one did not already regard Lachmann's Habilitationsschrift *Über die ursprüngliche Gestalt des Gedichts von der Nibelungen Noth* of 1816 and his Nibelungen studies as professionally foundational. In order to emphasize the nominal entry of German Studies into the newly forming university system of the early nineteenth century, reference was and still is made from the perspective of disciplinary history to the new establishment of an extraordinary (and unsalaried) professorship of German Language in 1810 at the newly founded Berlin University for Friedrich Heinrich von der Hagen.[8] However, Jacob Grimm's *Deutsche Grammatik (German Grammar)* of 1819, which became of considerable importance for the development of historical and comparative linguistics and text-critical editing, is usually cited as the central initial event in the history of the discipline. Heinrich Heine called it "a colossal work, a gothic cathedral", the preparation of which would actually have required "more than a human lifetime and more than human patience".[9]

There are good reasons why a more recent history of the discipline is rather hesitant about fixing and valorizing such memorial documents. The beginnings of the science of the German language and literature are now less associated with a specific event or commemorative document, but are described within the horizon of a mostly system-theoretical model of description as a concomitant phenomenon in the process of the formation of modernity.[10] From this perspective, the genesis and differentiation of a 'social system of science' into disciplinary subsystems, roughly estimated between the middle of the eighteenth and the middle of the nineteenth century, belong to the structural developments of the early and middle nineteenth century, which are to be considered in their processuality.[11] With a view to the formation of structures in this early period of German philology, some phenomena are particularly emphasized: Starting from the self-conception of a modern science as an institution that negotiates its objects and their claim to validity in a regulated manner in a public and contentious manner, the so-called 'science war' between the Brothers Grimm and Friedrich Heinrich von der Hagen between 1809/10 and 1813 thereby even again assumes a certain significance as a founding myth of the subject.[12] On a structural level, the historical moment of the dispute is closely linked to the development of the history of communication and conception in this early period of German philology. The formation of the science of German language and literature is shaped by a scholarly practice of communication, which in the early

---

[8] Still fundamentally Grunewald 1988.
[9] Heine 1987, p. 11 f.
[10] Koselleck 1979, p. XV. – Cf. also Décultot and Fulda (eds.) 2016.
[11] Still fundamental are the anthologies by Fohrmann and Voßkamp 1987, 1991 and 1994.
[12] Cf. Bluhm 1999.

nineteenth century experienced a tremendous concentration in the field of correspondence.[13] The developing networks not only led to an intensification of the scholarly exchange of knowledge and its verification, but also to the formation of 'communities of friends' on the basis of common interests, in which the groups were already emerging that would subsequently fight for the interpretative sovereignty of what could claim validity as a subject and procedure in the emerging science – and what could not. On the level of publications, this structural moment was reflected externally in reciprocal dedications, but also covertly in citation cartels and coordinated review strategies. An essential element of this community and group formation, which corresponded with the demarcation and discrediting of competing enterprises, was the interlocking of different scholarly projects and concepts in the field of German studies and the assertion and enforcement of this concerted program as exemplary and scholarly. Thus, in the common fixation on the so-called 'old German literature' in the coordination in particular between Jacob Grimm's history of language, Carl Lachmann's textual criticism, Georg Friedrich Benecke's lexicography and Wilhelm Grimm's history of reception, the nucleus of what was subsequently to endure as German philology emerged.[14] The sub-areas of this overall programme were themselves only separate fields of work within the framework of the much broader fields of work of the individual protagonists.

Part of the reality of the genesis of a career in the science of German language and literature is that it was a decades-long process that was by no means straightforward and continuous.[15] In practice, it is probably only in the last third of the nineteenth century that one can speak of a certain consolidation and actual implementation. This becomes particularly tangible if one directs one's gaze to the institutionalization as an academic subject at the universities and to its establishment as a school subject. The permanent constitution of the science of German language and literature cannot be separated from its anchoring as a school and university subject. It is a functional component of the state's efforts to shape and secure an educational system that is indebted to society's demand for specialists and administrators. According to a tabular overview compiled by Uwe Meves, the establishment of German studies seminars, which is generally regarded as "an indicator of the final integration of the subject of German studies into the university system",[16] only began in 1858 with Karl Bartsch's "Deutsch-philologisches Seminarium" at the University of Rostock and came to a provisional conclusion in 1895 with Wilhelm

---

[13] With a view to the history of the emergence of an early German philology, cf. Bluhm 1997; more recently Engel (ed.) 2019.

[14] Cf. Bluhm 2004.

[15] Cf. Uwe Meves: Die Institutionalisierung der Germanistik als akademisches Fach an den Universitätsneugründungen in Preussen, in: Meves 2004, pp. 335–368, esp. p. 335: "This process extended over six decades in Prussia. [...] It has by no means been a straight-line continuous path [...]."

[16] Uwe Meves: Die Gründung germanistischer Seminare an den preußischen Universitäten (1875–1895), in: Meves 2004, pp. 279–334, here p. 279. – Meves refers here to Burkhardt 1976, p. 66.

Storck's "German Studies Seminar" at the University of Münster.[17] In this context, one must "keep in mind" that – with a view to Prussia, for example – at almost all universities "mathematical and historical, mostly also modern-language seminars existed before the establishment of seminars in German studies".[18]

A comparable finding of a much later constitution of German studies in the educational system of the time than the talk of the beginnings of the science of German language and literature might suggest is offered by the reference to its establishment as a subject in schools. Although there had long been school activities that introduced German language and literature into the classroom, it was not until 1810, for example, that Prussia issued an examination edict for the training of grammar school teachers, which quite generally demanded "knowledge of the German language and literature", and it was not until 1831 that a "Reglement für die Prüfungen der Candidaten des höheren Schulamts" (Regulation for the Examinations of Candidates for Higher Education) came into force that "expressis verbis imposed an examination in the German language on prospective teachers in Prussia".[19] As a rule, however, the actual representatives of the subject were not represented at all on these examination boards, which seriously impaired the importance of the science of German language and literature as a subject of study; the examinations were generally taken over by representatives of other subjects – classical philologists, geographers or historians. It was not until 1866 that the composition of these examination boards changed fundamentally and made the appointment of a "specialist in German language and literature" obligatory.[20] Only then did the subject gain a secure basis as a university discipline and with regard to the training of German teachers.

3 On the Functional Context of Disciplinogenesis

The question of the beginnings and consolidation of the science of German language and literature cannot be detached from the functional conditional factors and the state-society requirements that made the discipline's career possible in the first place. In view of the often discontinuous and frequently coincidental development, one can hardly speak of an inevitable or necessary genesis from the beginning, nor of the one central or overpowering conditional factor that would have motivated or determined the events. In the process of the formation of a functionally organized

---

[17] Meves 2004, p. 281 f.
[18] Meves 2004, p. 283.
[19] Uwe Meves: "Wir armen Germanisten ...". Das Fach deutsche Sprache und Literatur auf dem Weg zur Brot-wissenschaft, in: Meves 2004, pp. 369–400, here p. 369. – On this subject comprehensively Uwe Meves: Die Aufnahme der altdeutschen Literatur und Sprache in die amtliche Bildungsplanung für das höhere Schulwesen in der neuhumanistischen Reformperiode in Preußen und ihre schulische Umsetzung, in: Meves 2004, pp. 171–277.
[20] Meves, "We poor Germanists ...", in: Meves 2004, p. 398.

modern bourgeois society, some of the many factors nevertheless deserve special attention. Here are just a few keywords: the science of German language and literature, as it finally emerged in the dispute of conceptions, especially in the early and middle nineteenth century, fitted in its specific 'order of knowledge' into the scientific profile of the contemporary secret leading disciplines from the fields of the natural sciences, or it understood how to position itself as a meaningful complement to the use-oriented 'exact' sciences. In this complementary, if not supplementary, character, it offers points of contact for a concept of education that is absorbed by utility, as was characteristic of New Humanism and as could be introduced, for example, into the civil service ethos of a modern administrative society.

Last but not least, the science of the German language and literature offered a program for creating meaning that was also politically acceptable, especially in the nineteenth century. For even if the long-lasting and hesitant, in parts even delayed course of the formation and consolidation of disciplines speaks against the frequently introduced notion of a 'triumph of a national science' borne by 'patriotic' euphoria, the functional connection with the process of nation-building in the nineteenth century must by no means be disregarded. The emerging science of German language and literature was moved by this impulse, especially in the first two decades of the century. There is ample evidence that an antagonism to Napoleonic France with its striving for hegemony and the dominance of French culture in Germany, understood as a form of cultural imperialism, played a decisive role in this process. The idea of German unity was to remain a point of reference in the following decades until the founding of the Reich in 1871. Against this background, the scholarship of German language and literature offered itself – even after 1871 – as a production site where the formation of a national identity could be promoted through the sifting, provision, scholarly legitimization, and mediation of memorial documents. In the reduction to a cultural tradition marked as 'German', a common past was contoured, which could be presented as supra-regional, vernacular and uniform and made serviceable as national culture for the legitimation of nation-state aspirations. The connection with the educational system, ultimately promoted by ministerial bureaucracy in the institutionalization as a university discipline and as a school subject, made this form of national identity formation a state task. Notwithstanding the systemic processes of self-organization that contributed to the development of the discipline in the formation of the science of German language and literature, it was above all deliberate political and administrative decisions that made the subject's career possible and subsequently guided it. They were ultimately connected with the pursuit and implementation of identity-political concepts for the purpose of nation-building.

The subject of German in today's schools and the subject of German Studies at today's universities in Germany are still functionally subjects to this nineteenth century assignment of tasks in their fundamental national-cultural structuring and orientation, despite manifold state, social, programmatic and other changes. Their mediators are – regardless of their personal educational program – still producers and promoters of a German national identity. German cultural history, as it is canonized in subject-specific ways, is still oriented and catalogued in schools and universities in terms of national language and national culture, which is a considerable narrowing with regard to the actual history of culture in Germany and certainly also with regard to future necessities. The task of contributing to the formation of a national identity, as the nineteenth and twentieth centuries claimed for their individual and above all social education, can hardly be regarded as sustainable today. The conservatism of current systems, familiar from systems theory, makes it unlikely that anything will change in the foreseeable future in this practice, which has been solidified by schools and universities, unless appropriate political and administrative measures intervene and initiate a reorientation.

4 A Look Ahead

Thus, at the end of this sketch and following the recent debate on the meaning and tasks of humanities and cultural studies today and tomorrow outlined at the beginning, let us at least briefly look at the present and future necessities and desirabilities. If one concedes that the humanities and cultural studies, at least through their mediating and reproducing instances of school and university, also have a community-building or community-promoting function in addition to their function of promoting individual education, then a new self-assurance with regard to content, formats and goals seems appropriate. This would then require a sober view of social conditions and developments as well as a certain readiness for utopia.

More than a sketch will not be attempted here. Parts of German didactics are obviously further along in the discussion than the subject sciences, subject historiography and the political discussion, so that corresponding borrowings from there are permitted. Anyone who deals with current teaching proposals and practical examples for schools today can only do so with direct reference to an analysis of current social developments and the challenges facing schools. The corresponding German didactic programmes quite explicitly break away from the guidelines of an essentialist concept of culture and its attachment to a "homogeneous culture, essentially linked to a people, a nation or a geographical area".[21] Aligned with concepts of multi-, trans- or interculturality, culture is rather understood as a dynamic space of change and heterogeneity. With regard to Germany and Europe, the point of reference for current and future school challenges is assumed to be 'plural migration societies', the reality of culturally heterogeneous and hybrid societies, "in which groups and communities with different cultural expressions of values, practices, forms of expression, patterns of understanding and behaviour are formed, which overlap, intermingle or also coexist in parallel."[22] With regard to Germany, people like to refer to the population structure and its prospective development, which, according to the Federal Statistical Office, actually shows 22.5% people with a

---

[21] Scherer and Vach 2019, p. 20.
[22] Scherer and Vach 2019, p. 11.

migration background in 2018 – with a clear upward trend. In relation to the process of political, social, economic, but also cultural integration movements in Europe, the aspect of plurality gains an additional dimension.

With outdated nation-state and national-cultural concepts of identity, as demanded by nation-building in the nineteenth century, this social development and its challenges will certainly no longer be successfully met today and in the future. Instead, an orientation towards a plural identity in the horizon of Europeanization and globalization seems more sustainable. The more recent and most recent concepts and programmes in parts of German didactics cannot be dealt with here.[23] However, following considerations from the canonical discussion in the field of German studies, some possible perspectives are outlined with regard to the science of German language and literature and its instances of mediation.[24] The school and the university are probably the most relevant institutions through which a reorientation adapted to social developments and challenges would have to take its course. In essence, this would mean a paradigm shift through the dissolution of the current subject-disciplinary structure in schools and in university teacher training. Corresponding school pedagogical concepts have existed for decades. In order to implement such a paradigm shift pointing to the future, the transfer of school subjects into a new structure with their own language education and cultural education areas would be one necessary organisational policy task. The other would be to detach university teacher training from the dominance of the subject areas – for example, German, English, Romance studies or other disciplines – and to transfer their subject-related scientific and didactic offerings into interdisciplinary curricula. The key to such adjustments, which are committed to the demands of the future, thus ultimately lies in the willingness and ability of political and ministerial decision-making bodies. Recognizing their influence on the development of subjects and their functional connection with concepts of identity politics is one of the insights that can be gained from a subject-historical view of the beginnings of the development of science, its institutionalization and transfer into the school system in the course of the nineteenth century. A transfer of the school subjects into a new structure in the future and the corresponding university restructuring doesn't imply an end of the science of German language and literature, but it would mean that it would have to reorient itself with regard to its content, formats and goals, find itself anew and in some respects perhaps even reinvent itself once again. It would then be in good company with other humanities and cultural studies, which would have to face a comparable reorientation. – But with this we are already entering another 'wide field'.

---

[23] Cf. for example Rösch 2017.

[24] Cf. esp. Lothar Bluhm: Was wir lesen sollen… Unmaßgebliche Überlegungen zu Kanon und literarischer Wertung heute und morgen. In: What we should read. Kanon und literarische Wertung am Beginn des 21. Jahrhunderts. Ed. by Stefan Neuhaus et al. Würzburg 2016, pp. 247–260.

References

Bluhm, Lothar: Die Brüder Grimm und der Beginn der Deutschen Philologie. Eine Studie zu Kommunikation und Wissenschaftsbildung im frühen 19. Jahrhundert. Hildesheim: Weidmann 1997.

Bluhm, Lothar: „compilierende oberflächlichkeit" gegen „gernrezensirende Vornehmheit". Der Wissenschaftskrieg zwischen Friedrich Heinrich von der Hagen und den Brüdern Grimm, in: Romantik und Volksliteratur. Hg. von Lothar Bluhm und Achim Hölter. Heidelberg: Winter 1999, S. 49–70. – Netzpublikation in: Goethezeitportal: URL: http://www.goethezeitportal.de/db/wiss/epoche/bluhm_wissenschaftskrieg.pdf (eingestellt am 12.01.2004).

Bluhm, Lothar: Wissenschaft als eine „Gemeinschaft von Freunden". Zur Verzahnung heterogener Wissenschaftsprojekte in der frühen Deutschen Philologie, in: Goethezeitportal. URL: http://www.goethezeitportal.de/db/wiss/epoche/bluhm_gemeinschaft.pdf (eingestellt am 12.01.2004).

Bluhm, Lothar: Was wir lesen sollen… Unmaßgebliche Überlegungen zu Kanon und literarischer Wertung heute und morgen, in: Was wir lesen sollen. Kanon und literarische Wertung am Beginn des 21. Jahrhunderts. Hg. von Stefan Neuhaus und Uta Schaffers. Würzburg: Königshausen & Neumann 2016, S. 247–260.

Burkhardt, Ursula: Germanistik in Südwestdeutschland: Die Geschichte einer Wissenschaft des 19. Jahrhunderts an den Universitäten Tübingen, Heidelberg und Freiburg. Tübingen: Mohr 1976.

Décultot, Elisabeth und Daniel Fulda (Hg.): Sattelzeit. Historiographiegeschichtliche Revisionen. Berlin: Oldenbourg Verlag 2016.

Engel, Karsten (Hg.): Wissenschaft in Korrespondenzen. Göttinger Wissensgeschichte in Briefen. Göttingen: Vandenhoeck & Ruprecht 2019.

Fohrmann, Jürgen und Wilhelm Voßkamp (Hg.): Von der gelehrten zur disziplinären Gemeinschaft. Sonderheft 1987: Deutsche Vierteljahrsschrift für Literaturwissenschaft und Geistesgeschichte (DVjs).

Fohrmann, Jürgen und Wilhelm Voßkamp (Hg.): Wissenschaft und Nation. Studien zur Entstehungsgeschichte der deutschen Literaturwissenschaft. München: Wilhelm Fink 1991.

Fohrmann, Jürgen und Wilhelm Voßkamp (Hg.): Wissenschaftsgeschichte der Germanistik im 19. Jahrhundert. Stuttgart: Metzler 1994.

Goethe, Johann Wolfgang von: Aus meinem Leben. Dichtung und Wahrheit. In: Werke. Hamburger Ausgabe in 14 Bänden. Hg. von Erich Trunz. Bd. 9. Autobiographische Schriften 1. München: dtv 1982.

Grimm, Jacob: Das Wort des Besitzes. In: Kleinere Schriften. Erster Band. Berlin: Ferdinand Dümmlers Verlagsbuchhandlung 1864.

Grunewald, Eckhard: Friedrich Heinrich von der Hagen 1780–1856. Ein Beitrag zur Frühgeschichte der Germanistik. Berlin, New York: de Gruyter 1988.

Hayer, Björn: Reißt den Elfenbeinturm ab! In Zeiten hitziger Debatten ist von den Kulturwissenschaften wenig zu hören. Dabei gilt es Diskursräume zu wahren oder zurückzuerobern. Ein Plädoyer für mehr Einmischung, in: Zeit online vom 3. Februar 2019 – https://www.zeit.de/kultur/2019-01/geisteswissenschaften-intellekt-literatur-digitale-medien-diskursteilnahme (aufgerufen am 04.02.2021).

Heine, Heinrich: Historisch-kritische Gesamtausgabe der Werke. Hg. von Manfred Windfuhr. Bd. 9. Elementargeister. Die Göttin Diana. Der Doktor Faust. Die Götter im Exil. Bearb. v. Ariane Neuhaus-Koch. Hamburg: Hoffmann und Campe 1987.

Herbold, Astrid: Weg vom Klischee. Eine Analyse, in: Zeit Campus vom 15. Mai 2019 – https://www.zeit.de/2019/21/geisteswissenschaften-studium-probleme-anerkennung-nutzen (aufgerufen am 04.02.2021).

Koselleck, Reinhart: Einleitung, in: Otto Brunner, Werner Conze, Reinhart Koselleck (Hg.): Geschichtliche Grundbegriffe. Bd. 1. Stuttgart: Klett Cotta 1979.

Meves, Uwe: Ausgewählte Beiträge zur Geschichte der Germanistik und des Deutschunterrichts im 19. und 20. Jahrhundert. Hildesheim: Weidmann 2004.

Rösch, Heidi: Deutschunterricht in der Migrationsgesellschaft. Eine Einführung. Stuttgart: Metzler 2017.

Scherer, Gabriela und Karin Vach: Interkulturelles Lernen mit Kinderliteratur. Unterrichtsvorschläge und Praxisbeispiele. Seelze: Kallmeyer in Verbindung mit Klett 2019.

Philology and Physics in Romanticism and Today

Christoph Strosetzki

Abstract If Romanticism and the philosophy of German Idealism brought a new impetus to physics and philology, and if physics and philology had both emerged from the propaedeutic tradition of the *artes liberales* at the beginning of the nineteenth century, the different development they have undergone in the ensuing two hundred years is astonishing. While physics now has numerous professorships in a wide variety of specialties, the philologies are still referred to sweepingly by uninitiated lawyers as the "language teaching" because they continue to be defined institutionally by national languages rather than by specialties, even though, like the physicists, they have their respective specialties.

At the time of the Romantic period, philology and physics were parts of the Faculty of Philosophy at German universities. In the following, therefore, a comparison of the development of the two subjects will be undertaken. First, some characteristics of the national philology at the time of Romanticism will be highlighted. Then, the path of physics up to Romanticism and its conception in Romanticism shall be briefly pointed out. And finally, a comparison between university physics and university modern philology today, using Romance studies as an example, will show how different the respective situations are. At the end then, there is a suggestion for the alignment of the conditions in both disciplines.

It was the spirit of Romanticism that influenced not only the new philologies, but also jurisprudence[1] and medicine.[2] In his inaugural lecture of April 30,

---
[1] Cf. Lieb and Strosetzki 2013.
[2] Cf. Engelhardt 2005, pp. 903–907.

C. Strosetzki (✉)
Romanisches Seminar, Universität Münster, Münster, Deutschland
e-mail: stroset@uni-muenster.de

© The Author(s), under exclusive license to Springer-Verlag GmbH, DE, part of Springer Nature 2023
C. Strosetzki (ed.), *200 Years of National Philologies*,
https://doi.org/10.1007/978-3-476-05925-3_16

1841, the founder of German studies, the jurist Jacob Grimm, stated an analogy between law and language, which he traced back to a folk spirit, a common folk custom and a common essence.[3] In 1846, he had been elected chairman of the first assembly of Germanists, to which philologists as well as lawyers were invited. German law, he argued, was far more influenced by poetry than Roman law, as manifested in the German epic poetry of the twelfth and thirteenth centuries. It was Carl Voretzsch who saw German and Romance studies united in the early phase under the umbrella of a Romantic science: "Romantic at that time meant the Middle Ages and modern times in contrast to classical antiquity; the Romantic literatures encompassed Germanic as well as Romance peoples."[4] That it was not easy for the modern philologies to emancipate themselves from the Latin of classical philology, which had been present in the discipline of the grammar of the *artes liberales* since the Middle Ages, is shown by Carl Wilhelm Mager's prohibition: "Nor is anyone who wants to call himself a philologist permitted access to another people, if he has not taken his way to it via Rome and Athens".[5] For Friedrich de la Motte Fouqué, Novalis, Wilhelm Heinrich Wackenroder and Ludwig Tieck, German cultural identity had already reached its zenith in the Middle Ages, when universal Christianity and social harmony prevailed.[6] In his *Lectures on Universal History,* Friedrich Schlegel sees Spanish history as the history of the development of the Germanic constitution in Spain, since there, in the Middle Ages, the Germanic constitution had defeated the spirit of Romanism, held its own despite Arab influence, and produced Christian values that endured until the *Siglo de Oro.*[7] Although the boundaries between the individual European peoples and nations became blurred with regard to the Middle Ages, the neo-philological subjects became increasingly differentiated in the course of the nineteenth century. In 1846, the journal *Archiv für das Studium der neueren Sprachen und Literaturen (Archive for the Study of Modern Languages and Literatures)* was founded for all new philologies, whereas the *Romanische Forschungen (Romance Research) was* limited to Romance studies from 1883 and the *Zeitschrift für Romanische Philologie (Journal of Romance Philology)* from 1877. The independence of Hispanic Studies from the framework of Romance Studies, on the other hand, is shown only since 1969 by *Iberoromania* and since 1977 by *Iberoamericana.* The differentiations thus follow the criterion of languages.

In the nineteenth century, the neo-philological subjects at universities emerged from the Faculty of Philosophy in the same way as the natural sciences. While in other European countries faculties of natural sciences had already emerged and gained independence in the first half of the century, this did not happen in German-speaking countries until the second half. While Leiden in 1811, Amsterdam in 1815

---

[3] Grimm 1966, p. 547 f.
[4] Voretzsch 1904, p. 2.
[5] Quoted from Christmann 1985, p. 14.
[6] Cf. Plessner 1959, p. 48 f.
[7] Schlegel 1960, pp. 174–179.

and Leuven in 1834 established a faculty of natural sciences, Vienna followed in 1872 and Frankfurt a. M. in 1912. Previously, Zurich in 1859, Munich in 1865 and Würzburg in 1873 had divided the Faculty of Philosophy into a philosophical and a scientific section. Physics was now divided into mechanics, thermics, molecular physics, electrics, acoustics and optics.[8]

Why are the German-speaking countries latecomers? Not least, this has to do with the influence of Romanticism and the philosophy of German Idealism on the Faculty of Philosophy. The Romantics, like the representatives of the philosophy of German Idealism, analogized the productive power of the absolute spirit to that of the individual spirit and the popular spirit. They thus gave preference to ideality over reality. For this very reason Don Quixote, with his striving for infinity, is for them a suitable modern myth. Just as, according to Friedrich Wilhelm Joseph Schelling, the absolute spirit created the world, so the individual subject creates his reality out of himself and with his spiritual creative power. Thus God becomes that cause in the world-process "which gives preponderance to the ideal over the real."[9] The same is true of creatures: "Finite beings, on the other hand, have only the freedom to set themselves eternally."[10] This means that reality explicitly represents what is already implicit in the idea. "Nature, according to this doctrine, is nothing but the idea fallen apart."[11] To illustrate this, Schelling cites geometry and light. In both examples, something starts from a point and lays itself upon the objects of reality, be they geometrical models, be they the rays of light from the sun.

In scholasticism, theology and philosophy were combined into a total system, so that physics, like philology, had its place in the basic philosophical studies and was linked to logic and metaphysics. In Aristotle, every thing strives for the perfection of its essence, its form. Therefore, natural processes as well as ethical actions are equally final. Although there were alchemical laboratories in the seventeenth century and mechanistic Cartesianism was emerging, physics in universities was Aristotelian and taught in the late scholastic tradition, with school philosophers seeing themselves not as researchers but as transmitters of a tradition concerned only with ordering, justifying, and preparing materials. Physics, like philology, works with transmitted texts, is contemplative and not concerned with mastery of nature. At Catholic universities the Aristotelian tradition continued until the middle of the eighteenth century, while the mechanistic one prevailed earlier at Protestant ones, mediated by Christian Wolff. Since people were critical of the mechanistic method on religious grounds because of its lack of teleology, efforts along the lines of Leibniz to combine the mechanistic with the Aristotelian method, i.e., a mechanistic physics with a teleological view of nature, were popular.[12] By the end of the eighteenth century, the paradigm shift from Aristotelian to mechanistic physics was

---

[8] Cf. Weber 2002, pp. 211–213.
[9] Schelling 1989, p. 97.
[10] Schelling 1989, p. 106.
[11] Schelling 1989, p. 65.
[12] Cf. Lind 1992, pp. 54–58.

complete, and thus the cosmos, hitherto meaningfully ordered according to divine plan, had become a world machine with events caused without purpose. Newton's later change from mechanical to inductive and experimental physics of forces could not have been greater, since both are concerned with the changes of bodies as movements. Natural philosophy became natural science, turning the Aristotelian question, "Why is nature as it is?" into the question, "How does it work?" This answered Karl Marx's phrase: "Philosophers have only interpreted the world differently, but what matters is to change it." For now, through mathematical descriptions and constructions, the steam engine, the railroad, and the radio set came into being.[13]

As already stated above for philology, Romanticism and the philosophy of German Idealism brought a new impulse to physics as well. By starting again from philosophical and literary premises, they take a step backwards for a short time. Based on the idea of the unity of man and nature, the knowledge of nature is given the task of bringing man closer to nature, as a glance at Karl Wilhelm Gottlob Kastner's *Grundriß der Experimental-Physik*, which was designed for use in the basic lectures at the university and appeared in 1810, shows.[14] He assumes with Friedrich Schelling that nature is a manifestation of the divine spirit, that nature and spirit are therefore one and that the human spirit has a part in the spirit of nature. Every physicist, he says, strives to find his own laws of life in the life of the whole. He approaches nature spiritually in order to explore its spirituality. In doing so, he does not make nature a mere object, but seeks the idea of the whole, which is that of the true, beautiful, and good in nature. In this search the explorer stands by the side of the artist and the priest. Nature is not only the object of knowledge, but also of admiration and worship. Romanticism contrasts the metaphor of the machine with the organism or world-soul. All organisms have a soul, so that nature is a dialectical unity of productivity and product, in Schelling's sense of *natura naturans* and *natura naturata*. Kastner even relates this conception to inorganic nature and speaks of *inorganic life* or *anorganisms*. The history of nature is teleologically defined as the determination of the higher developmental potentialities of the spirit. Evolutionary theory becomes ideal genesis and nature nothing but the representation of the activities of the original spirit or God, whereby scientific education teaches to see the whole and absolute in nature.

As late as the eighteenth century, the educational goal of the secondary school was the erudite who had acquired a certain body of knowledge and had shown in disputations that he was able to deal with scientific literature.[15] By the beginning of the nineteenth century, as already mentioned, the Faculty of Arts had emerged from its propaedeutic tradition of the *artes liberales* and had become an equal faculty in which physics was one among other subjects. At first the professor of physics gave only a one- to two-semester basic lecture in addition to private seminars. Even in 1860, in the eighth edition of his widely distributed work "Lehrbuch der Physik zum

---

[13] Cf. Coy 2003, p. 1.
[14] Cf. in the following Lind 1992, pp. 279–295.
[15] Cf. Lind 1992, pp. 314–324.

Gebrauche bei Vorlesungen und zum Selbstunterricht" ("Textbook of Physics for Use in Lectures and for Self-Instruction"), Wilhelm Eisenlohr does not completely abandon the teleological method when he wants "nature" to mean: "partly the epitome of all things perceptible to the senses, the whole physical world; partly the totality of all properties, forces and relationships of a thing; but partly also the first cause of all things".[16] After emphasizing the influences of physics on the trades and wealth of nations, he goes on to discuss the positive effect of physics on religious and moral feeling: "By it we everywhere learn to admire the wisdom and greatness of the Creator, by learning how, by the application of the simplest means, the most manifold and wonderful ends are accomplished, and what spirit of order, harmony, and power pervades the whole universe."[17] He then goes on to treat of bodies, wave motion, sound, light, heat, magnetism, electricity, and electrodynamics.

In his book *Grundzüge der Physik als Compendium zu seinen Vorlesungen* (*Basic Principles of Physics as a Compendium to his Lectures*), Georg Simon Ohm undertakes to take into account the scanty previous mathematical knowledge of his students, "most of whom come from the humanistic educational institutions",[18] in the arrangement of his material. In the division of natural science, he distinguishes between inner world and outer world, inner thing and outer thing, or inner and outer nature, the latter being the object of natural science and the former the object of soul science. Nor does he refrain from assuming a common cause: "Both inner and outer nature flow together into one common origin, in the creator of the world who is incomprehensible to us worms."[19] To the extent that Romantic natural philosophy gives way to positivism, however, teleological thinking disappears, and with it the common ground between physics and philology that was once again formulated in Romanticism.

If we now take a leap into the year 2019, comparing the two disciplines, we are struck by how many new sub-disciplines physics is divided into and how many new professorships have been created as a result. In the Department of Physics at the University of Münster, there are currently 36 professorships, three for Applied Physics, two for Dynamics at Interfaces, one for Electron Microscopy, two for Experimental Physics, one for Experimental Physics with a focus on Physics of Responsive Nanosystems, one for Experimental Physics and Gender Research in Physics, three for Solid State Theory, one for Solid State Quantum Optics and Nanophotonics, three for geophysics, one for interfacial physics, one for integration and manipulation of quantum emitters, three for nuclear physics, one for materials physics, another for surface physics, one for spin phenomena in low-D systems, five for theoretical physics, one for theoretical physics with a focus on ultrafast optics in nanostructured solids, one for the theory of active soft matter, and four for didactics of physics.

---

[16] Eisenlohr 1860, p. 1.
[17] Eisenlohr 1860, p. 3.
[18] Ohm 1854b, vol. 2, p. III.
[19] Ohm 1854a, vol. 1, p. 1.

At the Technische Universität München there are 28 professorships for Experimental Physics [Quantum Optics, Photonics and Optoelectronics (2), Biophysics (2), Laser Spectroscopy (2), Solid State Physics (2), Laser Physics (4), Hybrid Nanosystems (2), Medical Physics (3), Soft Condensed Matter (3), Elementary Particle Physics (3), BioMolecular Optics (2), Medical Physics (1), Systems Biophysics (1), Physics of Nanosystems (1)], for Theoretical Physics 19 professorships [Solid State Physics (2), Particle Physics (2), Statistical Physics (3), Mathematical Physics (5), Astroparticle Physics (3), Computational and Plasma Physics (2), Nanophysics (2)] and for Didactics of Physics one. If one compares this number of 48 professorships and the variety of disciplines with the list given by Eisenlohr in 1860, according to which he divided physics into bodies, wave motion, sound, light, heat, magnetism, electricity and electrodynamics, then a rapid development and differentiation of the disciplines in physics becomes apparent.

What is the situation in modern modern philology? Let this be demonstrated by the example of Romance Studies. As if clinging to the doctrine of the popular spirits of Romanticism, professorships are still defined on the basis of languages. There are professorships in Romance Studies with a special focus on French and Spanish literatures, with a special focus on French and Italian literatures, with a special focus on Spanish literature or Latin American literatures. At best, the text of the advertisement still indicates that experience in media studies or intercultural studies is desirable.

Since Romance studies, like other new philologies, still define its sub-disciplines according to the different languages, it is not surprising if the philologies, whether practised as literary or linguistic sciences, are referred to sweepingly as "language teaching" by the uninitiated lawyer, for example. Nor is it surprising that the Pisa study treats university philological subjects no differently from language teaching institutes such as the Berlitz or Benedict schools, as if they were only concerned with acquiring communicative competence in a foreign language.[20] Using Romance studies as an example, the question will now be asked whether the retention of the division of disciplines as it was in the nineteenth century is due to the fact that there have been no further developments beyond the interpretation of important authors, the analysis of genres, epochs and currents.

However, a look at the focal points indicated by the professors of Romance Studies with a literary studies orientation on the respective websites of the universities proves diversity and innovation. The professors' internet statements in March 2019 show, where they exist, a willingness to cooperate with other disciplines when a focus is stated as "literature and ...". Interdisciplinarity documents foci such as literature and philosophy, literature and ethics, literature and economics, science and literature. The same applies to topics such as exchange relations between religious and literary discourses, literature and psychoanalysis, mysticism and literature. Literature is associated with quite abstract focal points, such as literature, culture and violence or literature and dream in modernity, as well as very concrete

---

[20] Cf. Klieme et al. 2010; Graf 2017, pp. 112–120.

ones that would hardly have the potential to form the basis of a new discipline. I only mention focal points such as opera and literature, tango and literature, or literature and the coffee house.

The latter focal points, however, also illustrate that communication is not always easy even between subject representatives of Hispanic Studies, for example when one specializes in the tango and the other in the coffee house. The difficulty of communication among the subject representatives of Romance Studies, even if they have professorships with the same language combination, can be illustrated by a few more examples.

Will the one whose focus is "Kant's writings in translations" have anything to say to the one whose focus is "Spanish African discourse"? The one who works on "bande dessinée" will have little to say to the one whose focus is "Literary Discourses on Food in Early Modern and Modern Times." Nor does "Francophone Atlantic" have much to do with the "concept of 'sensibilité' in eighteenth-century French literature," any more than "Poetics of Friendship" has little to do with the "representation of violence in social proximity" or the "Literary and Cultural History of Venice in the Eighteenth Century" has little to do with the "'hero' act – heroization as a form of ontological rubrication." This shows that the similarities suggested by the same or by affine languages are only superficial and formal. They have no relevance to content.

In view of this situation, would it not make more sense to divide up the philological subjects according to content-related criteria, as physics does? If one takes another look at the focal points in Romance studies given on the Internet, then there are certainly topics that would be suitable for naming their own sub-disciplines of philology. These could include research fields in literary studies defined in terms of content, such as "history of concepts and history of ideas", "genealogies of the occidental subject" or "literary anthropology". "Dialogue and Dialogue Theory" or "Historical Discourse Analysis" would also be possible. These as well as the following topics have already been identified as research foci on the internet: "Cultures of Memory", "History of Intellectuals and Science", "Dialogue between the Humanities and the Natural Sciences", "Intercultural Hermeneutics / Transcultural Processes", "Economies and Money in Literary Texts from the Middle Ages to Modernity" or "Postcolonial Studies". All of these areas can be found among the Romance Studies foci on the Internet and could form sub-disciplines of philology, and this would be best done even before disciplines such as cultural geography and ethnology claim them as their own.

If focal areas were to be designated as sub-disciplines of Romance philology, then in a first step job advertisements could in future read: "Professorship in Romance philology with special consideration of literary anthropology" or "Professorship in Romance philology with special consideration of historical discourse analysis". It would become clear that philological subjects have as many sub-disciplines as physical ones. The misunderstanding that philology is primarily about language acquisition would then be ruled out from the outset. Perhaps, too, in view of the numerous sub-disciplines, the necessity of increasing the number of posts along the lines of physics would become apparent. Certainly, however, it would become clear who as a subject representative has what in common with another in terms of content and can enter into a process of intellectual exchange.

In summary, it can be stated: As long as physics was still Aristotelian or scholastic, it worked, like philology, with a canon of writings to be discussed and transmitted. The texts were teleologically oriented towards meaning, just as nature is. This changed with the mechanistic worldview, although the interlude of Romanticism and German Idealism in physics left a lasting impression. At that time, philosophical and literary axioms became the premises of a physical world view – a symbiosis that seems strange from the perspective of the twenty-first century.

Let us return to the comparison of philology and physics. How can the former learn from the successes of the latter? Should literary studies, like linguistics, set up laboratories to collect and mathematically exploit static data? Does the future lie in the *digital humanities*? Quite the contrary. Modifying the Marxian dictum quoted above, it can be said: "Physics and technology have radically changed the world in the last 200 years, but it depends on finally interpreting it again."[21] And here it is not only philosophy that is called upon, but also philology.

References

Christmann, Hans Helmut: Romanistik und Anglistik an der deutschen Universität im 19. Jahrhundert: Ihre Herausbildung als Fächer und ihr Verhältnis zu Germanistik und klassischer Philologie. Stuttgart: Steiner 1985.
Coy, Wolfgang: Eine Einheit der Wissenschaften?, in: Tagesspiegel-Sonderseiten: Humboldt-Uni, 14.4.2003, S. 1–2.
Eisenlohr, Wilhelm: Lehrbuch der Physik zum Gebrauche bei Vorlesungen und zum Selbstunterricht. Stuttgart: Krais und Hoffmann 1860 (8. Auflage; die erste erschien 1836).
Engelhardt, Dietrich von: Medizin der Romantik, in: Werner E. Gerabek (Hg.) et al.: Enzyklopädie Medizingeschichte. Berlin, New York: de Gruyter, Berlin 2005, 903–907.
Graf, Dittmar: Die schiefe Tour von PISA – Wieso die Vorzeigestudie nicht wissenschaftlich ist, in: Skeptiker (Zeitschrift), 03.2017, S. 112–120.
Grimm, Jacob: Kleinere Schriften, VIII, Vorreden, Zeitgeschichtliches und Persönliches. Hildesheim, Olms: Weidmann 1966.
Klieme, Eckhard et al. (Hg.): PISA 2009. Bilanz nach einem Jahrzehnt. Waxmann. Münster u. a.: Waxmann 2010.
Lieb, Claudia/Strosetzki, Christoph (Hg.): Philologie als Literatur- und Rechtswissenschaft. Germanistik und Romanistik 1770–1870. Heidelberg: Winter 2013 (Beihefte zum Euphorion, Heft 67).
Lind, Gunter: Physik im Lehrbuch. 1700–1850. Berlin, Heidelberg: Springer 1992.
Ohm, Georg Simon: Grundzüge der Physik als Compendium zu seinen Vorlesungen. Nürnberg: J. L. Schrag 1854a, Bd. I.
Ohm, Georg Simon: Grundzüge der Physik als Compendium zu seinen Vorlesungen. Nürnberg: J. L. Schrag 1854b, Bd. II.
Plessner, Helmuth: Die verspätete Nation, Stuttgart: Kohlhammer 1959.
Schelling, Friedrich Wilhelm Joseph: Einleitung in die Philosophie. Stuttgart: Frommann-Holzboog 1989.

---

[21] Cf. Coy 2003, p. 2.

Schlegel, Friedrich: Vorlesungen über Universalgeschichte (1805–1806), in: Jean-Jacques Anstett (Hg.): Kritische Friedrich-Schlegel-Ausgabe. München, 1960, Bd. 14.

Voretzsch, Carl: Die Anfänge des Romanischen Philologie an den deutschen Universitäten und ihre Entwicklung an der Universität Tübingen. Tübingen: Laupp 1904.

Weber, Wolfgang E. J.: Geschichte der europäischen Universität. Stuttgart: Kohlhammer, 2002.

Printed in the USA
CPSIA information can be obtained
at www.ICGtesting.com
LVHW011143150324
774517LV00041B/1715